THE WHITE INDIANS OF MEXICAN CINEMA

SUNY series in Latin American Cinema

Ignacio M. Sánchez Prado and Leslie L. Marsh, editors

THE WHITE INDIANS OF MEXICAN CINEMA

RACIAL MASQUERADE THROUGHOUT THE GOLDEN AGE

MÓNICA GARCÍA BLIZZARD

Cover: *La Zandunga* (1938). Photo courtesy of Mil Nubes-Foto (Roberto Fiesco).

Published by State University of New York Press, Albany

This book is freely available in an open access edition thanks to TOME (Toward an Open Monograph Ecosystem)—a collaboration of the Association of American Universities, the Association of University Presses, and the Association of Research Libraries—and the generous support of Emory University and the Andrew W. Mellon Foundation. Learn more at the TOME website, available at: openmonographs.org.

Except where otherwise noted, the text of this book is licensed under a Creative Commons Attribution-NonCommercial-NoDerivatives 4.0 International License (CC BY-NC-ND 4.0). https://creativecommons.org/licenses/by-nc-nd/4.0/

© 2022 Mónica García Blizzard

All rights reserved

Printed in the United States of America

For information, contact State University of New York Press, Albany, NY
www.sunypress.edu

Library of Congress Cataloging-in-Publication Data

Name: García Blizzard, Mónica, author.
Title: The white indians of Mexican cinema : racial masquerade throughout the golden age / Mónica García Blizzard.
Description: Albany : State University of New York Press, [2022] | Series: SUNY series in Latin American cinema | Includes bibliographical references and index.
Identifiers: LCCN 2021054823 (print) | LCCN 2021054824 (ebook) | ISBN 9781438488035 (hardcover : alk. paper) | ISBN 9781438488059 (ebook) | ISBN 9781438488042 (pbk. : alk. paper)
Subjects: LCSH: White people in motion pictures. | Ethnicity in motion pictures. | Motion pictures—Mexico—History and criticism. | Motion pictures—Social aspects—Mexico.
Classification: LCC PN1993.5.M4 G373 2022 (print) | LCC PN1993.5.M4 (ebook) | DDC 791.430972—dc23/eng/20220121
LC record available at https://lccn.loc.gov/2021054823
LC ebook record available at https://lccn.loc.gov/2021054824

10 9 8 7 6 5 4 3 2 1

Per Alessandro, Lucia e Tomás.

Contents

List of Illustrations		ix
Acknowledgments		xiii
Introduction		1
Chapter 1	Idealized Pre-Columbian Womanhood	63
Chapter 2	Taming the Tehuana	93
Chapter 3	Revolutionary Politics, Colonized Aesthetics	123
Chapter 4	Reframing *Mestizaje*: White Mayans, Indigenous Spirituality, and Cenote Suicides	177
Chapter 5	*María Isabel*: A White *Indita* for Modern Mexico	209
Chapter 6	*Indios*, Desire, and the White Mexican Woman	239
Conclusion		281
Bibliography		287
Index		301

Illustrations

Figure I.1 The cartoon titled "Buen juez" (Good Judge) appeared in *Excélsior* on August 31, 1927.   26

Figure I.2 Still showing *María Candelaria*'s (in)famous breach of indexicality with Dolores del Río and Pedro Armendariz playing Indigenous Mexicans (1944).   39

Figure 1.1 Medea de Novara as Indigenous royalty in *Zítari* (1931).   76

Figure 1.2 Medea de Novara as a Spanish aristocrat in *Tribu* (1935).   77

Figure 1.3 Naya is initiated into the Mayan belief system as a baby in *Chilam Balam* (1957).   87

Figure 1.4 Chilam Balam blesses Mayan youth with holy water during the coming-of-age ritual in *Chilam Balam* (1957).   87

Figure 2.1 The Tehuana protagonist, Lupe (Lupe Vélez), dances at a local wedding in *La Zandunga* (1938).   101

Figure 2.2 Lupe Vélez's image as a White Mexican star is used to advertise Hinds beauty cream in *Cinelandia*, February 1931, 52.   104

Figure 2.3 Close-up of the teary-eyed Tehuana protagonist, Lupe (Lupe Vélez), in *La Zandunga* (1938).   107

Figure 2.4	The Tehuana protagonist, Lupe (Lupe Vélez), lounges on a hammock while fully dressed in *La Zandunga*.	111
Figure 2.5	Linda (Margarita Mora) holds her head high as Diego Banderas and his cronies attempt to shame her in *Tierra de pasiones* (1943).	119
Figure 3.1	Joaquín (Carlos López Moctezuma) and Luis (Julián Soler) are morally dubious criollo *señoritos* in *La india bonita* (1938).	127
Figure 3.2	Anita Campillo as the "india bonita," Lupe, in *La india bonita* (1938).	129
Figure 3.3	The virtuous and authentically Mexican Indigenous couple, Miguel and Lupe, presented through whiteness-as-indigeneity in *La india bonita* (1938).	130
Figure 3.4	Anita Campillo playing the non-Indigenous Carmela in the Spanish-language Hollywood production *La cruz y la espada* (1934).	132
Figure 3.5	Consuelo Frank as the Indigenous María in *El indio* (1939).	138
Figure 3.6	María Candelaria (Dolores del Río) is saddened when blocked from selling her flowers in *María Candelaria* (1944).	143
Figure 3.7	A shot of María's intransigent community in *María Candelaria* (1943).	143
Figure 3.8	An indigenous-as-indigenous model poses for the criollo painter in *María Candelaria*.	145
Figure 3.9	María Candelaria as seen by the criollo painter.	149
Figure 3.10	The criollo painter gasps in astonishment upon seeing María Candelaria for the first time.	150
Figure 3.11	Margarita Cortés as the comparatively racialized antagonist, Lupe, in *María Candelaria* (1944).	151
Figure 3.12	De la Garza's gaze toward Maclovia produces pleasure.	159
Figure 3.13	Maclovia is gazed upon by de la Garza and the spectator.	160

Illustrations   xi

Figure 3.14 Maclovia (María Félix) and Sara (Columba Domínguez) occupying opposite sides of the frame in *Maclovia* (1948). 161

Figure 3.15 Maclovia (María Félix) and Sara (Columba Domínguez) in asymmetrical positions of the frame in *Maclovia* (1948). 162

Figure 3.16 Columba Domínguez as the scorned Indigenous antagonist, Sara, in *Maclovia* (1948). 163

Figure 3.17 In *Raíces* (1955), Teodalo stands by his daughter, Xanath. 172

Figure 3.18 Close-up of Alicia del Lagos as Xanath in "La potranca" (*Raíces*, 1954). 173

Figure 3.19 "La potranca" associates the young Xanath with a filly, or mare, under the age of four. 174

Figure 4.1 Deseada (Dolores del Río) explains to a Mayan painter (Wilbert Puerto) that he learned the contents of his artwork "antes de nacer" (before birth) in *Deseada* (1951). 197

Figure 4.2 Impossible love between Deseada (Dolores del Río) and Manuel (Jorge Mistral) causes much suffering in *Deseada* (1951). 201

Figure 5.1 Silvia Pinal playing an Indigenous maid in *María Isabel* (1968). 212

Figure 5.2 María Isabel is literally reflected in the image of the Virgin of Guadalupe. 219

Figure 5.3 María Isabel overreacts to a model skeleton. 223

Figure 5.4 Silvia Pinal in an advertisement for Colgate soap that aligns her with Mexican Whiteness. 227

Figure 6.1 While held as prisoners by the Indigenous tribe, Leonor (Medea de Novara, center left) and her circle are treated well by Tumitl (Miguel Contreras Torres, center right). 244

Figure 6.2	Though Leonor and Tumitl do not share the same religion, *Tribu* suggests that "ante Dios están unidos" (they are united before God).	248
Figure 6.3	Coyote Iguana (Armando Silvestre) takes Lola Casanova (Meche Barba) prisoner with the intention of marrying her.	251
Figure 6.4	Pedro Infante as the title character in *Tizoc* (1957).	259
Figure 6.5	The criolla María (María Félix) dressed as a Tehuana and Tizoc (Pedro Infante) find common ground in nature.	261
Figure 6.6	Tizoc (played by Pedro Infante in brownface) daydreams that María is dancing with a Whitened version of himself in *Tizoc* (1957).	264
Figure 6.7	In Tizoc's daydream, María gazes desirously at a Whitened version of himself.	264
Figure 6.8	The parodic film *El violetero* (1960) reproduces the visual motifs of *María Candelaria* for comedic effect.	270
Figure 6.9	At the end of *El violetero* (1960), neither Teresa nor the bourgeois party guests suspect that Lorenzo Miguel (Germán Valdés) is an Indigenous man.	272
Figure 6.10	Sombra and Ana kiss in *Güeros* (2014).	279

Acknowledgments

Though the process of writing a book can feel like a solitary experience, it is in fact the result of valuable encounters with many individuals. Because these people are often unaware of the role they play throughout the many years during which curiosity, expertise, and research develop, I wish here to recognize them and their contribution to making this volume possible.

Teachers and mentors are among the first to cultivate a passion for learning and set us on the path of intellectual inquiry. I would not have contemplated continuing my studies in the area of Latin American literatures and cultures were it not for two formidable professors and scholars at the University of Notre Dame who suggested that I had "madera de investigadora" (the makings of a researcher), María Olivera Williams and Encarnación Juárez Almendros. They, along with the Italianists Theodore Cachey and John Welle, encouraged me warmly to keep going. Thank you for the nudge.

This project evolved through numerous seminars I took as a graduate student in the Department of Spanish and Portuguese at the Ohio State University. I thank Abril Trigo, Ana del Sarto, and Fernando Unzueta for expanding my horizons and for always challenging me to think more deeply. At the dissertation stage, I benefited greatly from the mentorship and suggestions of Guisela Latorre and Paloma Martínez Cruz, whose work and way of being in academia continue to inspire me. I also thank Ignacio Corona for his contributions to my project at that early phase. Most importantly, my work would not exist without the guidance, kindness, and excellence of Laura Podalsky, who for years helped me to think through complex ideas and scores of films. Thank you for your dedication, without which none of this would have been possible.

Several entities and individuals enabled me to conduct research for this book. I thank the Center for Latin American Studies at the Ohio State University, which provided funding through a Tinker grant in 2013 for preliminary research. I am grateful to Angel Martínez from the Filmoteca at the Universidad Autónoma de México for providing me with access to dozens of films and for sharing his encyclopedic knowledge of Mexican cinema with me. I also thank the Filmoteca at the Universidad Autónoma de México and Mil Nubes-Foto (Roberto Fiesco) for their permission to include several images in this book, which greatly help to bring the films to life in this textual medium. A warm thank-you to Gabriela Ramírez Thomas, who welcomed me into her home during my stay in Mexico City.

A Dean's Graduate Enrichment Fellowship from the Ohio State University supported the writing of early portions of this manuscript. Several small grants from the same institution and from Kenyon College allowed me to present my ideas at professional conferences, where I received valuable feedback. I thank the Center for Faculty Development and Excellence at Emory University for the Scholarly Writing and Publishing Grant that supported this project in its final stages and Allison Adams for her warm encouragement throughout the writing process. I am grateful to Phil MacLeod and the Robert W. Woodruff Library for making a variety of resources available to me, including the Brill Classic Mexican Cinema Online Collection with the support of the Department of Spanish and Portuguese at Emory. I express special thanks to the Fox Center for Humanistic Inquiry within the Emory College of Arts and Sciences for the TOME (Toward an Open Monograph Ecosystem) subvention funded with support from the Andrew W. Mellon Foundation, which enables the widest possible access to this volume.

This book has benefited in no small measure from colleagues who graciously agreed to read and comment on early drafts of its chapters. To Juan Sebastián Ospina León, Jennifer Alpert, and Manuel Cuellar, my deepest thanks for your thoughtful comments and encouragement. I am immensely grateful to Jaqueline Avila and Oswaldo Mejía for their advice and support in locating images. Conferences allowed me to encounter many other colleagues who contributed to this project through their incisive questions and suggestions, including Sergio de la Mora, Victoria Ruétalo, Dolores Tierney, Ernesto Acevedo-Muñoz, Enrique García, Vinicius Navarro, Nilo Couret, Rielle Navitsky, Nicolas Poppe, David S. Dalton, Carolyn Fornoff, and Diana Horton. I offer a special thanks to Laura Isabel Serna for her guidance, generosity, and example of excellence.

Acknowledgments

At my home institutions throughout my postgraduate journey, I have received invaluable support from numerous colleagues. Thank you to Daniel Hartnett, Travis Landry and Clara Román Odio at Kenyon College and to James Melton, María M. Carrión, Karen Stolley, Hernán Feldman, Javier Villa-Flores, Yanna Yannakakis, and Tom Rogers at Emory University for their encouragement and kindness.

I am deeply appreciative to everyone at SUNY University Press involved with moving this project forward. To Ignacio Sánchez Prado and Leslie Marsh, thank you for supporting the inclusion of my work in your Latin American Cinema series. The revision and production phases of this project coincided with the extraordinarily challenging circumstances of the COVID-19 pandemic. I would like to express my gratitude to Rebecca Colesworthy for guiding me through the publishing process with clarity and care in the face of just about anything. I also thank the two anonymous reviewers who contributed greatly to the improvement of my work, as well as to Isis Sadek, whose editing wizardry helped to shape it into its present form.

To Patricia Arroyo Calderón, Jaime Omar Salinas Zabalaga, Raúl Diego Rivera Hernández, Daniela Salcedo, Axel Presas, Manuel Cuellar, Inés Nam, and Stephanie Kornexl-Kaufmann, thank you for years of intellectual and personal companionship, which have been a source of solidarity, strength, and motivation.

To my parents, Marco Antonio García Guzmán and Cecilia Blizzard de la Garza, this book would not exist if you had not shown me many *Méxicos, los de adentro y los de afuera*. Thank you for giving me an appreciation of language and culture that no displacement can erode. *Mamá, eres una guerrera*. Your example of perseverance has made all things possible. To my siblings, Chech and Coco, thanks for cheering me on in your own way.

Alessandro, your love has kept me grounded, sane, and whole through everything. Thank you. Lucia and Tomás, your unrelenting joy is truly radical and revolutionary. Thank you for sharing it with me. *Questo, come tutto, è per voi tre.*

Introduction

When many US and European spectators first encounter mainstream Mexican films and *telenovelas*, their reaction is frequently one of bewilderment. Often these spectators cannot help but ask something to the effect of "Why is everyone so White?"[1] What they mean, of course, is that the predominance of people with European epidermal schemas[2] in film and television produced in Mexico clashes forcefully with their own racialized understanding of Mexicanness and their (often unquestioned) acceptance that, with respect to themselves, Mexicanness is radical alterity.

Though the mediatic image of White preponderance has always contrasted starkly with the country's demography, as Charles Ramírez Berg and Dolores Tierney have observed, Whites have still enthroned themselves as the universal image of Mexican society in film and media, in part because of their political and economic dominance.[3] Local media

---

1. In this book I capitalize the words "White," "Whiteness," "Black," and "Blackness" to differentiate racial categories from the colors white and black. I capitalize the words "Indian," "Indigenous," and "Indigeneity" to indicate that I am referring to First Peoples as opposed to the more general definition of the word indigenous, which can refer to people who are native to any place. When quoting other scholars who use these terms, I reproduce the words as they appear in those sources.

2. Following Frantz Fanon and Hugo Cerón-Anaya, the term "epidermal schema" in this book designates "how the most obvious external features humans possess (skin color, hair texture, nose shape, lip size, and body fat) are used to determine racial categories and social belonging." Hugo Cerón-Anaya, *Privilege at Play: Class, Race, Gender, and Golf in Mexico* (New York: Oxford University Press, 2019), 94, note 5; Frantz Fanon, *Black Skin, White Masks* (New York: Grove Press, 2008), 89–119.

3. Charles Ramírez Berg, *Cinema of Solitude* (Austin: University of Texas Press, 2010), 137; Dolores Tierney, *Emilio Fernández: Pictures in the Margins* (Manchester: Manchester University Press, 2012), 86; Richard Dyer, "Introduction," in *The Matter of Images: Essays on Representation* (New York: Routledge, 1993).

producers established racialized norms of representation by which heroes and protagonists have been largely represented by actors whose phenotypes conform to the physical requirements of Whiteness in Mexico, while those with epidermal schemas that do not fall within the parameters of Mexican Whiteness are often relegated to the roles of villainous or comedic characters.[4] In recent years, Mexican actor Tenoch Huerta has publicly identified these norms as racist practices within the national film industry, which, in his own words, limit Mexican men of color like himself to the roles of "jodido, sufridor y . . . ratero" (the fucked, the suffering and . . . the thief).[5]

When this norm is not adhered to, racist backlash ensues. The case of Alfonso Cuarón's 2018 film *Roma*, which featured an actress of Mixtec origin, Yalitza Aparicio, is illustrative. Aparicio's centrality in the film produced racist indignation in the form of insults and calls to disqualify her from the Ariel Awards (the annual awards held by the Mexican Academy of Film),[6] a sentiment ostensibly exacerbated by the international acclaim the film garnered, including an Oscar nomination for Aparicio's performance. Throughout 2018 and 2019, the fact that this "*india*"[7] was representing Mexico on the world stage through the prestigious medium of auteur cinema at international festivals and award shows was, according to many Mexicans, a problem.[8]

---

4. Ramírez Berg, *Cinema of Solitude*, 57; see also Tierney, *Emilio Fernández*, 85–87; Ignacio Sánchez Prado, *Screening Neoliberalism: Transforming Mexican Cinema, 1988–2012* (Nashville: Vanderbilt University Press, 2014), 204. On similar racialized casting norms in Hollywood, see Richard Dyer, "Coloured White, Not Coloured," in *White* (London and New York: Routledge, 1997), 59.

5. E. Camhaji, S. Corona, and G. Serrano, "El racismo que México no quiere ver," *El País*, November 27, 2019, https://elpais.com/sociedad/2019/11/27/actualidad/1574891024_828971.html. Unless otherwise noted, all translations in this book are mine.

6. Sergio de la Mora, "Roma: Repatriation Versus Exploitation," *Film Quarterly* 72, no. 4 (summer 2019): 46–53.

7. In present-day Mexico, the terms *india* and *indio* are a pejorative way to refer to people who identify as Indigenous or have Indigenous ancestry; however, historically, the term has not always been deployed as a slur. See Antonio Zirión Pérez, "Hacia una descolonización de la mirada: la representación del indígena en la historia del cine etnográfico en México (1896–2016)," in *Repensar la antropología mexicana del siglo XXI*, ed. Maria Ana Portal Ariosa (Mexico City: Universidad Autónoma Metropolitana, 2019), 366.

8. I thank Patricia Arroyo Calderón for first pointing out to me the relevance of the racist attacks on Aparicio for this volume.

The position of Whiteness as the norm[9] in Mexican film and media is particularly perverse in light of the country's majority mestizo demography. The degree of mediatic distortion carried out by this norm and the virulence with which it is defended confers on Mexican film and media's privileging of Whiteness a unique ideological force that this book uncovers. That ideological force is the coloniality of power. Through this term, sociologist and political theorist Aníbal Quijano has suggested that the experience of Spanish colonialism established asymmetrical power relations according to the racialized distribution of labor defined during that period.[10] His concept also refers to how political, economic, and social inequalities have persisted along racial lines in the centuries since Latin American republics' independence from Spain.[11] Furthermore, as elaborated by Walter Mignolo,[12] the term *coloniality* exceeds what Stuart Hall has called the economic approach to racism and refers *also* to the ever evolving cultural and ideological structures of "dominance" that have accompanied racism's original "'economic nucleus.'"[13] In this sense, the coloniality of power has much in common with what Homi Bhabha has referred to as "colonial discourse as an apparatus of power."[14]

In Mexico, one of the clearest manifestations of the coloniality of power is the continued social and aesthetic valuing of Whiteness that has persisted long after colonial rule. As in all societies forged in colonialism and coloniality,[15] Whiteness in Mexico confers social, economic, and

---

9. Richard Dyer, "Whiteness: The Power of Invisibility," in *White Privilege: Essential Readings on the Other Side of Racism*, ed. Paula Rothenberg (New York: Worth Publishers, 2005).

10. Aníbal Quijano, "Coloniality of Power, Eurocentrism, and Latin America," *Nepantla: Views from the South* 1, no. 3 (2000): 553–80.

11. Mabel Moraña, Enrique D. Dussel, and Carlos A. Jáuregui, "Introduction," in *Coloniality at Large: Latin America and the Postcolonial Debate*, ed. Mabel Moraña, Enrique D. Dussel, and Carlos A. Jáuregui (Durham, NC: Duke University Press, 2008), 2, 17.

12. Walter D. Mignolo, "The Conceptual Triad: Modernity/Coloniality/Decoloniality," in Walter D. Mignolo and Catherine E. Walsh, *On Decoloniality: Concepts, Analytics, Praxis* (Durham, NC: Duke University Press, 2018), 139–40.

13. Stuart Hall, "Race, Articulation and Societies Structured in Dominance," in *Essential Essays/Stuart Hall Vol. 1*, ed. David Morley (Durham, NC: Duke University Press, 2019), 172–213.

14. Homi Bhabha, "The Other Question: Stereotype, Discrimination and the Discourse of Colonialism," in *The Location of Culture* (New York: Routledge, 1994), 100–1.

15. "Colonialism in its most literal form refers to particular political relations; coloniality refers rather to relations of power and to conceptions of being and knowing that

aesthetic privilege to those who are perceived to possess it. This reality permeates all aspects of social existence and is prominently manifested in the country's (audio)visual cultural production. Mexican cinema has been a key instrument serving to reinforce a local ideal of Whiteness through the exaltation of White Mexican bodies on-screen and the steering of spectatorial desire toward those bodies.

This book addresses a specific display of the ubiquity of Whiteness in Mexico's audiovisual landscape and one that speaks to the intensity with which the showcasing of Whiteness is inextricably tied to colonized notions of beauty and desire: its historical pervasiveness even in fiction films that explicitly claim to represent Indigeneity. This volume builds on the excellent existing scholarship pointing to the racial politics in Mexican cinema during the Golden Age (roughly from the mid-1930s to the mid-1950s)[16]—a period of film production frequently credited with having a profound impact on Mexican culture and society. Expanding on the valuable work of Joanna Hershfield, Charles Ramírez Berg, Andrea Noble, and Dolores Tierney, among others,[17] this volume examines the

---

produce a world divided between legitimate human subjects, on the one hand, and others considered not only exploitable but dependent, but fundamentally dispensable, possessing no value, and denoting only negative or exotic meaning in the various orders of social life, on the other." Nelson Maldonado-Torres, "The Decolonial Turn," trans. Robert Cavooris, in *New Approaches to Latin American Studies: Culture and Power*, ed. Juan Poblete (New York: Routledge, 2018), 119.

16. One can take as a start date for the Golden Age 1936, the year in which Fernando de Fuentes's film, *Allá en el Rancho Grande*, achieved notable commercial success within Mexico and abroad. See García Riera, "The Impact of *Rancho Grande*," in *Mexican Cinema*, ed. Paulo Antonio Paranaguá, trans. Ana M. López (London: British Film Institute, 1995), 128–32; Rosario Vidal Bonifaz, *Surgimiento de la industria cinematográfica y el papel del estado en México, 1895–1940* (Mexico City: Miguel Angel Porrúa, 2010). A plausible end date for the period is 1957 because of the financial difficulties of the national industry at that time and the death of its most emblematic male star, Pedro Infante. On this, see Eduardo de la Vega Alfaro, "The Decline of the Golden Age and the Making of the Crisis," in *Mexico's Cinema: A Century of Film and Filmmakers*, ed. Joanne Hershfield and David Maciel (Wilmington, DE: Scholarly Resources, 1999), 165–91; Carl J. Mora, *Mexican Cinema: Reflections of a Society* (Berkeley: University of California Press, 1989), 99; Sergio de la Mora, *Cinemachismo: Masculinities and Sexuality in Mexican Film* (Austin: University of Texas Press, 2006), 70, 77.

17. Joanne Hershfield, *Mexican Cinema/Mexican Woman, 1940–1950* (Tucson: University of Arizona Press, 1996); Joanne Hershfield, "Race and Ethnicity in the Classical Cinema," in *Mexico's Cinema: A Century of Film and Filmmakers*, ed. Joanne Hershfield and David Maciel (Wilmington, DE: Scholarly Resources, 1999), 81–100; Ramírez Berg,

duration of a local, idiosyncratic form of racial masquerade[18] that I term whiteness-as-indigeneity.[19] From a decolonial perspective[20] grounded in the history of race relations in Mexico, this volume elucidates how, throughout the Golden Age, the White Indians of Mexican cinema manifest the unresolved tension between two ideological formations. On the one hand was the government's twentieth-century postrevolutionary discourse that symbolically celebrated Indigeneity, and, on the other, was the persistent, long-standing valorization of a local construct of Whiteness that began with colonialism and was transformed through subsequent discourses of modernity during the nineteenth and twentieth centuries. A result of this

---

Cinema of Solitude; Andrea Noble, *Mexican National Cinema* (London; New York: Routledge, 2006); Tierney, *Emilio Fernández*; David S. Dalton, *Mestizo Modernity: Race, Technology, and the Body in Postrevolutionary Mexico* (Gainesville: University of Florida Press, 2018); Jacqueline Avila, *Cinesonidos: Film Music and National Identity During Mexico's* Epoca de Oro (Oxford: Oxford University Press, 2019), 164–65; Natasha Varner, *La Raza Cosmética: Beauty, Identity, and Settler Colonialism in Postrevolutionary Mexico* (Tucson: University of Arizona Press, 2020).

18. My use of the term "racial masquerade" is inspired by the work of Michael Rogin, who has used the term to elucidate the function of blackface in the United States. For Rogin, the use of blackface by Irish and Jewish immigrants was a means through which they cast off the stigma of immigration and positioned themselves as US Americans. See Michael Rogin, "Making America Home: Racial Masquerade and Ethnic Assimilation in the Transition to Talking Pictures," *Journal of American History* 79, no. 3 (December 1992): 1050–77; and *Blackface, White Noise* (Berkeley: University of California Press, 1998).

19. As is the case with "blackface," I do not capitalize "whiteness-as-indigeneity" throughout the book because this hyphenated term refers to a trope in visual representation and not to group identities.

20. If, as José Rabasa asserts, "[t]o reflect on the postcolonial, no longer as a moment posterior to the formal independence, implies becoming conscious that colonial continuities entail inevaible linguistic, cultural, and political legacies" (José Rabasa, "Postcolonialism," in *Dictionary of Latin American Cultural Studies*, ed. Robert McKee Irwin and Mónica Szurmuk [Gainesville: University Press of Florida, 2012], 254), this volume can be understood as a postcolonial one in a general sense. However, while postcolonial studies, as developed in Anglophone academies, has tended to center the subaltern's possibilities of articulation, the Latinamericanist decolonial perspective tends to center "how coloniality of power was formed, transformed, and managed in its history of more than 500 years" (Mignolo and Walsh, *On Decoloniality*, 10). Because this volume is fundamentally interested in how cinema operates as an agent of such dominance and in elucidating obfuscfated mechanisms of that dominance, the term "decolonial" most accurately names the perspective taken here.

tension, whiteness-as-indigeneity is the limit case of the racist norms that have structured audiovisual production in Mexico. Like its hemispheric cousin, blackface, whiteness-as-indigeneity is characterized by a "tendentiously flawed mimesis."[21] However, instead of seeking to ridicule the racialized subject, the Mexican trope—not unlike the Whitening of Roma people in Spanish cinema as analyzed by Eva Woods Peiró[22]—works in the opposite direction, infusing the racialized subject with the dignity and desirability that coloniality confers upon Whiteness.

To understand how the reelaborated vestiges of colonial racial hierarchies reemerge in visual mediums such as twentieth-century cinema, it is necessary to approach the subject of Whiteness in the Mexican context by considering the evolution of racial categories and their role in shaping projects of national identity.

The Persistent Privilege of Whiteness in Mexico

The constructs of the Indian and of Indigeneity are European inventions that homogenized the original inhabitants of what came to be known as the Americas[23] and cast them as Other vis-à-vis the colonizer. The precise meaning of the term and who is considered an Indian has evolved over time under what Mexican anthropologist Paula López Caballero has termed "national regimes of alterity,"[24] which have each brought with them new terms to designate the constructed Otherness of the native inhabitants and their progeny, including terms such as *autóctonos, indios, pueblos originarios* (the autochthonous, Indians, original inhabitants, etc.) as well as the "constant slippage and strategic ambiguity" of the terms Indian, mestizo, and *campesino*.[25] Whiteness, which in the local Mexican racial

---

21. Robert Stam and Louise Spence, "Colonialism, Racism and Representation," *Screen* 24, no. 2 (March 1983): 6.

22. Eva Woods Peiró, *White Gypsies: Race and Stardom in Spanish Musicals* (Minneapolis: University of Minnesota Press, 2012).

23. Edmundo O'Gorman, *La invención de América: el universalismo de la cultura de Occidente* (Mexico City: Fondo de Cultura Económica, 1958).

24. Paula López Caballero, *Indígenas de la nación: etnografía histórica de la alteridad en México* (Mexico City: Fondo de Cultura Económica, 2017), 45.

25. Rick López, *Crafting Mexico: Intellectuals, Artisans, and the State after the Revolution* (Durham, NC: Duke University Press, 2010), 10.

formation functions as the polar opposite of Indigeneity,[26] is an equally fabricated and ever-evolving social identity. Throughout the book, my use of the terms "White," "Whiteness," "Indian," "Indigenous," and "Indigeneity" are not meant to reify the notion that such hermetic racial groups exist as verifiable scientific realities. Rather, I use the terms to refer to the constructed nature of these ethnoracial categories in Mexico specifically, and to the very real social, economic, and emotional effects that the perception of one's belonging to these categories has in lived experience.

Furthermore, my treatment of Whiteness in Mexico refers to a person's ability to locate themselves on the "right" side of what Mignolo has termed modernity/coloniality—the "set of diverse but coherent narratives" produced by "the Western Christian version of humanity, complemented by secular de-Goding narratives of science, economic progress, political democracy, and lately globalization . . ."[27] In the Mexican context, modernity/coloniality has constructed Indigeneity as the bane of these discourses, fixating on the following as points of supposed inferiority in various stages: Indigenous paganism, alternative ways of knowing, models of economic subsistence, communal organization, apathy toward the nation-state and its "democracy," protections for local economies, and so forth. In Homi Bhabha's terms, this is the process by which the subjects of the (post)colonial discourse of power execute the "containment" of the colonized and produce "that limited form of otherness . . . called the stereotype."[28] Because of the ambivalence of (post)colonial discourse, not only is the pejorative position of the colonized within it ever shifting as the discourse evolves through time, but the placement of the colonized is also unstable *within* a given phase of the discourse.[29]

Moreover, as Satya P. Mohanty has argued, the process of racialization not only "creates stereotypes of the colonized as 'other' and as inferior . . .

---

26. Federico Navarrete Linares, *México racista: Una denuncia* (Mexico City: Grijalbo, 2016), 153. The formation of this racial discourse must be understood in the context of the erasure of Afro-Mexican populations in official discourse and cultural production throughout the nineteenth and twentieth centuries. See Hernández Cuevas.

27. Mignolo, "Conceptual Triad," 139–40.

28. Bhabha, "The Other Question," 111.

29. Bhabha, "The Other Question," 117–18. To add an example of "ambivalence" from the Mexican experience to those provided by Bhabha, the Mexican in the United States is both an irremediably lazy individual *and* one who is taking away jobs from Euro-Americans. See Ella Shohat and Robert Stam, *Unthinking Eurocentrism: Multiculturalism and the Media* (New York: Routledge, 1994), 199.

the colonizer too develops a cultural identity that survives well past the formal context of colonial rule."[30] In other words, the ongoing process of pejoratively racializing the colonized necessarily also yields the fabrication of a shifting but always privileged category of Whiteness defined by its correlation to the current regime of modernity. To name this aspect of Whiteness, I borrow and expand a term elaborated by Latin American philosopher Bolívar Echeverría, *blanquitud*. For him, *blanquitud* refers to an individual's internalization of a specific discourse of modernity—the "ethos puritano capitalista" (puritanical capitalist ethos) that values above all else a high degree of productivity and the external, material wealth that such productivity yields.[31] For my purposes in this book, *blanquitud* refers not only to this "puritanical capitalist ethos"—the current regime of modernity that Echeverría has brilliantly theorized—but also to the previous discourses of Western modernity that have taken root in Mexico beginning with the Spanish conquest and continue to exist in residual forms. In this sense, the discursive and performative dimension of Whiteness that I refer to as *blanquitud* is an aggregate of the discourses of Western modernity in Mexico.

At the same time, however, Whiteness and Indigeneity are not merely discursive or performative positionalities, but ones with a very real embodied component that imposes limits to performativity for those with racialized epidermal schemas.[32] To refer to the quality of having genealogical ties to Europe and an epidermal schema that is read as European, this book uses the term *blancura*.

In what follows, I provide a brief outline of the ways in which the definitions of Whiteness in Mexico have been functions of the colonial matrix of power,[33] evolving from the sixteenth century to the twentieth

---

30. Satya P. Mohanty, "Drawing the Color Line: Kipling and the Culture of Colonial Rule," in *The Bounds of Race: Perspectives on Hegemony and Resistance*, ed. Dominick LaCapra (Ithaca: Cornell University Press, 1992), 314.

31. Bolívar Echeverría, *Modernidad y blanquitud* (Mexico City: Ediciones Era, 2019), 59–62.

32. As Bhabha reminds us, "The difference of the object of discrimination is at once visible and natural—colour as the cultural/political sign of inferiority or degeneracy, skin as its natural 'identity.'" "The Other Question," 114. See also Richard Dyer's concept of "white people's right to be various" in Dyer, "Coloured White, Not Coloured," in *White*, 49.

33. Mignolo, "Conceptual Triad."

to reflect the prevailing discourse of modernity of a given period while, simultaneously, the justification of Indigenous inferiority reflected Indigenous people's supposed incompatibility with each of those discourses. Throughout the past five centuries, the ability to embody Mexican Whiteness—in its various discursive and corporal definitions—has been a persistent source of privilege.

Spanish colonialism is the underlying historical reality that has structured the asymmetrical positing of different ethnoracial identities in Mexico, though these have since continued to evolve in complex ways. The fact of colonial dominance meant that access to political power, land, and wealth were greater depending on one's proximity to Spanishness. Of course, not all Spaniards or genealogical claims of Spanish origin were equal. In the fifteenth century, the concept of *limpieza de sangre* (purity of blood) evolved in Spain to distinguish Jews and Muslims who had recently converted to Christianity (respectively known as *conversos* and *moriscos*) from people whose families had been Christian for more than two generations.[34] The 1449 *limpieza de sangre* statutes prevented these new Christians from holding public office in Spain, and the establishment of the Inquisition in 1478 heightened their persecution.[35] The principles of *limpieza de sangre* were applied in New Spain, with Indigenous people becoming "pure of blood" upon conversion to Christianity, while Africans and their descendants did not have a clear path to attaining this status because of the perception of their ties with Islam, which became the justification for their enslavement.[36] The casta painting genre in New Spain—more a reflection of the elite's hope that neat boundaries among racial groups could be named and maintained than a historical document of how the colonial order operated—corroborated the idea that Indigeneity could smoothly fold into Spanishness.[37] While these images show that the descendant of an Indigenous person could be considered Spanish over just a few generations, these same images suggest that an Afro-descendant's

---

34. María E. Martínez, *Genealogical Fictions: Limpieza De Sangre, Religion, and Gender in Colonial Mexico* (Stanford, CA: Stanford University Press, 2008); Peter Wade, *Race and Sex in Latin America* (New York: Pluto Press, 2009), 67–68.

35. Wade, *Race and Sex*, 67.

36. Wade, *Race and Sex*, 68.

37. Magnus Mörner, *Race Mixture in the History of Latin America* (Boston: Little, Brown and Company, 1967), 59; Illona Katzew, *Casta Painting: Images of Race in Eighteenth-Century Mexico* (New Haven: Yale University Press, 2004).

Blackness could unexpectedly resurface even after several generations of mixing with Spaniards.[38] The name given to an Afro-descendant whose phenotype prominently manifested Black ancestry after several generations of genealogical Whitening in these paintings, *torna atrás*, literally suggests regression, thus underscoring Whitening as the ideal direction of one's lineage in the colonial context.

Despite the relative privilege of Indigenous people according to these representations, they were in effect deemed a childlike variant of humanity.[39] In practice, having *converso*, Indigenous, or African heritage in New Spain "could create suspicion and possibly exclude a person from public office, university entrance or ordination in the Church"[40]—which constituted nearly all of the avenues to political power and/or wealth. Furthermore, the stigma of illegitimacy, which had already been an obstacle to political and economic ascent in Spain, kept many mestizos from being able to acquire purity of blood status.[41] In sum, in New Spain, the more one could approximate Whiteness in the form of a legitimate Spanish lineage untainted by *converso*, Indigenous, or African heritage, the greater one's educational, economic, and political opportunities. In this context, Whitening did not necessarily refer to ensuring one's offspring had a chromatically lighter appearance; rather, it meant securing a specific legal status that some Spaniards and criollos (the progeny of Spaniards born in the Americas) enjoyed because of their genealogies.[42]

After Mexican independence from Spain, the 1821 Plan of Iguala established the legal equality of all of the republic's inhabitants, and the following year Congress ordered the omission of racial classifications in all legal documents.[43] This shift brought Mexico closer, at least discursively, to the European model of modern nationhood, which required a substantial degree of homogeneity among fellow co-nationals. However, despite the

---

38. Katzew, *Casta Painting*.

39. Anthony Pagden, *The Fall of Natural Man: The American Indian and the Origins of Comparative Ethnology* (Cambridge: Cambridge University Press, 1982), 57–108.

40. Wade, *Race and Sex*, 69.

41. Mörner, *Race Mixture*; Wade, *Race and Sex*, 69.

42. Rachell Sánchez-Rivera, "What Happened to Mexican Eugenics?: Racism and the Reproduction of the Nation" (PhD diss., University of Cambridge, Queens College, 2019), 62.

43. Moisés González Navarro, "El mestizaje mexicano en el período nacional," *Revista Mexicana de Sociología* 30, no. 1 (1968): 35–52.

elimination of the term "Indian" as a legal category,[44] governing elites were aware of the need to negotiate the internal ethnic and racial heterogeneity of the population for the purposes of producing national cohesion.[45] Within this negotiation of internal difference, the construct of Indigeneity and the identification of its proper place and function within the new nation became an ongoing concern. These anxieties about Indigeneity did not emerge in a vacuum; rather they built on and evolved previous ideas. As Rachell Sánchez-Rivera has argued, in the nineteenth century "preconceived notions of honorability, respectability and purity of blood were subsumed within new scientific ideas to manage and control reproduction, framed within the terms of an 'ideal' mixing of people consequently determining the ideal Mexican citizen after the Independence in 1821."[46]

Fundamentally, Indigenous people were a source of frustration for governing elites in the nineteenth century because of the former's perceived incompatibility with elite designs of "progress"—a Eurocentric ideological orientation shaped by the Enlightenment, social Darwinism, and positivism.[47] From the elite perspective, part of the problem was that Indigenous people did not perceive themselves as national subjects. As Mexican historian Beatriz Urías Horcasitas observes, prominent public and academic figures of the period such as Francisco Pimentel and Rafael de Zayas Enriquez complained that Indigenous people lacked any sense of belonging to the Mexican nation-state.[48] Still, the greatest impediment that Indigenous people posed for national development according to elites was their supposedly unproductive use of the land according to modern,

---

44. González Navarro, "El mestizaje mexicano," 35, Alicia Castellanos Guerrero, "Para hacer nación: discursos racistas en el México decimonónico," in *Los caminos del racismo en México*, ed. José Jorge Gómez Izquierdo (Mexico City: Plaza y Valdés, S.A., 2005), 91–92; Rodolfo Stavenhagen, "El Indigenismo mexicano: Gestación y ocaso de un proyecto nacional," in *Raza y política en Hispanoamérica*, ed. Tomás Pérez Vejo and Pablo Yankelevich (Madrid: Iberoamericana Vervuert, 2018), 219.

45. Claudio Lomnitz-Adler, *Exits from the Labyrinth* (Berkeley: University of California Press, 1992), 263–80; José Jorge Gómez Izquierdo, "Racismo y nacionalismo en el discurso de las élites mexicanas," in Gómez Izquierdo, ed., *Los caminos del racismo*, 121.

46. Sánchez-Rivera, "What Happened to Mexican," 64–65.

47. E. Bradford Burns, *The Poverty of Progress: Latin America in the Nineteenth Century* (Berkeley: University of California Press, 1980), 18.

48. Beatriz Urías Horcasitas, *Historias secretas del racismo en México (1920–1950)* (Mexico City: Tusquets Editores México, 2007), 43–48.

nineteenth-century standards.[49] Within a vision of economic development based on the exporting of raw materials on a massive scale, Indigenous people's landownership and their alternative use of that land for subsistence purposes was cast as a serious economic liability for the nation.[50] The new nineteenth-century legal framework in which all Mexicans were, at least nominally, equal under the law led to the erosion of Indigenous people's previous condition of semiautonomy, rights to communal lands, and other protections.[51]

The so-called "guerras de castas"—Indigenous uprisings that took place in various regions of the country aiming to regain appropriated lands—greatly heightened the urgency of "el problema del indio" (the Indian question) for elites.[52] In the north, José María Leyva Cajeme led the uprising of the Yaquis in Sonora, governing a Yaqui state from 1875 to 1886 until the government sold the Yaquis to henequen plantation owners in Yucatan.[53] The Tzotzil Mayans in Chiapas rose up under the leadership of Pedro Días Cuscat from 1867 to 1870, while Manuel Lozada led Indian resistance to hacendado encroachment in Jalisco and present-day Nayarit from the 1850s until 1873.[54] The Indigenous uprising of greatest magnitude by multiple measures was the Caste War of Yucatan in which Mayans fought against Whites and mestizos on the peninsula from 1847 into the twentieth century, achieving self-governance for a period of time.[55] The zeal with which elites held the exploitation of private lands to be crucial to national "progress" is clear in the calls to annihilate those Indigenous groups who rebelled against the expropriation of their lands.[56] These conflicts and the debates surrounding them laid bare the endurance of a racialized perspective in governance and the persistence of heterogeneous

---

49. Castellanos Guerrero, "Para hacer nación," 100.

50. Burns, *Poverty of Progress*, 76, 78, 134.

51. Regina Martínez Casas, Emiko Saldívar, René D. Flores, and Christina A. Sue, "The Different Faces of Mestizaje: Ethnicity and Race in Mexico," in *Pigmentocracies: Ethnicity, Race, and Color in Latin America*, ed. Edward Telles (Chapel Hill: University of North Carolina Press, 2014), 40.

52. Castellanos Guerrero, "Para hacer nación," 110.

53. Burns, *Poverty of Progress*, 110–11.

54. Burns, *Poverty of Progress*, 111–12.

55. Burns, *Poverty of Progress*, 112.

56. Castellanos Guerrero, "Para hacer nación," 107.

ethnoracial identities in Mexico despite the erasure of racial language in official documentation. Indigeneity was now an undesirable categorization because it acquired the connotation of being antithetical to "progress" and national economic interests.[57]

Another dimension of elite anxieties about Indigeneity was linked to the emergence of positivism in the nineteenth century and the implications of Lamarckian understandings of heredity, which had a unique endurance in Mexico.[58] Believing that the propensity toward alcoholism, destitution, illness, crime, and prostitution were inheritable characteristics, scientists in emerging disciplines such as social hygiene, anthropology, sociology, psychiatry, and legal medicine saw "in society's poorest sectors a latent and imminent threat of national degeneration."[59] In this context, Indigenous people in the second half of the nineteenth century became one of the many social groups categorized as degenerate, in multiple senses of the word.[60] For instance, anthropologists Francisco Martínez Baca and Manuel Vergara's 1892 study of crime associated Indigeneity with lawlessness and "social deviation."[61] For sociologist Rafael de Zayas Enríquez, the biological heredity of Indigenous people was intrinsically degenerative, meaning that they were destined to disappear because each successive generation was increasingly afflicted with disease and vice.[62] In this context of scientism, anthropometrics often functioned as "proof" of Indigenous people's supposed biological and genetic inferiority.[63] As Oliva López Sánchez observes, during the Porfiriato (the period between 1876 and 1911 during which Porfirio Díaz served as president for seven terms), some scientists concluded that Mexican women's bodies were not well suited for childbirth because of their pelvic measurements, which were smaller than those of

---

57. Martínez Casas et al., "Different Faces," 41.

58. Urías Horcasitas, *Historias secretas*, 108, 114; Sánchez-Rivera, "What Happened to Mexican," 91–114.

59. Fernanda Núñez Becerra, "La degeneración de la raza a finales del siglo XIX. Un fantasma 'científico' recorre el mundo," in Gómez Izquierdo, ed., *Los caminos del racismo*, 67–88. See also Urías Horcasitas, *Historias secretas* and Sánchez-Rivera, "What Happened to Mexican."

60. Núñez Becerra, "Degeneración."

61. Urías Horcasitas, *Historias secretas*, 47.

62. Urías Horcasitas, *Historias secretas*, 48.

63. Beatriz Urías Horcasitas, "Medir y civilizar," *Ciencias*, no. 60 (October–March 2001): 28–36.

European women.[64] The implication of their studies is that racial mixture produced female bodies that were inadequate for reproduction[65] and, more specifically, that the biological contribution of Indigeneity was to blame for this deficiency. In these ways, nineteenth-century scientific paradigms and practices reinforced previous racial hierarchies, casting Indigenous people among society's most wretched and rationalizing under scientific auspices the superiority of upper-class subjects who exhibited hygienic, moral, racial, educational, and cultural ideals.[66]

To address the threat that, according to elites, Indigeneity posed to the progress and development of the nation, liberals proposed various forms of assimilationism.[67] This strategy for nation-building found expression in the writings of politicians and intellectuals such as Vicente Riva Palacio and Justo Sierra in the late nineteenth century[68] and later in Andrés Molina Enriquez's *Los grandes problemas nacionales* completed in 1910—all of which pointed to *mestizaje* as the avenue for achieving national cohesion and progress in Mexico.[69] The proposal that a thorough mixing of the country's Indigenous and European elements would bring about national cohesion and vitality flew in the face of contemporary European pronouncements on racial mixture, such as those by Arthur de Gobineau,[70] which saw in miscegenation "the epitome of human degeneration."[71] Still, because the liberal discourse in the second half of the nineteenth century cast Indigeneity as an undesirable location of biological and cultural origin from which one needed to evolve, it constitutes what Alicia Castellanos Guerrero understands as the renewed Mexican racism of the nineteenth

---

64. Olivia López Sánchez, "La mirada médica y la mujer indígena en el siglo XIX," *Ciencias*, no. 60 (October–March 2001): 44–49.

65. Sánchez-Rivera, "What Happened to Mexican," 66.

66. Núñez Becerra, "Degeneración," 74–75.

67. Castellanos Guerrero, "Para hacer nación," 89–115.

68. Martínez Casas et al., "Different Faces," 42.

69. Luis Villoro, *Los grandes momentos del indigenismo en México* (Mexico City: El Colegio de México, 1996), 217.

70. Castellanos Guerrero, "Para hacer nación," 100.

71. Alexandra Stern, "Mestizofilia, biotipología y eugenesia en el México posrevolucionario: Hacia una historia de la ciencia y el Estado, 1920–1960," *Relaciones* 21, no. 81 (2000): 53–91.

century, distinct but informed by the previous racial hierarchies.[72] While Spanishness still featured as part of the White ideal—evident in the centrality that speaking the Spanish language and sharing the Catholic faith had as markers of assimilation[73]—the understanding of Whiteness as it evolved in the nineteenth century also incorporated the nations of the North Atlantic, whose technological advancements and capitalist projects Mexican elites aspired to imitate.[74] In this way, nineteenth-century assimilationism continued to privilege Whiteness and introduced mestizaje as a desirable ethnoracial identity.

For governing elites in the second half of the nineteenth century, one of the strategies for creating a mestizaje that would result in national progress involved promoting the immigration of Whites from North America and Europe.[75] This plan was the topic of impassioned debates in the national congress, and it was supported by various political figures, including the prominent intellectual Justo Sierra.[76] The arrival of large quantities of White immigrants, liberals hoped, would "improve the race" and mitigate cultural and technological backwardness in Mexico.[77] At the same time, naturalization laws were put in place to block migrants deemed undesirable for Mexican mestizaje, including Jewish, Japanese, Afro-Caribbean, and Chinese people.[78]

In addition to promoting biological mestizaje, politicians and intellectuals such as Manuel Orozco y Berra and Francisco Pimentel also saw education as a vehicle to assimilate Indigenous Mexicans into a hegemonic criollo/mestizo culture.[79] The idea that Indigenous people could become intellectually equal to Whites through a Western education departed from

---

72. Castellanos Guerrero, "Para hacer nación"; Núñez Becerra, "Degeneración."

73. Castellanos Guerrero, "Para hacer nación," 93.

74. Burns, *Poverty of Progress*, 7.

75. Burns, *Poverty of Progress*, 31; Castellanos Guerrero, "Para hacer nación," 89–115; Urías Horcasitas, *Historias secretas*, 50; Erika Pani, *Para pertenecer a la gran familia mexicana: procesos de naturalización en el siglo XIX* (Mexico City: El Colegio de México, 2015); Sánchez-Rivera, "What Happened to Mexican," 67.

76. Castellanos Guerrero, Gómez Izquierdo, and Pineda, "Racist Discourse," 218, 229; Gómez Izquierdo, "Racismo y nacionalismo," 107, 148.

77. Castellanos Guerrero, "Para hacer nación," 106–7.

78. Sánchez-Rivera, "What Happened to Mexican," 67

79. Castellanos Guerrero, "Para hacer nación," 103–7; Gómez Izquierdo, "Racismo y nacionalismo," 120.

the biological racism of the day according to which Indigenous people were irremediably inferior to Europeans and their descendants. However, the premise of assimilationism through education was, nonetheless, that Indigenous people's culture kept them in a state of backwardness and that they therefore needed to be improved through Eurocentric culture. That some of the most illustrious men of the century had either partial or full Indigenous ancestry—José María Morelos, Benito Juárez, Ignacio Altamirano, and Porfirio Díaz—seemed to confirm liberals' hopes for the role of education. The Sociedad Indianista Mexicana, founded at the end of the Porfiriato, embodied the belief in Indigenous regeneration through both foreign migration and schooling.[80] In sum, by both exposing Indigenous people to Western education and increasing the presence of Europeans and Euro-Americans in the national gene pool, nineteenth-century Mexican intellectuals and politicians invested in nation building hoped to create a more homogenous and Whiter citizenry.

In contrast to the colonial period in which genealogical Whiteness possessed a greater weight,[81] the nineteenth century illustrates an important transformation of racial understandings in Mexico. Because, as we have seen, by then Indigeneity connoted both material poverty and backwardness, degrees of social Whitening were indeed possible through a combination of economic success and acculturation.[82] Cultural and material transformations now allowed for a greater fluidity of racial and ethnic identities than had previously been possible. However, the sociopolitical landscape remained a racist one, preserving its "link between essentialist representations of race and social structures of domination," the criteria that according to sociologists Michael Omi and Howard Winant define any racist social project.[83]

---

80. Guillermo Bonfil Batalla, "Andrés Molina Enriquez y la Sociedad Indianista Mexicana: El indigenismo en vísperas de la Revolución," *Anales del Instituto Nacional de Antropología e Historia* 47, tome XVIII (1965): 217–32; Urías Horcasitas, *Historias secretas*, 50.

81. Martínez, *Genealogical Fictions*.

82. Alan Knight, "Racism, Revolution, and Indigenismo: Mexico, 1910–1940," *The Idea of Race in Latin America, 1870–1940*, ed. Richard Graham (Austin: University of Texas Press, 1990), 71–113; Navarrete Linares, *México racista*.

83. Michael Omi and Howard Winant, "Racial Formation," in *Race Critical Theories: Text and Context*, ed. Philomena Essed and David Theo Goldberg (Malden, MA: Blackwell Publishers, 2002), 136.

After the Mexican Revolution and under a corporatist model, the new government reaffirmed commitments to progress and modernity, which now meant achieving comparable levels of technological sophistication, health, and economic growth with the United States and Western Europe.[84] This endeavor involved extending resources to Indigenous and *campesino* populations as well as incorporating them into the nation-state. These interrelated projects of *indigenismo* and *mestizaje*[85] also inaugurated a new national discourse that made Indigenous people and mestizos its protagonists in an effort to visibly exalt the new national subjects. However, Whiteness (*blancura* and *blanquitud*) continued to hold value in Mexico, which is reflected in the official postrevolutionary ideology that incorporates aspects of Indigeneity symbolically, but exalts its Whitened counterpart, mestizaje,[86] as the nation's common "fictive ethnicity."[87] As social scientists Regina Martínez Casas, Emiko Saldívar, René D. Flores, Christina A. Sue, and colleagues have noted, "Indigenista policy . . . played a central role in constructing and defining mestizos as being *non*indigenous individuals."[88] On the one hand, Indigeneity now functioned as a symbol of Mexican particularity; on the other, it played a fundamental role in the cult of mestizaje as a marker of the distance that the mestizo had traveled into modernity and into Mexican national subjectivity.[89]

---

84. Lomnitz-Adler, *Exits*, 278; Urías Horcasitas, *Historias secretas*, 18–19; Paul Schroeder Rodríguez, *Latin American Cinema: A Comparative History* (Berkeley: University of California Press, 2016), 13.

85. Knight, "Racism, Revolution," 86.

86. Lomnitz-Adler, *Exits*, 278–79.

87. Etienne Balibar, "The Nation Form: History and Ideology," *Race Critical Theories: Text and Context*, ed. Philomena Essed Goldberg and David Theo (Malden, MA: Blackwell Publishers, 2002), 223–24; Joshua Lund, *The Mestizo State: Reading Race in Modern Mexico* (Minneapolis: University of Minnesota Press, 2012). See also Gómez Izquierdo's use of the term "la fábula del mestizaje," Navarrete Linares's concept of "la leyenda del mestizaje" in *México racista*, and Palou's description of mestizaje as "social fiction" in *El fracaso del mestizo*.

88. Martínez Casas et al., "Different Faces of Mestizaje," 44 (emphasis in original).

89. Sarah Radcliffe and Sallie Westwood, *Remaking the Nation: Place, Identity and Politics in Latin America* (London and New York: Routledge, 1996.) As Radcliffe and Westwood point out, the dynamic of defining the self through the discourse of the Other has been explored by postcolonial scholars of the Anglophone world Edward Said, Stuart Hall, and Homi Bhabha.

To realize their project for a modern mestizo Mexico, postrevolutionary Mexican politicians and intellectuals adapted nineteenth-century perspectives toward Indigenous people but essentially pursued the same assimilationist approach rooted in racism.[90] Within the inherited positivist and evolutionist framework in which Mexican intellectuals and politicians continued to operate after the Revolution, Indigenous people were not racially inferior in a biological sense, but they could not contribute substantially to Mexican modernity beyond providing the archaeological and historical markers that endowed the nation with symbolic specificity.[91] For José Vasconcelos, the secretary of public education from 1921 to 1924 who put forth a utopic vision of racial amalgamation in Latin America, Indigenous people's contribution to mestizaje consisted of their "countless number of properly spiritual capacities."[92] Echoing their nineteenth-century counterparts' faith in education as a force of national amalgamation, some of the most emblematic postrevolutionary efforts to "improve" Mexican citizenry include the Cultural Missions designed by Vasconcelos, which from 1921 to 1924 traveled to rural areas for the purpose of priming young Mexicans for instruction in modern public schools.[93] Also, from 1926 to 1932 the Casa del Estudiante Indígena in Mexico City housed and educated rural Indigenous male youths with the goal that they would return to their communities to spread a civic sensibility and modernization.[94] In subsequent decades, influential anthropologists such as Alfonso Caso and Gonzalo Aguirre Beltrán would continue supporting *indigenista* policies that prioritized integration and acculturation, albeit with their own nuances.[95]

---

90. Urías Horcasitas, *Historias secretas*, 16–61, 122; Gómez Izquierdo, "Racismo y nacionalismo," 167, 169, 179; Sánchez-Rivera, "What Happened to Mexican," 24–27, 31, 75.

91. Urías Horcasitas, *Historias secretas*, 80–81.

92. José Vasconcelos, *The Cosmic Race/La raza cósmica: A Bilingual Edition*, trans. Didier T. Jaén (Baltimore: Johns Hopkins University Press, 1979), 32.

93. David G. Tovey, "The Role of the Music Educator in Mexico's Cultural Missions," *Bulletin of the Council for Research in Music Education*, no. 139 (winter 1999): 1–11.

94. Alexander S. Dawson, "'Wild Indians,' 'Mexican Gentlemen,' and the Lessons Learned in the Casa del Estudiante Indigena, 1926–1932," *The Americas* 57, no. 3 (January 2001): 329–61; Stern, "Mestizofilia," 85; Urías Horcasitas, *Historias secretas*, 52.

95. Guillermo de la Peña, "The End of Revolutionary Anthropology?: Notes on Indigenismo," *Dictablanda: Politics, Work, and Culture in Mexico, 1938–1968*, ed. Paul Gillingham and Benjamin T. Smith (Durham: Duke University Press, 2014), 284–85. See also Avila, *Cinesonidos*, 116.

Introduction 19

Those preoccupied with engineering an ideal Mexican citizenry shared with their Porfirian counterparts the desire to minimize the presence of elements deemed "degenerative" in the national gene pool.[96] Though the concerns of Mexican eugenicists exceeded the Indigenous question—targeting alcoholism, prostitution, and socioeconomic marginality as well—twentieth-century eugenicist doctors frequently established links between Indigenous people and tendencies toward delinquency and mental illness.[97] In addition, Mexican eugenicists of the period considered vagrancy and alcoholism to be Indigenous traits.[98]

The academics, doctors, intellectuals, and politicians who belonged to the Sociedad Eugénica Mexicana para el Mejoramiento de la Raza (Mexican Society of Eugenics for the Improvement of the Race), founded in 1931, perceived a need for "social prophylaxis"—measures intended to safeguard the health, vitality, and ideal of mestizaje among the Mexican citizenry.[99] Members of the group, including the "father" of Mexican anthropology, Manuel Gamio, at times voiced recommendations very similar to those suggested throughout the previous century and its political regimes. For instance, group members played a role in drafting the migration law of 1926, which distinguished potential immigrants as either "assimilable" or "unassimilable," resulting in the denial of naturalization to many Jewish and Chinese applicants and the favoring of immigrants from Spain.[100] In addition, Gilberto Loyo, a demographer close to President Plutarco Elías Calles; and Alfredo Saavedra, a surgeon, professor, and the Society's first president, supported the immigration of White foreigners to Mexico.[101] The Society's members eschewed traditional racial determinism, especially during and after the Nazi regime.[102] However, as Sánchez-Rivera observes, the group merely replaced biological racism with cultural racism—which, according

---

96. Urías Horcasitas, *Historias secretas*, 108; Sánchez-Rivera, "What Happened to Mexican," 29–88.

97. Urías Horcasitas, *Historias secretas*, 117; Sánchez-Rivera, "What Happened to Mexican," 114.

98. Sánchez-Rivera, "What Happened to Mexican," 72–73.

99. Stern, "Mestizofilia"; Urías Horcasitas, *Historias secretas*, 113; Sánchez-Rivera, "What Happened to Mexican," 76–118.

100. Sánchez-Rivera, "What Happened to Mexican," 73, 81.

101. Urías Horcasitas, *Historias secretas*, 120; Sánchez-Rivera, "What Happened to Mexican," 77–78.

102. Stern, "Mestizofilia," 80–81; Sánchez-Rivera, "What Happened to Mexican," 84–88.

to Etienne Balibar, uses the concept of culture to reproduce hierarchies of people who are supposedly incompatible with one another.[103] In sum, newly armed with twentieth-century pseudoscience, Mexican intellectuals and politicians understood Whiteness (*blancura* and *blanquitud*) as the key ingredient that would ensure an ideal blending of the Mexican citizenry into a healthy and modern mestizo people, producing "solutions" whose justifications may have been new, but whose substance certainly was not.

Twentieth-century *indigenismo-mestizaje* (this hyphenation reflecting that they were two sides of the same coin)[104] was predicated on the inferiority of Indigeneity and therefore was a racist national construct. As Gómez Izquierdo explains, "Indigenist ideology is based on a racist view of the Indian to define its policies of assimilation or integration into national culture . . . Being mestizo is better than being an Indian, it represents progress towards Mexico's dreamed-of europeanization."[105] Ultimately, as numerous scholars have concluded, indigenismo-mestizaje is a particularly pernicious racist ideology precisely because it pretends to be raceless.[106] This social history results in a complex reality in Mexico in which "Indian ancestry has been proudly acknowledged . . . [but] society . . . clearly values whiteness as both a status symbol and as an aesthetic."[107]

In recent years, social scientists have noted the contradiction between the raceless discourse of Mexican mestizaje and the privileging of Whiteness that exists in everyday society.[108] Specifically, Mónica Moreno Figueroa observes that "passing towards 'whiteness'—in its peculiar Mexican ver-

---

103. Sánchez-Rivera, "What Happened to Mexican," 84–88; Etienne Balibar, "Is there a "Neo-Racism?," in Etienne Balibar and Immanuel Wallerstein, *Race, Nation, Class: Ambiguous Identities* (New York: Verso, 1991), 25.

104. Knight, "Racism, Revolution," 86.

105. Gómez Izquierdo, "Racismo y nacionalismo," 181.

106. Castellanos Guerrero, Gómez Izquierdo, and Pineda, "Racist Discourse," 221; Gómez Izquierdo, "Racismo y nacionalismo," 117–81; René Flores and Edward Telles, "Social Stratification in Mexico: Disentangling Color, Ethnicity, and Class," *American Sociological Review* 77, no. 3 (2012): 486–94; Mónica Moreno Figueroa, "Distributed Intensities: 'Whiteness,' Mestizaje and the Logics of Mexican Racism," *Ethnicities* 10, no. 3 (2010): 387–401; Martínez Casas et al., "Different Faces."

107. Lomnitz-Adler, *Exits*, 280.

108. Andrés Villarreal, "Stratification by Skin Color in Contemporary Mexico," *American Sociological Review* 75, no. 5 (2010): 652–78; Moreno Figueroa, "Distributed Intensities," 391; Martínez Casas et al., "Different Faces"; Cerón-Anaya, *Privilege at Play*.

sion—is still a goal for the inhabitants, a problematic area in terms of identity and a non-spoken rule of social stratification."[109] Her findings and those of other scholars[110] point to Whiteness as an enduring form of physical capital[111] in Mexican society. In his elaboration of the term, sociologist Chris Shilling expands on Bourdieu's analysis of the body, explaining that through the notion of physical capital, the body can be understood as a "possessor of power, status and distinctive symbolic forms which is integral to the accumulation of various resources" allowing for "the development of bodies in ways that are recognized as having value in social fields . . ."[112] Given the racist nature of the Mexican "social field" outlined here, the Whiteness (*blancura* and *blanquitud*) of the Mexican body—understood not strictly in chromatic terms, but as a combination of physical features, hair texture, classed speech patterns, dress, wealth, body height and build, gait, hygiene, posture, and mannerisms—is a source of power that confers social and economic advantage.[113]

As I hope the historical outline above makes clear, the term "Whiteness" as used in this book is tied specifically to Mexican social and historical realities. This contextual understanding of Whiteness is in tune with Omi and Winant's concept of "the racial formation," which refers to a historically and socially situated project within which human bodies and social structures are represented and organized.[114] Several decades earlier,

---

109. Moreno Figueroa, "Distributed Intensities," 391.

110. Christina A. Sue, *Land of the Cosmic Race: Race Mixture, Racism, and Blackness in Mexico* (Oxford: Oxford University Press, 2013); Gómez Izquierdo, "Racismo y nacionalismo," 117–81; Cerón-Anaya, *Privilege at Play*.

111. Chris Shilling, *The Body and Social Theory* (London: Sage Publications, 1993), 14.

112. Shilling, *Body and Social Theory*, 127.

113. On labor discrimination of Indigenous people in Mexico, see Castellanos Guerrero, Gómez Izquierdo, and Pineda, "Racist Discourse in Mexico," 223; on the preference of White Mexicans as marriage partners, see Castellanos Guerrero, Gómez Izquierdo, and Pineda, "Racist Discourse in Mexico," 233–35; and Sue, *Land of the Cosmic Race*. On other forms of social discrimination based on a lack of Whiteness, see Moreno Figueroa, "Distributed Intensities," 387–401; on the limits of economic capital and the heightened importance of physical Mexican Whiteness within the elite, see Hugo Nutini, *The Mexican Aristocracy: An Expressive Ethnography* (Austin: University of Texas Press, 2008), 69, 74; and Cerón-Anaya, *Privilege at Play*, 101.

114. Michael Omi and Howard Winant, *Racial Formation in the United States: From the 1960s to the 1990s* (New York: Routledge, 1994), 126; see also Hall "Race, Articulation and Societies," 210–11.

sociologist Harry Hoetink had already alluded to the ways in which various definitions of Whiteness are contextual, as in, for example, the existence of a "white Iberian somatic norm image" in the Caribbean that is distinct from and darker than that of northwestern Europe.[115] This same White Iberian ideal—the visage of the first Western discourse of modernity imposed in what is now Mexico[116]—still serves as the baseline definition of *blancura* in the country, according to which criollo and mestizo bodies are read as physically White in the Mexican context.[117] Furthermore, because Mexican modernity is characterized by multitemporal simultaneity,[118] the physical construct of Whiteness in Mexico is a spectrum reflecting the personifications of all subsequent Western discourses of modernity. The boundaries of Mexican Whiteness, therefore, are the "Iberian variant of Hispanic whiteness, a white face with dark-brown to black hair"[119] on the darker end and the blond, blue-eyed, Anglo US-inspired phenotype on the lighter end.

I wish to emphasize that all of the other cultural and economic markers (*blanquitud*) listed above inform the local construct of Whiteness. This confluence of factors has led Regina Martínez Casas and colleagues to demonstrate that skin-color distinctions in Mexico are highly ambiguous and do not determine the way Mexicans self-identify ethnically or racially.[120] For this reason, the terms "Indian" and "Indigenous" are also

---

115. Hoetink defines the term "somatic norm image" as "the complex of physical (somatic) characteristics which are accepted as a group as its norm and ideal. Norm because it is used to measure aesthetic appreciation; ideal because usually no individual ever in fact embodies the somatic norm image of the group." Harry Hoetink, *Caribbean Race Relations* (Oxford: Oxford University Press, 1967), 120.

116. Mignolo, "Conceptual Triad," 139.

117. Nutini, *Mexican Aristocracy*, 62; Eugenia Iturriaga, *Las élites de la Ciudad Blanca: Discursos racistas sobre la Otredad* (Mérida: UNAM, 2016).

118. Aníbal Quijano, "Modernity, Identity, and Utopia in Latin America," trans. John Beverly, *Boundary 2* 20, no. 3 (1993): 149; Néstor García Canclini, *Hybrid Cultures: Strategies for Entering and Leaving Modernity*, trans. Christopher L. Chiappari and Silvia L. López (Minneapolis: University of Minnesota Press, 1995), 3; Ana M. López, "Early Cinema and Modernity in Latin America," *Cinema Journal* 40, no. 1 (fall 2000): 49; Paul Schroeder Rodríguez, *Latin American Cinema: A Comparative History* (Berkeley: University of California Press, 2016), 1–14.

119. Woods Peiró, *White Gypsies*, 27.

120. Martínez Casas et al., "Different Faces," 36–80.

similarly constructed and signal a combination of physical, cultural, and socioeconomic markers.

Yet despite the multifaceted nature of Mexican Whiteness, the physical dimension (*blancura*) does at times operate as a defining boundary that one cannot dress, dye, exercise, or surgically alter one's way out of. Here, the work of anthropologist Hugo Cerón Anaya is highly illustrative. Cerón-Anaya perceptively disentangles the relationship between race and class in Mexico by challenging the full accuracy of the familiar adage "money Whitens." He demonstrates that although lower- and middle-class individuals with darker epidermal schemas can impact how they are racialized through increased wealth, consumption, and cosmetic changes to their body, money's Whitening effect diminishes among the upper-middle and upper class, where nonpurchasable forms of Whiteness, such as family pedigree and a White Mexican phenotype, are of extreme importance.[121] Thus, although the Mexican racial formation is a landscape characterized by ambiguity, there remains a crucial relationship between one's body and the latitude available for one to position the self within the colonial matrix of power.

Indigenista Visual Production and Cultural Anxiety

Critics have debated the role that cultural production has played in the construction of the nation as an idea and in the formation of national subjectivities and identities. Following Benedict Anderson's well-known study of print capitalism for the creation of national imaginaries[122] and Homi Bhabha's discussion of narratives as texts that simultaneously perform the nation while casting their contents as national signifiers,[123] Radcliffe and Westwood have demonstrated the crucial role of cultural production in the formation of national subjectivities in Latin America.[124] In light of

---

121. Cerón-Anaya, *Privilege at Play*, 101. See also Nutini, *Mexican Aristocracy*, 51–76.

122. Benedict Anderson, *Imagined Communities: Reflections on the Origins and Spread of Nationalism* (London: Verso, 2006).

123. Homi K. Bhabha, "Dissemination: Time, Narrative, and the Margins of the Modern Nation," in *Nation and Narration*, ed. Homi K Bhabha (London and New York: Routledge, 1990), 291–322.

124. Radcliffe and Westwood, eds., *Remaking the Nation*, 14.

Nestor García Canclini's observation that Mexico's cultural profile was established more through visual production than through literature,[125] it follows that visual cultural production is a privileged locus for understanding the role of culture in the forging of twentieth-century Mexican nationalism.[126] For this reason, various scholars have carried out studies highlighting how different manifestations of Mexican cultural production operated within the nationalist project of indigenismo-mestizaje by featuring visual constructs of Indigeneity.[127]

Indeed, visual representation was a central concern for the architects of the new postrevolutionary nationalist campaign. One of the foremost figures of this impulse, the anthropologist Manuel Gamio, specifically addressed the country's culturally stratified patterns of artistic production and consumption as a symptom of the nation's lack of cohesion. In his 1916 treatise, *Forjando patria*, Gamio advocates for a fusion in the artistic preferences of Mexicans: "Cuando la clase media y la indígena tengan el mismo criterio en material de arte, estaremos culturalmente redimidos, existirá el arte nacional, que es una de las grandes bases del nacionalismo" (When the middle class and the indigenous class have the same criteria regarding art, we shall be culturally redeemed, national art will exist, which is one of the great bases of nationalism).[128] In concert with

---

125. García Canclini, *Hybrid Cultures*, 118.

126. John Mraz, *Looking for Mexico: Modern Visual Culture and National Identity* (Durham, NC: Duke University Press, 2009).

127. The bibliography on this topic is vast. Here is a sampling of works that address diverse forms of visual cultural production: Anne Doremus, "Indigenism, Mestizaje, and National Identity in Mexico during the 1940s and the 1950s," *Mexican Studies/Estudios Mexicanos* 17, no. 2 (2001): 375–402; Joanne Hershfield, "La Moda Mexicana: Exotic Women," in *Imagining La Chica Moderna: Women, Nation, and Visual Culture in Mexico, 1917–1936* (Durham, NC: Duke University Press, 2008); Rick A. López, *Crafting Mexico: Intellectuals, Artisans, and the State after the Revolution* (Durham, NC: Duke University Press, 2010); Ruth Hellier-Tinoco, *Embodying Mexico: Tourism, Nationalism & Performance* (New York: Oxford University Press, 2011); Shelley E. Garrigan, *Collecting Mexico: Museum, Monuments, and the Creation of National Identity* (Minneapolis: University of Minnesota Press, 2012); Robin Adèle Greeley, "Muralism and the State in Post-Revolution Mexico," in *Mexican Muralism: A Critical History*, ed. Alejandro Anreus, Leonard Folgarait, and Robin Adèle Greeley (Berkeley: University of California Press, 2012), 13–36; Ageeth Sluis, "Camposcape: Naturalizing Nudity," in *Deco Body, Deco City: Female Spectacle and Modernity in Mexico City, 1900–1939* (Lincoln: University of Nebraska Press, 2016), 101–36.

128. Manuel Gamio, *Forjando patria* (Mexico City: Editorial Porrúa, S.A., 1960), 39–40.

this vision, Vasconcelos famously commissioned artists to create works that would portray the Mexican people and aimed to provide the country with an aesthetic that it could call authentically national.[129]

The results of these efforts were the now well-known murals painted by figures such as Diego Rivera, José Clemente Orozco, and David Alfaro Siqueiros. Although he did not adhere strictly to Vasconcelos's views,[130] Rivera explicitly engaged the theme of Indigeneity in paintings such as *The Great City of Tenochtitlan* (1945) located in the Palacio Nacional in Mexico City, which "depicts an idealized view of the Aztec capital."[131] In other works such as *The World of Today and Tomorrow* (1929–1935) (also located in the Palacio Nacional), he envisions the nation's central subjects as the peasant, the soldier, and the worker, and conceives of them as the evolved descendants of Mexico's Indigenous people. While such works prominently displayed Indigeneity and mestizos of color, it is important to keep in mind that indigenista cultural production (and indigenismo itself) was as preoccupied with modernity as it was with Indigeneity. As Adèle Robin Greeley points out, a major motive for the creation of the murals in the first place was the desire of President Alvaro Obregón (in office from 1920 to 1924) to mitigate the image of Mexico as an uncivilized country, especially following the violence of the armed phase of the Revolution.[132]

Interrogating indigenista visual production in Mexico during the mid-twentieth century allows us to address the tension between the official indigenismo-mestizaje ideology and the continued valuing of Whiteness that was both colonially inflected and ever evolving in response to subsequent regimes of modernity. Although starting from the early 1920s there was a highly visible promotion of Indigenous themes in the realm of Mexican cultural production, what I wish to point out is that in light of a history of racialized Othering, having the Indigenous and peasant populations suddenly become the privileged objects of aesthetic expression was not an unproblematic proposal. Figure I.1 is a cartoon that appeared in

---

129. Mary K. Coffey, *How a Revolutionary Art Became Official Culture: Murals, Museums, and the Mexican State* (Durham, NC: Duke University Press, 2012), 5–7.

130. Susan Dever, *Celluloid Nationalism and Other Melodramas: From Post-Revolutionary Mexico to Fin De Siglo Mexamérica* (Albany: State University of New York Press, 2003), 22.

131. Andrea Noble, "Latin American Visual Cultures," in *The Companion to Latin American Studies*, ed. Philip Swanson (London: Arnold, 2003), 154–71.

132. Greeley, "Muralism and the State," 13–36.

Figure I.1. The cartoon titled "Buen juez" (Good Judge) appeared in *Excélsior* on August 31, 1927.

Excélsior, a conservative newspaper directed toward a middle- and upper-class readership,[133] on August 31, 1927. The cartoon is titled "Buen juez"

---

133. Arno Bukholder de la Rosa, "El periódico que llegó a la vida nacional. Los primeros años del diario *Excelsior* (1916–1932)," *Historia Mexicana* 58, no. 4 (April–June 2009):

(Good judge), and it shows an Indigenous woman who has brought her son to a beauty pageant for children as she is met with the confusion of one of the pageant's judges.[134] "Ma'am, how dare you bring such an ugly little boy?" the judge asks the woman. When she responds that "Don Diego" is one of the judges for the pageant, the judge remains confused and asks what Diego Rivera's participation in the pageant has to do with anything. To this the woman responds, "Well, the boy looks just like the ones he painted in the Secretariat of Public Education." The cartoon suggests that just because Diego Rivera is painting Indigenous people in state-sanctioned murals in public buildings for all to see, this does not necessarily mean that they are aesthetically venerable according to Mexican public opinion.[135] It hints at the idea that pictorial indigenismo had yet to interpellate lighter-skinned elites, but at the same time allows the reader/viewer interpretative latitude. Most importantly, the cartoon points to the fact that there was contention about whether or not Indigenous people were fit for celebratory artistic representation and debate about how they should be rendered.

Anxiety surrounding the visualization of Indigeneity is also evident in relation to other mediums and practices that sought to showcase *lo mexicano*—understood as a hegemonic criollo/mestizo take on Indigeneity and rural Mexico.[136] In the 1920s and 1930s, Mexican intellectuals and

---

1370; Adriana Zavala, *Becoming Modern, Becoming Tradition: Women, Gender, and Representation in Mexican Art* (University Park: Penn State University Press, 2011), 190.

134. Based on the signature that appears on the cartoon, the cartoonist who drew it is presumably Ernesto García Cabral, one of the most prominent Mexican ilustrators of the first half of the twentieth century. Though, as Carlos Monsiváis explains, Cabral did eventually create picturesque images of Mexican people, in this cartoon he appears to be problematizing this mode of artistic representation. See Monsiváis, "Ernesto García Cabral y el nuevo darwinismo: 'El hombre desciende de la caricatura,'" in *La vida en un volado: Ernesto el Chango García Cabral*, ed. María José Moyano (Mexico City and Barcelona: CONACULTA-INAH/Lunwerg Editores, 2005).

135. For Adriana Zavala, this cartoon mocks the very possibility of "Indian" beauty. See Zavala, *Becoming Modern*, 190.

136. "Part official construct, part popular narrative, lo mexicano emerged in the 1920s as the organizing motif for a society devastated by revolutionary turmoil and in search of a unifying identity." Gilbert M. Joseph, Anne Rubenstein, and Eric Zolov, "Assembling the Fragments: Writing a Cultural History of Mexico Since 1940," in *Fragments of a Golden Age: The Politics of Culture in Mexico Since 1940*, ed. Gilbert M. Joseph, Anne Rubenstein, and Eric Zolov (Durham, NC: Duke University Press, 2001), 7.

business entrepreneurs helped the Mexican government develop its own version of a national exoticism that was shaped by Euro-American visions of Mexico and by national discourses that were central to postrevolutionary national identity,[137] This internal form of Orientalism[138] idealized and re-created rural Mexico, placing a specific emphasis on images of women because "it equated the exotic with the feminine."[139]

As a result, images of what Joanne Hershfield has called the "domestic exotic" and what Ageeth Sluis has termed the "camposcape" appeared in multiple mediums including high art, advertisements of various kinds, and postcards.[140] Within this new national aesthetic, *la india bonita* featured as a motif.[141] For Sluis, the dressing up of "deco bodies" (characterized by their slender shapes and fashionable late-1930s makeup with very thin eyebrows, full lashes, and a light complexion) in Indigenous garb across visual mediums was a way for the cultural industry to simultaneously convey modernity and authenticity.[142] Natasha Varner has used the term *india bonita* to draw connections among multiple forms of visual culture including beauty pageants, tourism posters, film, and photography to point to how postrevolutionary cultural elites reconstructed images of the female Indigenous body in a manner that was in fact "a project of erasure."[143] As David S. Dalton has illustrated, another cultural strategy for manifesting embodied Mexican specificity and modernity in the postrevolutionary period was to represent Indigenous bodies fused with technologies to convey their transformation into modern mestizos.[144]

Read together, these scholars analyze two embodied proposals for visualizing Mexican modernity, which are inversions of each other. The first

---

137. Hershfield, *Imagining la Chica Moderna*, 130; Varner, *La Raza Cosmética*.

138. I use Said's term "Orientalism" here as interpreted and recast by Stuart Hall to refer broadly to dominant Eurocentric forms of "racialized knowledge of the Other." Edward Said, *Orientalism* (New York: Vintage Books, 1978); Stuart Hall, "The Spectacle of the 'Other,' " in *Representation: Cultural Representations and Signifying Practices*, ed. Stuart Hall (London: Sage Publications & Open University, 1997), 260.

139. Ageeth Sluis, *Deco Body, Deco City*, 102; Varner, *La Raza Cosmética*.

140. Hershfield, *Imagining la Chica Moderna*, 128–53; Sluis, *Deco Body, Deco City*, 103; Varner, *La Raza Cosmética*.

141. Hershfield, *Imagining la Chica Moderna*, 127–55; Varner, *La Raza Cosmética*.

142. Sluis, *Deco Body, Deco City*, 105.

143. Varner, *La Raza Cosmética*, 13.

144. Dalton, *Mestizo Modernity*, 18.

uses the White Mexican body to signify modernity and folkloric accessories to denote *mexicanidad*; in the second, the Indigenous body is used to evoke Mexicanness, while technology conveys modernity. In this book, I maintain that the two proposals will not function as true equivalents in the Mexican cultural landscape because of one crucial factor: the aesthetic, romantic, and sexual desirability that will remain tied to Whiteness because of the nation's discriminatory racial history and the multifaceted legacy of coloniality. I suggest that while the association with technologies may have served to transform Indigenous bodies into modern mestizo ones, this juxtaposition was not enough to supplant (or even approach) the White Mexican body's status as the pinnacle of aesthetic value in society (especially for women), which in turn had a determinant effect on the representation of beauty and desirability as White in the modern visual medium of Mexican cinema.

The inability of the Mexican person of color to be upheld as simultaneously modern and desirable can be gleaned from the existing work of several scholars. Hershfield's analysis of illustrated magazines of the time featuring *la india bonita* provides insight into the racial politics at work in the appropriation of Indigenous culture: "*la india's* skin color was not something to be emulated, [but] her colorful, non-Western dress habits were a fashion rage among various sectors of elite society."[145] Furthermore, Laura Isabel Serna's analysis of how Mexican women of color who attempted the flapper hairstyle and other modern fashion trends were openly ridiculed in local print culture points to a tension with respect to beauty, modernity, and race.[146] Quoting a 1924 article by journalist Carlos Serrano in *Revista de revistas*, Serna notes,

> Middle-class observers clucked "in many of the dark faces that carry the imperturbable stamp of the race," the [flapper] style ends up being "unsympathetic and ridiculous." In designating modern styles as the province of those with fair skin, these sorts of comments reinforced Mexico's racial hierarchy . . .[147]

---

145. Hershfield, *Imagining la Chica Moderna*, 152.
146. Laura Isabel Serna, *Making Cinelandia: American Films and Mexican Film Culture Before the Golden Age* (Durham, NC: Duke University Press, 2014), 132–34.
147. Serna, *Making Cinelandia*, 133.

Serna's observation points to how the Mexican woman of color was held to be incompatible with a modernity that was also aesthetically desirable, making her participation in modern fashions appear absurd to the middle and upper class in Mexican society. The women's lack of *blancura* apparently disqualified them from taking on modern trends tied to *blanquitud*.

Because of the racialized dynamics of aesthetic value and desire, it is the specific combination of a White epidermal schema and stylized Indigenous garb that "wins" as a hegemonic national visual symbol (ubiquitous in twentieth-century cinema, calendar art, and advertisements). These representations have greater currency because the impermanence of the local embellishments and the more permanent Whiteness of the body anchor Mexico's claim to modernity in a manner that reinforces the long-standing colonized valuing of Whiteness as universally desirable in the Mexican racial formation.

Indeed, White Mexican bodies have had the luxury of adorning themselves with folkloric paraphernalia because these impermanent additions to the body do not threaten the White body's social privilege, which is safely secured by more permanent physical markers of Whiteness—a dynamic that Dyer has referred to as "white people's right to be various."[148] In this sense, I distance myself from Varner's analysis of a broad range of visual mediums that include dark-skinned Indigenous women as examples of *indias bonitas* because my focus suggests the nonequivalency of these examples.[149]

But to which iteration of modernity does this White Mexican body masqueraded as Indigenous correspond? When tasked with representing an Indigeneity that is both modern and desirable, twentieth-century cultural producers resort to using the visage of the *first* project of Western modernity introduced in what is now Mexico: an Iberian physical schema. By this point, Iberianness was sufficiently inscribed in local society and displaced from a global hegemonic position (having become the decayed alter ego of Anglo-US imperialism)[150] so as to be associated with Mexican tradition vis-à-vis looks disseminated from western Europe and the United States.

---

148. Dyer, "Coloured White, Not Coloured," in *White*, 49. See Federico Navarrete Linares's discussion of the role of clothing in granting bodies access to spaces of privilege in *México racista*, 52.

149. Varner, *La Raza Cosmética*, 13.

150. On the waning of Spain's global hegemonic position in contradistinction to US imperialism and its discourse of modernity, see María DeGuzmán, *Spain's Long Shadow: The Black Legend, Off-Whiteness, and Anglo-American Empire* (Minneapolis: University of Minnesota Press, 2005), xvii, xxiii. See also Woods Peiró, *White Gypsies*, 14, 19.

At the same time, a physical appearance that connoted Iberianness was still "superior" to the Indigenous physical schemata within a Eurocentric worldview. For this reason, the Iberian physical schemata—the darkest variant of Mexican Whiteness—became the canvas of choice onto which the signifiers of Indigeneity could be layered through folkloric embellishment. This visual code will define whiteness-as-indigeneity in cinema throughout the twentieth century with many White Mexican actresses transforming themselves physically into Indigenous characters simply by wearing long dark braids.

Filmic representations of Indigeneity in Mexico were also produced in the midst of a complex racial climate in which some aspects of Indigeneity were officially praised while others were unofficially disparaged. Such films often fulfilled an internally colonial function, reifying a criollo/mestizo subject position by making Indigenous Mexicans the "objects of spectacle."[151] Additionally, Indigenous-themed films were charged with other meanings and missions because of the significance of cinema as a medium that was uniquely associated with modernity.[152] Although government officials attempted to use muralism as an assertion of Mexico's modernity by marrying avant-garde aesthetics with local themes, and despite Vasconcelos's belief that it was impossible to develop film as a national form,[153] cinema eventually did become the most important channel through which the country would assert its aspirational status as a modern nation-state throughout the twentieth century. International recognition of Mexican films was one way in which the nation sought to proclaim its arrival as a sophisticated peer among North American and Western European countries. Through their participation in the modern art form of cinema, Mexican filmmakers sought to be recognized in international contexts as producers of films that were both exemplars of artistic quality *and* identifiably Mexican.[154] Mexican films about Indigeneity

---

151. Stam and Spence, "Colonialism, Racism," 4; Noble, *Mexican National Cinema*, 87–88.

152. Linda Williams, *Playing the Race Card: Melodramas of Black and White from Uncle Tom to O. J. Simpson* (Princeton: Princeton University Press, 2001), 22.

153. de la Vega Alfaro, "Origins, Development and Crisis of the Sound Cinema (1929–64)," in *Mexican Cinema*, ed. Paulo Antonio Paranaguá, trans. Ana M. López (London: British Film Institute, 1995), 79.

154. In this sense, Emilio Fernández's indigenista films were successful. *María Candelaria* (1944) won a special noncompetitive prize at the Cannes festival, and *La perla* (1945) won awards at the Venice Film Festival and at the US Golden Globes. See Tamara Falicov, "The Interlocking Dynamics of Domestic and International Film Festivals,"

are therefore rich spaces in which the search for Mexican singularity and external recognition, the racialized associations between Indigeneity and backwardness (both at home and abroad), and the national aspiration to be modern are carefully negotiated.

Mexican films about Indigeneity have been addressed by scholars in a variety of ways. Overwhelmingly, the literature on the subject is dominated by analyses of Emilio "El Indio" Fernández's indigenista films from the 1940s and those films that are considered to be precursors to his work.[155] This genealogy features Sergei Eisenstein's unfinished *¡Qué viva México!* (1932), Carlos Navarro's *Janitzio* (1935), Fred Zinnerman's *Redes* (1936),[156] and on occasion the early silent films *De raza azteca* (1921), Guillermo Calles's *El indio yaqui* (1926), and *Raza de bronce* (1927).[157] Scholarship has tended to address these films because Fernández's work is often considered to be most emblematic of the postrevolutionary government's aims for incorporating Indigenous people into the national community while exalting them on a symbolic and aesthetic level.[158] When films that represent Indigenous people have been discussed outside the postrevolutionary indigenista narrative, they are often mentioned in isolation and

---

in *The Routledge Companion to Latin American Cinema*, ed. Marvin D'Lugo, Ana M. López, and Laura Podalsky (New York: Routledge, 2018), 268.

155. See Daniel Chavez, "The Eagle and the Serpent on the Screen: The State as Spectacle in Mexican Cinema," *Latin American Research Review* 45, no. 3 (2010): 115–41; Laura Podalsky, "Patterns of the Primitive: Sergei Eisenstein's ¡Qué Viva México!," in *Mediating Two Worlds: Cinematic Encounters in the Americas*, ed. John King, Ana M. López, and Manuel Alvarado (London: British Film Institute, 1993), 25–39; Hershfield, "Race and Ethnicity"; Noble, *Mexican National Cinema*; Martin Lienhard, "La noche de los mayas," *Journal of Latin American Cultural Studies* 13, no. 1 (2004): 35–96; Tierney, *Emilio Fernández*; Claudia Arroyo Quiroz, "Fantasías sobre la identidad indígena en el cine mexicano del periodo post-revolucionario," in *Identidades. Explorando la diversidad*, ed. Laura Carballido (Mexico City: Universidad Autónoma Metropolitana-Anthropos, 2011), 149–70.

156. See Podalsky, "Patterns of the Primitive"; Tierney, *Emilio Fernández*, 77–80; Hershfield, "Race and Ethnicity"; Mora, *Mexican Cinema*, 40–42, 58–69; Aurelio de los Reyes, *El Nacimiento de* Que Viva México! (México, D.F: Universidad Nacional Autónoma de México, Instituto de Investigaciones Estéticas, 2006).

157. Chávez, "The Eagle and the Serpent," 117; Jorge Ayala Blanco, *La aventura del cine mexicano en la época de oro y después* (Miguel Hidalgo: Grijalbo, 1993), 145.

158. Báscones Antón, "La negación,"; Tierney, *Emilio Fernández*, 80–81.

studied within the development of the Mexican film industry;[159] thus they are not analyzed in ways that foreground the significance of their specific contents. Furthermore, much of the film studies tradition within the Mexican academy has tended to privilege historical and sociological approaches[160] rather than engagement with textual readings that allow us to interpret how these Indigenous-themed films produce meaning.

Many early films prior to the Golden Age have not been studied in detail because of their obscurity and lack of commercial success. Furthermore, Indigenous-themed films made toward the end of the Golden Age and after have largely been ignored or underanalyzed, in part because they are perceived to be plagued with the same general lack of quality and artistic merit that scholars attribute to Mexican films from the late 1950s through the late 1970s.[161]

Furthermore, scholarship on Mexican cinema in general traditionally has tended to privilege state policies and discourse as determining factors for the interpretation of films.[162] This emphasis is logical because the Mexican government played a significant role in the Mexican film industry beginning with the promotion of "quality cinema with a marked social content" during Lázaro Cardenas's government (1934–1940).[163] In 1942, the Banco Cinemátográfico (which later became the Banco Nacional Cinematográfico in 1947) "was funded primarily by the state to protect, promote and remodel" film production in the country.[164] The government also impacted distribution through the formation of Películas Mexicanas

---

159. Mora, *Mexican Cinema* and Aurelio de los Reyes, *Cine y sociedad en México*, vols. 1 & 2 (Mexico City: Universidad Nacional Autónoma de México, 1981).

160. Ayala Blanco, *La aventura*; Emilio García Riera, *Historia documental del cine mexicano* (Guadalajara: Universidad de Guadalajara, 1993–1994); Aurelio de los Reyes, *Cine y sociedad en México*, vols. 1 & 2; Carlos Monsiváis, "Se sufre pero se aprende," in *A través del espejo: el cine mexicano y su público*, ed. Carlos Monsiváis and Carlos Bonfil (Mexico City: Instituto Mexicano de Cinematografía, 1994); Sánchez Prado, *Screening Neoliberalism*, 9.

161. de la Vega Alfaro, "Decline"; Mora, *Mexican Cinema*; Ayala Blanco, *Aventura del cine mexicano*; Andrew Paxman, "Cooling to Cinema and Warming to Television: State Mass Media Policy, 1940–1964," in *Dictablanda*, ed. Paul Gillingham and Benjamin T. Smith (Durham, NC: Duke University Press, 2014), 308–15.

162. Chávez, "The Eagle and the Serpent," 115.

163. de la Vega Alfaro, "Origins," 82. See also Misha MacLaird, *Aesthetics and Politics in the Mexican Film Industry* (New York: Palgrave MacMillan, 2013), 24–25.

164. de la Vega Alfaro, "Origins," 85, 91.

S.A. in 1945 to handle distribution abroad and the creation of the mixed capital distributor, Películas Nacionales S.A., to carry out domestic distribution. Finally, in 1949 the Ley de Industria Cinematográfica was passed, proposing government financing for films of national interest, stricter censorship, and requiring governmental authorization for Mexican films screened abroad.[165] In light of the government's involvement in the film industry, official discourses about Indigenous communities at the moment films were produced are a pertinent factor that may have informed filmmaking decisions. For instance, we know that Emilio Fernández had to make modifications to *Río Escondido* (1948) after censors found the film to be "antirevolucionaria," or not in keeping with the ideals of the Revolution.[166]

However, while clearing censorship requirements was an important consideration,[167] film production of the Golden Age was also a function of other concerns, such as the market, the search for international recognition and prestige, and individual filmmakers' creative visions. Furthermore, as Andrew Paxman has argued, there is reason to believe that the state's role in Mexican film production and culture was less pronounced than has previously been argued because many of the state's measures regarding the industry had greater symbolic significance than real impact. Paxman observes, for instance, that when the Film Bank was created in 1942, it "was a largely private-sector bank, capitalized at 2.5 million pesos, the state committing a mere 10 percent."[168] Also, film quotas were passed but not necessarily enforced, and as a result, even during Mexican cinema's much celebrated Golden Age, the majority of the films exhibited were foreign, while few domestic productions were ever profitable.[169] In light of the priorities of industrialization, modernization, and the laissez-faire

---

165. "Ley de la industria cinemátografica," http://dof.gob.mx/nota_to_imagen_fs.php?cod_diario=196431&pagina=3&seccion=2; Roberto Ramírez Flores, "La Ley federal de cinematografía de 1949: la consolidación de un paradigma censor," *El ojo que piensa. Revista de cine iberoamericano*, no. 13 (2016), http://www.elojoquepiensa.cucsh.udg.mx/index.php/elojoquepiensa/article/view/246.

166. Matthew J. K. Hill, "The Indigenismo of Emilio 'El Indio' Fernandez: Myth, Mestizaje, and Modern Mexico" (MA thesis, Brigham Young University, 2009), 111.

167. Carlos Monsiváis, "Mexican Cinema: Of Myths and Demystifications," trans. Mike González, in *Mediating Two Worlds. Cinematic Encounters in the Americas*, ed. John King, Ana M. López, and Manuel Alavardo (London: British Film Institute, 1993), 140–41.

168. Paxman, "Cooling to Cinema," 303.

169. Paxman, "Cooling to Cinema," 299–320.

media policy in presidential terms (sexenios) after Cardenas, Paxman asserts that "the content of film and TV programming (newsreels and newscasts aside) was less important to the state than the proliferation of movie theatres and radios or TV sets."[170]

With regard to films about Indigenous people, the tendency to center the state has resulted in a lot of attention toward films that evidence ideological affinity with official state discourses of a particular period. For instance, *Redes* and *Janitzio* are frequently identified as examples of Cardenas's progressive social agenda that supported worker's rights and agrarian reform,[171] while Fernández's indigenista films are consistently read as examples of belated *cardenismo*.[172] However, there were other Indigenous-themed films produced during the Cárdenas presidency, such as *Tribu* (dir. Contreras Torres, 1935), *La india bonita* (dir. Helú, 1938), and *La Zandunga* (dir. de Fuentes, 1938), yet, because they have nothing to do with the official rhetoric of the period, they are largely understudied. As Paula Félix-Didier and Andrés Levinson have perceptively observed, "problems arise when attempts are made to establish close or direct ties between a political moment in the country's history and cultural production—as if it were possible to establish from a political perspective a cultural hegemony free of all contradictions."[173]

The tendency to center the state has yielded excellent scholarship and has, without a doubt, illuminated myriad aspects of filmic production in Mexico. However, when interrogating a pervasive and consistent racist code of cinematic representation, attempting to tie each film to a specific discourse during a *sexenio* (the six-year presidential term in Mexico) impedes an understanding of evident continuities, which the endurance of whiteness-as-indigeneity as a device exemplifies. Furthermore, a *sexenio*-centered approach also means that while connections

---

170. Paxman, "Cooling to Cinema," 306.

171. Alexander S. Dawson, *Indian and Nation in Revolutionary Mexico* (Tucson: University of Arizona Press, 2004), xxii.

172. Julia Tuñón, "Una escuela en celuloide. El cine de Emilio 'Indio' Fernández o la obsesión por la educación," *Historia Mexicana* 48, no. 2, special issue "Las imágenes en la historia del México porfiriano y posrevolucionario" (October–December 1998): 437–70; Dever, *Celluloid Nationalism*; Tierney, *Emilio Fernández*.

173. Paula Félix-Didiér and Andrés Levinson, "The Building of a Nation: La guerra gaucha as Historical Melodrama," in *Latin American Melodrama. Passion, Pathos, and Entertainment*, ed. Darlene J Sadlier (Urbana: University of Illinois Press, 2009), 53.

between some Indigenous-themed films have been consistently identified by scholars (such as the affinity between Emilio Fernández's *indigenista* films of the 1940s and Carlos Navarro's 1935 film *Janitzio*, in which Fernández acted), many others have never been explored. For instance, Emilio Fernández also played an Indigenous man in Miguel Contreras Torres's 1935 colonial-era drama, *Tribu*, a film that has very little ideological or aesthetic overlap with *Janitzio*, yet was released in the same year. The *sexenio* framework offers no meaningful way of reading these films together. The same is true for other aesthetically and ideologically dissimilar films about Indigeneity produced in temporal proximity in later decades, such as *Raíces* (dir. Alazraki, 1955) and *Chilam Balam* (dir. de Martino, 1957).

Instead of departing from the assumption that each film studied here must be somehow defined by the officialist rhetoric of the specific *sexenio* in which it was produced, this book's point of departure is that residual and emergent attitudes about race coexist in complex ways throughout the twentieth century, as is glaringly indicated by the very existence of whiteness-as-indigeneity throughout the period of cultural nationalism that championed *indigenismo*. Through a broad view of Indigenous-themed films, it becomes clear that ideologically divergent films about Indigenous people were produced in very close succession. Nearly all of these resorted to whiteness-as-indigeneity to convey those divergent messages. By privileging the films' aesthetic similarities while also identifying their discursive differences and the recurrence of those discourses, my hope is that this study can help provide a broader understanding of how cinema in Mexico has mediated a variety of conceptions about Indigeneity and the nation throughout the twentieth century.

Within these Indigenous-themed Mexican films, more often than not, women occupy the prominent roles, a fact that continues a long-standing local tendency to portray Indigeneity through the feminine.[174] Another reason for the prominence of female characters has to do with the param-

---

174. Tuñón, "Femininity, *Indigenismo*, and Nation: Film Representation by Emilio 'El Indio' Fernández," in *Sex in Revolution: Gender, Politics, and Power in Modern Mexico*, ed. Mary Kay Vaughan, Gabriela Cano, and Jocelyn H. Olcott (Durham, NC: Duke University Press, 2006), 95; Ana María Alonso, "Territorializing the Nation and 'Integrating the Indian': 'Mestizaje' in Mexican Official Discourses and Public Culture," in *Sovereign Bodies: Citizens, Migrants, and States in the Postcolonial World*, ed. Thomas Blom Hansen and Finn Stepputat (Princeton: Princeton University Press, 2005), 39–60; Analisa Taylor, *Indigeneity in the Mexican Cultural Imagination* (Tucson: Arizona University Press, 2009), 100; and Varner, *La Raza Cosmética*.

eters of the melodramatic mode, which was pervasive in postrevolutionary Mexican film production because "it responded to political and moral chaos by offering up 'truth' in the clearest and most melodious terms."[175] In melodrama, virtuous women are often protagonists because they have historically served as privileged vehicles for transmitting victimhood and emotionalism.[176] If, as Silvia Oroz has observed, one of the characteristics of Latin American melodrama is "[a] construção de uma imagem cinematografica nacional, que remete a um universo próximo do espectador" ([t]he construction of a national cinematic image, that references a universe close to the spectator),[177] one can see how Indigenous female lead roles in Mexican cinema were ideal vessels for melodrama in the local context. However, while on postcards intended for tourists Indigenous women could appear in rich epidermal shades,[178] their visualization in twentieth-century Mexican cinema is overwhelmingly White. In other words, in mainstream Mexican films, it is women whose epidermal schemas locate them as White in the local racial formation—understood in its multifaceted physical and cultural definition outlined above—who are cast in leading roles, even in Indigenous-themed films.

The obvious fact that this phenomenon is a breach of indexicality—often a point of contention within many discussions about race and representation in cinema—is not this book's primary focus. Robert Stam and Louise Spence have correctly observed that in scholarship about race and cinema, "the emphasis on realism has often betrayed an exaggerated faith in the possibilities of verisimilitude in art in general and the cinema in particular, avoiding the fact that films are inevitably constructs, fabrications, representations."[179] Richard Dyer echoes this position when he reminds us that cinema, like all other forms of representation, "never 'gets' reality."[180] While certainly noting the inconsistencies between characters' diegetic identities and those (more socially privileged ones) of the

---

175. Dever, *Celluloid Nationalism*, 77. See also Hershfield, *Mexican Cinema*, 43.

176. Jesús Martín-Barbero, *Communication, Culture and Hegemony: From the Media to Mediations*, trans. Elizabeth Fox and Robert A. White (London: Sage Publications, 1993), 117.

177. Silvia Oroz, *Melodrama: O cinema de lágrimas da América Latina* (Rio de Janeiro: FUNARTE, 1999), 100.

178. Hershfield, *Imagining la Chica Moderna*, 134–48; Varner, *La Raza Cosmética*, 107.

179. Stam and Spence, "Colonialism, Racism," 3; see also Shohat and Stam, *Unthinking Eurocentrism*, 191.

180. Dyer, "Introduction," in *The Matter of Images*, 3–4.

actors who play them, the primary purpose of this book is not merely to point out that the actors playing Indigenous people in Mexican cinema are not themselves Indigenous people. Rather, this book interrogates the existence of a pervasive racialized visual logic in Mexico that makes this Whitening approach to visualizing Indigeneity—and society in general—the rule in the local context. The method used here to interrogate this phenomenon—a constant across the periodizations of Mexican cinema usually used to explain stylistic changes[181]—is to critically engage the multiple discursive functions of Whiteness in the cinematic representation of Indigeneity in Mexico.

Commentary on this phenomenon has tended to consist of critiques of Emilio "El Indio" Fernández's indigenista films, most of which point to their breach of indexicality as a means of transmitting mestizo hybridity and/or an attempt to produce cosmopolitan appeal.[182] Within the discussion of this director's work, Dolores Tierney has expertly demonstrated how the use of Whiteness for the main characters in *María Candelaria* is a crucial device informed by the colonial hierarchy through which the film "reconciles indigenismo with the project of modernity in order to offer an idealized visualization of the indígena's place within the modernizing Mexican nation."[183] Expanding on Tierney's excellent work, and in conversation with other scholars who engage mid-twentieth-century Mexican racial masquerade in cultural production such as Hershfield, Sluis, Dalton, and Varner, I situate the corpus of films analyzed in *The White Indians of Mexican Cinema* within a racist visual tradition and argue that it can be understood through the coloniality of power and as the result of the colonization of both desire and subjectivity.

---

181. See Podalsky's critique of the "stagist approach" that highlights moments of rupture. "Unpacking Periodization," in *The Routledge Companion to Latin American Cinema*, ed. Marvin D'Lugo, Ana M. López, and Laura Podalsky (New York: Routledge, 2018), 64–65. See also Schroeder Rodríguez, *Latin American Cinema*, 1–14.

182. Ayala Blanco, *Aventura del cine mexicano*; Aurelio de los Reyes, *Medio siglo de cine mexicano (1896–1947)* (Mexico City: Editorial Trillas, 1987), 196–98; Zavala, *Becoming Modern*; Hershfield, *Mexican Cinema*; Noble, *Mexican National Cinema*; Marta Báscones Antón, "La negación de lo indígena en el cine de Emilio Fernándes," *Archivos de la Filmoteca* 40 (2002): 97, 101; Dalton, *Mestizo Modernity*; Salomé Aguilera Skvirsky and Carl Good, "Las cargas de la representación," *Hispanófila* 117 (2016): 143–44; Varner, *La Raza Cosmética*; Arroyo Quiroz, "Fantasías sobre le identidad indígena."

183. Tierney, *Emilio Fernández*, 95.

Figure I.2. Still showing *María Candelaria*'s (in)famous breach of indexicality with Dolores del Río and Pedro Armendariz playing Indigenous Mexicans (1944). Photo Courtesy of Mil Nubes-Foto (Roberto Fiesco). All rights reserved.

Whiteness-as-indigeneity takes as its canvas the imagined Iberian phenotype—the visage of the first project of Western modernity imposed in Mexico[184]—which by the twentieth century was so thoroughly inscribed into the local cultural landscape and displaced from a position of global hegemony as to take on the symbolism of local tradition, particularly in comparison with more contemporary ideals of feminine beauty created and disseminated by Hollywood and European cinema.[185] Whiteness-as-indigeneity is a phenomenon that not only is characteristic of Emilio

---

184. Mignolo, "Conceptual Triad," 139–40.

185. This dynamic is also evident in the representation of religion. The pious Catholicism of "good" Indians in Mexican cinema similarly evinces the process by which in twentieth-century representation, a feature of Iberian colonial modernity becomes the mark of Indigeneity because it contrasts with subsequent discourses of modernity.

Fernández's cinematic indígenismo, but also can be identified in (extant) films as early as 1931 and beyond the Golden Age.[186] This book treats whiteness-as-indigeneity as the crystallization of an uneasy process of ideological accommodation that takes on nuanced and varied stances in specific films spanning decades. Whiteness-as-indigeneity is an enduring and idiosyncratic form of on-screen racial masquerade, a racialized visual pact with the Mexican spectator based on shared colonized codes of beauty and subjectivity that were also applied to male representation. Although many aspects of the films analyzed here reflect the changes that scholars attribute to the shifts throughout the stages of Mexican film production, whiteness-as-indigeneity is an enduring device, a constant across periods. It is the endurance of the trope that is of primary interest in this study.

In addition to using critical race theory and decolonial thought to elucidate the racialized implications of whiteness-as-indigeneity in Mexican film, this book also aims to broaden what is understood as indigenista cinema to include films beyond those aligned with the political aims of indigenismo-mestizaje in a specific moment, administration, or policy. In a more general vein, inspired by Mexican philosopher Luis Villoro's definition of indigenismo as "the group of theoretical concepts and of processes of consciousness that, throughout the ages, have manifested indigeneity,"[187] I take indigenista films to be those that imagine and/or set out to convey Indigeneity from non-native perspectives and, in so doing, speak to the definition of the imagined criollo/mestizo national self. Through this perspective, I analyze a variety of films from different moments in the development of the Mexican film industry that explicitly, either diegetically or extradiegetically, convey the intention of representing Indigeneity.[188] In broadening the temporal, aesthetic, and ideological scope of the films we might consider indigenista, I aim to show the *variety* of indigenista proposals (*indigenismos*) regarding the place of Indigeneity in the modern Mexican national identity that can be gleaned from Indigenous-themed cinematic production throughout the Golden

---

186. Tierney, *Emilio Fernández*, 73–103.

187. "aquel conjunto de concepciones teóricas y de procesos concienciales que, a lo largo de las épocas, han manifestado lo indígena." Luis Villoro, *Los grandes momentos*, 13–14.

188. This approach is also influenced by the fact that the definition of Indigeneity in Mexico has been the subject of a long-standing debate. For a summary of the variety of positions on the subject, see Guillermo Bonfil Batalla, "El concepto del indio en América: categoría de situación colonial," *Anales de Antropología* 9 (1972): 105–25.

Age. Following Dolores Tierney and Susan Dever, who have argued that Mexican films from the Golden Age were "a porous amalgamation of ideas"[189] conveying "a range of contradictory ideologies,"[190] I suggest that this corpus of Indigenous-themed films transmit vying, if not conflicting, ideas about the place of Indigeneity in the nation. In exposing this plurality of positions, I aim to show how Mexican cinematic production registers a lack of consensus about what the place of Indigeneity should be in the modern national identity, which in turn suggests the instability of the supposedly hegemonic indigenismo-mestizaje project.[191]

Contextualizing Race and Gender On-screen

Theoretical debates about gender, race, and cinema inform this volume's approach to the filmic representation of Indigeneity, which insists on the centrality of local race relations and understandings. Laura Mulvey has famously argued that Hollywood cinema has produced representations of women that are products of the male gaze, through which the spectator (envisioned as male) is incited to "possess" the woman on-screen, therefore imposing subjective male positionality onto the spectator.[192] While Mulvey's approach is certainly pertinent to the ways in which Indigenous women in Mexican films from the first half of the twentieth century are presented as objects of desire, it is also true that, as bell hooks and Jane Gaines have noted, traditional feminist film theory is not helpful for understanding the racial dynamics at work in cinema.[193] In her approach to these connections, bell hooks has encouraged film scholars to consider the *local* realities in which films are produced and consumed. Through this emphasis, she has noted that the gaze of US Blacks toward cinema cannot be divorced from US racial history in which the Black gaze could

---

189. Dever, *Celluloid Nationalism*, 12–14.
190. Tierney, *Emilio Fernández*, 13–15.
191. de la Peña, "The End of Revolutionary Anthropology?," 292.
192. Laura Mulvey, "Visual Pleasure and Narrative Cinema," in *Literary Theory: An Anthology*, ed. Julie Rivkin and Michael Ryan (New York: Blackwell, 1998), 585–96.
193. bell hooks, "The Oppositional Gaze: Black Female Spectators," in *Feminist Film Theory: A reader*, ed. Sue Thornham (Edinburgh: Edinburgh University Press, 1999); and Gaines, "'White' Privilege and Looking Relations."

be considered an act of defiance or sexual aggression.[194] By highlighting contextual racial dynamics, hooks observes that the Black male gazers of White womanhood on-screen not only engaged in an act of possession (as Mulvey suggests), but that as spectators they were situated in a subject position that was violently denied to them in lived experience. In this way, hooks's work illustrates that films can have dramatically different implications depending on the racial contexts in which they are consumed and provides a point of entry to explore the gendered and racialized nature of cinema spectatorship in postcolonial contexts.

Among film theorists who have addressed the relationship between race and cinema, Richard Dyer has approached the issue of Whiteness specifically. He posits that Whiteness acquires its power because it attributes to itself a universal quality, an ability to represent anything because Whiteness claims not to be a particularizing quality.[195] Although Mexican film has used Whiteness in a similar way,[196] I suspect that in the case of Hollywood, the use of Whiteness to represent anything and everything is strongly rooted in the demographic reality and national narrative of the United States, particularly in the era of so-called classical cinema. Mexico, on the other hand, has always been a minority-majority country,[197] in which Whiteness has always been a particularizing quality because it has been tied to socioeconomic privilege and because it has historically included only a small minority of the population. In the Mexican (post)colonial context, it is both the rarity of Whiteness and its privilege—not its pervasiveness—that "generated a dominant image of the white man as spectacle."[198]

Though the image of White homogeneity in Mexican society has always contrasted starkly with the country's demography, as Charles Ramírez Berg and Dolores Tierney have noted, Whites have succeeded in fashioning themselves as the universal image of Mexico in film and

---

194. hooks, "The Oppositional Gaze."

195. Dyer, *White*, 3–12.

196. Tierney, *Emilio Fernández*, 95.

197. "Moreover, as opposed to racism in the United States, where blackness is marked (negatively) and 'whiteness' claims the majority position, in Mexican racism it is 'whiteness' that is marked (positively) and brownness claims the unmarked majority position." Lomnitz-Adler, *Exits*, 280.

198. Mohanty, "Drawing," 314

media, which their political and economic dominance has made possible.[199] The pervasiveness of this blatant distortion even in the majority-minority scenario of Mexico makes film and media's privileging of Whiteness the product of a unique ideological force: the coloniality of power and, more specifically, the colonization of desire and subjectivity. It manifests itself clearly in the ubiquity and veneration of White Mexican actors on-screen and off. Mexican films that state their intention to represent Indigeneity, yet still employ Whiteness to do so, are this system's limit case—a testament to the extent to which desire and subjectivity have been colonized, so much so that the indexically unfeasible (White Mexican women presented as Indigenous women) is preferable to the presentation of "Indigenous-looking" femininity (and masculinity) as desirable. By qualifying the meanings of cinematic Whiteness in the Mexican context, this volume also seeks to contribute to Anglo-American theorizations of race and cinema.

Colonizing Desire

One of the many aspects of the colonial experience that theorists have addressed is the impact of coloniality on the cross-racial dynamics of desire. In his well-known 1952 text, *Black Skin, White Masks*, Frantz Fanon suggests that the prohibition of sexual relations and marriage between Black men and White women during the colonial period in the Antilles causes Black men to experience desire toward the White woman because an intimate relationship with the White woman symbolizes both redress for the colonial subjugation and acceptance within White society.[200] Assuming the voice of a collective Black Antillean male subjectivity, he writes:

> I wish to be acknowledged not as black but as white . . . who but a white woman can do this for me? By loving me she proves that I am worthy of white love. I am loved like a white man . . . I marry white culture, white beauty, white whiteness.

---

199. Ramírez Berg, *Cinema of Solitude*, 137; Tierney, *Emilio Fernández*, 86; Dyer, "Introduction," in *The Matter of Images*.

200. Fanon, *Black Skin, White Masks*, 63–82. See also Lucía Strecher, "Las máscaras del deseo interracial: Fanon y Capécia," in *Frantz Fanon desde América Latina: Lecturas contemporáneas de un pensador del siglo XX*, ed. Elena Oliva, Lucía Strecher, and Claudia Zapata (Buenos Aires: Ediciones Corregidor, 2013), 258, 261.

When my restless hands caress those white breasts, they grasp white civilization and dignity and make them mine.[201]

When discussing the Black Antillean woman's desire to couple with a White man, Fanon suggests that the inclination is rooted in a wish to Whiten, and therefore improve, the prospects for future children. He also suggests that marrying a White man is a way to definitively disassociate oneself from Blackness and approach a more consolidated and convincing White identity.[202] In a similar vein, Albert Memmi's *The Colonizer and the Colonized* highlights the desire to marry the colonizer as an extension of the colonized's strategy to become like his oppressor by adopting everything from the colonizer's world as superior.[203] Both Fanon and Memmi reveal that in colonial contexts, sexual attraction and desire are far from arbitrary occurrences and can be understood as racialized phenomena. Of course, I do not mean that the colonized are never considered to be sexually desirable, but that the overwhelming tendency to exalt Whiteness as desirable in these contexts has a basis in colonial subjugation. Furthermore, as Fanon and Memmi argue, the way in which colonialism upholds the colonizer's body as more desirable contributes to a process of self-loathing in the colonized, and this fact is evidenced in various attempts at physical Whitening alongside the broader processes of socioeconomic and cultural Whitening.[204]

While the history of interracial marriage in Mexico has its own historical specificities, the experience of colonialism produced similar results to those described by Fanon and Memmi. Early during the conquest, the marriage of Spanish men and Indigenous women was looked upon favorably because of the lack of Spanish women in the Americas and because these unions were considered vehicles for conversion to Catholicism by the Spanish Crown.[205] Indeed, intermarriage was a part of Hernán Cortés's

---

201. Fanon, *Black Skin, White Masks*, 63.

202. Fanon, *Black Skin, White Masks*, 43–48.

203. "A blonde woman, be she dull or anything else, appears superior to any brunette. A product manufactured by the colonizer is accepted with confidence. His habits, clothing, food, architecture are closely copied, even if inappropriate. A mixed marriage is the extreme example of this audacious leap." Albert Memmi, *The Colonizer and the Colonized* (Boston: Beacon Press, 1991), 120–21.

204. Fanon, *Black Skin, White Masks*, 43–63; Memmi, *The Colonizer*, 121; Dyer, "Coloured White, Not Coloured," in *White*, 50.

205. Mörner, *Race Mixture*, 37.

initial strategy for supporting the conquest of New Spain.[206] The freedom to marry Indigenous women was made explicit in laws passed in 1501 and 1514.[207] However, as soon as Spanish women became available in New Spain, Spanish men rejected Indigenous women as marriage partners.[208] Subsequent laws continued to protect Spanish unions with Indians and with those of mixed Indigenous and Spanish ancestry (*mestizos* and *castizos*)[209] while discouraging unions between Spaniards and people of African ancestry.[210] However, the mere fact of legal protection does not mean that unions between Spaniards and Indigenous people were common or socially encouraged. Magnus Mörner has illustrated the distinction between the legal statuses and social statuses of different groups in New Spain.[211] He has shown that although Indigenous people had the highest *legal* status of those who were neither Spanish nor criollo, they had the lowest *social* status,[212] which was in turn tied to the racialized division of labor according to which they performed primarily physical tasks. Thus, despite the protected legal status of Indigenous people and the fact that their marriages with Spaniards and criollos were legal, they were less common because of the great socioeconomic distance that evolved between the groups.[213] Though their selection of marital partners changed, White men maintained "privileged access to non-white women's sexuality" while at the same time obstructing non-Whites' access to White women's sexuality.[214]

According to Douglas Cope, the significance of marriage for securing wealth and status made unions with non-Whites undesirable for Spanish and criollo families in New Spain, and phenotype served as a "sieve, filtering out unsuitable candidates for admission to Spanish families."[215] This relationship between phenotype and status can be corroborated by Alex-

---

206. Mörner, *Race Mixture*, 37.
207. Mörner, *Race Mixture*, 37.
208. Mörner, *Race Mixture*, 26.
209. Mörner, *Race Mixture*, 39.
210. Mörner, *Race Mixture*, 38.
211. Mörner, *Race Mixture*, 60.
212. Mörner, *Race Mixture*, 60.
213. For exceptions to this general tendency, see Mörner, *Race Mixture*, 65–66.
214. Wade, *Race and Sex*, 83.
215. Douglas R. Cope, *The Limits of Racial Domination* (Madison: University of Wisconsin Press, 1994), 25.

ander von Humboldt's observation of the social distinction that Whiteness (*blancura*) conferred in the Mexican context. During his trip to the country at the turn of the nineteenth century, he noted, "In Spain, it is a kind of title of nobility not to descend from Jews or Moors. In America, the skin, more or less white, is what dictates the class that an individual occupies in society. A white, even if he rides barefoot on horseback, considers himself a member of the nobility of the country."[216] Clearly, physical appearance mattered as a factor that informed one's social status and marriage prospects. In fact, as historian Federico Navarrete Linares points out, criollo families in Mexico were at times so desperate to Whiten their "tainted" lineages or preserve them that they were regularly willing to intermarry with White Spaniards even if they were of low socioeconomic status.[217]

After independence, as we have seen, acculturation and wealth (*blanquitud*) enabled individuals to shift their ethnoracial identities to White ones, giving way to greater mixture. However, the practice of Whitening continued, both through a preference for physically and genealogically Whiter marriage partners, especially among the elite, and through physical and cultural attempts to Whiten the self.[218] The historical practice of elite, White endogamy in Mexico and the negative characteristics attributed to Indigeneity over time have helped make Whiteness the aesthetic ideal in the country as well as an object of sexual and romantic desire. With this I do not mean that non-White bodies are never considered desirable by anyone in Mexico, but that, according to the dominant racial ideology, Whiteness (*blancura*, especially when paired with *blanquitud*) is constructed as aesthetically superior and more desirable, especially in the context of long-term and socially visible coupling.[219]

This racialized desire for White bodies has been documented throughout the history of Mexican cultural production. Referring to the country's literary texts, José Vasconcelos noted that "You find almost in every one of

---

216. Alexander von Humbolt, qtd. in Mörner, *Race Mixture*, 56.

217. Navarrete Linares, *México racista*, 72.

218. Knight, "Racism, Revolution," 100; Lomnitz, *Exits*, 278–79; Sue, *Land of the Cosmic Race*; Moreno Figueroa, "Distributed Intensities," 387–401; Navarrete Linares, *México racista*.

219. For a discussion of the coexistence of socially sanctioned desire toward White Mexican femininity and the disavowed desire toward non-White Mexican women, see Eugenia Iturriaga, "La ciudad blanca de noche: las discotecas como espacios de segregación," *Alteridades* 25, no. 50 (July–December 2015): 110.

our Indian or mestizo poets, dark of skin themselves, the ardent eulogy of the white hands, the pale cheek, of the amada."[220] Even in Ignacio Altamirano's foundational national novel *El Zarco*, which earnestly proposes the dark-skinned Indian, Nicolás as the ideal of manly virtue, Nicolás cannot match the blue-eyed bandit's handsome appearance, and the novel opts instead to establish Nicolas's moral superiority with his "beautiful soul."[221] Mexican cinema, television programs, and advertisements reinforce the supposed aesthetic superiority and desirability of Whites to this day.[222] Although I do not exclude that Mexican films have also sought to imitate the conventions of Whiteness in European and American films, what I wish to point out is that because beautiful bodies and faces are almost always requirements for film stars (especially for women),[223] Whiteness in Mexican film production has *also* been predominant because of the local process of the colonization of desire, which dictates that beauty is White according to a very specific set local bodily standards within the context of the local racial formation.[224]

Furthermore, this book seeks to elucidate how the Mexican cinematic experience is predicated on racialized and classed "looking relations."[225] For this reason, films have exploited the opportunity to offer the majority-non-White, nonelite audience the indulgence[226] of gazing upon and desiring White bodies in a manner that likely would not be possible for them in lived reality without facing some form of social sanction because, as Mónica Moreno Figueroa notes, "seeing is a racialized, gendered, and classed cultural practice . . ."[227] In addition to allowing people to gaze at racially privileged bodies, cinema spectatorship amplifies the scopophilic

---

220. Vasconcelos, qtd. in Knight, "Racism, Revolution," 100.

221. Ignacio M. Altamirano, *El Zarco* (Mexico City: Editorial Porrúa, 2010), 60.

222. Navarrete Linares, *México racista*, 27.

223. Martin Shingler, *Star Studies: A Critical Guide* (New York: Palgrave MacMillan, 2012), 72–79.

224. For a specific breakdown of physical features that are considered as being within and outside Mexican Whiteness, see Nutini, *Mexican Aristocracy*, 62–64.

225. Jane Gaines, "'White' Privilege and Looking Relations," in *Feminist Film Theory: A reader*, ed. Sue Thornham (Edinburgh: Edinburgh University Press, 1999).

226. As Richard Dyer has observed, "cultural media are only sometimes concerned with reality and are at least as much concerned with ideals and indulgence, that are themselves socially constructed," in "The Light of the World" in *White*, 83.

227. Mónica Moreno Figueroa, "Displaced Looks: The Lived Experience of Beauty and Racism," *Feminist Theory* 14, no. 2 (2013): 144.

dimension of this experience because, as Christine Gledhill reminds us, "[p]hotography and especially the close-up, offers audiences a gaze at the bodies of stars closer and more sustained than the majority of real life encounters."[228] In other words, Mexican cinema has capitalized on the effects of the colonization of desire and subjectivity, which include, for those who consciously or unconsciously still subscribe to those values, non-White Mexicans' desire to be White, White Mexicans' will to affirm themselves as desirable and beautiful, and both groups' desire toward White bodies as aesthetically, sexually, and romantically preferable.

Colonizing Subjectivity

Of course, there are other aspects of the discursive and epistemic violence of coloniality that have helped to produce the centrality of Whiteness in cultural production. Fanon also describes how the colonized subject's exposure to racialized discourses in comic books and history books impacts him, effectively alienating him from himself through a kind of discursive brainwashing[229]—the colonization of his subjectivity. He identifies with the White protagonist, the victor, and becomes complicit in the Othering of pejoratively racialized subjects. He therefore associates the Senegalese with the "wicked Negroes" of his texts and attributes to himself a White subjectivity, disavowing his own African ancestry.[230] Fanon's identification of how the colonized are coerced to identify with Whiteness not only is a characteristic of the Antilles, but also is constitutive of the coloniality of power across colonies.[231]

In the Mexican context, the colonial experience similarly created a cultural symbolic order (through, for example, historical and religious narrative) that privileged Whiteness as a preferred signifier of privileged social identity. This cultural symbolic order was not entirely replaced or eliminated through independence, revolution, or the Revolution's institutionalized cultural projects. Instead, these movements merely qualified the

---

228. Christine Gledhill, "Signs of Melodrama," in *Stardom: Industry of Desire*, ed. Christine Gledhill (New York: Routledge, 1991), 210.
229. Fanon, *Black Skin, White Masks*, 146–47.
230. Fanon, *Black Skin, White Masks*, 146–47.
231. See also Memmi, *The Colonizer*, 91, 104–5.

terms of White superiority through subsequent discourses of modernity. Although José Jorge Gómez Izquierdo does not refer to Fanon, his own study of how Mexican history books teach about Indigenous cultures brings him to a similar conclusion: their discourses serve the purposes of White supremacy in Mexico, aligning the pupil with the non-Indigenous subject, which results in psychological and emotional damage.[232]

This value and protagonism ceded to Whiteness is further evidenced in the generalized indifference toward the suffering and death of non-White Mexicans. As Mexican anthropologist Roger Bartra explains while debunking the notion that indifference toward death is an inherent characteristic of rural and Indigenous Mexican culture, "this fatalism has another origin, . . . the disdain of the dominant classes for the lives of those who find themselves in conditions of misery. There are people whose lives are not worth much in the eyes of their masters: the death of a Mexican Indian . . . occurs in the bosom of the undifferentiated 'masses'; such deaths can reach monstrous statistical proportions but do not threaten the civilized man."[233]

Echoing the theme of indifference, Navarrete Linares perceptively illustrates how the association between Indigeneity and poverty in Mexico has been thoroughly naturalized, producing generalized attitudes of detachment toward racialized socioeconomic marginality.[234] He explains how when a Facebook user in 2012 spotted a blond, light-skinned girl named Alondra begging for money on the streets of Guadalajara, a social media storm ensued. Insinuations that the girl must have been kidnapped prompted local authorities to temporarily remove the girl from the custody of her parents, who, after providing a legitimate birth certificate, were still required to provide DNA evidence to prove that Alondra was, in fact, their daughter. This wave of indignation over the socioeconomic marginality of one blond, light-skinned child—forceful enough to incite legal intervention—contrasts starkly with the generalized silence and indifference regarding the poverty in which numerous Indigenous and mestizo Mexican children live.

---

232. Gómez Izquierdo, "Racismo y nacionalismo," 142. For a parallel example of the process of racialization in Spanish history books, see Woods Peiró, *White Gypsies*, 16–17.

233. Roger Bartra, *The Cage of Melancholy: Identity and Metamorphosis in the Mexican Character*, trans. Christopher J. Hall (New Brunswick: Rutgers University Press, 1992), 60–61.

234. Navarete Linares, *México racista*, 76–79.

Luis Estrada's mordant satirical film, *La dictadura perfecta* (2014), masterfully re-creates the racialized dynamics at work throughout the case of Alondra, as explained by Navarrete Linares. In Estrada's film, a corrupt governor, Carmelo Vargas, and the most prominent Mexican television company, TVMX, collude to make the kidnapping of light-skinned, middle-class twin sisters national news to distract from the governor's rampant corruption. The film's display of how the Mexican media frame the girls' kidnapping as a tragedy while refusing to show the scores of dead bodies that emerge during their partnership with Vargas points to the racialized attitudes toward suffering and death in Mexico according to which the plight of middle-class White people is the stuff of tragedy and that of poorer Indigenous or mestizo Mexicans is unremarkable or ignored altogether.[235] For Elena Poniatowska, this racialized appraisal of human life is apparent in the Mexican state's mishandling of the "disappearance" of forty-three teacher trainees from the state of Guerrero in 2014.[236] In short, in Mexico Whiteness functions as perhaps the most important "frame" that determines "grievability."[237]

In light of this racial history and the persistence of highly racialized social attitudes, I suggest that Whiteness (*blancura*) is also dominant in Mexican cultural production (and in Mexican cinema specifically) because in the context of colonized subjectivity, physical Whiteness functions as a device for inciting identification between the spectator and the main characters in the diegeses (story worlds).[238] Charles Ramírez Berg has already alluded to some of the consequences of this phenomenon by observing that in twentieth-century Mexican film, Whiteness functions as a "marker of morality and social standing . . . light skin confers righ-

---

235. At the end of the film, the twins become what else but protagonists in their own telenovela, thus doubling the mediatic centrality they enjoy due to their little White bodies.

236. Luis Méndez, "México es racista—Poniatowska," *El Norte*, January 28, 2015, https://www.elnorte.com/aplicacioneslibre/articulo/default.aspx?id=450888&md5=a7d9542d-2e1168fcf306d6434e7adb2c&ta=0dfdbac11765226904c16cb9ad1b2efe.

237. "Forms of racism instituted and active at the level of perception tend to produce iconic versions of populations who are eminently grievable, and others whose loss is no loss, and who remain ungrievable." Judith Butler, "Precarious Life, Grievable Life," in *Frames of War: When Is Life Grievable?* (New York: Verso, 2016), 24.

238. For an analogous explanation of the entirely White landscape of Mexican advertising, see Federico Navarrete Linares's discussion of Indigenous and brown mestizo Mexicans as non-"aspirational" subjects in *México racista*, 59.

teousness and high social station; dark skin usually signifies a lower-class villain or clown."²³⁹ Leading roles, the primary point of identification for audiences in narrative cinema, are therefore almost exclusively played by actors who can conform to the physical boundaries of Mexican Whiteness. *Blancura* functions as a kind of passport for aspiring media figures, because according to the logic of the colonization of subjectivity, physical Whiteness qualifies them as deserving of centrality and attention. In this way, several stars in Mexico and throughout the Americas who originally lacked substantive *blanquitud* were able to capitalize on and enhance their *blancura* while presenting their lower-class affinity as charm or relatability, allowing them to rise to prominence in still-racist societies. Figures who have benefited by playing this "Whiteness game" include Pedro Infante in Mexico,²⁴⁰ Eva Perón in Argentina, Carmen Miranda in Brazil,²⁴¹ and Marilyn Monroe in the United States.

It is through the colonization of desire and subjectivity that we arrive at the situation in Mexico in which the national audiovisual repertoire has painted an overwhelmingly (and unrealistically) White picture of Mexico. Although the dynamics are different with respect to the US context, the ubiquity of Whiteness on-screen has also been a tool of White supremacy in Mexico.²⁴² Indeed, it is one of the most powerful manifestations of what Guillermo Bonfil Batalla has termed "el México imaginario" (the imaginary Mexico), which he defines as "a minority country organized according to norms, aspirations, and intentions of Western civilization that are not shared (or are from another perspective) by the rest of the national population . . . that sector that incarnates and impels the dominant project in our country."²⁴³

---

239. Ramírez Berg, *Cinema of Solitude*, 57. See also Marco Polo Hernández Cuevas's use of the term "white aesthetic" to describe a dymanic in Mexican cultural production in which "virtuosity is defiend by whiteness" in *African Mexicans and the Discourse of the Modern Nation*, XV. For an analysis of similar dynamics in Indian cinema, see Martin Shingler, *Star Studies*, 66.

240. For the significance of Pedro Infante's Whiteness for his stardom and appeal, see de la Mora, *Cinemachismo*, 86.

241. Marshall C. Eakin, *Becoming Brazilians: Race and National Identity in Twentieth-Century Brazil* (Cambridge: Cambridge University Press, 2017), 115.

242. hooks, "The Oppositional Gaze," 514.

243. Guillermo Bonfil Batalla, *México profundo: Una civilización negada* (México, D.F.: Secretaría de Educación Pública, 1987), 10. See also Echeverría, *Modernidad y blanquitud*, 240.

Clearly (to apply one of bell hooks's observations), Mexico is not as White as it wants to be.[244] And so we return to the bewildered European or US American spectator who upon encountering Mexican films and *telenovelas* for the first time cannot help but ask, "Why is everyone so White?" I have often heard many Mexicans react indignantly to this kind of question, and I have done so myself. "We have White people too," the response goes, beneath which one can read, "we have beauty, civilization, and modernity too." But like children and drunks who unwittingly reveal uncomfortable truths,[245] those who ask the ingenuous (and sometimes prejudiced) question reveal the fantasy for what it is: an aspirational and unconvincing mask.

Whiteness, Melodrama, and Hegemony

Speaking specifically about the Golden Age of Mexican cinema (lasting from about 1936 to 1957), both Jesús Martín-Barbero and Carlos Monsiváis have posited that film production from the period fulfilled a hegemonic role, helping to fashion Mexican spectators into national subjects.[246] On the one hand, the films reinforced the viewer's awareness of their existence within an "imagined community,"[247] but cinema also had a strong pedagogical and socializing function, serving as a "school" in which spectators could learn models of behavior that would be associated with what is typically Mexican.[248] While scholars have questioned the lessons surrounding gender

---

244. hooks, "The Oppositional Gaze," 514.

245. I am referring to the popular Spanish saying, "Los niños y los borrachos siempre dicen la verdad" (Children and drunk people always say the truth).

246. Martín-Barbero, *Communication, Culture and Hegemony*, 165–68; and Carlos Monsiváis, "Se sufre," 99–224. See also Oroz, *Melodrama*, 28; Noble, *Mexican National Cinema*, 70–79; Elena Lahr-Vivaz, *Mexican Melodrama: Film and Nation from the Golden Age to the New Wave* (Tucson: University of Arizona Press, 2016), 16–17.

247. Anderson, *Imagined Communities*; Shohat and Stam, *Unthinking Eurocentrism*, 103; Dever, *Celluloid Nationalism*.

248. Martín-Barbero, *Communication, Culture and Hegemony*, 165–68; and Carlos Monsiváis, "Se sufre," 99–224 and "Mexican Cinema," 142–43. See also Ana M. López, "Tears and Desire: Women and Melodrama in the 'Old' Mexican Cinema," in *Mediating Two Worlds: Cinematic Encounters in the Americas*, ed. John King, Ana M. López, and Manuel Alvarado (London: British Film Institute, 1993), 147–63; Noble, *Mexican National Cinema*; Lahr-Vivaz, *Mexican Melodrama*.

and sexuality that these didactic cultural products conveyed,[249] what has yet to be pointed out is that through the ubiquity of Whiteness, these films *also* contained a heavy-handed lesson about race through which Mexican Whiteness was upheld as the aesthetic and cultural ideal.

Furthermore, the didacticism of Golden Age cinema was effective precisely *because* it gave a White face to multiple groups within Mexican society. Nowhere is this dominance of Whiteness clearer than in the realm of melodrama. Because identification is an essential component of melodrama,[250] and, as we have seen, Whiteness operates as the preferred human type for inciting identification in the Mexican context, the main characters of melodrama in Mexico tend to be White independently of their socioeconomic situation or ethnicity in the diegeses. This function of Whiteness is predicated on the fact that as a performative tradition, melodrama used physiognomy to "charg[e] the visible appearance of the actors with ethical values and counter values."[251]

Whiteness functions as the colonially determined glue that allows a broad sector of Mexican society to identify with and desire characters who have stigmatized social identities (as well as nonstigmatized ones) because Whiteness interpellates[252] and appeals to spectators on the basis of their shared colonized desire and subjectivity.[253] Because "[s]tars reach their audiences primarily through their bodies,"[254] what Jesús Martín-

---

249. Hershfield, *Mexican Cinema*; Julia Tuñón, *Los rostros de un mito. Personajes femeninos en las películas de Emilio Indio Fernández* (Mexico City: CONACULTA, 2003); López, "Tears and Desire"; de la Mora, *Cinemachismo*; Héctor Domínguez-Ruvalcaba, *Modernity and the Nation in Mexican Representations of Masculinity: From Sensuality to Bloodshed* (New York: Palgrave Macmillan, 2007).

250. Peter Brooks, *The Melodramatic Imagination: Balzac, Henry James, Melodrama, and the Mode of Excess* (New Haven: Yale University Press, 1995), 4–5; Oroz, *Melodrama*, 17–35.

251. Martín-Barbero, *Communication, Culture and Hegemony*, 115.

252. I do not use the term "interpellation" in the Althusserian sense because I do not argue that all examples of Whiteness in cinematic Mexican melodrama can be understood as the functioning of the Ideological State Apparatus. Rather, I am employing this term in the broader sense of appealing or engaging spectators as a catalyst for the hegemonizing process. For a discussion of Golden Age melodrama as a manifestation of the Ideological State Aparatus in Mexico, see Lahr-Vivaz, *Mexican Melodrama*, 11.

253. Jesus Martín-Barbero argues that identification and desire are the primary factors on which stardom depends. *Communication, Culture and Hegemony*, 145.

254. Gledhill, "Signs of Melodrama," 201.

Barbero has identified as the "secret pact that bonded [movie stars'] faces with the desires and obsessions of their publics"[255] depended in Mexico on this White norm as its crucial factor. It is through Whiteness that a representative of the urban working class, Pepe "El Toro" (played by Pedro Infante in the 1948 film *Nosotros los pobres*), becomes one of the most cherished characters in all of Mexican cinema history. It is also through Whiteness that melodramatic Indigeneity works to endear itself to spectators through the faces of Dolores del Río and María Félix among many others. Or, to put it another way, the Whitening of marginalized social sectors in Mexican melodrama is their visual "re-semanticization through the hegemonic code"[256] according to which White bodies are valuable and desirable. If, as Roger Bartra has argued, a specific "formula" is needed to produce the "transposition of some selected aspects of lower-class struggles and feelings to the domain of national culture,"[257] then I argue that, with regard to cinema, Whiteness is that formula's key ingredient.

Although the formula yields a cinematic repertoire that dramatically distorts national reality,[258] it has functioned effectively because of the extent to which coloniality in Mexico entrenched itself as the metric of value. Therefore, what has caused Mexican audiences to receive these films with a celebratory reaction[259] is not the faithfulness of cinematic representation to their lived reality, because Mexican cinema, like Hollywood cinema, is largely a fantasy.[260] Rather, Mexican audiences have traditionally applauded the code of Mexican cinematic *irreality* because they recognize its patterns formed in a *local* experience of coloniality (as opposed to that of Hollywood). Therefore, even though Mexican melodrama indeed "references

---

255. "Above and the beyond the make-up and the commercial star industry, the movie stars who were truly stars for the people gathered their force from a secret pact that bonded their faces with the desires and obsessions of their publics," Martín-Barbero, *Communication, Culture and Hegemony*, 167.

256. "Gramsci has explained that there is no social legitimation without re-semantizication through the hegemonic code. Cinema was the living social mediation that constitutes the new cultural experience, and cinema became the first language of the popular urban culture." Martín-Barbero, *Communication, Culture and Hegemony*, 166.

257. Bartra, *Cage of Melancholy*, 171.

258. Alejandro Galindo, *Una radiografía histórica del cine mexicano* (Mexico City: Fondo de Cultura Popular, 1968); Bartra, *Cage of Melancholy*, 171–72.

259. Galindo, *Radiografía histórica*; Charles Ramírez Berg, *Cinema of Solitude*, 5.

260. Lahr-Vivaz, *Mexican Melodrama*, 15.

a universe close to the spectator,"[261] this in fact occurs in two different senses. The first is in the indexical sense of reproducing the sights and sounds a local spectator would recognize from their immediate environment—a long-standing feature of Latin American cinema production through which it offered something absent in Hollywood films.[262] The second is that Mexican melodrama also showcases the codes of local epistemological dominance that *obfuscate* that spectator's local reality. Even though it is true that Mexican film production throughout the Golden Age was highly influenced by Hollywood's norms (while also seeking a cosmopolitanism that could make it palatable in Europe),[263] because of the different positions that Indigeneity occupies in the US and Mexican racial formations and national projects, as well as the distinct parameters of Whiteness in both countries, Mexican cinema spawned and consistently deployed idiosyncratic "solutions" to filmic racial representation, such as whiteness-as-indigeneity.[264] As we have seen, this particular trope seeks to retain the markers of Whiteness that are advantageous in the context of the local racial formation for the sake of featuring an Indigenous character as compassion-worthy and desirable both romantically and sexually.

Furthermore, this idiosyncratic solution was also exportable to the rest of Latin America (a film market in which Mexican productions occupied a position of privilege during the Golden Age)[265] as well as to diasporic communities in the United States.[266] When Elena Lahr-Vivaz proposes that

---

261. Oroz, *Melodrama*, 100.

262. Paulo Antonio Paranaguá, *Tradición y modernidad en el cine de América Latina* (Madrid: Fondo de Cultura Económica de España, 2003), 15–31; Schroeder Rodríguez, *Latin American Cinema*, 21.

263. Ramírez Berg, *Classical Mexican Cinema*, 6; Monsiváis, "Mexican Cinema," 141; Aurelio de los Reyes, *Medio siglo de cine mexicano*, 197–99.

264. For studies on the representation of US Indigenous people in Hollywood cinema, see Peter C. Rollins and John E. O'Connor, eds., *Hollywood's Indian: The Portrayal of the Native American in Film* (Lexington: University Press of Kentucky, 2003); Angela Aleiss, *Making the White Man's Indian: Native Americans and the Hollywood Movies* (Westport: Praeger Publishers, 2005); M. Elise Marubbio, *Killing the Indian Maiden: Images of Native American Women in Film* (Lexington: University Press of Kentucky Press, 2006).

265. Robert McKee Irwin and Maricruz Castro Ricalde, *Global Mexican Cinema: Its Golden Age* (London: British Film Institute, 2013); Lahr-Vivaz, *Mexican Melodrama*, 18; Monsiváis, "Mexican Cinema," 140–41, 143.

266. Dever, *Celluloid Nationalism*; Colin Gunckel, *Mexico on Main Street: Transnational Film Culture in Los Angeles Before World War II* (New Brunswick: Rutgers University Press, 2015), 122–58.

Spanish-speaking spectators throughout the Americas "glimpsed themselves in Golden Age films,"[267] I suspect that part of what they were glimpsing was a shared experience of (originally Iberian) colonialism and coloniality.

It is important to keep in mind that the stars who would embody Mexican Whiteness on-screen were able to do so because they conformed to the contextual and ambiguous nature of Mexican Whiteness. As other scholars have already observed, many of these same actors (such as Lupe Vélez and Dolores del Río) were cast as ethnic Others within Hollywood's distinct Anglo-American Protestant construct of Whiteness.[268] According to Richard Dyer, within Hollywood's racial framework, "Latin whites" are more sexual and prone to "anything that can be characterized as low, dark and irremediably corporeal."[269] In this sense, during their US careers, Vélez and del Río operated as incarnations of what María DeGuzmán has called "off-whiteness" in referring to the liminal positionality that Spaniards and their descendants in the Americas occupy within the US racial formation and cultural imagination precisely because they incarnate a deposed project of empire and modernity vis-à-vis that of the United States after 1898.[270] The "alien whiteness" of these actresses generates Anglo-America's "drama of the repulsion of and attraction to" them; however, ultimately, off-whites are "abjected from the ideal body politic."[271]

Regarding Indigenous-themed films, Mexican whiteness-as-indigeneity is an instance in which, as Ana M. López has articulated with regard to the representation of women in Golden Age cinema, "conflicting voices and needs visibly erupt into the cinematic and social sphere."[272] Whiteness-as-indigeneity functions as a "solution" to an aesthetic challenge raised by the shift in the official ideology regarding Mexican national identity after the

---

267. Lahr-Vivaz, *Mexican Melodrama*, 18.

268. Joanne Hershfield, *The Invention of Dolores del Río* (Minneapolis: University of Minnesota Press, 2000); Ana M. López, "Are All the Latins from Manhattan?: Hollywood, Ethnography and Cultural Colonialism," in *Mediating Two Worlds: Cinematic Encounters in the Americas*, ed. John King, Ana M. López, and Manuel Alvarado (London: British Film Institute, 1993), 67–80; Paranaguá, *Tradición y modernidad*, 108.

269. Richard Dyer, "The Matter of Whiteness," in *White*, 28. See also Dyer, "Coloured White, Not Coloured," in *White*, 59.

270. DeGuzmán, *Spain's Long Shadow*, xi–xxxiii.

271. DeGuzmán, *Spain's Long Shadow*, xxi, xxiv, xxvii.

272. López, "Tears and Desire," 149.

Revolution.²⁷³ Whiteness-as-indigeneity operates as a palimpsest of discourses: beneath are the racialized vestiges of the colonial symbolic order that have not been entirely erased by the Revolution and continue to privilege Whiteness. Above is the new state-sponsored discourse urging Mexicans to value Indigenous people and peasants as worthy national subjects. Or, to use the vocabulary of Raymond Williams, we are seeing the relationship between the "residual" and the "emergent."²⁷⁴ In this way, the use of Whiteness for representing Indigeneity (before, after, and during the Golden Age) operates as a hegemonic maneuver and sophisticated, colonially inflected semiotic trick to facilitate the national and personal appropriation of Indigeneity precisely through the continued glorification of Whiteness. In this way, these films, though nominally about Indigenous people, are actually heavily invested in affirming the nonnative national self through their showcasing of "nuestra bella apariencia estética criolla/mestiza sancionada como la norma hegemónica" (our beautiful criollo/mestizo aesthetic appearance, sanctioned as the hegemonic norm).²⁷⁵ Through racial masquerade, whiteness-as-indigeneity is a tool for impelling spectators toward varied ideological positions regarding the place of the native in national culture.

The White Indians of Mexican Cinema

In writing about the White Indians of Mexican cinema during the mid-twentieth century, I engage in the process of marking the ubiquity of Whiteness as a racist phenomenon in Mexican cinema. As a body of work, spanning from the early 1930s to the end of the 1960s, this group

---

273. For Eva Woods Peiró, Whiteness similarly functions as a "solution" in cinematic representation that harmonizes competing racial ideas about Roma people and modernity in Spain. See *White Gypsies: Race and Stardom in Spanish Muscials*.

274. According to Raymond Williams, the "residual" can be understood as that which "has been effectively formed in the past, but . . . is still active in the cultural process, not at all as an element of the past, but as an effective element of the present. Thus certain experiences, meanings, and values which cannot be expressed or substantially verified in terms of the dominant culture, are nevertheless lived and practiced on the basis of the residue—cultural as well as social—of some previous social and cultural institution or formation. It is crucial to distinguish this aspect of the residual, which may have an alternative or even oppositional relation to the dominant culture . . ." Raymond Williams, *Marxism and Literature* (Oxford: Oxford University Press, 1977), 122.

275. Gómez Izquierdo, "Racismo y nacionalismo," 123.

of films illustrates how the use of Whiteness to represent Indigenous womanhood (and, to a lesser degree, manhood) promotes the codification of Indigeneity into the national narrative in specific and varied manners that ultimately privilege Whiteness and reinscribe Indigenous people as the objects of coloniality.

I would also like to state clearly what this book does not aim to accomplish. I am not arguing that these indigenista films effectively influenced the adoption of specific subjective attitudes toward Indigeneity. Such a study would require extensive information about the circulation and diffusion of the films as well as their financial accessibility and interviews with human subjects. It is a widely documented fact that the main audience for national films made during the Mexican Golden Age was urban populations, especially the working class. For the purpose of this volume, I am not concerned with researching more specifically who the spectators of the films analyzed here were because I do not claim to address the process through which the films' perspectives were absorbed, but rather the variety of messages about the relationship between Indigeneity and the nation that they put forth in doubly racialized terms. Nor am I engaged in a project that seeks to recover native voices or extensively denounce the films' inauthentic portrayal of Indigeneity. This study assumes, from the outset, the inauthenticity of the films with respect to the Indigenous cultures of Mexico, because the films are told from non-Indigenous perspectives and without the meaningful creative collaboration of Indigenous people. In other words, this book is preoccupied with how Mexican cinema functions as a tool of racialized dominance and not with analyzing subaltern forms of resistance in the realm of representation.

My approach to analyzing the films is influenced by Robert Stam, Louise Spence and Ella Shohat's delineations of the formal aspects of film and narrative that constitute a social group's representation within the medium.[276] Because narrative and visual details are the sites through which films convey their individual constructs and messages regarding Indigeneity, the analyses focus on the stylistic and narrative conventions used in the films. The purpose of these analyses is to tease out how the films depict Indigenous characters, how they position the spectator vis-à-vis Indigeneity, and how they instrumentalize Whiteness to craft various proposals regarding the relationship between Indigeneity and the

---

276. Stam and Spence, "Colonialism, Racism," 11–12, 17; Shohat and Stam, *Unthinking Eurocentrism*, 205–15.

nation. At the same time, following the insights of Dolores Tierney and Ana López, I concede and explore the possibility that the films' narrative and technical aspects can be at odds with their explicit hegemonic messages.[277]

Chapter 1 discusses two films that represent pre-Columbian natives and that, although from distinct moments in Mexican film history, similarly present them as glorified ancestors of the Mexican nation: *Zítari* (dir. Contreras Torres, 1931) and *Chilam Balam* (dir. de Martino, 1957). I suggest that in these films Whiteness serves to idealize the women as symbols of Indigeneity in a manner that is compatible with the indigenismo-mestizaje discourse but that, at the same time, harks back to late eighteenth- and nineteenth-century approaches to representing dignified Indigeneity. Chapter 2 focuses on two films about the Tehuana type (women from the Isthmus of Tehuantepec), *La Zandunga* (dir. de Fuentes, 1938) and *Tierra de pasiones* (dir. Benávides, 1943). It argues that whiteness-as-indigeneity is one of the many ways in which the films revise the regional figure's mythic reputation to make her more palatable for a national audience.

In Chapter 3, I address a set of films that contain specifically indigenista political discourses, *La India Bonita* (dir. Helú, 1938), *El Indio* (dir. Vargas de la Maza, 1939), *María Candelaria* (dir. Fernández, 1944), and *Maclovia* (dir. Fernández, 1948). I propose that in these contexts, the association of Whiteness and female beauty undermines the decolonial intent of their explicitly revolutionary messages. I also explore important exceptions to this trend in two notable films of the indigenista genre, *Jantizio* (1934) and *Raíces* (1955).

Chapter 4 argues that *La noche de los mayas* (dir. Urueta, 1939) and *Deseada* (dir. Gavaldón, 1951) reframe the origin story of Mexican mestizaje as a destructive tragedy and at the same time bolster cultural mestizaje through an unusual approach: the presentation of the Indigenous cosmovision as the legitimate source of truth. Here I argue that the Whiteness of the central Mayan maidens allows them to serve as conduits for spectatorial positioning within a supposedly non-Western belief system.

Chapter 5 analyzes a late manifestation of the *indita* genre starring Silvia Pinal (arguably the last diva of the Golden Age), *María Isabel* (1968) and its sequel, *El amor de María Isabel* (1970). In these films the protagonist personifies the ideal combination of modernity and tradition, which

---

277. See Tierney, *Emilio Fernández*, 17; López, "Tears and Desire."

enables her to function as the moral grounding for the Mexican male subject of the 1960s while retaining the requisite of Whiteness necessary to project her desirability and melodramatic centrality.

The book's final chapter discusses how the dynamics of the colonization of subjectivity and desire are also evident in the few films that depict Indigenous men as romantic interests, *Tribu* (dir. Miguel Contreras Torres, 1935), *Lola Casanova* (dir. Matilde Landeta, 1949), *Tizoc* (dir. Ismael Rodríguez, 1957), and the parodic film, starring Tin Tan (Germán Valdés), *El violetero* (dir. Gilberto Martínez Solares, 1960). This chapter also considers how the cross-racial patterns of desire and their obstruction persist well beyond the Golden Age in *El juicio de Martín Cortés* (dir. Alejandro Galindo, 1974) and *Batalla en el cielo* (dir. Carlos Reygadas, 2005), as well as how *Güeros* (dir. Alonso Ruizpalacios, 2014) counters these patterns by offering an alternative outcome.

The readings of the films will consider how the Whiteness of the characters, and at times that of the actors who play them, is constructed within and beyond the films. While nonsomatic factors such as wealth and education (*blanquitud*) are important for the inhabiting of a convincing White Mexican social identity in lived experience, because cinema is a visual medium, the visual and embodied aspects of Whiteness will have a heightened significance in determining which persons appear as white-as-Indigenous on-screen to function as objects of desire and as characters with whom spectators are meant to identify. Rather than simply classifying the actors based on my own reading of their phenotype (an inadequate method that would only serve to reveal my own racialized socialization), I rely on several approaches for analyzing Whiteness. First, for the purposes of reading physical White womanhood on-screen, I use as a guide the characteristics that anthropologist Hugo Nutini has identified as the boundaries of embodied Whiteness for women in Mexico, which I broaden only slightly to include the darkest variant of Mexican Whiteness marked by the dark eyes and hair of the imagined Iberian type discussed above,

> For females these standards include white, alabaster skin; medium blonde or auburn hair, straight or slightly curled; light eyes, preferably blue or greenish blue; medium height and thin body conformation; large, expressive eyes, with long lashes; fine, well-proportioned features; a small mouth and nose; and

above all elegance and gracefulness in every movement, from walking and sitting to gesticulating and resting.[278]

Nutini's observations serve as points of reference for reading both the extent to which characters' appearances conform to White womanhood (and manhood) through physical features, movement, and expression. Furthermore, I extend Nutini's indications regarding "elegance and gracefulness" to oral expression of the characters in sound films. In addition, I rely on the analysis of lighting, mise-en-scène, expository texts, opening credits, cinematography, movement, speech patterns, and the star texts of actors and actresses (where applicable) to illustrate how the films craft their performances as instances of whiteness-as-indigeneity.

By discussing the ways in which Whiteness creates meaning in these films, I hope to contribute to the process of "making whiteness strange"[279]—helping to dislodging it as the unquestioned, venerated, and "commonsense" convention for representing Mexican society.

---

278. Nutini, *Mexican Aristocracy*, 62.

279. Richard Dyer, "The Matter of Whiteness," in *White Privilege: Essential Readings on the Other Side of Racism*, ed. Paula Rothenberg (New York: Worth Publishers, 2005), 12.

1

Idealized Pre-Columbian Womanhood

Pre-Columbian Mexico has been an important part of the national imaginary since the decades following independence in the early nineteenth century.¹ The curation of artifacts from the period as well as local representations of the era have served to reify and preserve the notion of an undefiled authentic Mexican essence that also could be understood as a local version of classical antiquity.² With this imagined landscape of Indigenous purity as its background, the Mexican foundational narrative crystalized in both racialized and gendered terms, privileging the union of the Indigenous woman and Hispanic conquistador as the nation's first couple. The foundational narrative of Hernan Cortés and La Malinche, which Octavio Paz sanctions as legitimate national folklore in *El laberinto de la soledad*, is the most prominent example.³

---

1. Stacie G. Widdifield, *The Embodiment of the National in Late Nineteenth-Century Mexican Painting* (Tucson: University of Arizona Press, 1996), 79; Rebecca Earle, *The Return of the Native: Indians and Myth-Making in Spanish America, 1810–1930* (Durham, NC: Duke University Press, 2007), 21–46.

2. This tendency can be appreciated through Shelly Garrigan's discussion of the creation of Mexican archaeology as a nationalizing cultural endeavor in *Collecting Mexico: Museums, Monuments, and the Creation of National Identity* (Minneapolis: University of Minnesota Press, 2012), 65–105; Widdifield, *Embodiment*, 100.

3. "La Malinche" refers to the Indigenous woman, Malintzin, who assisted Hernán Cortés as a translator and intermediary. She also gave birth to his son, Martín Cortés. In the Mexican cultural imaginary, she occupies an ambivalent position as both the Indigenous "mother" of Mexican mesitzaje, but also as a traitor to her own Indigenous people because her collaboration facilitated the Spanish conquest. See Octavio

It is not surprising, therefore, that among twentieth-century Mexican films about Indigeneity, pre-Columbian and conquest-era Indians should surface, and that Indigenous women in particular should be central to these representations. This chapter explores two films with strong melodramatic elements that foreground idealized Indigenous womanhood as one part of their approach to aggrandizing pre-Columbian Indigeneity: *Zítari* (dir. Miguel Contreras Torres, 1931) and *Chilam Balam* (dir. Íñigo de Martino, 1957). Given that national film histories tend to highlight commercial and critical successes,[4] *Zítari*'s lack of distribution and *Chilam Balam*'s perceived artistic deficiencies largely explain why neither film has garnered much scholarly attention.

Without denying the limitations of either film, I suggest that a critical and comparative analysis of *Zítari* and *Chilam Balam* contributes to a more complex understanding of the construct of Indigeneity in twentieth-century Mexican cinema in the following ways. First, instead of excluding from *indigenista* cinema Indigenous-themed films that do not adhere to social realism or constitute an artistic accomplishment as conceived by film critics,[5] critically approaching *Zítari* (a melodrama from the very end of the silent era in Mexico) and *Chilam Balam* (a campy production from the twilight of the Golden Age) allows for a perspective of Mexican cinematic Indigeneity that extends beyond perceptions of prestige in favor of completeness and complexity. Second, by showing how both melodramatic films, although separated by more than two decades, employ similar strategies for elevating pre-Columbian natives to a legendary status within a national framework, I point to a line of continuity in the filmic construct of the Indian that traverses periods instead of interrogating the racial construct from a stagist point of view.[6] This approximation mirrors Colin Gunckel's

---

Paz, *El laberinto de la soledad* (Madrid: Ediciones Cátedra, 2016) and Roger Bartra, *The Cage of Melancholy: Identity and Metamorphosis in the Mexican Character*, trans. Christopher J. Hall (New Brunswick: Rutgers University Press, 1992).

4. Carl J. Mora, *Mexican Cinema: Reflections of a Society* (Berkeley: University of California Press, 1989); Andrea Noble, *Mexican National Cinema* (London; New York: Routledge, 2006).

5. Jorge Ayala Blanco, *La aventura del cine mexicano en la época de oro y después* (Miguel Hidalgo: Grijalbo, 1993).

6. Laura Podalsky has pointed to the limitations of a "stagist approach" to understanding Latin American cinema that emphasizes moments of rupture. "Unpacking Periodization," in *The Routledge Companion to Latin American Cinema*, ed. Marvin D'Lugo, Ana M. López, and Laura Podalsky (New York: Routledge, 2018), 64–65.

exploration of Indigeneity in Mexican horror films,[7] as it enables the identification and analysis of recurring racial tropes, which, not being frozen in a particular moment of cultural history, are also not contained within a given period of Mexican film history. In putting forth an analysis of *Zítari* alongside that of the chronologically distant *Chilam Balam*, I point to recurring ideological emphases and aesthetic strategies for rendering Indigeneity. Furthermore, I submit that while these films' approaches to Indigeneity are compatible with twentieth-century indigenismo-mestizaje in the general sense that they symbolically glorify Indigeneity, they also have roots in earlier moments of Mexican cultural history.

Both *Zítari* and *Chilam Balam* elevate the vicissitudes of temporally removed Indigenous protagonists to the level of legendary dramas. In their attempts to ennoble pre-Hispanic and colonial-era natives, the films position the twentieth-century Mexican nation as the inheritor of Indigenous-themed lore. This mode of *indigenismo* is not entirely new, but instead has much in common with what Luis Villoro has identified as the second moment of indigenismo in his seminal study, *Los grandes momentos del indigenismo en México*. For Villoro, the second phase of indigenismo must be understood in contradistinction to an earlier position articulated by sixteenth-century figures such as Hernán Cortés, who led the conquest of the Aztec empire in the early sixteenth century, and Fray Bernardino de Sahagún, the Franciscan friar and evangelizer best known for compiling the *Historia general de las cosas de Nueva España* (*General History of the Things of New Spain*). According to Villoro, both of their written records cast Mesoamericans as an immediate, contemporary presence and an imminent, demonic threat to Catholicism.[8] In contrast, at the end of the eighteenth century, the thinkers that Villoro understands as initiating a second phase, such as Francisco Javier Clavijero and Fray Servando Teresa de Mier, began to shift their construct of the Indian as both a temporally distant and positive cultural referent.[9] Clavijero and Teresa de Mier's writings aimed to redeem pre-Columbian natives on religious grounds by both framing their practices and beliefs as misunderstood parts of the Judeo-Christian tradition and suggesting the

---

7. Colin Gunckel, "*El signo de la muerte* and the Birth of a Genre: Origins and Anatomy of the Aztec Horror Film," in *Sleaze Artists: Cinema at the Margins of Taste, Style and Politics*, ed. Jeffery Sconce (Durham, NC: Duke University Press, 2007), 121–43.

8. Luis Villoro, *Los grandes momentos del indigenismo en México* (Mexico City: El Colegio de México, 1996), 30–55.

9. Villoro, *Los grandes momentos*, 149–69.

comparability of pre-Conquest Mesoamerican cosmovisions with those of other premodern civilizations.[10] Such arguments—because they refuted the religious justification for the conquest—constituted a positive refashioning of Indigeneity that served as an important ideological precursor to the independence movement and to the articulation of a national identity.[11]

Zítari and Chilam Balam echo some of the tropes for lauding Indigeneity that these cultural figures from the late eighteenth and early nineteenth centuries crafted and mobilized, specifically the presentation of ancient Indigenous religiosity as having value and the equivalency of temporally distant Mesoamericans to other pagan peoples. Although Zítari and Chilam Balam draw on these earlier strategies for framing Indigenous culture and religion, they also transmit a congruence with the official twentieth-century indigenismo-mestizaje discourse. As mentioned in the introduction, indigenismo-mestizaje underscored Indigenous peoples' contribution to the mixed makeup of modern Mexican society in selective terms. One of those contributions, according to José Vasconcelos, was Indigenous people's "countless number of properly spiritual capacities."[12] Therefore, even though Zítari and Chilam Balam reproduce long-established devices for recasting ancient Indigeneity as positive, the films also exalt the Indigenous contribution to the Mexican nation in a manner that was discursively compatible with popular nationalism's symbolic celebration of Indigenous Mexicans and mestizos.

---

10. In Francisco Javier Clavijero's *Historia antigua de México*, he suggests that the Indigenous people descended from the biblical Adam and Eve and that they experienced the great flood recounted in the book of Genesis. The proof of this, according to Clavijero, can be found in native beliefs, stories, and rituals that recount similar events. Clavijero rejects the earlier idea that the Indians were led by Satan and instead suggests that their error was the excess of their practices, but not their devotional intent. Clavijero put forth the notion that the Indians were comparable to any other pagan society in which similar rituals were common and that they were even less barbaric by comparison. Fray Servando Teresa de Mier casts Indigenous religions as misled versions of Christianity. He argues that the Indians had been converted to Christianity by St. Thomas, who was venerated by the Aztecs in the form of Quetzalcóatl, and that the god Huitzilopochtli was the native name for Christ, while the goddess Coatlicue was the Virgin Mary. See Villoro *Los grandes momentos*, 149–69.

11. Villoro, *Los grandes momentos*, 149–69.

12. José Vasconcelos, *The Cosmic Race/La raza cósmica: A Bilingual Edition*, trans. Didier T. Jaén (Baltimore: Johns Hopkins University Press, 1979), 32.

Furthermore, *Zítari* and *Chilam Balam*'s ennoblement of ancient Indigeneity also has much in common with mid-nineteenth-century Mexican history paintings that celebrate pre-Columbian Indigenous peoples as civilized and authentic precursors of the Mexican nation.[13] As Stacie G. Widdifield has observed, paintings such as Rodrigo Gutiérrez's *Deliberation of the Senate of Tlaxcala* (1875) drew explicit comparisons between the conquest-era natives and classical antiquity to suggest the cultural and political sophistication of the pre-Hispanic Mesoamerican world and by extension, that of the mid-nineteenth century Mexican republic.[14] Additionally, during that period, Mexican artists selected pre-Columbian legends about love and Indigenous royalty as worthy subjects of representation within the elite genre of history painting, of which José Obregón's *Discovery of Pulque* (1869) is an example.[15] This rendering of the encounter between the Toltec king, Tecpancaltzin, and the young Toltec woman, Xochitl, is presented as "noble and romantic" while offering a point of continuity with the nineteenth-century Mexican viewer through its display of the popular maguey-derived beverage, pulque.[16] Such paintings seek to elevate the place of Indigeneity in the national narrative by representing legendary historical episodes involving Mesoamerican nobles through a culturally prestigious form and in a highly stylized manner employing stoic poses, orderly political settings, and dignified clothing that evoke classical references. In a similar manner, the mid-twentieth-century melodramas *Zítari* and *Chilam Balam* celebrate Mesoamericans of the remote past as glorified figures with a connection to the national present in highly stylized terms that similarly privilege elegance and gravitas.

Crucial to the ennoblement of ancient Indigeneity in both films is the centrality of the white-as-indigenous pre-Columbian woman; Zítari in the film by the same title (played by Medea de Novara) and Naya in *Chilam Balam* (played by Lucy González). These films present the Indigenous woman from the pre-Hispanic period as a legendary character fit for appropriation into national lore through the following strategies: her privileged positioning in relation to spiritual practices, her function in

---

13. Widdifield, *Embodiment*, 78–121.
14. Widdifield, *Embodiment*, 103.
15. Widdifield, *Embodiment*, 91.
16. Widdifield, *Embodiment*, 91–92.

the melodrama as the primary point of emotive display and identification for the spectator, and her presentation as desirable in both narrative and technical terms. Because of the dynamics of the colonization of desire and subjectivity outlined in the introduction, in the melodramatic context of these films, Zítari and Naya's Whiteness functions as a racialized semiotic device for underscoring the pathos and desirability of the characters. When viewed from this perspective, not unlike the lightening of Xochitl in Obregón's painting,[17] the indexically illogical Whitening of the pre-Columbian protagonists in *Zítari* and *Chilam Balam* supports the films' overall portrayal of the women as glorious contributors to Mexicanness.

Zítari (1931)

Miguel Contreras Torres's 1931 short film *Zítari* is one of the earliest extant Indigenous-themed Mexican productions. It is a very late silent film, finished shortly before the release of the first Mexican sound production *Santa* (dir. Antonio Moreno, 1932).[18] Despite its late production date, *Zítari* exemplifies the characteristics that, according to Paul Schroeder Rodríguez, characterize silent Latin American narrative cinema, which was "made by an emerging criollo bourgeoisie using a small-scale, artisanal approach to production, distribution and exhibition, and espousing a Eurocentric worldview with correspondingly Europeanized aesthetics."[19] As we will see, the film aligns with what Schroeder Rodríguez terms "a criollo aesthetic" in that its "visual language and narrative structures are metropolitan but [its] atmospheres, concerns, and characters are local, national or regional."[20]

Zítari consists of two distinct parts: the first contains multiple views and panoramas of different archeological sites within the Mexican republic, while the second is a fictional narrative about the love between an Indigenous princess (Zítari) and a warrior who dies in battle (Mazatal). Scholars who have addressed the film have focused primarily on the circumstances of its production. Eduardo de la Vega Alfaro points

---

17. Widdifield, *Embodiment*, 91–95.
18. Mora, *Mexican Cinema*, 34–35.
19. Paul Schroeder Rodríguez, *Latin American Cinema: A Comparative History* (Berkeley: University of California Press, 2016), 19.
20. Schroeder Rodríguez, *Latin American Cinema*, 18.

out the ways in which Zítari is a product of the transition to sound in Mexico, concluding that, most likely, the narrative portion was filmed first without synchronized sound and that, wanting to take advantage of the enthusiasm surrounding the new technology, Contreras Torres later added the documentary portion containing voice over narration and music, as well as music to the originally silent narrative portion.[21] In addition, Gabriel Ramírez's discussion of the film cites an interview with Medea de Novara, the director's wife and the actress who plays the title role of Zítari, suggesting that Contreras Torres made the film more as a source of amusement for her than as an earnest commercial endeavor.[22] Though containing references to the work of those who have analyzed the sound version, the analysis of Zítari put forth here is based on the version of the film that contains the archeological sequence but relies on intertitles (instead of sound) to convey contextual information.

The suggestion that Mexican national identity is a productive lens through which to read Contreras Torres's work is not new. Mexican film scholars have regularly pointed out the director's investment in the topic[23] and have even described his filmography as "archi-nacionalista" (ultra-nationalist).[24] Indeed, prior to making Zítari, Contreras Torres had already made four films that in some way dealt with nationalistic themes: *El Zarco* (1921), *De raza azteca* and *El hombre sin patria* (both made in 1922), and *El águila y el nopal* (1929). My observation that his early Indigenous-themed film, Zítari, comments directly and indirectly on the national is therefore in line with broader readings of his oeuvre. In the case of Zítari specifically, Contreras Torres's work crafts the greatness of Mexico by highlighting the merit of pre-Hispanic peoples who lived on what eventually became the national territory.

The film's point of departure for glorifying Indigeneity is its featuring of archaeological sites within Mexico, which laborious state-funded projects

---

21. Eduardo de la Vega Alfaro, "La transición del 'mudo' al 'sonoro' en México y el caso de Zítari (Miguel Contreras Torres, 1931)," in *Cine mudo latinoamericano: Inicios, nación, vanguardias y transición*, ed. Aurelio de los Reyes and David M. J. Wood (Mexico City: UNAM, 2015), 235–50.

22. Gabriel Ramírez, *Miguel Contreras Torres, 1899–1981* (Guadalajara: Centro de Investigación y Enseñanza Cinematográficas, Universidad de Guadalajara, 1994); Mora, *Mexican Cinema*, 31.

23. De la Vega Alfaro, "Transición"; Ramírez, *Miguel Contreras Torres*.

24. Ramírez, *Miguel Contreras Torres*.

had fashioned into "the sacred and ordered space of modern ruins."[25] While the display of the preserved sites marks the modernity of the contemporary state,[26] *Zítari*'s opening expository text upholds the architectural accomplishments of pre-Hispanic cultures as sources of mystery and wonder with a passage written by American historian and Hispanist William H. Prescott, "Es imposible contemplar los misteriosos monumentos de una civilización ya perdida, sin tener viva curiosidad de saber quiénes fueron los arquitectos" (It is impossible to contemplate the mysterious monuments of a now lost civilization without becoming intensely curious to know who the architects were). The subsequent sequence showing Mesoamerican ruins in different parts of the country suggests not only a will to display the structures of pre-Columbian natives as grand achievements, but also a didactic impulse, as the sites are presented in terms of their geographical location within Mexico and the civilizations to whom the monuments are attributed. Finally, the archeological sequence implies that the survival of Indigenous engineering feats is also a testament to Mesoamerican greatness by suggesting that buildings in the United States may not be able to last as long as those structures have. The sound version of the sequence contains a voice-over that, in referring to the endurance of pre-Columbian structures, tendentiously asks, "¿Podremos decir lo mismo de los rascacielos neoyorkinos dentro de mil años?" (Will we be able to say the same of New York skyscrapers in a thousand years?).[27] In casting doubt on the permanence of Yankee high-rises, the question seeks to reaffirm the value of Mesoamerican antiquity vis-à-vis a modernity that it presents as comparatively foreign and uncertain. In sum, the film initially features archeology to suggest the ingenuity and value of pre-Hispanic peoples and, by extension, of Mexico.

Having displayed Mesoamerican ruins as laudable accomplishments in the first half, the film then repurposes their aura[28] by using an archaeological site as the setting of its tragic love story. The importance of the setting's structures for the aggrandizing representation of the pre-Hispanic

---

25. Quetzil E. Castañeda, "The Aura of Ruins," in *Fragments of a Golden Age: The Politics of Culture in Mexico Since 1940*, ed. Gilbert M. Joseph, Anne Rubenstein, and Eric Zolov (Durham, NC: Duke University Press, 2001), 455.

26. "Restored to authenticity by the genius of modern science, ruins are original copies: authentic inventions of modernity." Castañeda, "The Aura of Ruins," 456.

27. De la Vega Alfaro, "Transición," 247.

28. Castañeda, "The Aura of Ruins," 452–70.

Idealized Pre-Columbian Womanhood 71

characters in the film can be appreciated in the film's full title, which romantically casts one of the Mesoamerican structures as "el templo de las mil serpientes" (the temple of the thousand serpents), the place where ancient Indians worship "the goddess of love." In referring to the structure and the Indigenous deity in this general way, which lacks specific Mesoamerican names for the place and for the divine entity venerated there, the film re-presents the temple as general pagan artifact, and pre-Columbian beliefs as equivalent to classical traditions that also had a goddess of love and impressive worship sites.[29] Furthermore, by staging diegetic acts of religious worship at the archeological site, the film works to reinfuse the artifact with the sacred dimension to which it originally owes its aura.[30]

Zítari's mythification of chronologically remote Indigeneity proceeds to frame the love story as being rooted in "legend."[31] The choice of this particular word in the film's expository text suggests that the story has been handed down through time yet possesses a romantic quality, closer to the fable than to historical account.[32] In this way, *Zítari* elevates its pre-Columbian protagonists by suggesting that their belief system is a source of cultural value.[33] Furthermore, unlike some twentieth-century films that comment on native beliefs pejoratively,[34] in *Zítari*, the worthi-

---

29. During the midnight meeting between the two lovers, Zítari mentions her faith in the gods of war and love (whom the film evokes through these generally pagan designations): "Yo rogaré al Dios de la Guerra por vuestra salvación y que podáis regresar a pedir mi mano al Rey . . . Tengo fé en vuestro triunfo y la Diosa del amor velará por vuestro regreso" (I will beg to the god of war for your salvation and so that you can return to ask the king for my hand . . . I have faith in your triumph and the goddess of love will safeguard your return).

30. Walter Benjamin, "The Work of Art in the Age of Mechanical Reproduction," in *Illuminations*, ed. Hannah Arendt, trans. Harry Zohn (New York: Schocken Books, 1969), 217–52.

31. "La leyenda atribuye una romántica historia a la Diosa del Amor, que veneraban los indios en los altares del Templo de las mil Serpientes" (Legend attributes a romantic story to the Goddess of Love, whom the Indians venerated at the Temple of the thousand serpents).

32. The film explicitly distances itself from historical authority at the beginning of the archaeological sequence when an expository text renounces any claim to accuracy and disavows all "pretensión histórica" (historical pretense).

33. See also the analyses of *La noche de los mayas* and *Deseada* in chapter 4.

34. Such as *Tepeyac* (1917), *El signo de la muerte* (1939), *Lola Casanova* (1949), *Chilam Balam* (1955), *Tizoc* (1957), and *La momia azteca films* (1957–1958), among others.

ness of the Mesoamerican characters is not compromised by their pagan spiritual beliefs and practices. Any potentially problematic aspects of native religiosity, such as human sacrifices—the taboo par excellence[35]—are elided in this rendition. Also, there is no hint of the necessity of conversion in order to redeem or improve the Indians, as they are noble, grand, and fossilized figures whose beliefs in no way tarnish the image of their community or of the contemporary nation, which in part, descends from them (as the archaeological sequence implies). On the contrary, in the film pre-Columbian beliefs are a source of cultural achievements (the temples displayed at the beginning of the film) and legends (the way in which the love story is framed). Like the thinkers discussed in Villoro's second phase of indigenismo, Miguel Contreras Torres's film instantiates a rehabilitation of remote Indigeneity in the local imaginary via a reconsideration of Mesoamerican paganism. While the film does not attempt to do this by recasting a pre-Columbian belief system as a long-lost branch of Christianity, it does mobilize the notion of pagan equivalency to present remote Indigeneity as a nonstigmatized source for myths and legends for the contemporary nation.

One of the ways in which *Zítari* romanticizes what it presents as legendary pre-Columbian Indigeneity is by adhering to the conventions of melodrama in characterization and narrative. The protagonists—the honorable warrior Mazatal and the virtuous princess Zítari—are one-dimensional, innocent victims whose suffering unfolds because of Mazatal's adversary, who kills him in an act of vengeance. By initially portraying the couple's love as pure and intense through hyperbolic declarations of affection and loyalty in an idyllic garden, which functions visually and symbolically as the melodrama's "space of innocence,"[36] *Zítari* frames Mazatal's death as a tragic event. Through the film's absolute, personified contrast between good and evil and its dramatic focus on the thwarted aspirations of the

---

35. Gómez Izquierdo, "Racismo y nacionalismo en el discurso de las élites mexicanas," in *Los caminos del racismo en México*, ed. José Jorge Gómez Izquierdo (Mexico City: Plaza y Valdés, S.A., 2005), 143.

36. According to Peter Brooks, melodrama begins in the "space of innocence" (often an idyllic garden) representing the well-being of the protagonist prior to the intrusion on behalf of the villain. Peter Brooks, *The Melodramatic Imagination: Balzac, Henry James, Melodrama, and the Mode of Excess* (New Haven: Yale University Press, 1995), 29. See also Linda Williams, *Playing the Race Card: Melodramas of Black and White from Uncle Tom to O. J. Simpson* (Princeton: Princeton University Press, 2001), 7–8, 28.

central couple, the film mobilizes the hallmarks of the melodramatic mode. In so doing, *Zítari* imbues the pre-Columbian couple's vicissitudes with an epic quality,[37] echoing through narrative devices the film's initial claim that the Mesoamerican story is the stuff of legend.

Furthermore, the film links its version of a pre-Columbian worldview with the emotionalism that is characteristic of melodrama by tying the possibility of poetic justice for the lovers with the Indigenous characters' belief in a spiritual realm. This occurs when, upon Zítari's death, one of her subjects alludes to their afterlife as a place in which Zítari can be reunited with her beloved, "¡La muerte os arrebató soñadora princesa, pero el amor es más fuerte que la muerte, y allá en la eternidad juntaréis vuestras almas!" (Death has snatched you, dreamy princess, but love is stronger than death, and there in eternity will you join your souls!). By locating the lovers' yearned-for return to "the place of innocence" in a pre-Columbian version of an afterlife, and by ostensibly bearing out the power of the goddess of love through the protagonist's sudden death at her shrine, *Zítari*'s melodramatically charged representation of an ancient Mesoamerican cosmovision affirms it as a valid worldview within its cultural and temporal context. In this way, *Zítari* employs the conventions of melodrama to offer a glorified interpretation of pre-Columbian paganism, which contributes to the film's idealization of remote Indigeneity as a valuable aspect of Mexicanness.

In contrast to the humble *inditos* of the mid to late Golden Age of Mexican cinema who speak a pidgin Spanish and walk in short hop-like movements (of whom María Candelaria and Tizoc are the most widely known),[38] the pre-Columbian indigenista variant that *Zítari* belongs to aims for elegance and stateliness, attempting, like mid-nineteenth-century Mexican history painting,[39] to confer solemnity and nobility to the portrayal of temporally distant Indigenous people. In *Zítari*, the characters'

---

37. Brooks, *The Melodramatic Imagination*, 13–15.
38. Joanne Hershfield, "Race and Ethnicity in the Classical Cinema," in *Mexico's Cinema: A Century of Film and Filmmakers*, ed. Joanne Hershfield and David Maciel (Wilmington, DE: Scholarly Resources, 1999), 81–100; Dolores Tierney, *Emilio Fernández: Pictures in the Margins* (Manchester: Manchester University Press, 2012), 73–102; Yásnaya Aguilar, "El efecto Tizoc," July 4, 2012, https://web.archive.org/web/20190510094735/http://archivo.estepais.com/site/2012/el-efecto-tizoc/. For *María Candelaria*, see chapter 4; for *Tizoc*, see chapter 6.
39. Widdifield, *Embodiment*, 78–121.

movements on-screen are slow, stoic, and dramatic. Zítari's royal status, the lovers' ardor, and the characters' religious devotion create multiple opportunities for affected bodily movements that take up considerable space in the frame, such as dramatic bowing, arm-raising, and hand-kissing. Additionally, their costumes are elaborate and serve to convey either their military status or noble condition. Furthermore, when individual characters speak to each other, the dialogue in the intertitles uses the "vosotros" form for the second-person singular, which by the twentieth century functioned in peninsular Spanish to convey the second-person plural and did not appear in Mexican Spanish. Because in *Zítari* the "vosotros" form is used for the second-person singular when Zítari and Mazatl speak to each other, it operates as an aural affectation that locates the Indigenous characters in a removed temporal realm and elevates the register of their speech. Echoing visual references to classical artwork in paintings such as José Obregón's *Discovery of Pulque* (1869) or Rodrigo Gutiérrez's *Deliberation of the Senate of Tlaxcala* (1875),[40] *Zítari* crafts a version of ancient indigeneity through aestheticization, which seeks to attribute a palpable degree of gravitas and aplomb to pre-Columbian Mesoamericans. In so doing, the film attempts to glorify them and, by extension, the Mexican nation that in part descends from ancient Indigeneity.

In addition to the aural and visual devices mentioned above, part of the way in which *Zítari* crafts the protagonists' mythical aura is through a differentiated approach to displaying filmed bodies as representative of Indigeneity. Zítari's opening credits include information that highlights the aspects of the film that are meant to reinforce its authenticity, including on-location filming at historical sites. When it comes to the film's on-screen participants, the film's text creates a distinction between the two actors who play main roles, on the one hand, and the rest of the cast, on the other, referring to the former by name (Medea de Novaro and Matías Santoro) and to the latter as "aborígenes mexicanos" (aboriginal Mexicans). In this way, the film marks a distinction between those it presents as indexically Indigenous versus those whose bodies signify Indigeneity in the film purely through dramatization.[41] Because it is precisely the

---

40. Widdifield, *Embodiment*, 78–121.

41. Claudia Arroyo Quiroz identifies a similar distinction in her analysis of Emilio Fernández's films, which she articulates as a contrast between visualizing Indigenous characters through an "ethnographic body" as opposed to through "the bodies of stars which are constructed as an object of contemplation." Claudia Arroyo Quiroz, "Fantasías

idealized Zítari and Mazatal who are not presented through indexically Indigenous bodies, the film deploys Whiteness (through the semiotic trick of whiteness-as-indigeneity) as one of the film's visual strategies for conveying the greatness of the pre-Columbian lovers in the postcolonial Mexican context.

Following Hugo Nutini's outline of the physical projection of White femininity in Mexico (a combination of *blancura* and *blanquitud*),[42] Zítari manifests White Mexican womanhood through her tall and slender body, large eyes, light eye color, fine facial features, thin manicured eyebrows, graceful movements on-screen, as well as through her eloquent and elevated register of Spanish in the intertitles. Furthermore, the acting trajectory of Medea de Novara (born Hermine Kindle Flutcher in Liechtenstein, and wife of the prominent Mexican director Miguel Contreras Torres) further bears out that the actress' body was read as White in Mexico. De Novara's career confirms Richard Dyer's observation regarding the license afforded to Whiteness to represent any character regardless of its diegetic race or ethnicity.[43] While in *Zítari*, Medea de Novara plays an Indigenous princess, in Contreras Torres's 1934 film *Tribu*,[44] she plays a European noblewoman in New Spain during the early colonial period who interacts with an Indigenous tribe (effectively placing her in a diametrically opposed position to the one she occupies in *Zítari*). De Novara is perhaps best-known for having played, no fewer than four times, the role of Empress Carlota of Mexico, the Belgian-born wife of the Austrian archduke (and, later, second emperor of Mexico), Maximilian.[45] The fact that de Novara played both European and Mesoamerican royalty in the Mexican context of production (as well as the Middle Eastern biblical figure Mary Magdalene)

---

sobre le identidad indígena en el cine mexicano del periodo post-revolucionario," in *Identidades. Explorando la diversidad*, ed. Laura Carballido (Mexico City: Universidad Autónoma Metropolitana-Anthropos, 2011), 159. See chapter 4 for a parallel discussion of the role of credits in *La noche de los mayas* (1939).

42. Hugo Nutini, *The Mexican Aristocracy: An Expressive Ethnography* (Austin: University of Texas Press, 2008), 62.

43. Richard Dyer, "Coloured White, Not Coloured," in *White* (London; New York: Routledge, 1997).

44. See chapter 5.

45. *Juárez y Maximiliano*, dir. Miguel Contreras Torres, 1934; *La paloma*, dir. Miguel Contreras Torres, 1937; *The Mad Empress*, dir. Miguel Contreras Torres, 1939; *Caballería de imperio*, dir. Miguel Contreras Torres, 1942.

Figure 1.1. Medea de Novara as Indigenous royalty in *Zítari* (1931). Photo courtesy of Mil Nubes-Foto (Roberto Fiesco). All rights reserved.

highlights the flexibility and privilege afforded to her precisely because her body and persona were read as White there. Furthermore, her career points to the colonially inflected tolerance for the disavowal of indexicality in the representation of Indigeneity in Mexico (whiteness-as-indigeneity) and the intransigence regarding the representation of diegetic Whiteness as anything other than indexically White.[46]

In a manner parallel to *María Candelaria* as analyzed by Dolores Tierney,[47] *Zítari*'s deployment of Whiteness to transmit legendary pre-Columbian womanhood creates the need to layer Indigeneity onto the White body through other visual markers. This fact is a recurring characteristic

---

46. Can one recall or fathom a Mexican film in which the Empress Carlota is played by a nonWhite Mexican actress?

47. Tierney, *Emilio Fernández*, 73–102.

Figure 1.2. Medea de Novara as a Spanish aristocrat in *Tribu* (1935). Photo courtesy of Mil Nubes-Foto (Roberto Fiesco). All rights reserved.

of the Indigenous-themed genre and, as I explore in the rest of the book, occurs in many different ways depending on how films frame Indigeneity in relation to the contemporary Mexican nation. *Zítari*'s approach to Indigenizing the White body, because the film aims for distanced idealization, involves overstated and formal garb, elaborate headdresses, large jewelry, stoic bodily movements, and mise-en-scène that places the character on or near pre-Columbian archeological sites at every opportunity. In this way, the film attempts to transmit Zítari's nobility through bodily Whiteness while at the same conveying her diegetic Indigeneity through visual elements connected to social or cultural prestige. Through its combination of embodied Whiteness and a diegetic Indigeneity, *Zítari* promotes an understanding of the native as a distanced and glorified precursor of Mexicanness in racialized visual terms.

Furthermore, in *Zítari*, it is the white-as-indigenous title character who functions as the primary point of identification in the melodrama.

In keeping with the conventions of the mode, the film presents Zítari as a virtuous protagonist through her loving devotion to Mazatal both in life and after his death. In addition, despite the fabricated accusations that he betrayed her with another woman before dying, Zítari continues to believe in her beloved's virtue, which aligns her with truth and rectitude. Furthermore, and also in keeping with the conventions of melodrama, the film puts her at the center of the narrative as the suffering victim of the antagonist's misdeeds. Visually, the film emphasizes the title character's privileged status within the melodrama through the frequent use of the close-up, which, by displaying her extreme emotional states, heightens the film's pathos. The film highlights the title character's emotional state in this manner on three occasions: the evening before her beloved's departure, the day of his departure when she gifts him her ring, and when she receives news of his death. Zítari is the character who is captured on camera most often through this cinematic device, which serves the double function of emphasizing her anguish and also showcasing her white-as-indigenous face. By locating emotional intensity in the white-as-indigenous body, the film mobilizes the racialized semiotic privilege of Whiteness to establish her as the melodrama's compassion-worthy victim, which in turn serves to idealize her as a pre-Columbian legend.

Miguel Contreras Torres's two-part short film puts forth a celebratory representation of pre-Columbian Indigeneity by lauding its architectural achievements and by making it the context of a melodramatic love story of two noble characters, which it elevates to the status of legend. *Zítari* mobilizes various strategies for depicting the ancient Mesoamericans as distant, quasi-mythical ancestors of Mexican *mestizaje*. Like cultural figures from the late eighteenth and early nineteenth centuries, Contreras Torres offers a noncondemnatory perspective on an ancient Mesoamerican cosmovision. By employing the concept of an Indigenous worldview as an instrument of melodrama, the film uses paganism to heighten pathos while also suggesting the veracity of Mesoamerican beliefs within their remote temporal and cultural context. Furthermore, *Zítari*'s highly stylized approach to cinematic indigenismo aims for gravitas and aplomb, not unlike nineteenth-century Mexican history painting that referenced classical models to fashion stately pre-Columbians.[48] Even though the film's style is compatible with the emergent indigenismo-mestizaje discourse of the

---

48. Widdifield, *Embodiment*, 78–105.

postrevolutionary period in the general sense that it glorifies Indigeneity, it is strongly embedded in residual cultural and aesthetic perspectives on Indigeneity.[49] Part of the film's exaltation of ancient Mesoamericans rests on the colonially inflected semiotic privilege of the White body, onto which the film layers a solemn and formal diegetic Indigeneity. The anchoring of the film's melodramatic intensity to the white-as-indigenous woman cements the character's pathos and her exalted status as a legendary, proto-Mexican in racialized terms. As we will see, *Chilam Balam* similarly aims to dignify pre-Columbian Indigeneity, but places an explicit emphasis on its role in the forging of Mexican mestizaje.

Chilam Balam (1957)

Íñigo de Martino's directorial debut, *Chilam Balam* (1955),[50] is a product of what has been identified by scholars as the decline of the Golden Age of Mexican cinema.[51] Although dwindling financial investment is considered one of the causes of the lack of artistic quality in the films made during this period, it does not appear that *Chilam Balam* lacked financial backing. Emilio García Riera highlights that the CLASA Films Mundiales producers spent large sums of money on sets and jewelry for the film.[52] Moreover, *Chilam Balam* is ostensibly an attempt to create a Mexican film comparable to Hollywood's successful biblical and classical epics of the period, such as *Samson and Delilah* (dir. Cecil B. DeMille, 1949), *Quo Vadis* (dir. Mervyn LeRoy, 1951), and *The Ten Commandments* (dir. Cecil B. DeMille, 1956). Like these Hollywood productions, *Chilam Balam* foregrounds religious conflict to dramatize the prevailing of the Judeo-Christian tradition while

---

49. Raymond Williams, *Marxism and Literature* (Oxford: Oxford University Press, 1977), 122.

50. María Luisa Amador and Jorge Ayala Blanco confirm that the film was in theaters for only two weeks beginning on February 13, 1957. María Luisa Amador and Jorge Ayala Blanco, *Cartelera cinematográfica 1950–1959* (Mexico City: CUEC, 1985), 252.

51. Eduardo de la Vega Alfaro, "The Decline of the Golden Age and the Making of the Crisis," in *Mexico's Cinema: A Century of Film and Filmmakers*, ed. Joanne Hershfield and David Maciel (Wilmington, DE: Scholarly Resources, 1999), 165–91; Mora, *Mexican Cinema*.

52. Emilio García Riera, *Historia documental del cine mexicano*, vol. 8, *1955–1956* (Guadalajara: Universidad de Guadalajara, 1994), 122–25.

also promising a superior visual experience through up-to-date filmic technology. Coverage of *Chilam Balam*'s production process in the film magazine *Cinema Reporter* beginning in 1955 positioned the film in this way. Articles in the magazine sought to whet the reader's appetite for the film by promising a "film epopéyico, a colores y pantalla panorámica"[53] (epic film, in color and widescreen) as well as an "ambiciosa superproducción" (ambitious superproduction).[54] *Cinema Reporter*'s coverage also insinuated the equivalency of de Martino's film and Hollywood epics by suggesting that the Mexican film's prints were admired in Los Angeles, "en los laboratorios norteamericanos, acostumbrados a la calidad y espectacularidad de las grandes super-producciones, causó gratísima impresión el material mexicano, despertando gran interés" (in the North American laboratories accustomed to the quality and spectacularity of the great superproductions, the Mexican material made a pleasing impression, generating great interest).[55]

However, despite the evidence of robust financial investment and the trappings of an epic production, (which more often than not result in unintentional humor),[56] *Chilam Balam* is no cinematic masterpiece.[57] Possessing "the proper mixture of the exaggerated, the fantastic, the passionate, and the naïve," and exhibiting both "the spirit of extravagance" and "a seriousness that fails,"[58] *Chilam Balam* belongs squarely to the world of camp, while, by contrast, *Zítari* does not quite "fail" enough to receive this designation.

Here I call attention to the ways in which *Chilam Balam* participates in similar strategies of ennobling temporally removed Indians with respect to Miguel Contreras Torres's earlier film; however, unlike *Zítari*, *Chilam Balam* firmly establishes Catholicism as foundational requisite for the Mexican nation. The difference between the presentation of Catholicism in *Zítari* and *Chilam Balam* bears some relation to the postrevolutionary government's shifting attitude toward the religion in the span of time in which the two films were produced. The first Cristero Rebellion, which opposed the anti-

---

53. "Chilam Balam, un film mexicano de raíces históricas," *Cinema Reporter*, November 30, 1955, 4.
54. "Terminó su rodaje Chilam-Balam," *Cinema Reporter*, December 21, 1955, 30.
55. *Cinema Reporter*, January 11, 1956, 4.
56. García Riera, *Historia documental del cine*, vol. 8: 122–25.
57. Mexican film critic Jorge Ayala Blanco has suggested that the film is of such poor quality that it is not even worthy of analysis. Jorge Ayala Blanco, *Aventura del cine mexicano*, 150.
58. Sontag, Susan, "Notes on Camp," in *Camp: Queer Aesthetics and the Performing Subject: A Reader*, ed. Fabio Cleto (Edinburgh: Edinburgh University Press, 2008), 53–65.

clerical objectives within the Mexican Revolution, took place between 1926 and 1929.[59] In the early 1930s, when former President Plutarco Elías Calles (1924–1928) unofficially retained power, anticlerical legislation passed in almost every Mexican state.[60] However, President Lázaro Cardenas (1934–1940) began to pull away from his predecessors' antagonistic relationship to the Catholic Church in Mexico starting in 1935,[61] and President Manuel Ávila Camacho (1940–1946) attempted to symbolically resolve the tension between the PRI and Mexican Catholics by publicly declaring himself a man of faith.[62] In light of this history, it is logical that the filmic portrayal of Catholicism as a fundamental component of the Mexican nation can be found in a post-Ávila Camacho production like *Chilam Balam*.[63]

However, though casting Catholicism as a foundational element, *Chilam Balam* also portrays the native belief system as proof of the Indigenous culture's worth as an admirable aspect of the future Mexican nation's mestizaje. Furthermore, in *Chilam Balam*'s reimagining of the nation's foundational couple consisting of the Indigenous woman and the Spanish conquistador, the white-as-indigenous conquest-era woman takes on legendary significance. The melodramatic centrality of the white-as-indigenous female protagonist locates her as the film's primary point of identification and desire, which underscores her idealization as the deserving Indigenous progenitor of the Mexican nation.

Like *Zítari*, De Martino's *Chilam Balam* is a fictitious extrapolation from a Mayan artifact, in this case, the several books written in the sixteenth and seventeenth centuries in the Yucatán peninsula known as the Books of Chilam Balam.[64] The film reimagines the story these texts tell about a *chilan* (a pre-Hispanic oracle or prophet) who "was believed to have foretold the arrival of the Spanish conquistadors and the new religion they aggressively

---

59. Ben Fallaw, *Religion and State formation in Postrevolutionary Mexico* (Durham, NC: Duke University Press, 2013), 4.

60. Martin Austin Nesvig, "Introduction," in *Religious Culture in Modern Mexico*, ed. Martin Austin Nesvig (Lanham, MD: Rowman & Littlefield, 2007), 2–3; Fallaw, *Religion*, 4.

61. Fallaw, *Religion*, 220.

62. Fallaw, *Religion*, 21.

63. Ben Fallaw, *Religion and State formation in Postrevolutionary Mexico* (Durham, NC: Duke University Press, 2013), 1–12; Martin Austin Nesvig, "Introduction," in *Religious Culture in Modern Mexico*, ed. Martin Austin Nesvig (Lanham, MD: Rowman & Littlefield, 2007), 1–13.

64. Timothy Knowlton, *Maya Creation Myths: Words and Worlds of the Chilam Balam* (Boulder: University Press of Colorado, 2010), 2.

promoted."[65] In the film, Naya (Lucy González) is the daughter of the Mayan leader and prophet, Chilam Balam (Carlos López Moctezuma), and she is destined to be sacrificed to the gods. Naya is courted by a Mayan suitor, Bakal, but refuses his proposal. After jumping into a sinkhole (or cenote, as they are called in southern Mexico and Central America) to simulate the completion of her self-sacrifice to the gods, Bakal attempts to rape Naya, and she kills him in self-defense. Having foretold the arrival of the Spanish and the end of his people's sovereignty, Chilam Balam finds Naya and they flee, defying their high priest and leader, Ah K'in Chel. The Mayans track down Naya and Chilam Balam with the intention of bringing them to justice, but Naya's second sacrifice to the gods is postponed when the Spanish conquistadores arrive just in time to save her. Even though Chilam Balam has fallen out of favor with his people, he temporarily allies with them against the Spanish. As a part of this alliance, Chilam Balam offers to take the Spanish to Chichén Itzá under the pretext of leading them where they can find gold, while in reality, he is setting them up to be ambushed by several Mayan groups. Along the way, a love triangle forms between Naya, her new (and very jealous) Indigenous suitor from the coast, A'Kan, and the Spanish soldier, Francisco de Montejo. When the Spanish arrive in Chichén Itzá, the Mayans attack them and are defeated. Ah K'in Chel, Chilam Balam, and A'kan all perish in the conflict. Naya and Francisco marry, and their bond fulfills her father's prophesy as they come together to form the foundation of a new people.

Like the archaeological footage, intertitles, and voice-over narration in *Zítari*'s first half, *Chilam Balam*'s preamble highlights the cultural achievements of pre-Columbian Mayans. The didactic mode of address in this instance (complete with a shot of a map of Mexico and close-up of the Yucatán Peninsula) similarly seeks to educate the spectator and elevate the ancient Mesoamericans as noble contributors to Mexican patrimony. In particular, the film exalts the ancient Maya by highlighting the longevity of their society and the various areas of their knowledge and expertise, ". . . por más de doce siglos floreció la más brillante civilización del nuevo mundo, la de los pueblos Mayas. Sus conocimientos matemáticos y astronómicos fueron extraordinarios, pero en lo que mayormente destacaron fue como escultores y arquitectos" (for more than twelve centuries flourished the most brilliant civilization of the new world, that of the Maya peoples. Their mathematical and astronomical knowledge was extraordi-

---

65. Knowlton, *Maya Creation Myths*, 2.

nary, but they were most distinguished as sculptors and architects). As in *Zítari*, the pre-Columbian monuments in particular function as symbols of Indigenous greatness and are featured in panoramic shots in the film's opening sequence. Other moments in the film echo this initial and explicit visualization of the ruins, for example, through the staging of important moments of the story at archeological sites, most notably, the culminating final battle between the Mayans and Spanish at Chichén Itzá. In short, both films display pre-Columbian monuments as a way of crafting an elevated, temporally distanced perspective toward Indigeneity. As in the case of Miguel Contreras Torres's film, *Chilam Balam* will use the archaeological emphasis to create a link with Mayan spirituality, which it posits as further proof of the evolved and ancient nature of Indigenous culture.

Whereas both films discussed in this chapter call attention to pre-Columbian spiritual practices, in *Zítari* they are rendered as entirely unproblematic, while *Chilam Balam* suggests that they are an aspect of Indigeneity that must be overcome for the foundation of the Mexican nation to occur. The most obvious way in which *Chilam Balam* suggests this is through the depiction of human sacrifice as a cause of suffering for the film's protagonists, and the dramatization of that anguish on more than one occasion. The second sacrifice scene, which takes place after Naya's tribe discovers that she has survived the cenote offering, is perhaps the more dramatic of the two. As she is tied to two posts, close-up shots that display her suffering and physical struggle align the spectator with her will and not the native cosmovision according to which she must die. On this occasion, the Spanish soldiers arrive just before she is supposed to be killed.[66] The film clearly casts the interruption of Naya's human sacrifice in a positive light when, as the Spanish soldiers approach the Mayans, triumphant nondiegetic music plays, establishing them as heroic figures for their intervention. In particular, the low-angle shot of Francisco de Montejo as he arrives to cut Naya free and the dramatic opening of his helmet to the sound of culminating music establish him as her hero and prefigure their romantic union. Here the diegetic dynamic of "white men . . . saving brown women from brown men,"[67] codified in cinema as

---

66. Following Linda Williams's analysis of events that take place "just in the nick of time," the saving of Naya in this way contributes to the film's alignment with the melodramatic mode. See Williams, *Playing the Race Card*, 31–35.

67. Gayatri Chakravorty Spivak, "Can the Subaltern Speak?" in *Marxism and the Interpretation of Culture*, ed. Cary Nelson and Lawrence Grossberg (Urbana: University of Illinois Press, 1988), 271–314.

"the rape and rescue trope,"[68] suggests the superiority of the colonizers and justifies their dominance, as well as that of their faith system.

Chilam Balam further detracts from Mesoamerican religion by contrasting the practice of human offerings with the concept of sacrifice in Catholicism. As Naya interacts with the Spaniards, both Francisco and a friar take turns catechizing her. In one of these interactions, the friar juxtaposes both faith systems, arguing that the presence of sacrifice in the Catholic faith is preferable to the native understanding of the concept when he says to her, "Tus dioses han sido imaginados crueles y temibles. No hay más que un sólo Dios, Naya. Es todo amor y lejos de exigir sacrificios, él sacrificó su vida por amor . . ." (Your gods have been imagined as cruel and fearsome. There is only one God, Naya. He is all love and far from demanding sacrifices, he sacrificed his life for love . . .). By associating native sacrifices with deities who are frightening and upholding Christian sacrifice as an example of love, the priest and the film suggest that Christianity is preferable to the Indigenous belief system. Furthermore, the narrative structure of the film, which requires the defeat of the Mayan religion for the protagonist to live and for the film's central couple to unite romantically, works to align the spectator with the priest and conquistador's religious stance, and not with the Mayan cosmovision that precludes the happy resolution of the melodramatic conflict.

Despite the film's condemnation of human sacrifice via melodramatic staging, in many ways *Chilam Balam* also uses the portrayal of the Mayan belief system as a way to demonstrate the value and complexity of the pre-Columbian people and, by extension, their worthiness as a component of Mexican mestizaje. For instance, the film's opening voice-over commentary establishes that the film's action takes place at a time when the Maya no longer possessed their previous "splendor and power"; however, it suggests that the surviving "rites and customs" were what remained of their earlier greatness.[69] As we shall see, this linking of native religious practices with cultural complexity and sophistication will be borne out visually throughout the film. Furthermore, while the voice-over does suggest that the practice of offering human sacrifices was

---

68. Ella Shohat and Robert Stam, *Unthinking Eurocentrism: Multiculturalism and the Media* (New York: Routledge, 1994), 156.

69. ". . . Los habitantes de Chichén Itzá . . . sólo conservaban de sus antepasados las costumbres y los ritos" (The inhabitants of Chichén Itzá . . . conserve only their ancestors' customs and rites).

primitive, it also presents the tradition in an apologetic light by pointing out that Mesoamericans shared the practice with other ancient peoples.[70] In this way, while *Chilam Balam* suggests that pre-Columbian human sacrifice was misguided, it avoids a blanket condemnation through pagan equivalency and also points to pre-conquest Mayan religiosity as having cultural value.

Even as *Chilam Balam* suggests that Mayan spiritual beliefs have no place in the future Mexican nation that will descend from the conquistador (Francisco de Montejo) and the Indigenous woman (Naya), overall, the film paints a nuanced picture of the Mesoamerican ceremonies that suggests the value of Indigenous beliefs as cultural points of reference. For example, the mise-en-scène of the scene that depicts the coming-of-age ritual for young men and women presents the ceremony, and by extension the pre-Columbian people, as civilized. As the scene begins, two single-file lines of men and women descend the steps of a pre-Columbian structure with solemnity. When they have reached their final places, the four priests officiating the ceremony stand stoically, and the head priest speaks to them with gravitas. As opposed to transmitting the various parts of the rite as arbitrary actions with no clear significance,[71] the head priest specifies for the participants and the spectator what different actions mean within the ritual: "Agua sagrada para que estén purificados . . . humo para que tengan espírtu de hombres. Flores para que tengan espiritu de mujer" (Sacred water so that you may be purified . . . smoke so you will have the spirit of men. Flowers so you may have the spirit of women). By displaying this native ritual as having a system of signification and providing access to that system, *Chilam Balam* uses the ritual to afford the natives cultural complexity. Overall, the scene depicts the natives' spiritual practice as orderly and meaningful.

Furthermore, the system of signification provided closely matches those with which the Mexican spectator would be familiar. The coming-of-age ritual divides its participants based on essentialized gender identities and initiates each group into separate roles as adults. Moreover, the

---

70. "Su limpio cielo azul inspiró el color sagrado de los sacrificios en que, como en todas las civilizaciones primitivas, ofrendaban a la divinidad sus propias vidas . . ." (Their clear blue sky inspired the sacred color of the sacrifices in which, as in all primitive civilizations, they offered up to divinity their own lives . . .)

71. As Bill Nichols notes, in cinema "The Other [. . .] rarely functions as a participant in and creator of a system of meanings . . ." See *Representing Reality: Issues and Concepts in Documentary* (Bloomington: Indiana University Press, 1991), 205.

ritual itself is reminiscent of the Catholic sacrament of confirmation in which young people take on an adult identity in the church, and many of the details used in the diegetically Mayan ceremony have parallels in the Catholic sensorium. These include the way in which the native priest sprinkles water on the participants and the use of smoke (recalling the use of holy water and incense). Similarly, early in the film, Naya experiences the mezmeck ceremony as a baby, during which she receives various gifts from different priests. The purpose and symbolism of each gift is explained, again supporting the portrayal of the Mayan belief system as complex and allowing for a parallel with another Catholic practice, baptism. By presenting native rituals as having a hermeneutic legitimacy that is different from, but not alien to, the religious and gendered cultural references of the Mexican spectator, the film presents the native rituals as an intricate, organized, and solemn form of cultural expression, and its participants as distanced but elevated spiritual subjects.

In addition to the film's presentation of Mayan ceremonies, narrative aspects of the film also support its portrayal of Mayan religious beliefs as holding value. The clearest way in which *Chilam Balam* does this is by showing that the title character's prophesy,[72] which is repeated multiple times throughout the film, actually turns out to be true. Furthermore, the majority of the narrative is a visualization of how the prophecy is fulfilled, particularly through the final battle scene and through Naya's marriage. Thus, although the film suggests the superiority of Catholicism and the misguided nature of human sacrifice, by showing that the Mayan cosmovision affords Chilam Balam accurate ways of knowing, the film ascribes to it a notable degree of cultural validity. In this way, like *Zítari*, *Chilam Balam* legitimizes diegetic Indigenous beliefs as a part of its approach to dignifying temporally remote Indians as eminent Mexican ancestors.

The film further ennobles the Mesoamerican characters by emphasizing their strong sense of ethics and honor. For instance, after Naya and

---

72. "He visto en las estrellas que vendrán hombres blancos y barbados por el mar de oriente, y su sangre se mezclará con la nuestra, primero en el suelo por el odio, y luego en los cuerpos por el amor. Y nacerá otro pueblo que ni será el de ellos, ni será el de nosotros, y traerán un madero cruzado con otro, de gran virtud contra los demonios que arrojará de los templos a nuestros dioses." (I have seen in the stars that white bearded men will come through the Eastern sea, and their blood will mix with ours, first in the ground because of hatred, and later in the flesh because of love. And another people will be born that will not be theirs nor ours. And they will bring a wooden beam crossed with another, of great strength against demons, and which will force our gods from the temples).

Figure 1.3. Naya is initiated into the Mayan belief system as a baby in *Chilam Balam* (1957). Filmoteca UNAM Collection. All rights reserved.

Figure 1.4. Chilam Balam blesses Mayan youth with holy water during the coming-of-age ritual in *Chilam Balam* (1957). Filmoteca UNAM Collection. All rights reserved.

Chilam Balam have been discovered by the head priest of their tribe, Naya complains to her father about the fate they will face when they return to Chichén Itzá. Chilam Balam's response conveys that he is a man of principle with a strong ethical code according to which he is willing to accept "la muerte sí, pero no la deshonra, ni la entrega, ni la traición" (death, yes, but neither dishonor, surrender, nor treason). Although ultimately the film presents Chilam Balam as fighting on the wrong side (against Catholicism and the men who bring it), he dies fighting the Spanish soldiers despite having been offered the opportunity to live in exchange for accepting surrender. In this way, his honorable death (complete with dramatic nondiegetic music and the use of his last breaths to repeat his prophesy) cements his status as a tragic and noble savage. In displaying Chilam Balam's uncompromising commitment to his people and beliefs, for which he is willing to pay the ultimate price, the film presents the film's title character as a valiant pre-Columbian Indian who, although incompatible with the Mexican nation's future, was an indisputably honorable figure.

Like *Zítari*, *Chilam Balam* endeavors, through stylistic devices, to confer dignity and gravitas to its temporally removed Mesoamericans to create an idealized representation. In this case, however, the result is a markedly campy aesthetic. First, the Spanish the Mayans speak is characterized by a contrived syntax and lexicon that aspire to be poetic. For example, after the death of Chilam Balam's wife and his period of mourning, Ah K'in Chel tells the prophet, "Es hora ya de que apartes las sombras que nublan tu corazón" (It is time for you to push aside the shadows that cloud your heart). This kind of dialogue (like the emotional hyperbole, "vosotros" form, and religious references in *Zítari*'s dialogue) is meant to signal the temporal distance between the spectator and the pre-Columbian Mayans through speech, as well as to attribute to them a stoic quality. Instead, the aural dimension of the film's indigenista aesthetic comes across as a sometimes comedic, strained aural affectation. Furthermore, the costumes of the Mayan characters are overstated, especially those of important Indigenous men such as Ah K'in Chel and Chilam Balam, who are rarely without a cape, and whose headdresses are at times very elaborate and tall to the point of visibly inhibiting the actors' movements and occupying large portions of the frame.[73] In addition, their speech and movements are slow and measured; their facial expressions are stoic,

---

73. See García Riera, *Historia documental del cine*, vol. 8: 124.

Idealized Pre-Columbian Womanhood

and they do not show emotion, even in distressing situations. Through language, costuming, and acting style, *Chilam Balam*, like *Zítari*, attempts to portray pre-Columbian natives as stately and noble ancient peoples.

Within the film's aspiration to represent elevated pre-Columbian Indigeneity, Naya emerges as the idealized Indigenous woman who is fit to form the nation's foundational couple with the Spanish conquistador Francisco de Montejo. Naya functions as a highly sanitized equivalent to Malinche in many ways. The most obvious manner in which the film suggests that she is fit to form the new nation is through her disposition to receive Christianity. Before the arrival of the Spanish, Naya did not accept her destiny according to her people's beliefs, which was to be sacrificed to appease Mayan deities. While never betraying her people during the conflict with the Spanish (which is the primary indictment contributing to the historical Malinche's ambiguous status in the national consciousness), after the Mayans are defeated, she embraces both Francisco and Catholicism. The film clearly suggests that Catholicism is a precondition for the foundation of the nation both through Chilam Balam's prophesy, which links the emergence of a new people to the defeat of Mayan gods,[74] as well as through visual devices. During the film's final shot, a portion of the prophesy is repeated through voice-over narration while triumphant nondiegetic music plays: "¡Y de la sangre de esas dos razas, nació una nueva, joven y vigorosa!" (And from the blood of those two races was born a new, young, and vigorous one!). As this commentary sounds, Naya and Francisco appear in the center of the frame, holding hands and standing in front of a small crucifix. The film's concluding image is that of their clasped hands with a crucifix between them. In this clear allegory of the foundation of the Mexican nation, Naya now represents the part of pre-Columbian Mexico that has been sanitized through Christianity in order to participate in mestizaje. In this way, the film elevates her to legendary status as the deserving Indigenous woman in the nation's foundational couple.

Furthermore, the fact that throughout the film Naya occupies a central position in the melodrama affords her an epic aura that supports her importance in the film's symbolic founding of the Mexican nation.

---

74. ". . . y traerán un madero cruzado con otro, de gran virtud contra los demonios que arrojará de los templos a nuestros dioses." (. . . and they will bring a wooden beam crossed with another, of great strength against demons, and which will force our gods from the temples).

Chilam Balam privileges Naya in melodramatic terms in the following ways. Initially, her inner conflict about her fate as a human sacrifice is the central source of tension in the film. *Chilam Balam* clearly seeks to create the spectator's investment in Naya by dramatizing her anguish during both of the attempts to sacrifice her. Later, the arrival of the Spanish creates additional tension that impacts Naya directly. For example, she is sexually assaulted by Spanish men on two separate occasions, underscoring her position as victim. In more general terms, the entire conflict between the Mayans and the Spanish creates a narrative structure in which Naya's fate hangs in the balance because her future depends on the outcome of the encounter. The diametrically opposed results that the conflict could have for Naya, certain death at the hands of the Mayans or loving unification with Francisco, are the central source of the film's suspense.

Chilam Balam dramatizes Naya's conflicted state, as she is pushed to choose between Catholicism and Mayan beliefs as well as between Francisco and her father, who metonymically represent their opposing worldviews. After confessing tearfully to her father that now her "corazón es del hombre blanco" (heart belongs to the White man), the film's editing and mise-en-scène emphasize her inner strife on a visual level. An extreme long shot of Naya in between a large crucifix in the foreground and the Mayan temple in the background shows that she is literally and metaphorically in between the two faith systems and the men who personify them in her life. By illustrating Naya's inner struggle in visual terms and displaying the distress it causes her, the film reinforces the white-as-indigenous Naya as the innocent primary point of identification in the fraught encounter between two peoples. In positioning her as the central site of its melodramatic intensity, *Chilam Balam* suggests that Naya is deserving of the celebratory outcome in which she emerges as the mother of Mexico.

The film further produces Naya as the idealized pre-Columbian woman fit for Mexican mestizaje by marking her as the most desirable woman in the diegesis through the repeated advances on behalf of multiple Indigenous and Spanish men. Initially, one of Naya's fellow tribesmen, Bakal, asks to marry her and eventually attempts to have intercourse with her by force. Later, a native man from the coast, A'Kan, also courts her. When the Spaniards arrive, two different Spanish soldiers attempt to rape her, but they are killed by her former suitor's bow and arrow. Finally, Naya is desired by the virtuous Spanish soldier, who courts and finally marries her. By presenting Naya as the most sexually and romantically coveted woman, *Chilam Balam* further underscores her exceptionality and value.

Disavowing indexicality, *Chilam Balam* visualizes Naya's desirability through the colonially inflected device of whiteness-as-indigeneity and the deliberate display of the white-as-indigenous body. Naya's on-screen presence projects White Mexican womanhood in the context of the local racial formation through her tall, slender body; light skin color; large eyes; graceful movements; high-pitched voice; and delicate, timid tone as she articulates Spanish. Like *Zítari*, *Chilam Balam* layers Indigeneity onto the White body through costume. Furthermore, the film's costuming, mise-en-scène, and camera language call attention to her white-as-indigenous body as a source of pleasure. The close-up is used frequently to capture Naya's face, which supports her melodramatic centrality and presents her as physically appealing. Additionally, during the second sacrifice scene when she is saved by the Spanish, Naya wears a costume that is both short and low-cut, exhibiting large portions of her bare skin and therefore helping to produce her to-be-looked-at-ness.[75] Though Naya's whiteness-as-indigeneity is an indexically illogical choice for representing pre-Columbian womanhood, through the colonization of subjectivity and desire, we can understand how in the Mexican context Naya's Whiteness is a colonially inflected, raced semiotic device to signal her central narrative role and the desirability that the film attributes to her. Therefore, paradoxically, *Chilam Balam* instrumentalizes the White Mexican female body to underscore Naya's eminence as the worthy Indigenous progenitor of the Mexican nation.

Conclusion

Separated by more than two decades, both *Zítari* and *Chilam Balam* draw on similar strategies for dignifying temporally remote Mesoamericans as valuable contributors to Mexican mestizaje. These strategies bear resemblances to the work of cultural figures from the late eighteenth and early nineteenth centuries who sought to rehabilitate Indigeneity in the local cultural imagination through a reconsideration of paganism. The films' approaches to Indigeneity also echo mid-nineteenth-century history paintings that attempted to dignify the pre-Columbian world through

---

75. Laura Mulvey, "Visual Pleasure and Narrative Cinema," in *Literary Theory. An Anthology*, ed. Julie Rivkin and Michael Ryan (New York: Blackwell, 1998), 585–96.

classical aestheticization. In both films, pre-Hispanic monuments as well as spiritual beliefs and practices function as evidence of Indigenous people's cultural achievement, complexity, and value. These qualities are externalized aesthetically through elevated verbal registers, stoic acting styles, diegetically Indigenous regalia, and whiteness-as-indigeneity. In these stately visions of remote pre-Columbians, the tying of melodramatic intensity to white-as-indigenous bodies underscores their epic quality as legendary proto-Mexican figures.

Zítari and *Chilam Balam* are particularly telling examples of the ways in which the dynamics of the colonization of desire and subjectivity operate in Mexican cinema because in the diegeses, the women are pre-Columbian Mesoamericans, making the films' disavowal of indexicality especially pronounced in these cases. Zítari and Naya's whiteness-as-indigeneity can be understood as part of a racialized visual logic used in Mexican cinema according to which Whiteness underscores centrality in melodramatic narrative as well as physical desirability in women. Within the broader discourse of these films, which aims to aggrandize and dignify temporally remote Indigeneity, the women's whiteness-as-indigeneity elevates them as idealized Mesoamericans whose stories are the stuff of an exalted Indigenous-themed Mexican lore.

2

Taming the Tehuana

Throughout the nineteenth and twentieth centuries, the women of the Isthmus of Tehuantepec (Tehuanas) drew attention from both international visitors to the region and domestic cultural figures. Ageeth Sluis has noted that cultural production from both centuries participated in the creation of the "camposcape"—an idealization of the countryside "as a site of national authenticity, origin, and beauty"[1]—in which "the Tehuana emerged as an . . . ambiguous figure who embodied seduction, unbridled female sexuality, independence, beauty, and strength but also represented the soul of southern, *indígena* Mexico."[2] Mexican cinema's Golden Age representation of the Tehuana, therefore, had to contend with a preexisting mythology about the regional type that contained elements that were at odds with the conventions of ideal womanhood in mid-twentieth-century filmic melodrama, including unabashed attitudes toward sexuality and nudity, dominant social and economic positions,[3] and the phenotypical and aural markers of Indigeneity in Mexico.

As Ana M. López reminds us, Mexican cinema produced between the 1930s and 1950s "was family entertainment—by design and by commercial imperatives, broader-based"; this required, among other things, a careful

---

1. Ageeth Sluis, *Deco Body, Deco City: Female Spectacle and Modernity in Mexico City, 1900–1939* (Lincoln: University of Nebraska Press, 2016), 102.

2. Sluis, *Deco Body, Deco City*, 105. See also Joanne Hershfield's concept of the "domestic exotic" in *Imagining La Chica Moderna: Women, Nation, and Visual Culture in Mexico, 1917–1936* (Durham, NC: Duke University Press, 2008), 127–55.

3. Analisa Taylor, "Malinche and Matriarchal Utopia: Gendered Visions of Indigeneity in Mexico," *Signs* 31, no. 3 (2006): 815–19.

management of the representation of sexuality and desire.[4] This chapter explores two melodramatic films with Tehuana protagonists[5] that were created within the commercial and industrial thrust of the Golden Age, *La Zandunga* (dir. Fernando de Fuentes, 1938) and *Tierra de pasiones* (dir. José Benávides Jr., 1943). It illustrates how both Tehuana-themed films temper multiple aspects of this type's earlier representation to generate a nonthreatening cinematic regional type for broad consumption. In this process of refashioning, Mexican Whiteness plays a key role in the creation of a Tehuana that functions as a desirable woman, physically and romantically, and as a compelling melodramatic character in the local context.

Nineteenth- and Early Twentieth-Century Representations of the Tehuana in Mexico

In the nineteenth century, Tehuanas were objects of observation and admiration in widely differing contexts. In travel writing, a foreign fascination with the Tehuana converted her into an embodiment of the rural landscape that she inhabited.[6] French travel accounts from this period, such as those of Mathieu de Fossey and Charles Brasseur (who wrote in the 1830s and 1860s, respectively), depicted Isthmus women as arrogant and portrayed their ornate clothing and practice of nude river bathing in an alluring manner.[7] The liberal Oaxacan intellectual Manuel Martínez Gracida, on the other hand, took a great interest in patrician Tehuanas, who for him were evidence of a local, aristocratic, and, at the same time, autochthonous civilization in the region, which he exalted as an ideal example of local identity and culture.[8]

---

4. Ana M. López, "Tears and Desire: Women and Melodrama in the 'Old' Mexican Cinema," in *Mediating Two Worlds: Cinematic Encounters in the Americas*, ed. John King, Ana M. López, and Manuel Alvarado (London: British Film Institute, 1993), 152–53.

5. *La Zandunga* and *Tierra de pasiones* are ideal for studying the refashioning of the regional type in Mexican cinema because in them, the Tehuana characters are protagonists. For a film with Tehuanas as secondary characters or part of background folklore, see *Tehuantepec* (dir. Miguel Contreras Torres, 1954). For a later Golden Age film that is largely repetitive of *La Zandunga*, see *Zandunga para tres* (dir. Roberto Rodriguez, 1954).

6. Sluis, *Deco Body, Deco City*, 109–10, 133.

7. Deborah Poole, "An Image of 'Our Indian': Type Photographs and Racial Sentiments in Oaxaca, 1920–1940," *Hispanic American Historical Review* 84, no. 1 (2004): 66.

8. Poole, "An Image of 'Our Indian,'" 53.

In the twentieth century, non-Zapotec artists and writers who traveled to Tehuantepec created "enticing myths of the place as a matriarchal utopia" that constructed the Tehuana as a charismatic, self-reliant, and sexually licentious figure.⁹ These myths have endured in the Mexican cultural landscape in part because of the prominence of those who contributed to them, including Cube Bonifant, Miguel Covarrubias, Diego Rivera, Frida Kahlo, Sergei Eisenstein, Tina Modotti, Graciela Iturbide, and Elena Poniatowska.¹⁰ As Analisa Taylor has perceptively observed, the representations that created the myth of Tehuantepec are projections "in which travelers, journalists, artists, and writers have found in the isthmus an ideal location for their own longings for a space outside the confines of patriarchal domination and capitalist alienation."¹¹ Both this mythology and the Tehuana's epidermal schema underwent revision for the type to represent *lo mexicano*¹² in a highly visible way.

According to Deborah Poole, significant changes to how photographers rendered the Tehuana influenced the process through which the regional type became a national symbol.¹³ While the photographic records of North American scientist Frederick Starr from the late nineteenth century represented the people of the Isthmus in order to argue for the existence of observable racial categories among them, his photographs, as well as those of Martínez Gracida before him, did not circulate widely.¹⁴ Instead, it was the development of commercial photography featuring Tehuanas in the early twentieth century that gave the type national visibility.¹⁵ In particular, the work of foreign photographers based in Mexico City, Charles Waite and Hugo Brehme, who, by the early years of the twentieth century, were photographing women in Mexico City dressed in Tehuana clothing, helped to "transform the Tehuana from an ethnologically curious Oaxacan

---

9. Taylor, "Malinche and Matriarchal Utopia," 815–16.
10. Taylor, "Malinche and Matriarchal Utopia," 815–19; Sluis, *Deco Body, Deco City*, 127.
11. Taylor, "Malinche and Matriarchal Utopia," 819.
12. "Part official construct, part popular narrative, lo mexicano emerged in the 1920s as the organizing motif for a society devastated by revolutionary turmoil and in search of a unifying identity." Gilbert M. Joseph, Anne Rubenstein, and Eric Zolov, "Assembling the Fragments: Writing a Cultural History of Mexico Since 1940," in *Fragments of a Golden Age: The Politics of Culture in Mexico Since 1940*, ed. Gilbert M. Joseph, Anne Rubenstein, and Eric Zolov (Durham, NC: Duke University Press, 2001), 7.
13. Poole, "An Image of 'Our Indian,'" 63–64.
14. Poole, "An Image of 'Our Indian,'" 55–63.
15. Poole, "An Image of 'Our Indian,'" 63–64.

type to a symbol of the Mexican woman as both sexual being and bearer of the nation."[16] The Tehuana's new place on the national stage is perhaps most evident in her inclusion as a part of the 1910 centennial celebration, which upheld her as a representative of Mexicanness.[17]

While it is clear that, after the armed phase of the Revolution, the Tehuana crystallized into a national symbol,[18] the diverse approaches to her visualization suggested a latent anxiety about the proper place and function of her Indigeneity. On the one hand, a racially marked Tehuana image was deployed in prestigious visual art forms, notably in the paintings of Diego Rivera and Frida Kahlo, the photography of Tina Modotti, and the "Sandunga" segment of Sergei Eisenstein's now famous film shot in the country beginning in 1930, ¡Qué viva México!. On the other hand, in more quotidian forms of representation, images of performed Indigenous femininity through "deco-bodies" (which Sluis defines as "white, thin and tall"[19]) were more widely disseminated than those of actual Indigenous women living in Mexico City.[20] While the former "presented culture industries with a movable *camposcape* that traveled across imagery yet signified both Mexican authenticity and modernity,"[21] images of Indigenous women in the city "produced anxiety rather than pleasure."[22]

The impulse to Whiten highly visible images of the Tehuana was not limited to the context of Mexico City, but also surfaced in their home state of Oaxaca. The 1932 the festivities commemorating the 400th anniversary of the founding of Oaxaca City included an "Homenaje Racial," in which five delegations, each "supposedly representing a discrete cultural territory within the state, would render homage to the city of Oaxaca."[23] Each group consisted of one main female ambassador and an entourage of other women from her place of provenance; however, the primary ambassadors consistently had much Whiter epidermal schemas than the

---

16. Poole, "An Image of 'Our Indian,'" 64.
17. Poole, "An Image of 'Our Indian,'" 67.
18. Taylor, "Malinche and Matriarchal Utopia," 815; Sluis, *Deco Body, Deco City*, 109–10, 133, and Deborah Poole, "An Image of 'Our Indian.'"
19. Sluis, *Deco Body, Deco City*, 134.
20. Sluis, Deco Body, *Deco City*, 123
21. Sluis, *Deco Body, Deco City*, 123.
22. Sluis, *Deco Body, Deco City*, 118.
23. Poole, "An Image of 'Our Indian,'" 76–77.

rest of their entourage.[24] Strategies for making the Tehuana visible in early twentieth-century Mexico therefore varied with respect to whether or not they displayed bodies that could be read as Indigenous at the level of phenotype in the local context. The desire to Whiten the Tehuana across visual displays and regions speaks to a lingering hesitation about visually privileging the nonWhite female in the postrevolutionary cultural landscape.

Deborah Poole and Ageeth Sluis have accurately suggested that photographs and pageantry displaying White bodies dressed in Tehuana vestments were a visual strategy for conveying both modernity and Mexican authenticity. In line with these observations, here I turn my attention to film and argue that Whitening is one of the several ways in which narrative Golden Age cinema refashions the Tehuana as a type compatible with the dominant values of Mexico's postrevolutionary attempt at cultural hegemony. On the one hand, following the discussion of the colonization of subjectivity and desire in the introduction, White Tehuanas in cinema create a way for diegetically Indigenous female characters to be presented as desirable women and emotional centers of melodrama in the Mexican context. On the other hand, these films simultaneously mitigate multiple other aspects of the Tehuana's representation, including her previously crafted sexuality, nudity, financial independence, and social dominance over males.[25] In this sense, the Golden Age representation of the Tehuana follows a similar pattern to that of Mario Moreno's version of the urban lumpenproletariat male type, "el pelado." Critics and scholars have demonstrated how Moreno's character, Cantinflas, incrementally revised the "pelado," transforming his meaning in the national cultural imaginary from a potential threat and incarnation of supposed Mexican psychological deficiency to being one of the best-loved representatives of Mexican identity at home and abroad.[26] *La Zandunga* and *Tierra de pasiones* similarly refashion the Tehuana, creating a version of

---

24. Poole, "An Image of 'Our Indian,'" 76–77.

25. The "Sandunga" segment of Sergei Eisenstein's *¡Qué viva México!* emphasizes all of these characteristics and also features a Tehuana with epidermal schema that align with the parameters of indigeneity in Mexico.

26. See Samuel Ramos, *El perfil del hombre y la cultura en México* (Madrid: Espasa Calpe, S.A., 1951); Carlos Monsiváis, "Cantinflas: That's the Point!," in *Mexican Postcards*, ed. and trans. John Kraniauskas (New York: Verso, 2000), 88–105; Roger Bartra, *The Cage of Melancholy: Identity and Metamorphosis in the Mexican Character*, trans. Christopher J. Hall (New Brunswick: Rutgers University Press, 1992), 125–29; Jeffrey M. Pilcher, *Cantinflas and the Chaos of Mexican Modernity* (Wilmington, DE: Rowman and Littlefield, 2001).

the regional type that is compatible with patriarchal, racist, and nationalist values, and in so doing, the films illustrate how cinema participated in the extraction and transformation of the regional figure into an uncontroversial national symbol.

La Zandunga (1938)

At a time when the viability of a Mexican film industry was not universally apparent, Fernando de Fuentes's 1936 international box-office hit, *Allá en el Rancho Grande*, had demonstrated that national films could capture the attention of spectators in Mexico and across the Spanish-speaking world by combining elements from the popular genre theater with local folklore.[27] This success was due in no small part to the advent of sound.[28] On the one hand, the technological development laid bare Hollywood's inability to produce appealing sound films in Spanish for the Spanish-speaking market.[29] On the other hand, sound created an opportunity for Latin American film producers to capitalize on the popularity of musicians as a strategy for making successful films.[30] In the wake of *Rancho Grande*, de Fuentes and other filmmakers attempted to repeat its success with similar formulas, creating the *comedia ranchera* genre.[31] Set in Tehuantepec, *La Zandunga* is a regional variation of this genre, containing its requisite combination of melodramatic moments, comic relief, and staged folklore. Emilio García Riera draws a direct comparison between *La Zandunga* and *Allá en el Rancho Grande* by suggesting that both films rely heavily on folklore that is equally "adulterado y maquillado" (adulterated and

---

27. Emilio García Riera, "The Impact of *Rancho Grande*," in *Mexican Cinema*, ed. Paulo Antonio Paranaguá, trans. Ana M. López (London: British Film Institute, 1995), 128–32.
28. Marvin D'Lugo, "Aural Identity, Geneaologies of Sound Technologies, and Hispanic Transnationality on Screen," in *World Cinemas: Transnational Perspectives*, ed. Kathleen Newman and Natasa Durovicova (New York; London: Routledge, 2009), 160–85.
29. García Riera, "Impact of *Rancho Grande*"; D'Lugo, "Aural Identity," 160–85.
30. D'Lugo, "Aural Identity."
31. Eduardo de la Vega Alfaro, "Origins, Development and Crisis of the Sound Cinema (1929–64)," in *Mexican Cinema*, ed. Paulo Antonio Paranaguá, trans. Ana M. López (London: British Film Institute, 1995), 83.

made-up).[32] Despite infusing the *comedia ranchera* formula with regional flair and the repatriated star power of Lupe Vélez, who was working in Hollywood at that time, *La Zandunga* underperformed commercially.[33]

La Zandunga takes place in the town of San Lorenzo on the Isthmus of Tehuantepec and tells the story of a young Tehuana, Lupe (played by Lupe Vélez), who is in love with a sailor from Veracruz, Juancho (played by Arturo de Córdova). Within the film, local custom dictates that Tehuanas are not to be courted by nonlocal men, which threatens Lupe and Juancho's union. The primary person enforcing this custom is Ramón (played by Rafael Falcón) a Tehuano who is also in love with Lupe. When Juancho leaves the Isthmus to make money so that he can marry Lupe, Ramón courts her. After not hearing from Juancho for several months and fearing that she has been abandoned, Lupe succumbs to the pressure from nearly everyone in her town and agrees to marry Ramón. Juancho finally returns "in the nick of time"[34] during another couple's wedding festivities. Although Lupe tearfully says she will remain with Ramón, he recognizes that she truly loves Juancho and releases her from their engagement so that she and Juancho can be happy together.

La Zandunga clearly participates in the visualization of what Sluis has termed the "camposcape" by depicting the Isthmus town of San Lorenzo in romanticized terms "as a site of national authenticity, origin, and beauty"[35] and featuring Tehuana women as personifications of the idealized space. This glorified representation of the domestic as exotic relies on two factors: on the one hand, the fabrication[36] and exhibition of the Isthmus as

---

32. Emilio García Riera, *Historia documental del cine mexicano*, vol. 1, *1929-1937* (Guadalajara: Universidad de Guadalajara, 1993), 301-2.

33. García Riera, "Impact of *Rancho Grande*."

34. Juancho's arrival after Lupe has become engaged to another man, but before she has gone through with the marriage, is an example of the melodramatic convention identified by Linda Williams in which a timely intervention spares the protagonists the sad fate of being "too late." See Linda Williams, *Playing the Race Card: Melodramas of Black and White from Uncle Tom to O. J. Simpson* (Princeton: Princeton University Press, 2001), 31-35. See also Jesús Martín-Barbero, *Communication, Culture and Hegemony: From the Media to Mediations*, trans. Elizabeth Fox and Robert A. White (London: Sage Publications, 1993), 118.

35. Sluis, *Deco Body, Deco City*, 102.

36. Emilio García Riera criticizes the film's representation of the Isthmus as egregiously inauthentic in *Historia documental del cine*, vol. 1: 301-2.

simultaneously alien and alluring, and on the other, reminders that the space is in fact a part of the Mexican nation.

The film's staging of the Isthmus as exotic "camposcape" occurs through multiple technical devices including mise-en-scène, cinematography, and sound. The narrative pretext for much of this display is wedding ceremonies, which occur twice and are presented as involving various folkloric customs. *La Zandunga*'s opening sequence transmits the community's preparation for a wedding, visualized through shots of white-as-indigenous Tehuana women putting on their traditional headdresses, the decoration of carts and bulls, and the gathering of people in the town square decked out in their finest regional clothing. The first wedding also involves an elaborate procession, captured through a long shot, which allows for the display of the local townspeople's dress. Both weddings in the film provide the opportunity for extended dance scenes whose durations extend far beyond their narrative purpose of establishing the context of the marriage festivities. The length of the dance scenes as well as the multiple camera angles used to capture them amount to the exhibition of the dances as folkloric spectacle.[37] In addition to scenes related to wedding festivities, *La Zandunga* participates in the creation of the "camposcape" through shots of Tehuanas working happily in the fields while regional, angelic-sounding nondiegetic music plays in the background and various shots of Tehuana women carrying wares on their heads. Furthermore, many of the film's scenes are shot outdoors, which contributes to the idealization of the Isthmus through the constant presence of sunshine, lush foliage, and vegetation in the film's mise-en-scène. Through these visual and sonic devices, *La Zandunga* crafts a representation of the Isthmus as a beautiful, alluring, and distinct space, particularly in contrast to the urban contexts in which Golden Age cinema was largely consumed.

While the film presents the Isthmus as exotic and idealized through its display of dress and dance, it also clearly identifies the space as a part of the Mexican nation and as subject to modernizing forces of national integration. The clearest way in which *La Zandunga* establishes the broader

---

37. For the processes through which the dance traditions of Indigenous and rural Mexicans became a feature of postrevolutionary national culture, see Ruth Hellier-Tinoco, *Embodying Mexico: Tourism, Nationalism & Performance* (New York: Oxford University Press, 2011) and Manuel Cuellar, *Choreographing Mexico: Festive Performances and Dancing Histories of a Nation* (Austin: University of Texas Press, 2022).

Figure 2.1. The Tehuana protagonist, Lupe (Lupe Vélez), dances at a local wedding in *La Zandunga* (1938). Screen capture from film.

Mexican context is when an opening expository text identifies that the film takes place "En México . . . en un pueblo del Istmo de Tehuantepec" (In Mexico . . . in a town on the Isthmus of Tehuantepec). Furthermore, the character of the town mayor, Don Catarino, who becomes involved in all of the local people's affairs, represents the town's belonging to national political and governmental structures. His recurring presence throughout the film as well as his legitimate political authority are ways in which *La Zandunga* differs from other Indigenous-themed Golden Age films (such as *María Candelaria* or *Río Escondido*) in which a connection between Indigenous people and national political structures is tenuous or absent. Furthermore, Don Catarino's baton visually represents his political authority, and his insistence that its white, red, and green colors be reconditioned is a detail that hints at both his national subjectivity and the commitment with which he inhabits his role as mayor. In this way, even though *La Zandunga* presents San Lorenzo as an exotic space, the film also clearly emphasizes that the area where the story unfolds is part of the Mexican national reality.

The fact that the Isthmus town, San Lorenzo, belongs to a broader national space becomes a source of tension in the film when Ramón and other local men want to impose endogamy. Specifically, the Tehuanos try to bar Lupe from marrying her boyfriend from Veracruz, Juancho, and plan to physically assault the fiancé of her friend Marilú because he is from a neighboring town. Though the Tehuanos from San Lorenzo desist from attacking Marilú's fiancé, they resolve to break with the local custom of decorating the groom's house before Marilú's wedding as a way of protesting the groom's outsider origins. As a representative of the national, Don Catarino convinces the men to accept greater integration by accepting Marilú's fiancé and keeping their custom of decorating the groom's home. In this way, the nationalizing forces of modernity that Don Catarino personifies are the means through which local tradition is preserved and evolves. Furthermore, Don Catarino's authority creates a space for Lupe to choose between her two suitors, the local Ramón, and Juancho from Veracruz, without the pressure of compulsory adherence to the town's endogamous custom. By making possible the "mixed" union between Lupe and Juancho, Don Catarino is a force of national integration and helps to push the town beyond a purely localist perspective and practice. In this way, while the film exhibits the Isthmus of Tehuantepec as "camposcape," it also suggests that even the nation's exotic and traditional spaces must evolve in the context of a twentieth-century national modernity.

La Zandunga's "camposcape" visualizes the Tehuana through whiteness-as-indigeneity, particularly through the on-screen presence of the film's protagonist, Lupe, played by Lupe Vélez. To unpack the layers of meaning at work in Vélez's interpretation of this role, one must consider the nature of her star persona in Mexico. Working in Hollywood starting in the late 1920s, Lupe Vélez was sometimes treated as a problematic incarnation of Mexican womanhood by the Mexican press in relation to traditional norms regarding class, gender, and the appropriate performance of Mexican identity.[38] Her behavior was perceived as being characteristic of the lower class, vulgar, and indicating a lack of culture. This characterization was even more prominent when compared to Dolores del Río, a contemporary Mexican actress also working in Hollywood whose star text associated her with aristocracy, refinement, and morality.[39] Furthermore, the Mexican press accused Lupe Vélez of being unfavorably Americanized, and therefore unpatriotic, which Rosa Linda Fregoso has perceptively understood as an indication of elite "anxieties about the solidity and sta-

---

38. Rosa Linda Fregoso, *MeXicana Encounters: The Making of Social Identities on the Borderlands* (Berkeley: University of California Press, 2003), 112–18.

39. Fregoso, *MeXicana Encounters*, 112.

bility of Mexican national identity during the 1930s."[40] Finally, Lupe Vélez challenged traditional gender norms for women in Mexico, embracing independence and sexual freedom, due to which she was cast as a negative influence on Mexican women.[41]

Although Lupe Vélez was criticized on many fronts, she still possessed an important form of capital that allowed her to work both in Hollywood and Mexico and be considered a beauty icon in her home country. Vélez has a physical appearance that was coded as White in Mexico (*blancura*), even if she did not originally possess some of the aspects of a White socioeconomic identity in Mexico (*blanquitud*), such as affluence and an aristocratic pedigree, as was the case with Dolores del Río.[42] In addition to her physical *blancura*, Vélez's successful film career in Hollywood did imbue her with another form of *blanquitud*—the type that Bolivar Echeverría understands as the success and wealth derived from participation in capitalist production wedded to modern technology.[43]

The following advertisement, which appeared in the newspaper *El Universal Ilustrado* on June 13, 1929, illustrates the centrality of Vélez's White identity (*blancura*) and her connection to the motion picture industry (*blanquitud*) for the purpose of selling a beauty cream in Mexico (see figure 2.2). The text of the advertisement makes clear that Vélez is a model of beauty because of her skin color. It also casts Lupe's endorsement of the product within a national framework by mentioning that the cream protects her complexion in the different environments within the Mexican republic,[44] keeping it "deliciosamente blanco, fresco y juvenil" (deliciously white, fresh, and youthful). Furthermore, the fact that here Vélez appears "wearing nothing but a Spanish shawl"[45] hints that her Mexican Whiteness may be linked to Spanish origins, or at the very least, that it allows her to carry off a Spanish look. By emphasizing that Vélez possesses

---

40. Fregoso, *MeXicana Encounters*, 112.

41. Fregoso, *MeXicana Encounters*, 113–15.

42. Joanne Hershfield, *The Invention of Dolores del Río* (Minneapolis: University of Minnesota Press, 2000), 1–16.

43. Bolívar Echeverría, *Modernidad y blanquitud* (Mexico City: Ediciones Era, 2019), 59–62.

44. Hershfield, *Imagining la Chica Moderna*, 150–52.

45. Hershfield, *Imagining la Chica Moderna*, 150.

Figure 2.2. Lupe Vélez's image as a White Mexican star is used to advertise Hinds beauty cream in *Cinelandia*, February 1931, 52.

light skin—"a mark of feminine beauty in Mexico"[46]—in a manner that also inscribes her as a Mexican national subject with potential ties to Spanishness, the advertisement reveals that although in the United States Vélez was constructed as an ethnic Other against the US WASP notion of Whiteness,[47] in her home country she was able to participate in White Mexican womanhood and to profit from its privileges.

The fact that Velez's Whiteness (*blancura*) is a component of her attractiveness and stardom would seemingly conflict with the parameters of the role she plays in *La Zandunga*, in which the actress is meant to incarnate an exotic, southern, and Indigenous Mexican woman. Instead, Lupe's whiteness-as-indigeneity functions as a hegemonic maneuver meant to impel Mexican spectators toward the admiration and emotional connection to a regional type, therefore working to nationalize the Tehuana. *La Zandunga* produces the protagonist's whiteness-as-indigeneity in multiple ways. First, the film invites a conflation between the identity of the star, Lupe Vélez, and that of the Tehuana character in the film through the protagonist's name, Lupe. The significance of Vélez's stardom as a draw for the film is evident because her name features prominently in opening credits, stating the film's title as a vehicle for the star, "Lupe Vélez en *La Zandunga*" (Lupe Vélez in *La Zandunga*).

Lupe's embodied on-screen presence closely follows classic studio cinema's visual parameters for leading female characters. Lupe appears in the form of a tall, slender body with light skin; large eyes; full, made-up lashes; visible eyeshadow; thin, manicured eyebrows; and lipstick. The character's Indigeneity is layered on through folkloric costume, hairstyles, and a peppering of Spanish anachronisms in her speech.[48] Following the dynamics of the colonization of desire and subjectivity present in the Mexican audiovisual landscape as outlined in the introduction, I argue that in *La Zandunga*, Lupe is presented through whiteness-as-indigeneity because she functions as both an object of desire and a source of identification for the spectator throughout the melodrama.

---

46. Hershfield, *Imagining la Chica Moderna*, 152.

47. Ana M. López, "Are All the Latins from Manhattan?: Hollywood, Ethnography and Cultural Colonialism," in *Mediating Two Worlds: Cinematic Encounters in the Americas*, ed. John King, Ana M. López, and Manuel Alvarado (London: British Film Institute, 1993), 72–73.

48. For a parallel dynamic in *María Candelaria*, see Dolores Tierney, *Emilio Fernández: Pictures in the Margins* (Manchester: Manchester University Press, 2012), 80–95.

The film clearly presents Lupe as a physically and romantically desirable character. This is evident when three different men, Juancho, Ramón, and Don Atanasio, actively pursue her, and the tensions that result from this love quadrangle are the forces that move the plot forward. The film produces her desirability in visual terms, exalting her white-as-indigenous face and body through close-ups and medium close-ups. On multiple occasions, the film also produces her to-be-looked-at-ness[49] through three-point lighting and the use of the soft-focus lens, which at key moments make her entire head appear to radiate light. In this sense, *La Zandunga* deploys the conventions through which, according to Richard Dyer, cinema has visually idealized White female beauty. As he explains, throughout the history of film, "[i]dealised white women are bathed and permeated by light. It streams through them and falls on them from above. In short, they glow . . . The light within or from above appears to suffuse the body."[50] Lupe's Whiteness as glorified by studio-era lighting conventions is a manifestation of raced beauty standards for women in commercial Mexican cinema. Furthermore, her Whiteness functions as the key factor through which *La Zandunga* manifests the Tehuana not only as a beautiful ornament (the way in which Indigenous Tehuanas from the Isthmus had been photographed in Mexico since the nineteenth century[51]) but also as a worthy object of aesthetic and romantic desire for a broad Mexican audience.

In addition to functioning as the object of desire within the film, the white-as-indigenous Lupe is also the emotional center of the melodrama. Even though *La Zandunga* is largely a comedy, creating space for Vélez to tell jokes and carry out pranks in a manner that is consistent with her other comedic roles, it contains several melodramatic elements that relate to Lupe's character directly. While Lupe is presented as mischievous and feisty, she also embodies the good female protagonist who is a victim of unjust circumstances—a convention of the melodramatic mode.[52] The film portrays Lupe's goodness through her filial piety, almost marrying a man

---

49. Laura Mulvey, "Visual Pleasure and Narrative Cinema," in *Literary Theory: An Anthology*, ed. Julie Rivkin and Michael Ryan (New York: Blackwell, 1998), 585–96.
50. Dyer, "The Light of the World," in *White* (London; New York: Routledge, 1997), 122.
51. Hershfield, *Imagining la Chica Moderna*, 137–44.
52. Martín-Barbero, *Communication, Culture and Hegemony*, 117.

whom she does not love (Ramón) to please her father. The film further characterizes Lupe as a victim through a side plot involving an older man to whom her father is indebted, Don Atanasio. He demands that Lupe's father repay his debt immediately, requiring either Lupe's hand in marriage or their banana grove if he cannot pay. Furthermore, the film conveys that Lupe suffers intensely because of the absence of the man she truly loves, Juancho, and the conflict between what her fellow townspeople pressure her to do (marry Ramón) and her true wishes. In fact, when this conflict reaches its climax during the film's final scene, Don Catarino (the voice of authority and reason within the film) sums up the circumstances that make Lupe a melodramatic heroine: "¿Qué no ven que lo que van a hacer es sacrificar a una muchacha buena no más por sus habladas? (Don't you see that just because of your boasting, you are going to sacrifice a good woman?) Therefore, although *La Zandunga* is a comedy, its characterization of Lupe obeys melodramatic conventions by portraying her as a virtuous young woman whose suffering is central to the film.

In concert with its melodramatic narrative architecture, the film's technical devices underscore Lupe's sadness and suffering throughout the film, clearly fashioning her as the character with whom the spectator is meant to identify. While cinematography is essential to this process (see figure 2.3), *La Zandunga* most closely adheres to the melodramatic

Figure 2.3. Close-up of the teary-eyed Tehuana protagonist, Lupe (Lupe Vélez), in *La Zandunga* (1938). Screen capture from film.

tradition in a scene in which Lupe, alone in her bedroom, proclaims her suffering and longing in song form. The song's lyrics draw attention to the protagonist's sorrow with lines such as "Mírame que triste estoy / Se me fue el hombre que quiero / Y me muero por su amor . . . / Solo tengo tristeza y dolor . . ." (Look at how sad I am / The man I love has left me / And I am dying for his love . . . / I only have sadness and pain . . .). The film promotes pathos during Lupe's song both through the slow and sad melody of the music and through the constant use of the close-up throughout the performance, which magnifies her sorrowful facial expressions. Through these techniques, *La Zandunga* reproduces the hallmarks of melodrama that work to tie the spectator to the emotional distress of the female protagonist.

Because of the dynamics of the colonization of subjectivity outlined in the introduction, Lupe's whiteness-as-indigeneity is crucial to the operation of pathos in *La Zandunga*'s melodramatic apparatus. The film's attempt to generate an emotional bond with the white-as-Indigenous Tehuana in the person of Lupe Vélez is a factor that operates toward the nationalization of a regional type. The deployment of whiteness-as-indigeneity foregrounds the physical capital of the White Mexican female body (which, as the advertisement above suggests, was considered beautiful according to hegemonic, racialized standards in Mexico) to solicit the approval and compassion of Mexican spectators for a person who belongs to a regionally specific and racially marked type. In other words, *La Zandunga* mobilizes the privilege of White womanhood within the local Mexican racial formation as a basis for establishing an emotional connection between a diverse range of spectators and a particular regional Other, the Tehuana.

La Zandunga's Whitening of the Tehuana, which allows her to function as an object of desire and compassion, is just one of the ways the film modifies the regional type to refashion her for broad consumption within a commercial Mexican film industry. The film also mitigates other aspects of the preexisting mythology about the Tehuana that had associated the type with a dominant role in her local community, frequent sexual activity, a casual attitude toward nudity, distance from bourgeois life, and participation in commerce.[53] Notably, some of the film's "solutions" for toning down the Tehuana also interface with Lupe Vélez's star text by creating opportunities for the display of her capacity for screwball comedy[54] and

---

53. Sluis, *Deco Body, Deco City*, 101–35.
54. According to Rosa Linda Fregoso, Lupe Vélez "was one of the most accomplished and popular screwball comedians of the time." In *MeXicana Encounters*, 116.

by tempering the star's own controversial reputation for independence and sexual freedom.

One of the notable ways in which *La Zandunga* tempers the Tehuana is by recasting her reputation for having a dominant position in her community[55] as mischief, impudence, and irreverence for authority through Lupe's behavior. Through her actions, Lupe is not able to hold power or agency in her life; instead, she pokes fun at the men who do. For example, when Don Atanasio (the unappealing older suitor) insists on seeing Lupe so he can convince her to marry him, she tricks him into thinking that he is unwell so that she can slip away. Furthermore, Lupe displays humorous irreverence toward male authority when she greets the town mayor by tapping him on his round belly with exaggerated familiarity, thus mocking his constant performance of political decorum and gravitas. By ridiculing male power and privilege with spunk, Lupe stands out from her dramatic counterparts in other Indigenous-themed films from the period (such as those by the Fernández-Figueroa team). The compromise that *La Zandunga* strikes in the creation of a melodramatic-yet-still-feisty Indigenous heroine constitutes a vehicle for Lupe Vélez to exercise her comedic prowess in a manner that is consistent with her career trajectory and spirited star personality.

Yet, crucially, Lupe's spirit does not amount to agency in her own life. Even though Lupe stands up to Don Atanasio, her family loses the banana grove anyway, and even though she makes fun of the mayor, he is the only person with the power to stop the Tehuanos from imposing endogamy. Furthermore, it is only through men that Lupe exerts influence or makes decisions. This point is clearest when Juancho does return and she has the opportunity to choose between her two suitors. Lupe's spirited nature recedes entirely as she sadly says she wants to remain with Ramón because of pressure from her father and the town. It is only when Ramón tells her she can choose whom she truly loves that she finally does. By replacing the idea of the Tehuana's social agency with an ultimately ornamental and inconsequential feistiness, *La Zandunga* fashions a version of

---

55. Sergei Eisenstein's "Sandunga" segment in *¡Qué viva México!* (shot in Mexico in 1932) in particular emphasizes a matriarchal social arrangement on the Isthmus. The film highlights female agency by presenting Tehuanas as the money- and decision-makers in their society. As Laura Podalsky has noted, Eisenstein's emphasis on the power of Isthmus women is central to his portrayal of Tehuantepec as the "womb of civilization." See Laura Podalsky, "Patterns of the Primitive: Sergei Eisenstein's ¡Qué Viva México!," in *Mediating Two Worlds: Cinematic Encounters in the Americas*, ed. John King, Ana M. López, and Manuel Alvarado (London: British Film Institute, 1993), 34.

the regional type that is consistent with patriarchal norms according to which men are society's dominant agents.[56] In this way, the film creates a more submissive rendition of the regional type, which through adherence to social gender norms could be more easily appropriated by Mexican society at large.

La Zandunga also curbs other aspects of the Tehuana's characterization in cultural production from the nineteenth and early twentieth centuries,[57] such as her casual attitudes toward nudity and sexuality. The costumes that the actresses playing Tehuanas wear in the film appear to be inspired by Juana Catalina Romero's nineteenth-century version of local dress made according to "Porfirian (and Victorian) fashion sensibilities," which included "European lace, ruffles, petticoats, and velvet."[58] The modest nature of the regional vestments presented in the film contrasts greatly with Claudio Linati's 1830 lithograph of the regional type,[59] *cronista* Cube Bonifant's 1921 description of Tehuanas' "dark skin, fresh and throbbing under clear silks and pale ribbons, showing through their white transparent trajes,"[60] and Sergei Eisenstein's display of a bare-breasted Tehuana lounging outdoors with complete nonchalance in *¡Qué viva México!*. In particular, the scene in which a fully dressed Lupe lounges on a hammock (see figure 2.4) invites comparisons with the one when Concepción in Eisenstein's film similarly rests outside, but nude from the waist up. Most likely, the cinematic depiction of the Tehuana's scanty traditional dress would have been considered scandalous, especially on a White Mexican actress, and almost certainly would have hampered the distribution and exhibition of a commercial film like *La Zandunga*.[61] By opting for a modest version of Tehuana dress, the film tempers the regional type for the broadest possi-

---

56. Such male power over Lupe's life is not the only way in which the film reveals an investment in defining and guarding Mexican manhood. After Ramón accepts Juancho and Lupe's union and calls for everyone to resume the wedding festivities, Juancho asserts in admiration, "Es muy hombre" (He is a real man), thus protecting Ramón from the perception of emasculation for having lost Lupe.

57. Sluis, *Deco Body, Deco City*, 105.

58. Sluis, *Deco Body, Deco City*, 108.

59. Sluis, *Deco Body, Deco City*, 107.

60. Cube Bonifant, "Una pequeña Marquesa de Sade para un Oscar Wilde pequeño," *El Universal Ilustrado*, April 21, 1921, 9; qtd. in and trans. Sluis, *Deco Body, Deco City*, 127.

61. For a parallel taboo surrounding white-as-indigenous nudity, see the analysis of *María Candelaria* in chapter 4.

Figure 2.4. The Tehuana protagonist, Lupe (Lupe Vélez), lounges on a hammock while fully dressed in *La Zandunga*. Photo courtesy of Mil Nubes-Foto (Roberto Fiesco). All rights reserved.

ble commercial consumption, while still referencing some aspects of the previously established iconography used to represent her.

Despite opting for more conservative costuming, the film does reference the Tehuana's supposed nonchalance toward nudity. This may be a result of the fact that the *cronista* Salvador Novo, who defended Mexican nudism,[62] collaborated on the film's script. However, the film carefully crafts its presentation of Tehuana nudity in both technical and narrative terms to mitigate its scandalous potential. *La Zandunga* presents Tehuana nudity when the unmarried women accompany Marilú to the river so that she can bathe in preparation for her wedding. When the medium shot is used on Marilú in this scene, her body appears submerged in the water with her hands and hair covering her breasts, impeding the exposure of

---

62. Sluis, *Deco Body, Deco City*, 129–30.

her body. The tame approach to visualizing her body is also evident in the use of the extreme long shot when Marilú emerges from the river, which renders her naked body visually inaccessible to the spectator. Furthermore, the use of the shot-reverse-shot while the women make flattering observations about Marilú's physique during her bath suggest her exposed nudity during the scene, but do not fully visualize the body that the women are complimenting. Furthermore, when Lupe jokes openly about Marilú's nudity in comments such as "¡El pedacito de dulce que se va a llevar el sinvergüenza de José Antonio! . . . ¡Ahora nos damos cuenta por qué está tan loquito por ti!" (What a treat that rascal José Juan is going to snag. Now we realize why he's so crazy about you!), the film also hints at Lupe's own relaxed attitudes about the subject. In this way, the film references the association between the regional type and nudity that earlier representations of the Tehuana had suggested, but *La Zandunga* tempers its representation by carefully contextualizing it in relation to marriage while also using cinematography, editing, and suggestive dialogue to avoid visually exposing a nude female body.

La Zandunga also revises the Tehuana's class status and socioeconomic agency. While Lupe supposedly undergoes hardship because Don Atanasio strips her family of their banana grove, in visual terms, Lupe appears as a member of the bourgeoisie throughout the film. The colonial-style house in which she and her father live is sturdy and comfortably furnished. Lupe has no shortage of beautiful clothing and always appears on-screen comely coiffed and made-up. Therefore, the film crafts the socioeconomic presentation of her daily reality as one that can be interpreted as visually middle-class.

Furthermore, the Tehuana's mythic commercial prowess and agency in the marketplace[63] are almost entirely absent here, creating the image of a woman who relies on men for long-term economic stability. Sluis has pointed out that "much of the Tehuana's revolutionary or postrevolutionary allure resulted from discourses about her economic power" of which the market was the "cornerstone."[64] However, Lupe is only presented as active in the market when the character is at her lowest: after Juancho has left and her family has lost their primary form of sustenance. In addition, the short scene in which Lupe sells flowers in the market serves more as a

---

63. Taylor, "Malinche and Matriarchal Utopia," 115; Sluis, *Deco Body, Deco City*, 111–12, 134.

64. Sluis, *Deco Body, Deco City*, 111, 134.

pretext for a conversation between Ramón and Lupe than as a display of her commercial activity. Lupe's presence in the marketplace is therefore more associated with powerlessness than with agency, especially because her father implies that, despite her efforts, Lupe is not able to support them.

Instead, the film suggests that Lupe's path to economic stability lies in her future union with Juancho, who leaves the Isthmus for several months precisely to accumulate wealth for the couple to be able to marry. This representation contrasts markedly with the well-known "Sandunga" sequence in Sergei Eisenstein's *¡Qué viva México!*, in which it is the main Tehuana character, Concepción, who acquires the gold necessary for her wedding. *La Zandunga* directly contradicts the mythology of female independence and financial power in Tehuantepec that Eisenstein's film reinforced. Instead, the economic situation of the Isthmus conveyed in de Fuentes' film, and the proposed solution, situate the region within a national framework in asymmetrical and gendered terms. *La Zandunga* presents the Isthmus as a beautiful but underdeveloped corner of the country from which one must migrate (at least temporarily) to achieve economic stability. By transforming the Tehuana into an economically powerless figure, Lupe's dependence mirrors the implied economic dependence of her region, and she becomes an iteration of the regional type who does not pose a threat to male economic dominance.

In sum, *La Zandunga* crafts a cinematic Tehuana who conforms to normative racial, gender, and class attitudes of the day, resulting in a white-as-indigenous protagonist who is ultimately docile, modest, and ostensibly bourgeois. The second filmic rendering of Isthmus women I explore here similarly tempers the regional type for commercial consumption. However, it does so by foregrounding her within a context of tyrannical abuse of power that recalls the historical narrative of the Mexican Revolution.

Tierra de pasiones (1943)

A dramatic poem by Mexican writer Miguel N. Lira is the inspiration for José Benavides's 1943 film, *Tierra de pasiones*.[65] The film transfers the setting from Lira's native Tlaxcala to the fictional town of Tehuanchitán

---

65. Emilio García Riera, *Historia documental del cine mexicano*, vol. 2, *1938–1942* (Guadalajara: Universidad de Guadalajara, 1993), 288.

(supposedly) in Tehuantepec[66] but retains themes that evoke the Mexican Revolution through a story that centers a small-town strongman and those who suffer because of his abuse of power.[67] Like the *comedias rancheras*, Benavides's film bears a resemblance to several Latin American and Spanish films from the 1920s and 1930s whose stories revolve around overthrowing "the traditional right of *pernada* (which gave landowners sexual access to peasant women) with an emphasis on local colour."[68] *Tierra de pasiones*, however, lacks the comic relief and cheerful musical entertainment that counterbalanced the dramatic content in *comedias rancheras*.

In the film, Linda Maldonado (played by Margarita Mora) and Máximo Tépal (played by Jorge Negrete) are two Tehuanos in love who wish to get married. Máximo leaves Tehuanchitán to make money for his future life with Linda. In his absence, Diego Banderas, the recently appointed (not elected) town mayor, concocts a scheme to be the first to have sex with Linda. Banderas arranges for Linda to marry one of his debtors, Salvador Peredo, so that he can sleep with her on the wedding night. When Máximo returns, Banderas and his men unjustly accuse him of attempting to buy land with stolen money, and after a fight with the strongman, Máximo flees to the mountains with a group of men. Banderas succeeds in forcing the marriage between Linda and Salvador; however, Linda thwarts the men's plan when she reveals that she has already had sexual relations with Máximo. Shortly after this revelation, Máximo descends into the town to take Linda away with him to the mountains, and she informs him that she is pregnant. Linda's stay with Máximo is cut short because another woman, Camila, falsely asserts that she is romantically involved with Máximo. Months later when Linda and Maximo's baby boy is born, Diego Banderas prepares his baptism to lure Máximo into returning to the town, resulting in a confrontation between the two, which ends in Máximo's death. Linda predicts that her son will avenge his father's death, which comes true when the film flashes forward to show Máximo Tépal (junior) confronting and finally killing Diego Banderas. In keeping with melodramatic conventions, this defeat comes "too late" for Linda and Máximo (senior) to have a happy life together,

---

66. The town's fictional name appears to combine those of two districts in the state of Oaxaca, Tehuantepec and Juchitán.
67. García Riera, *Historia documental del cine*, vol. 2: 288.
68. García Riera, "The Impact of *Rancho Grande*," 128–30.

but also "in the nick of time," allowing the son to avenge his father's death and reestablish justice.[69]

Tierra de pasiones visualizes the Isthmus of Tehuantepec through strategies similar to those that we find in *La Zandunga*; however, Benávides's film presents these folkloric and paradisiacal elements in a way that highlights the destructive nature of Diego Banderas's tyrannical authority and the virtue of his victims. For instance, the film's initial sequence—a flash-forward to the moment just before Máximo's son avenges his father—features elaborate folkloric dancing to the sound of local music, however, the dancing scene lacks a celebratory tone. Diego Banderas forcefully calls for the dancing to take place when he believes that Maximo's son has rejected the opportunity to avenge his father. Therefore, even if the dancing scenes in both films appear to be similar in visual terms, they produce opposite effects. In *La Zandunga*, the context of the joyful marriage in which local dancing occurs contributes to the film's overall portrayal of the Isthmus as a mostly jubilant haven within Mexico, while the initial dancing scene in *Tierra de pasiones* presents the performance of folklore as an extension of the strongman's unchecked power.

Similarly, the presentation of rural scenery, nudity, and music in *Tierra de pasiones* all highlight regional specificity in a manner that throws into relief the negative effect of repressive and arbitrary rule there. When the film flashes back to Linda and Máximo's youth at the beginning of the film, it characterizes both protagonists in idealized ways through pastoral clichés tied to the region. Máximo is shown walking his herd of goats against a lush backdrop while he sings a marimba-infused ranchera that proclaims his pure love. The bright lighting, medium close-up, and low camera angle used while Máximo belts out the song conveys him as a representative of positive masculine values within the film—a portrayal in line with Jorge Negrete's wholesome and dignified star text.[70] The film cites the familiar association

---

69. Following Franco Moretti, Linda Williams has discussed the salience of lost time in the pathos of melodrama. Furthermore, she suggests that ". . . the spectacular essence of melodrama seems to rest in those moments of temporal prolongation when 'in the nick of time' defies 'too late.'" See Williams, *Playing the Race Card*, 31–35.

70. Sergio de la Mora, *Cinemachismo: Masculinities and Sexuality in Mexican Film* (Austin: University of Texas Press, 2006), 80. On the connection between singing and masculinity in Golden Age Mexican cinema, see Jacqueline Avila, *Cinesonidos: Film Music and National Identity During Mexico's* Epoca de Oro (Oxford: Oxford University Press, 2019), 150–92.

between Tehuanas and nudity by introducing Linda as she is bathing with friends in the river. The initial visualization of the film's virtuous protagonists in what is supposed to be a natural setting in Tehuantepec alongside the aural and visual references to Isthmus culture (the marimba and Linda's nudity) fashion Tehuantepec as a *locus amoenus*. This initial idealization of the film's regional location and its Tehuano protagonists constitutes what Peter Brooks has termed the trope of the "space of innocence": the place where melodrama begins prior to the intrusion of the villain, and where it can end happily if justice is restored.[71] According to Linda Williams, this "space of innocence" is tied to the display of the protagonist's good character because it the place where "virtue can take pleasure in itself."[72] In *Tierra de pasiones*, the regionally specific "space of innocence" is an important way in which the film calls attention to Diego Banderas's intervention and destruction of Tehuanchitán's peaceful atmosphere where, were it not for him, the lovers could have been happy together.

Perhaps the most frequently cited aspect of diegetic isthmus culture that is meant to lend *Tierra de pasiones* regional specificity is the practice of examining the bride on her wedding day and decorating her wedding cart with red flowers if she is a virgin and white ones if she is not. In the film, the local custom also includes hanging up a large clay pot in front of the new couple's home if the bride is a sexual novice and hanging up a broken pot if the bride has had previous sexual experience. Beyond their function as staged folklore, the display and repeated discussion of these supposedly regional customs are central to the film's condemnation of Diego Banderas's attempts to bed Linda through a sham marriage and to publicly shame her. In other words, foregrounding these customs helps to establish Linda's victimhood because the strongman cruelly weaponizes them against her. Thus, instead of showcasing regionally specific content merely for the sake of spectacle, as occurs in *La Zandunga*, *Tierra de pasiones* presents the practices of the Isthmus in a manner that serves the purpose of denouncing injustice—a central characteristic of melodrama[73]—

---

71. Peter Brooks, *The Melodramatic Imagination: Balzac, Henry James, Melodrama, and the Mode of Excess* (New Haven: Yale University Press, 1995), 29.

72. Williams, *Playing the Race Card*, 7, 28.

73. Linda Williams, "'Tales of Sound and Fury . . .' or, The elephant of Melodrama," in *Melodrama Unbound across History, Media, and National Cultures*, ed. Christine Gledhill and Linda Williams (New York: Columbia University Press, 2018), 214. See also Martín-Barbero, *Communication, Culture and Hegemony*, 116.

in a manner that would have had a particularly strong resonance in the postrevolutionary period.

Moreover, the representation of the Tehuana herself in *Tierra de pasiones* is in line with the more general way in which the film features regional characteristics to call attention to the struggle against strongmen's oppression. Specifically, the film repurposes aspects of the Tehuana's famed reputation, such as her independence, social dominance, and overt sexuality, to fashion Linda as a protorevolutionary heroine who challenges caudillismo. By putting some of the Tehuana's characteristics in the service of her protorevolutionary reframing, *Tierra de pasiones* reformulates the regional type in a manner that makes her compatible with broader national narratives and suggests her suitability for appropriation on a national scale. Alongside the positioning of the Tehuana on the right side of injustices that recall those denounced during the Revolution, *Tierra de pasiones* further crafts Linda as a regional type with broad national appeal through her white-as-Indigenous on-screen presentation, which both signals and makes possible her centrality as melodramatic victim and desirable female in the Mexican context. Therefore, the re-presentation of the Tehuana in *Tierra de pasiones* nationalizes a regional figure in narrative terms that are expedient during the postrevolutionary cultural moment and in visual terms that conform to raced requirements of female beauty and protagonism in Mexican cinema.

The presentation of nudity in *Tierra de pasiones* is just as tame as that in *La Zandunga*, with Tehuanas wearing modest versions of regional vestments and a bucolic bathing scene that suggests the nudity of submerged female bodies but avoids their exhibition. However, the film's treatment of Tehuana sexuality departs from conservative norms in cultural representation that associate the virginity of women with their general virtue as characters. In this film, the Tehuana's reputation for unabashed sexuality takes the form of Linda having sexual relations with Máximo before marriage, an action that is treated as taboo in many Golden Age films. Here, however, Linda's sexual activity is linked to her status as heroine in the protorevolutionary narrative because it is through this action that she foils the caudillo's plan to take her virginity against her will. Furthermore, the film itself criticizes the villain's use of sexual conservatism to carry out unjust acts when, as Máximo Tépal arrives in Tehuanchitán to whisk Linda away, he shoots down the broken pot Banderas had strung up over Linda and Salvador's future home to shame Linda for her sexual past. Moreover, the film condones Linda's sexual autonomy on another level: in freely choosing to have sex with Máximo, she conceives the film's hero, who later avenges his father and reestablishes justice by ending the caudillo's rule.[74] *Tierra de pasiones* uses the Tehuana's regional specificity to attribute to Linda a sexual action that would normally be coded as immoral in the time and place when and where the film was made, but that, within the context of the narrative, constitutes a defiance of injustice and leads to the defeat of caudillo rule.

The Tehuana's characteristics of dominance and independence in *Tierra de pasiones* follow a pattern of selection and attenuation. The Tehuana's reputation for financial independence and enterprising market activity is nowhere to be found in the film, as Linda appears to be the daughter of a patrician family and depends entirely on Máximo to make money for the couple to get married. *Tierra de pasiones* does, however, take up the Tehuana's reputation for self-reliance, as Linda refuses to be the victim of Diego Banderas and his crony, Salvador Peredo. When the latter intends to examine Linda on their wedding day, Linda—understanding fully that she has been the object of the men's plot—confronts him defiantly and orders him to notify Banderas of his failure: "Ve a decirle a Diego Banderas que no podrá cobrar" (Go tell Diego Banderas that he won't be collecting). Linda further demonstrates resolve when Banderas attempts to disgrace her by ensuring that her wedding cart is decorated with white flowers—signifying her nonvirginal status—and parading her throughout the town. Linda, however, refuses to be shamed and instead holds her head high with pride throughout the procession. In addition to the fortitude with which she opposes Banderas, Linda exercises agency in defying Máximo when she decides to return to Tehuanchitán on her own. While Linda never exerts dominance over the film's hero, her independence and ability to defend herself cast her as his worthy female counterpart. In this way, *Tierra de pasiones* transforms the Tehuana's famed social dominance into the capacity to confront male instigators of injustice and mirror the male hero's courage.

Alongside its selection and reframing of some aspects of the Tehuana's reputation, like *La Zandunga*, *Tierra de pasiones* further modifies this figure by employing whiteness-as-indigeneity to represent the Tehuana on-screen. Here, too, Whiteness is central to the way Mexican melodrama signals the compassion-worthy female protagonist. Indeed, Linda's character is at

---

74. As Jesús Martín-Barbero explains, the hero who reimposes justice is a fundamental figure in melodrama. See *Communication, Culture and Hegemony*, 118.

Figure 2.5. Linda (Margarita Mora) holds her head high as Diego Banderas and his cronies attempt to shame her in *Tierra de pasiones* (1943). Filmoteca UNAM Collection. All rights reserved.

the center of the film's melodramatic plot. Her misfortunes begin when, through no fault of her own, she becomes the plaything of powerful men. The film calls further attention to Linda's suffering when she is forced to marry against her will, and later when Máximo is shot in front of her. In tandem with this characterization, *Tierra de pasiones* presents Linda as the film's compassion-worthy female victim within Mexican melodrama through her whiteness-as-indigeneity. Visually and aurally, *Tierra de pasiones* produces Linda's Whiteness through her tall, slim body; fine facial features; large eyes; manicured eyebrows; graceful movements; and clear pronunciation of dominant Mexican Spanish. Because of the local colonization of subjectivity, these visual and aural signifiers that connote Whiteness are privileged semiotic devices for promoting identification, which here are mobilized through melodramatic conventions. By using whiteness-as-indigeneity to re-represent its protorevolutionary Tehuana female protagonist, *Tierra de pasiones* produces a regionally specific Other as a victim of caudillo injustice in visual terms that can be experienced as normative in a still-racist, postcolonial Mexican context.

The fact that whiteness-as-indigeneity plays a role in the film's idealization of Linda can be further appreciated if one compares how another Tehuana in the film—Camila, a woman who is vying for Máximo's affection—is presented on-screen. Camila attempts to separate Máximo and Linda through deception and manipulation, and Máximo explicitly rejects Camila when she offers herself to him sexually on more than one occasion. Furthermore, Camila defies the patriarchal structure: she seemingly has no family, she camps out with Máximo and his men, and she attempts to separate a budding family. Linda's antagonist is played by an actress, Margarita Cortés, who does not conform as closely to the epidermal schema of White womanhood (*blancura*) within the local racial formation because of her darker skin, and she often appears darkly lit in the film, emphasizing that she is a wayward woman.[75] Through the difference in the actresses' appearances and the way in which lighting associates them with light and dark through the illumination of their faces, in *Tierra de pasiones* Whiteness functions to differentiate the Tehuana who personifies good moral character and resistance to injustice from her ostensibly "darker" female antagonist.[76]

In addition to how Linda's whiteness-as-indigeneity conveys her position as virtuous female sufferer within this Mexican melodrama, her Whiteness is also significant for her central function as the object of desire for multiple male characters. Among the men who desire Linda are her lover Máximo Tépal, Diego Banderas, and Salvador Peredo. Their attraction toward her constitutes the film's fundamental conflict, making Linda's desirability a primary component of its structure. Considering the raced codes of the colonization of desire, the on-screen presentation of Linda's

---

75. Margarita Cortés also plays the antagonistic Indigenous woman, Lupe, in *María Candelaria*, discussed in chapter 3.

76. A similar dynamic occurs in *María Candelaria* (1946), in which Margarita Cortés plays the role of "Lupe," the Indigenous female rival of María Candelaria who helps to bring about the protagonist's tragic death. The analysis presented here is analogous to the racialized and gendered patterns that bell hooks observes among Black Americans, ". . . the fair-skinned black woman who most nearly resembled white women was seen as the 'lady' and placed on a pedestal while darker-skinned black women were seen and bitches and whores," in *Ain't I a Woman: Black Women and Feminism* (New York: Routledge, 2015), 110.

Whiteness is the chief way in which *Tierra de pasiones* codifies her desirability in the local context. The film further suggests her appeal in other ways. Her name, for instance, hints at her pleasing physical appearance because it means "beautiful" in Spanish. Also, visual elements such as the character's elaborate hairstyles, makeup, and the use of the close-up and bright lighting craft her appearance as visually attractive. In particular, the scene in which the spectator first encounters Linda establishes her as a nymph-like creature, as she is nude and bathing in a brightly lit bucolic setting. Medium close-up shots display her exposed light skin and face as her hair flows in the water and flowers stream past her. Linda's physical Whiteness, her name, and the film's camerawork and mise-en-scène thus work together to present Linda as a cinematic Tehuana who conforms to the raced requirements of on-screen feminine attractiveness in Mexico. The crafting of Linda's Whiteness functions as a device in the film to render this Tehuana's reframing as protorevolutionary heroine (marked by virtue, melodramatic centrality, and physical appeal) visually legible according to the local raced hierarchization of female bodies.

Conclusion

Both Golden Age melodramas set in the Isthmus of Tehuantepec discussed in this chapter, *La Zandunga* and *Tierra de pasiones*, draw on ideas about the Isthmus as both a domestic and exotic national space as well as on aspects of the Tehuana's mythic reputation that had circulated in earlier Mexican cultural production. While *La Zandunga* displays the Isthmus as an idealized rural location in the style of the *comedia ranchera*, including folkloric elements such as dancing, music, and pageantry, *Tierra de pasiones* references these elements to highlight how cruel caudillo rule wreaks havoc in an otherwise paradisiacal place. Both films revise the mythology surrounding Tehuanas, modifying her presentation to suit a broad national audience in different ways. *La Zandunga* recasts the Tehuana's famed dominance as irreverence, her sexuality as colorful humor, and her marketplace prowess as bourgeois vulnerability. In this way, the film tames the mythic Tehuana, adapting her to patriarchal societal norms while at the same time providing a vehicle for the film's star, the comedic actress with a reputation as a liberated and modern woman, Lupe Vélez.

On the other hand, *Tierra de pasiones* modifies the Tehuana to position her as a protorevolutionary heroine who stands up to strongman rule.

Here the Tehuana's reputation for unbridled sexuality is recast as an act of resistance: the film justifies Linda's premarital relations with her lover as the catalyst for the villain's eventual undoing. Additionally, the film tempers the Tehuana's reputation for social dominance by transforming it into Linda's ability to confront injustice at the hands of powerful men and go against the wishes of her family, while entirely omitting the idea of Tehuana economic power.

The two films advance their respective discourses on the Tehuana through their use of whiteness-as-indigeneity. In both instances the representation of the Tehuana as White serves to locate the films' protagonists as the emotional centers of the melodramas and signal on a visual level their desirability as women in the racially inflected Mexican context. By taming the Tehuana in ways that make her more compatible with dominant patriarchal norms, national narratives, and racially determined criteria for female beauty, *La Zandunga* and *Tierra de pasiones* re-create and disseminate the regional type as an anodyne figure.

3

Revolutionary Politics, Colonized Aesthetics

The films discussed in the previous two chapters relate to *indigenismo* thematically in the broad sense that they feature Indigenous characters and their respective scenery, therefore aligning with postrevolutionary nationalism's symbolic celebration of the nation's native roots and identity. Those explored here, *La india bonita* (dir. Antonio Helú, 1938), *El indio* (dir. Armando de la Maza, 1939), *María Candelaria* and *Maclovia* (dir. Emilio Fernández 1944 and 1948, respectively), as well as *Janitzio* (dir. Carlos Navarro, 1935), and *Raíces* (dir. Benito Alazraki, 1955), are more closely tied to the political dimension of the indigenismo and *mestizaje* discourses in that they convey the plight of Indigenous people within an oppressive social structure. In doing so, these films either implicitly or explicitly infer the necessity of the Mexican Revolution of 1910 and the need to overturn a racially stratified social order. To create these critiques, the films use whiteness-as-whiteness to represent criollo or European men from a privileged class who either wittingly or unwittingly abuse their position to the detriment of Indigenous communities (adversely affecting the Indigenous female protagonists specifically). By calling attention to the coloniality of power as wielded by White men in Mexico, the films are, to varying degrees, invested in revolutionary politics.

However, through the aesthetic choice of whiteness-as-indigeneity for representing virtuous and beautiful (diegetically) Indigenous women, the four melodramas listed above betray an adherence to both the colonization of subjectivity and the colonization of desire, which establish Whiteness as the preferred device for inciting identification and conveying physical appeal. Therefore, while this corpus of films discursively rejects the political manifestations of coloniality, it upholds coloniality's gendered aesthetic implications, according to which female desirability is measured by its approximation to Whiteness. By highlighting the limits of revolutionary indigenismo and mestizaje discourses in these melodramatic, Indigenous-themed films, this chapter ultimately points to the way in which discursively decolonial cultural artifacts can, in effect, reify deeply rooted, racist ways of valuing bodies in Mexico. Furthermore, the chapter explores *Janiztio* and *Redes* as significant counterexamples that do not follow the trend of whiteness-as-indigeneity because (among other reasons) they do not adhere to the same conventions of melodrama, which, as I suggest in the introduction, favor Whiteness to signal desirability and identification in Mexican cinema.

The six films are grouped based on their production contexts, which inform their aesthetic tendencies. *La india bonita* and *El indio* were made in the initial stage of industrial filmmaking in Mexico when the privileging of nationally oriented themes was an evident trend, limited technological possibilities resulted in simple camerawork, and a robust star system was not yet in place. The second group of films, *María Candelaria* and *Maclovia*, represent a peak in the aestheticization of rural Mexico on film during the industrial and commercial heyday of the Golden Age and feature the most significant female figures of the Mexican star system, Dolores del Río and María Félix. Finally, even though *Janitzio* was made in the preindustrial period and *Raíces*'s production coincided with the decline of the Golden Age, both films coincide in their rejection of studio-era norms and commercial aspirations. Thus, despite the more than twenty years that separate the two films, they employ similar strategies for rendering Indigeneity, in part because of both films' marginal status with respect to industrial filmmaking.

La india bonita (1938)

Antonio Helú's *La india bonita* closely adheres to the conventions of the comedia ranchera genre in that it is a comedic film set in rural Mexico containing musical numbers and humorous interludes.[1] As Natasha Varner observes, the film's title comes directly from the beauty pageant held

---

1. Emilio García Riera, "The Impact of Rancho Grande," in *Mexican Cinema*, ed. Paulo Antonio Paranaguá, trans. Ana M. López (London: British Film Institute, 1995), 128–32.

in Mexico City in 1921[2] organized by leading cultural figures, including Manuel Gamio, with the aim of promoting the desirability of Indigenous women to White Mexican men to bolster mestizaje.[3] For several scholars, this pageant captures the racial and gendered dynamics at work in postrevolutionary Mexican popular nationalism.[4] Helú's film builds its plot around the pageant, which it thoroughly reimagines and showcases in line with "a growing indigenist ethos of the late 1930s that celebrated select aspects of many different Indigenous cultures."[5]

In the film, Joaquín (played by Carlos López Moctezuma) is the son of a ranch owner, but lives in Mexico City. He and his friend Luis (played by Julián Soler) take a break from city life to visit Joaquín's family ranch in an unidentified rural area of Mexico. They concoct a plan to seduce two of the Indigenous girls from the ranch, Lupe (played by Anita Campillo) and Ana María, by entering them into the *india bonita* contest, which is taking place in the capital. In the city, they hope to bed the women away from the watchful eyes of their boyfriends and community. The women's boyfriends, Manuel (played by Emilio Tuero) and Jacinto, suspect the privileged men's ignoble intentions and oppose the trip, but cannot prevent it from going forward. While on the trip as Lupe's chaperone, her mother, Gertrudis, finds out about Joaquín's intentions with her daughter. Gertrudis returns to the ranch to alert Joaquín's father, Gonzalo, because Lupe and Joaquín are in fact brother and sister. Gertrudis and Gonzalo travel to the city along with Manuel and Jacinto to stop the bachelors from pursuing Lupe and Ana María. Lupe wins the *india bonita* contest, and Lupe and Ana María are happily reunited with their boyfriends, whom they marry shortly after.

Helú's film has been criticized for being "excessively conventional" and narratively negligible.[6] Here I explore how, on the one hand, this seemingly

---

2. Natasha Varner, *La Raza Cosmética: Beauty, Identity, and Settler Colonialism in Postrevolutionary Mexico* (Tucson: University of Arizona Press, 2020), 88–91.

3. Rachell Sánchez-Rivera, "What Happened to Mexican Eugenics?: Racism and the Reproduction of the Nation" (PhD diss., University of Cambridge, Queens College, 2019), 98–101.

4. Rick A. López, "The India Bonita Contest of 1921 and the Ethnicization of Mexican National Culture," *Hispanic American Historical Review* 82, no. 2 (2002): 291–328; Adriana Zavala, *Becoming Modern, Becoming Tradition: Women, Gender, and Representation in Mexican Art* (University Park: Penn State University Press, 2011), 161–67; Varner, *La Raza Cosmética*; Sánchez-Rivera, "What Happened to Mexican."

5. Varner, *La Raza Cosmética*, 91.

6. Jorge Ayala Blanco, *La aventura del cine mexicano en la época de oro y después* (Miguel Hidalgo: Grijalbo, 1993), 148; Julianne Burton-Carvajal, "Mexican Melodramas

innocuous film registers the idea of a raced abuse of power on behalf of elite males and, on the other, it implements whiteness-as-indigeneity as a visual strategy for presenting a version of Mexican femininity as both authentically national and desirable.

La india bonita does not explicitly mention the Revolution as armed conflict, and as a film with clear ties to the *comedia ranchera* genre, it largely represents the hacienda as a place characterized by jovial social harmony.[7] However, the film differs with respect to widely known examples of the genre, such as *Allá en el Rancho Grande* (dir. Fernando de Fuentes, 1936), in which the possibility of transgression on the part of the landowner is only hinted at, and the dangers of the city are entirely out of the frame.[8] *La india bonita* blends a moral anxiety about the effects of urban culture with a revolutionary subtext through its reference to White male power that has the ability to exert itself through private injustices along racial, gendered, and class lines. In the following dialogue in which Luis (Julián Soler) and Joaquín (Carlos López Moctezuma) concoct their plan, the film exposes how men who enjoy advantages because of their class and race abuse their position for the sexual exploitation of Indigenous women:

> LUIS. ¡Hombre! Supongo que no querrás casarte con ella. (Come on! I don't suppose you'd want to marry her.)
> JOAQUIN. Claro que no. (Of course not.)
> LUIS. Pues ahí tienes. Lo que no puedes hacer aquí, lo podrás hacer en México . . . en México podemos hacer con ellas lo que nos dé la gana. Las muchachas se pierden de todos modos, aquí o en la ciudad, con la diferencia de que aquí caerán en manos de algún indio y se pasarán toda la vida encerradas en la hacienda . . . (Well there you have it. What you cannot do here, you can do in Mexico City . . . there we can do with them what we want. Young women lose their way anyhow, here

---

of Patriarchy: Specificity of a Transcultural Form," in *Framing Latin American Cinema: Contemporary Critical Perspectives*, ed. Ann Marie Stock, trans. Ambrosio Fornet (Minneapolis: University of Minnesota Press, 1997), 211.

7. Eduardo de la Vega Alfaro, "Origins, Development and Crisis of the Sound Cinema (1929–64)," in *Mexican Cinema*, ed. Paulo Antonio Paranaguá, trans. Ana M. López (London: British Film Institute, 1995), 83.

8. Marvin D'Lugo, "Aural Identity, Geneaologies of Sound Technologies, and Hispanic Transnationality on Screen," in *World Cinemas: Transnational Perspectives*, ed. Kathleen Newman and Natasa Durovicova (New York and London: Routledge, 2009), 172–73.

Figure 3.1. Joaquín (Carlos López Moctezuma) and Luis (Julián Soler) are morally dubious criollo *señoritos* in *La india bonita* (1938). Filmoteca UNAM Collection. All rights reserved.

or in the city, with the difference that here they will end up in the hands of some Indian and will spend their entire lives shut away on the ranch).

By showing that White members of the upper urban and landowning class consider pretty Indigenous girls to be beneath marrying, while at the same time staking strong claims of sexual entitlement over them, *La india bonita* evidences the abuse of power on the part of members of the elite, albeit within a larger comedic framework. Set in the postrevolutionary period, *La india bonita* translates the idea of a political conflict between men of distinct racial and class positions into an analogous rivalry over the love and honor of the Indigenous woman. The film's revolutionary resonance consists of its insistence on portraying the diegetically Indigenous man as the worthy and moral romantic subject.[9]

---

9. In this sense, my reading of *La india bonita* aligns with Jaqueline Avila's reconsideration of the progressive potential of *Allá en el Rancho Grande*, whose narrative, visual, and musical elements celebrate the foreman despite the overarching hacienda structure in which the landowner is boss. See Avila, *Cinesonidos*, 176–77.

Because of their intentions to seduce and abandon, which the film presents as a dishonorable course of action,[10] the film casts Luis and Joaquín as the film's antagonistic force threatening the genuine affection shared by the primary Indigenous couple, Lupe and Miguel. *La india bonita* uses whiteness-as-whiteness to signal the morally dubious and high-handed male, while whiteness-as-indigeneity is used to present the characters who occupy the moral and diegetic center of the film. Beyond this point, in *La india bonita* the white-as-indigenous Lupe and Miguel also represent Mexican authenticity. The film presents this genuine national quality as being tied to the idealized countryside—or "camposcape"[11]—through an explicit contrast between the countryside and the city. Prior to leaving for Mexico City to take part in the contest, for instance, Lupe's uncle makes a brief speech in which he extols the virtues of Indigenous women from the countryside in a way that associates them with Mexican authenticity: "Allá tendrán muchas catrinas guapas, pero inditas, mexicanas puras como las que aquí tenemos, no las tienen allá" (Over there they may have many fancy ladies, but *inditas*, pure Mexican women like the ones we have here, they don't have there). Through this speech, the film suggests that Lupe is representative of the Mexican essence because of her Indigenous background and rural upbringing.

Similarly, the film presents Miguel as Lupe's true equal because he is tied to the land, unlike the *patrón*'s son, who over the course of multiple years has only spent a few days on the hacienda, or his friend, who initially can only stomach the thought of spending a couple of days in the rural environment. The film associates Joaquín and Luis's lack of experience in the countryside with their shady moral character (the supposed evidence of the city's corrupting influence) and their incapacity to impress through musical ability. For example, when Joaquín and Luis try to serenade Lupe and Ana María as a part of their plot to coax them, they are upstaged by Miguel's impressive singing and forced to leave without being noticed by

---

10. For example, Joaquín's father refers to Luis as a "sin vergüenza" (shameless person) when Ana María's boyfriend, Jacinto, reveals to him that Joaquín and Luis have taken both girls to the city.

11. Ageeth Sluis uses the term "camposcape" to refer to the way in which the countryside was idealized in the early twentieth century Mexico in written and visual production as a privileged site of Mexican authenticity and purity. In *Deco Body, Deco City: Female Spectacle and Modernity in Mexico City, 1900–1939* (Lincoln: University of Nebraska Press, 2016), 101–3.

Figure 3.2. Anita Campillo as the "india bonita," Lupe, in *La india bonita* (1938). Filmoteca UNAM Collection. All rights reserved.

the women, which suggests the superiority of Miguel's rustic manhood and romantic prowess. Later, when Miguel interrupts the *india bonita* contest to reclaim his beloved, he takes the attention away from Luis (who is serving as the contest's master of ceremonies) by belting out a love song as he makes his grand entrance. The film suggests that Miguel's singing is far more impressive than Luis's hosting through the crosscut editing of the scene, which presents the musical number as undermining Luis's orchestration of the event. Furthermore, as Miguel sings, he hands flowers to members of the audience, further reinforcing his association with the countryside. Miguel is therefore the embodiment of authentic Mexican masculinity who is deserving of Lupe, which the film establishes through his tie to the *camposcape*, his moral integrity, and his musical ability.

Regarding diegetically Indigenous womanhood, *La india bonita* uses whiteness-as-indigeneity as a strategy to present desirable and compassion-worthy female Indigeneity through Anita Campillo's embodiment of Lupe. The character's on-screen appearance is characterized by the following

Figure 3.3. The virtuous and authentically Mexican Indigenous couple, Miguel and Lupe, presented through whiteness-as-indigeneity in *La india bonita* (1938). Filmoteca UNAM Collection. All rights reserved.

attributes read as White in the local racial formation: a tall and slender body, light skin complexion, fine facial features, large eyes, full lashes, and thin, manicured eyebrows. The film further underscores Lupe's Whiteness through her graceful movement and gesticulation, especially in contrast with the other inhabitants of her *rancho* whose characters fulfill a purely comedic function in the tradition of the popular theater. While, for example, the unnamed quarrelling husband and wife characters beat each other, producing slapstick humor and displaying rude facial gestures, because Lupe's plotline is a melodramatic one (complete with the surprise revelation of her true parentage), her gestures and movements are contained, graceful, and noncomedic. Last, Lupe's sweet tone of voice and clear articulation of dominant Mexican Spanish contrasts with the class and racialized speech patterns of her comedic male counterparts, such as her uncle, Panteleón, whose speech is full of colloquialisms. *La india bonita* therefore crafts Lupe as white-as-Indigenous for melodramatic purposes through corporeal, kinetic, and linguistic markers.

The fact that the film's "india bonita" (pretty Indian girl) is a woman without embodied or aural markers associated with Indigeneity within the Mexican racial formation and who is made up according to cosmetic trends of the day speaks to the "problem" that the concept of Indigenous beauty posed in the cinematic realm. The salience of the colonization of desire in this film's portrayal of appealing Indigenous femininity is evident in the contrast between the *india bonita*'s appearance in this film and the appearance of the woman who won the actual *india bonita* contest in Mexico City in 1921, María Bibiana Uribe. In real life, somatic Indigenous markers were admissible in the contest, if not expected characteristics of the contestants,[12] while in cinema, they are categorically absent in the character whose central role engages melodramatic conventions.

Furthermore, of the two potential candidates for representing the hacienda in the film's contest (Lupe and Ana María), the woman with a physical appearance that most closely aligns with parameters for female Whiteness is selected to take part in the competition (Lupe is taller and slenderer than Ana María, her face is less round, and her facial features are finer). A glimpse at Anita Campillo's career trajectory, which included a variety of non-Indigenous leading roles in both Mexican and US productions, further suggests that the actress embodied cosmopolitan bodily ideals. In addition to appearing alongside John Wayne in *The Man from Utah* (dir. Robert N. Bradbury, 1934),[13] Anita Campillo was featured in at least two of the (now infamous) Spanish-language sound films made in Hollywood in the 1930s, *La cruz y la espada* (dir. Frank Strayer, 1934) and *La Buenaventura* (dir. William C. McGann, 1934). Campillo's acting career illustrates that she enjoyed "white people's right to be various."[14] By Whitening "la india bonita" in the body of Anita Campillo, Helú's film uses whiteness-as-indigeneity to present the embodiment of a genuine feminine Mexican essence that could also be read as desirable according to a colonially inflected hierarchization of female bodies.

As in other Indigenous-themed films, *La india bonita*'s "solution" for representing appealing Indigenous womanhood requires the layering of

---

12. López, "The India Bonita Contest"; Adriana Zavala, *Becoming Modern*, 161–67.
13. Varner, *La Raza Cosmética*, 79.
14. Richard Dyer, "Coloured White, Not Coloured," in *White* (London and New York: Routledge, 1997), 49.

Figure 3.4. Anita Campillo playing the non-Indigenous Carmela in the Spanish-language Hollywood production *La cruz y la espada* (1934). *Cinelandia*, July 1942, 13.

folkloric garb on the White Mexican female body.[15] This aesthetic choice in the film is particularly salient and problematic because *La india bonita* repeatedly marks a sharp contrast between the countryside and the city in part by calling attention to the differences in the physical appearances of women from both areas. For example, early in the film, Joaquín's father makes a point of telling Lupe that she is "monísima" (really beautiful) and that women like her can't be found easily in the city: "¿A poco crees que en la ciudad hay muchas como tú? ¡Qué más quisieran!" (Do you think that in the city there many like you? They wish!). The contrast is repeated later when Lupe's uncle sends her off with the speech mentioned above, in which he marks a distinction between "catrinas guapas" (fancy ladies)

---

15. Dolores Tierney, *Emilio Fernández: Pictures in the Margins* (Manchester: Manchester University Press, 2012), 84.

and "inditas, mexicanas puras" (*inditas*, pure Mexicans). The irony of the film's association of Lupe with Indigenous beauty—including Miguel's referring to her as "prieta mia" (my darkie) in one of his ballads—is that while Lupe is wearing garments and accessories that mark her as a rural woman of Indigenous extraction, she otherwise physically embodies the cosmopolitan beauty standards of her day. In *La india bonita*, Lupe's whiteness-as-indigeneity muddles the visual distinction between "catrinas" and "inditas."[16] The negation of this visual contrast in cinema, which *did* exist in the Mexican press,[17] points to how cinema in Mexico has functioned as a peculiar space where an insistence on the aesthetic superiority of White Mexican femininity has persisted with remarkable (and colonially determined) tenacity.

El indio (1939)

Armando Vargas de la Maza directed *El indio* in 1938, an adaptation of Gregorio López y Fuentes's 1935 novel by the same title. *El indio* echoes the privileging of national themes and rural settings that became popular in the wake of *Allá en el Rancho Grande*;[18] however, like *Tierra de pasiones* (discussed in chapter 2), the film departs markedly from the lighthearted genre through its dramatic tone and focus on caudillo-orchestrated injustice. We might refer to both films as *dramas rancheros*.

While *El indio* has been criticized for its "touristic and melodramatic vocation" and for helping to pave the way for an acritical indigenist cinema,[19] unlike *La india bonita*, the film explicitly situates itself within a militant and

---

16. For a discussion of the contrast between urban and rural models of femininity in Mexican print culture in the first decades of the twentieth century, see Joanne Hershfield, *Imagining La Chica Moderna: Women, Nation, and Visual Culture in Mexico, 1917-1936* (Durham, NC: Duke University Press, 2008); Ageeth Sluis, *Deco Body, Deco City: Female Spectacle and Modernity in Mexico City, 1900-1939* (Lincoln: University of Nebraska Press, 2016); López, "The India Bonita Contest."

17. Both Rick López and Adriana Zavala discuss the visual and discursive distinctions between participants in the "India bonita" and "La mujer más bella" contests in the Mexican press in 1921. See López, "The India Bonita Contest," 304-5 and Zavala, *Becoming Modern, Becoming Tradition*, 161-66.

18. García Riera, "The Impact of Rancho Grande."

19. Emilio García Riera, *Historia documental del cine mexicano*, vol. 2, *1938-1942* (Guadalajara: Universidad de Guadalajara, 1993), 34.

political framework. From the opening expository text, *El indio* contextualizes the events it recounts in relation to the Mexican Revolution: "la revolución ha logrado la redención del indio . . . estos hechos se desarrollaron en una época que precedió al periodo revolucionario actual" (the Revolution has achieved the Indian's liberation . . . these events took place in a period previous to the contemporary revolutionary moment). With this text, the film signals that it will address racialized injustice, but, in a manner similar to the expository text in *María Candelaria*, de la Maza's film carefully locates this dynamic as a reality of the prerevolutionary period that has been eradicated at the time of the film's production.[20]

The plot in *El indio* centers the politics of the Revolution by highlighting the White landowning class' greed and exploitation of Indigenous labor. The story follows a group of Indigenous people who toil endlessly for a criollo landowner, Gonzalo, and receive scarce compensation. In addition to enforcing unjust working conditions for the Indigenous laborers, the landowner becomes convinced that their tribe possesses ancient treasures long buried for safekeeping. He tortures one of the community's members, Julián, because he denies knowing the treasure's location. The Indigenous people kill one of Gonzalo's men in retribution for Julián's torture, to which Gonzalo responds by burning down their town. The landowner also attempts to access the treasure by taking advantage of the rivalry between two Indigenous men, Julián and Felipe (played by Pedro Armendáriz), who are both in love with the same Indigenous woman, María (played by Consuelo Frank). When Gonzalo attempts to rape María, Felipe rallies Indigenous peoples from different areas in an uprising that the film presents as part of the Mexican Revolution.[21]

A significant part of the revolutionary critique in *El indio* occurs through its condemnation of Gonzalo as the personification of the prerevolutionary landed elite who exerts power through economic, physical, and structural oppression. The film emphasizes that brutality and injustice

---

20. As Dolores Tierney observes, the film on which *María Candelaria* was partially based, *Janitzio* (discussed below), is also set in the prerevolutionary period and bears similar implications. See *Emilio Fernández*, 79.

21. Alfredo B. Crevenna's 1954 film, *La rebelión de los colgados*, similarly frames a local uprising of Indigenous people against a tyrannical criollo as part of the Mexican Revolution of 1910. I do not focus on this film here because the Indigenous female character's role is a minor one in the diegesis, and the desirability of Indigenous characters is not a salient aspect of the film in technical or narrative ways.

characterize the labor arrangement on Gonzalo's estate. The film opens with a shot of three diegetically Indigenous men toiling to the point of exhaustion. When one of them falls to the ground, he is immediately lashed by an overseer. Later, when the Indigenous laborers collect their weekly payment, they receive only meager sums or a ration of corn in exchange for their hard work because they are indebted to the estate. By explicitly depicting the unjust labor arrangement on Gonzalo's estate, the film aligns the circumstances of the fictional Indigenous group with the well-known grievances raised during the Mexican Revolution.

El indio further casts Gonzalo as a tyrannical figure by highlighting his use of both violence and influence. In the aftermath of Julian's punishment and the burning of the town, the film suggests that, in addition to deploying excessive force, Gonzalo's class exerts power through shady political relationships. In a hearing in which Gonzalo and several Indigenous peasants present their case before the governor, the law sides with Gonzalo, and afterward the landowner offers to pay the governor for his "assistance." The governor's response, as well as the knowing handshake and smiles they exchange, suggests an entrenched level of corruption in the governing structures run by White men: "cuando sea usted diputado, podrá ayudarme en otros negocios" (when you will hold office, you can help me with other matters). By indicating Gonzalo's economic exploitation of Indigenous laborers, his use of unwarranted force toward them, and his nefarious arrangements with political figures, *El indio* positions him at the center of its revolutionary critique and suggests that violent revolt is the only recourse available to the Indigenous peasants.

Visually, the film uses distinct strategies for presenting Whiteness to mark the landed elite and the righteous Indigenous rebels. On the one hand, *El indio* uses whiteness-as-whiteness to mark the oppressive landowning class. The film signals Gonzalo's Whiteness through his dress, Spanish accent, and phenotypical markers that are read as White in the Mexican racial formation. On the other hand, the film uses whiteness-as-indigeneity to distinguish the main Indigenous characters in the diegesis (María and Felipe) from both their elite oppressors and the secondary Indigenous characters. In line with the explanation of the colonization of subjectivity and its predominance in melodrama outlined in the introduction, in *El indio*, whiteness-as-indigeneity signals the film's protagonists and primary points of identification. In addition to exhibiting the gendered virtues of traditional twentieth-century Mexican society (forthrightness, honor, and bravery in the case of Felipe; and modesty, beauty, and chastity in María's case), Felipe and María's love story is the plot's sentimental center. *El indio*'s use of whiteness-as-indigeneity marks the diegetically Indigenous Mexicans who overthrow the unjust criollo order as the new protagonists of the emerging postrevolutionary nation.[22]

Beyond María's role within the film's central couple, in *El indio* she is the object of desire for several men across racial and class lines. The film's strategy for presenting her as both desirable and Indigenous employs the then in vogue "deco-body," which features slender shapes, long lines, an androgynous body shape, fashionable late 1930s makeup, thin eyebrows, full lashes, and a light completion.[23] Here the Indigenous woman is coded as desirable for a Mexican audience through her aesthetic refashioning according to the cosmopolitan beauty standards of the day.

Even though a robust star system was not yet in place at the time *El indio* was made, press coverage of the actress, Consuelo Frank, just a few years later confirms that she embodied normative ideals of female beauty in Mexico at the time. A feature in *Cinema Reporter* from 1945 asserts that "durante toda una etapa fue la mujer más hermosa de nuestro cine, y su atractivo en el público fue siempre indiscutible. Es toda una figura con señorío, gracia y múltiples capacidades" (during an entire period she was the most beautiful woman of our cinema, and among the public her appeal was always undeniable. She is a leading figure with dignity, grace, and multiple abilities).[24] The article even suggests that Consuelo Frank's beauty and talent were underserved in the types of roles she took in films like *El indio*: "no había temas para ella, como no fueran los peligrosos y deleznables temas rurales . . ." (there were no subject matters for her that went beyond the dangerous and poorly made rural themes . . .). In suggesting that Frank's cosmopolitan appearance and air were an awkward fit for films set in provincial areas, the article hints that these films put forth disingenuous representations of rural Mexicans.

Close-ups of Frank playing María throughout *El indio* function as part of the cinematic conventions of melodrama because they highlight the character's emotional states, but at the same time, this cinematic device features María's whiteness-as-indigeneity as desirable on an aesthetic level.

---

22. According to Garcia Riera, *El Indio* contains "una idealización absoluta del héroe nativo" (an absolute idealization of the native hero). In *Historia documental del cine*, vol. 2: 34.

23. Sluis, *Deco Body, Deco City*, 105.

24. *Cinema Reporter*, "Una personalidad," April 14, 1945, 8–9.

More importantly, however, her whiteness-as-indigeneity is also the means through which the film presents María as the corrupt criollo order's most helpless and compassion-worthy victim. The fact that the film assigns her this status is apparent in that Gonzalo's attempt to rape María is the last indignation that finally instigates her community's armed rebellion. This point is remarkable considering that prolonged economic exploitation, Julián's unjust punishment, and even the razing of their town previously had not been enough to spur them into action. María's Whiteness helps to transmit the urgency of the revolutionary cause by visually instrumentalizing the long-standing privileged treatment of White bodies in Mexico according to which their violation or suffering is perceived as egregious and "grievable," while the violation of non-White bodies is deemed tolerable or is ignored altogether.[25]

In this sense *El indio* functions analogously to the examples of melodrama described by Linda Williams, which "stag[e] a recognition of virtue through the visible suffering of the endangered white woman."[26] As Williams explains, in Hollywood "[i]nter-racial (non-white on white) rape is represented as bestiality storming the citadel of civilization."[27] This Mexican film with a revolutionary message adapts the Hollywood trope. *El indio* uses the white-as-Indigenous woman, alongside dramatic music during the attempted rape scene, to represent unchecked criollo control as horrific and to interpellate[28] the Mexican spectator toward an ideological position that affirms the necessity of the Revolution. In this way, María's whiteness-as-indigeneity serves the purpose of bolstering the film's revolutionary message, while at the same time reinforcing the raced privilege of White bodies on a semiotic level.

---

25. Roger Bartra, *The Cage of Melancholy: Identity and Metamorphosis in the Mexican Character*, trans. Christopher J. Hall (New Brunswick: Rutgers University Press, 1992), 62–64; Federico Navarrete Linares, *México racista: Una denuncia* (Mexico City: Grijalbo, 2016), 23–41, 88–90; Albert Memmi, *The Colonizer and the Colonized* (Boston: Beacon Press, 1991), 86; Judith Butler, "Precarious Life, Grievable Life," in *Frames of War: When Is Life Grievable?* (New York: Verso, 2016), 24.

26. Linda Williams, *Playing the Race Card: Melodramas of Black and White from Uncle Tom to O. J. Simpson* (Princeton: Princeton University Press, 2001), 100.

27. Richard Dyer, "The Matter of Whiteness," in *White* (London and New York: Routledge, 2017), 26.

28. I employing this term not in the Althusserian sense, but rather in the broader sense of appealing or engaging spectators in a manner that promotes an ideological view.

Figure 3.5. Consuelo Frank as the Indigenous María in *El indio* (1939). Screen capture from film.

María Candelaria (1944)

Emilio Fernández's 1944 film, *María Candelaria*, is among the most widely studied and commented-on in Mexican film history because, at least in part, of its iteration of the indigenismo and mestizaje discourse and its visual genealogy.[29] In this bona fide Golden Age melodrama, it is the incongruity among different sectors of the population in prerevolutionary Mexico that leads to a tragic outcome. The film tells the story of María Candelaria (Dolores del Río), an Indigenous woman from Xochimilco

---

29. Tierney, *Emilio Fernández*, 77–83. See also Andrea Noble, *Mexican National Cinema* (London and New York: Routledge, 2006), 79–90; David S. Dalton, *Mestizo Modernity: Race, Technology, and the Body in Postrevolutionary Mexico* (Gainesville: University of Florida Press, 2018), 100–39; Claudia Arroyo Quiroz, "Fantasías sobre la identidad indígena en el cine mexicano del periodo post-revolucionario," in *Identidades. Explorando la diversidad*, ed. Laura Carballido (Mexico City: Universidad Autónoma Metropolitana-Anthropos, 2011), 149–70.

who is ostracized from her community because of her mother's reputation for transgressing its sexual norms. By selling flowers, she hopes to repay her debt to a mestizo strongman, Don Damián, and marry her beloved, Lorenzo Rafael (Pedro Armendáriz). However, the community does not allow her to sell flowers, and later María contracts malaria after Don Damián refuses to distribute quinine to the Indigenous people. In a moment of desperation, Lorenzo Rafael steals the medicine for María as well as a dress for her to wear on their wedding day—an act that eventually lands him jail. In exchange for helping María negotiate Lorenzo Rafael's release, a criollo artist asks to paint María. After painting her face, the artists requests to paint her nude body, to which María reacts by running away in distress. Even though he completes the painting using the nude body of another Indigenous woman as his model, María's community interprets the resulting image as evidence of her sexual immorality, for which they stone her to death.

Regarding the film's connection to the politics of the Revolution and the postrevolutionary era, scholars have concluded that *María Candelaria* suggests isolation as the only viable path to protecting Indigenous people[30] and opts to praise a dead Indigenous person rather than contend with the social and economic struggles of Indigenous communities in 1940s Mexico.[31] However, if we foreground the fact that, in the diegesis, the Revolution has not yet occurred, one can also conclude that *María Candelaria* presents its tragedies as a result of a faulty prerevolutionary governing structure that does not effectively rule or integrate different social sectors. In other words, the Mexico of *María Candelaria* lacks a competent corporatist government. In this prerevolutionary nightmare, Indigenous people take justice into their own hands, freely victimizing exceptional, innocent natives such as María Candelaria and Lorenzo Rafael, and dubious subjects such as Don Damián are able to exercise authority arbitrarily. Furthermore, criollos know so little about their Indigenous co-nationals that they unintentionally violate them. Given that the local priest and the painter prove incompetent for protecting María and José Rafael, instead of embodying the future, an ideal modernity, or European

---

30. Tierney, *Emilio Fernández*, 83.
31. Susan Dever, *Celluloid Nationalism and Other Melodramas: From Post-Revolutionary Mexico to Fin De Siglo Mexamérica* (Albany: State University of New York Press, 2003), 40.

values worthy of imitation,[32] I suggest that they can be read as part of a defective social order that is also responsible for María's death alongside what the film presents as Indigenous barbarity. The painter and the priest indeed embody a project of modernity,[33] but it is the *first* project of Western modernity introduced through Iberian colonialism,[34] which, as presented in *María Candelaria*, has survived throughout the long nineteenth century and continues to wreak havoc in a prerevolutionary early twentieth-century Mexico. These oblivious criollos must therefore also be reformed, and their attempts at mediation on behalf of Indigenous Mexicans must be supplanted through the Revolution for the good of the nation.

By featuring, although in a highly romanticized vein, the plight of Indigenous people and attributing that suffering to a lack of competent mediation among the various sectors of the population, *María Candelaria*—not unlike *El indio*—points to the necessity of the Revolution and justifies the governing order that resulted from it—one distinct from the criollo patriarchy represented by the priest and artist.[35] In making corporatist government the film's structuring absence, *María Candelaria*—like many other Latin American studio-era films—promotes it as an alternative order for modernizing society.[36] In sum, the modernity *María Candelaria* advocates for is that of postrevolutionary corporativism, and a central way the film advances this proposal is by characterizing the preexisting project of criollo modernity as fatally inadequate.

Scholars have skillfully pointed to the ways in which *María Candelaria* separates the female protagonist and Lorenzo Rafael as exceptionally virtuous Indians vis-à-vis the other members of their community, whom the film portrays as backwards and savage.[37] In particular, Dolores Tier-

---

32. Tierney, *Emilio Fernández*, 90; Paul Schroeder Rodríguez, *Latin American Cinema: A Comparative History* (Berkeley: University of California Press, 2016), 106.

33. Tierney, *Emilio Fernández*, 95

34. Walter D. Mignolo, "The Conceptual Triad: Modernity/Coloniality/Decoloniality," in Walter D. Mignolo and Catherine E. Walsh, *On Decoloniality: Concepts, Analytics, Praxis* (Durham, NC: Duke University Press, 2018), 139–40.

35. E. Bradford Burns, "The Patriarchal Preference," in *The Poverty of Progress: Latin America in the Nineteenth Century* (Berkeley: University of California Press, 1980), 72–85.

36. Schroeder Rodríguez, *Latin American Cinema*, 88–115.

37. Tierney, *Emilio Fernández*, 88–95; Noble, *Mexican National Cinema*, 89–90; Schroeder Rodríguez, *Latin American Cinema*, 104.

ney has pointed to the film's use of lighting and White somatic markers to argue that the film associates María and Lorenzo Rafael with virtue and the criollo characters (the painter and priest), who for her represent modernity.[38] The contrast between the film's indigenist impulse and the alignment of the film's protagonists with criollo characters results, for Tierney, in a representation of Indigenous Mexicans that is "incoherent" and "schizophrenic."[39]

While the argument presented here is indebted to Tierney's perceptive observations of how the film constructs the characters' Whiteness in multifaceted ways, I propose an alternative understanding of how the film's racial masquerade operates and what it accomplishes. In light of the ways in which the colonization of subjectivity primes postcolonial subjects to identify with Whiteness,[40] White epidermal schemas (*blancura*) operate in *María Candelaria* as a semiotic device to visually render the unique social and moral identity of María and Lorenzo Rafael as separate from the well-meaning but dangerously oblivious criollos, the Indigenous people presented as backwards, and unenlightened mestizos (Don Damián). In this way, María and Lorenzo Rafael's whiteness-as-indigeneity marks them as the authentically Mexican couple according to a coherent pattern of racialized representation of cinematic Indigeneity, as also evidenced in *La india bonita* and *El indio*. Furthermore, because in this reading the criollos represent a defective social order—not the future or the project of postrevolutionary modernity, but an expiring criollo patriarchy—the protagonists' affinity with them is in fact the source of their tragedy. If María Candelaria and Lorenzo Rafael are "antithetical to the modern Mexican state,"[41] it is only because—in contrast to their counterparts in *El indio*—they are too compliant with the existing criollo order and no alternative project is yet underway. María Candelaria and Lorenzo Rafael are in fact such a modern Mexican state's ideal candidates,[42] but their embeddedness within criollo patriarchy obstructs their ability to envision or bring about such a project. The racialized semiotic dynamic of whiteness-

---

38. Tierney, *Emilio Fernández*, 90.
39. Tierney, *Emilio Fernández*, 75, 84.
40. Frantz Fanon, *Black Skin, White Masks* (New York: Grove Press, 2008), 146–47. See also Memmi, *The Colonizer*, 91, 104–5.
41. Tierney, *Emilio Fernández*, 95.
42. Dalton, *Mestizo Modernity*, 115.

as-indigeneity serves to anchor the spectator's identification with María and Lorenzo Rafael as the melodrama's tragic characters—quintessential Mexicans who are orphans of a competent, modern state—with whom the spectator is meant to identify.

One of the clearest scenes in which somatic difference, underscored by the film's editing, highlights the difference between the film's noble Indians and the unredeemable natives is when María Candelaria rows toward the market place to sell flowers, and the community forms a barrier, impeding her from doing so. There are many aspects of these shots that firmly establish María as the primary point of identification. Andrea Noble has already suggested that in this film "collective cinematic identity by definition functions . . . to prevent close spectatorial identification" with the large Indigenous group.[43] In addition, the way in which this confrontation between the María and the group is rendered visually promotes the spectator's association with María when the extreme long shot of her being thwarted by the community position her as its defenseless and isolated victim. As Claudia Arroyo Quiroz has observed, the series of short medium close-ups, which switch from showing María to showing different members of the community and then María again, emphasizes the Indigenous community's unified opposition to her (see figures 3.6 and 3.7),[44] prefiguring the dynamics of her lapidation later on. The fact that the editing keeps returning to shots of María indicates that the film privileges her experience of the event, and the spectator is therefore meant to identify with her. In addition, the medium close-ups of María are taken from a high angle, emphasizing her vulnerability, while several shots of those in the Indigenous community are taken from a low angle, which may mimic María's point of view but also imbue her adversaries with a menacing quality.

Furthermore, as Jacqueline Avila has illustrated, the use of sound in the scene is crucial to privileging María's subjectivity.[45] The nondiegetic music builds up dramatically at the point of confrontation when it is clear to María that she will not pass. After she understands this, the "music reinforces María Candelaria's emotions and functions not only as a marker of oppression but also as a physical indication of her desperation and

---

43. Noble, *Mexican National Cinema*, 89.
44. Arroyo Quiroz, "Fantasías sobre la identidad indígena," 155–56.
45. Jacqueline Avila, *Cinesonidos: Film Music and National Identity During Mexico's Epoca de Oro* (Oxford: Oxford University Press, 2019), 143–44.

Figure 3.6. María Candelaria (Dolores del Río) is saddened when blocked from selling her flowers in *María Candelaria* (1944). Screen capture from film.

Figure 3.7. A shot of María's intransigent community in *María Candelaria* (1943). Screen capture from film.

loss,"[46] further underscored through the medium close-up. Alongside these aural and editing effects, Dolores del Ríos's somatic Whiteness within the Mexican racial formation (which operates alongside her White star text)[47] also contributes to the way in which the film promotes the spectator's identification with her character in this scene. In juxtaposing medium close-ups of the Indigenous people in her community with those of María, the film showcases their phenotypical difference, which serves as a visual tool of moral differentiation. The members of the community who are presented through indigeneity-as-indigeneity[48] here are precisely those whom the film casts as vindictive, unreasonable, unjust, and predatory, while the white-as-indigenous María incarnates the characteristics that are represented as exemplary: piety, selflessness, and chastity.[49] While I agree with Claudia Arroyo Quiroz that this differentiated approach to Indigenous representation within the same film in part constitutes an effort to infuse the melodrama with "autenticidad antropológica" (anthropological authenticity),[50] I suggest that, via the colonization of subjectivity, Whiteness functions to locate María as the film's privileged point of identification and as a device to convey "the nobility of María Candelaria's Indianess"[51] to Mexican audiences.

Of course, the fact that María Candelaria is an object of desire for men across race and class lines within the diegesis is a crucial factor that must be taken into consideration when understanding the weight of whiteness-as-indigeneity in cinematic representation as a vestige of the coloniality of power. The film calls attention to María's appeal because the development of the plot depends directly on Don Damián, the painter, and Lorenzo Rafael's struggle to possess her.[52] Visually, as Dolores Tierney has

---

46. Avila, *Cinesonidos*, 144.

47. Joanne Hershfield, *The Invention of Dolores del Río* (Minneapolis: University of Minnesota Press, 2000), 57–67; Tierney, *Emilio Fernández*, 87–88.

48. Clauda Arroyo Quiroz understands the film's strategy for visualizing the antagonistic Indians as the projection of an "ethnographic body." See Claudia Arroyo Quiroz, "Fantasías sobre la identidad indígena," 159.

49. For a detailed reading of how lighting in María Candelaria also emphasizes María Candelaria and Lorenzo Rafael's Whiteness, see Tierney, *Emilio Fernández*.

50. Arroyo Quiroz, "Fantasías sobre la identidad indígena," 156–58.

51. Hershfield, *The Invention of Dolores del Río*, 62. See also Aurelio de los Reyes, *Medio siglo de cine mexicano (1896–1947)* (Mexico City: Editorial Trillas, 1987), 196–98.

52. Noble, *Mexican National Cinema*, 81.

Figure 3.8. An indigenous-as-indigenous model poses for the criollo painter in *María Candelaria*. Screen capture from film.

perceptively explained, the film's use of lighting brightens Maria's appearance in a manner that is consistent with Western visual conventions according to which a woman's appeal is rendered through luminosity.[53] In addition to the film's lighting, *María Candelaria* also uses whiteness-as-indigeneity in the somatic sense to convey diegetic Indigenous feminine desirability, thereby also reinscribing a colonized hierarchy of female bodies, even as the film advocates for the dismantling of internal colonial social relations in Mexico.[54] While *La india bonita* and *El indio* also portray Indigenous beauty through whiteness-as-indigeneity, Fernández's films take full

---

53. Tierney, *Emilio Fernández*, 94.
54. While this reading emphasizes how *María Candelaria* taps into a legacy of coloniality, in Natasha Varner's analysis (which presupposes an affinity between the film and the Vasconcelian perspective), *María Candelaria* establishes a mestiza appearance as "the beauty of the future." In *La Raza Cosmética*, 115–18.

advantage of the more advanced technology available in Mexico by the mid-1940s to aestheticize the racial masquerade through elaborate filmic techniques. In *María Candelaria*, these techniques put forth clearer differentiations between the desirability of whiteness-as-indigeneity and that of other diegetically Indigenous females throughout the film.

The opening images in *María Candelaria* consist of an Eisenstein-influenced montage of pre-Columbian stone figures and a final mask, which dissolves into a shot of a diegetically Indigenous woman that has the same facial structure as the mask.[55] As Joanne Hershfield has noted, through these images, Fernández "specifically links that past through his presentation of Mexico's 'eternal' Indianness."[56] While Andrea Noble has suggested that María too "is linked to the imagistic dialogue between pre-Columbian past and post-Columbian present," which is made explicit when the painter refers to her as "una india de pura raza mexicana" (an Indian of pure Mexican race),[57] María Candelaria in not presented on-screen in a comparable way to the woman who personifies eternal Indianness in the beginning of the film and with whom María is supposed to share this enduring essence. María's complexion is lighter and is brightened repeatedly through illumination, and she also has finer facial features.[58] Although, according to Hershfield and Noble, both women are meant to personify pre-Columbian authenticity, within the film there is an important distinction between the two that explains why they appear through such different embodiments: while the function of the model within the film is merely ornamental, María's diegetic function requires that she be presented as an object of romantic and sexual desire, and melodramatic identification, which, because of how the coloniality of power has impacted cultural production in Mexico, has historically required Whiteness in its national cinema.

---

55. Tierney, *Emilio Fernández*, 82.

56. Joanne Hershfield, *Mexican Cinema/Mexican Woman, 1940–1950* (Tucson: University of Arizona Press, 1996), 55.

57. Noble, *Mexican National Cinema*, 82.

58. Adriana Zavala observes that the Indigenous model at the beginning of the film and Nieves, the model who stands in for María Candelaria's body in the film's infamous painting, "conform to one standard of Indian beauty," while Dolores del Río "embodied an elite, *criollo* (and Western) standard of beauty and culture." In *Becoming Modern, Becoming Tradition*, 268. Tierney, *Emilio Fernández*, 91–94.

Furthermore, the fact that the film never shows the artist's infamous painting on-screen betrays a self-consciousness regarding the difference between the visibly ethnic femininity featured in twentieth-century pictorial indigenismo (à la Diego Rivera), of which the painting is supposed to be an example,[59] and the White requirement of female Indigeneity in Mexican (melodramatic) cinema. The fact that the painting is supposed to simultaneously capture two different and contradictory approaches to rendering Indigenous female beauty—pictorial indigenismo that exalts Indigenous bodies and Dolores del Río as diegetically Indigenous protagonist—results in the impossibility of the painting's representation on film.[60] In other words, the film can display pictorial indigenismo in the making (as the model sits for the painter) and whiteness-as-indigeneity (in the fashioning of María Candelaria), but no single image can do both simultaneously.[61]

The tension surrounding the painting's impossibility is also the result of the racialized sensibilities surrounding female nudity in different visual mediums. Because of the influence of classical art, the painting of nude women came to constitute a long-accepted genre in that medium, while female nudity in publicly visible photography and film, because of those mediums' association with indexicality, has historically provoked a distinct set of attitudes and anxieties. Race is a significant factor in the constitution of these attitudes and anxieties. Insofar as the cinematic representation of nonWhite people was informed by a Eurocentric demarcation between

---

59. According to García Riera, Diego Rivera was the inspiration for the character of the artist in *María Candelaria*. In Emilio García Riera, *Historia documental del cine mexicano*, vol. 3, *1943–1945* (Guadalajara: Universidad de Guadalajara, 1993), 67. Also, Dolores Tierney notes that "[t]he artist's model who appears in the film is played by Nieves, who often posed for Rivera." In *Emilio Fernández*, 82.

60. As Laura Podalsky has noted, the visual omission of the painting allows the film to avoid asking if the "film [is] a more reliable representation of the indigenous community than the painting of the artist." In "Disjointed Frames: Melodrama, Nationalism, and Representation in 1940s Mexico," *Studies in Latin American Popular Culture* 12 (1993): 57–74.

61. For Andrea Noble, the impossibility of showing the painting in the film is the result of a different tension: one between the pre-Columbian gaze, which she believes the Indigenous antagonists exhibit, and a modern Mexican gaze she believes was in formation at the time the film was made. Noble, *Mexican National Cinema*, 82–85.

"historifiable" and "ethnographiable" people[62] and operated "on a continuum with zoology, anthropology, botany, entomology, biology and medicine,"[63] nonWhite nakedness on film had a distinct status from that of White nakedness. While filmic nudity of nonWhite women presented through the ethnographic gaze was not typically considered obscene, White female nudity—rarely subjected to the same ethnographic visual representation—would have been considered scandalous in the Mexican mid-twentieth century. We can appreciate this difference in the pseudo-anthropological "Sandunga" segment of Sergei Eisenstein's 1932 film, *¡Qué Viva México!*, which features a dark-skinned Indigenous woman, Consuelo, appearing undressed from the waist up. Another example can be found in the photography of popular mid-twentieth-century magazines, such as *Hoy*, whose cover on August 6, 1938, featured a photograph titled "Indígena in Cosoleacaque" by Rafael Carrillo in which an Indigenous woman appears unclothed from the waist up.[64] However, equivalently public displays of White Mexican women's nakedness in photography and film would have been considered worthy of censorship. Indeed, the first Mexican film to display a nonethnographic or intentionally pornographic shot of a nude woman, *La mancha de sangre* (dir. Adolfo Best-Maugard), was censored in part for its nudity.[65] Thus, the irrepresentability of the nude portrait in *María Candelaria* also stems from the fact that presenting a nude Dolores del Río on film, even if only in painting form, would likely still have been considered pornographic[66]—or at the very least, it would have been highly incompatible with her star text as an elegant and well-mannered aristocrat.

---

62. Fatimah Tobing Rony, *The Third Eye: Race, Cinema, and Ethnographic Spectacle* (Durham, NC: Duke University Press, 1996), 8.

63. Ella Shohat and Robert Stam, *Unthinking Eurocentrism: Multiculturalism and the Media* (New York: Routledge, 1994), 106–7.

64. John Mraz, "Today, Tomorrow and Always: The Golden Age of Illustrated Magazines in Mexico, 1937–1960," in *Fragments of a Golden Age: The Politics of Culture in Mexico Since 1940*, ed. Gilbert M. Joseph, Anne Rubenstein, and Eric Zolov (Durham, NC: Duke University Press, 2001), 130.

65. Emilio García Riera, *Historia documental del cine mexicano*, vol. 1, *1929–1937* (Guadalajara: Universidad de Guadalajara, 1993), 288–89.

66. For a parallel example of the permissibility of Indigenous female nudity and anxiety surrounding White female nudity in Argentine film, see Victoria Ruétalo, *Violated Frames: Armando Bó and Isabel Sarli's Sexploits* (Berkeley: University of California Press, 2022).

Revolutionary Politics, Colonized Aesthetics 149

Figure 3.9. María Candelaria as seen by the criollo painter. Screen capture from film.

While avoiding the display of María Candelaria's nudity, the film does establish her desirability by presenting her to the spectator through the desirous gaze of male characters, thus cementing her to-be-looked-at-ness from their perspective.[67] This occurs, for example, when the painter first sees María as she approaches the market—an encounter that prompts "his sexual desire for María Candelaria, masked behind his artistic desire to paint her."[68] When the artist first sees María, an eyeline match from his perspective displays her as an object of wonder and captures his reaction as he gasps in astonishment (figures 3.9 and 3.10). As Laura Mulvey has illustrated, camera language of this kind places the spectator into the position of desire for the fetishized woman, inciting the viewer to do the

---

67. Laura Mulvey, "Visual Pleasure and Narrative Cinema," in *Literary Theory: An Anthology*, ed. Julie Rivkin and Michael Ryan (New York: Blackwell, 1998), 585–96.

68. Zavala, *Becoming Modern, Becoming Tradition*, 244.

Figure 3.10. The criollo painter gasps in astonishment upon seeing María Candelaria for the first time. Screen capture from film.

same.[69] Only María, the white-as-Indigenous woman, provokes this kind of reaction or is presented through editing in a manner that suggests her appeal for men in the diegesis.[70]

Furthermore, other women in the community, whom the film presents as having closer cultural ties to Indigeneity, are either cast as possessing undesirable, antagonistic characteristics or as being utterly ridiculous. For example, María's rival for the affection of Lorenzo Rafael, Lupe (played by Margarita Cortés),[71] is not desired by Lorenzo Rafael (whom she fancies) or any other male in the story. Visually, she is not consistently presented through close-ups or bright lighting, as María is. Additionally, the film

---

69. Mulvey, "Visual Pleasure."

70. For the discussion of María's Whiteness as a device to facilitate female desire, see Zavala, *Becoming Modern, Becoming Tradition*, 244.

71. Margarita Cortés also plays the antagonistic indigenous woman, Camila, in *Tierra de pasiones*, discussed in chapter 2.

Figure 3.11. Margarita Cortés as the comparatively racialized antagonist, Lupe, in *María Candelaria* (1944). Screen capture from film.

more closely associates Lupe with Indigeneity both because of her superstitious beliefs and because she is the only character to speak in Nahuatl, which she does in moments of anger.[72] In visual terms, the film clearly places the women in opposition to each other, most notably when María directly confronts Lupe. Much like the confrontation between María and the entire *pueblo*, the alternation of medium close-ups of María and Lupe with dramatic nondiegetic music in the background suggests that they embody opposing values. These close-ups also highlight the extent to which María's physical presence on-screen adheres to the physical criteria for Whiteness for women in Mexico,[73] while Lupe's does not. Specifically, María's eyes are rounder and larger, while Lupe's are more slanted, and María's nose is finer than that of Lupe. In this way, the film emphasizes

---

72. Tierney, *Emilio Fernández*, 84–85.

73. Hugo Nutini, *The Mexican Aristocracy: An Expressive Ethnography* (Austin: University of Texas Press, 2008), 62.

María's on-screen presence as an instance of whiteness-as-indigeneity vis-à-vis her rival, Lupe, who is comparatively racialized to emphasize her negative character traits.

In addition to Lupe, the other Indigenous woman who receives a notable amount of screen time is the *huesera* (bone doctor) who visits María Candelaria when she is on the verge of dying from malaria. Beyond being presented as very old and past the age when she could be physically appealing, the *huesera* functions as the ignorant foil to the doctor who is an expert in Western medicine.[74] The scene is meant to be humorous, and its comedy depends on highlighting the *huesera*'s mispronunciation of words in Spanish and the implied baselessness of her healing practices. By presenting the *huesera* as unattractive, foolish, and more closely tied with Indigenous culture, the film suggests that the white-as-indigenous María is the only possible version of native womanhood that can be simultaneously all of the following: a paragon of Indigenous authenticity (as the painter mentions at the beginning of the film), ornamental (fit for pictorial representation), and desirable (sought after by multiple men in the diegesis for sexual and/or romantic satisfaction).

While the breach of indexicality in the casting of María Candelaria is remarked on by nearly every scholar and critic who has written about the film in the past thirty years, at the time the film was released, some Mexican press coverage both made it clear that Dolores del Río was not herself an Indigenous woman, but also foregrounded nationalism to praise del Río's appropriateness for the role. The title of an article that appeared in *Cinema Reporter* in February 1945 hints at the complex logic behind this view of del Río's performance: "De *Ramona* a *María Candelaria*. Lolita ama a las indias mexicanas. Lolita ya es nuestra" (From *Ramona* to *María Candelaria*. Lolita loves Indigenous Mexican women. Lolita is now ours).

On the one hand, this article (complete with glamourous photographs of the interview on which it is based) reifies the distance between Dolores del Río's star persona and Indigenous Mexican women.[75] It casts del Río as a highly refined and delicate woman, even to the point of suggesting that the filming requirements for *María Candelaria* were challenging because her "constitución física no está hecha para las rudezas" (physical

---

74. Dalton, *Mestizo Modernity*, 100–39.

75. Ana M. López, "From Hollywood and Back: Dolores del Río, A Trans(National) Star," *Studies in Latin American Popular Culture* 17 (1998): 5–28; Hershfield, *The Invention of Dolores del Río*, 1–16; Tierney, *Emilio Fernández*, 87.

constitution is not made for roughness).[76] On the other hand, the article crafts a celebratory narrative in which *María Candelaria* constitutes del Río's inhabiting *mexicanidad*.

In this narrative, during del Río's time in Hollywood, "estaba perdida para el pueblo mexicano" (she was lost to the Mexican people).[77] This alienation from her home country is paralleled in her interpretation of the leading role in *Ramona* (dir. Edwin Carewe, 1928) in which she played a half-Indigenous woman just after the United States' incursion into Mexican California. The article presents del Río's Ramona as removed from Mexican authenticity by referring to the character as "auqella otra indita fabricada en Hollywood" (that other little Indian woman fabricated in Hollywood).[78]

The article's narrative turns when it presents del Río's absence from her homeland as the impetus for her love of Indigenous Mexican women. In del Río's words, "'. . . los problemas indios siempre me han interesado; siento gran cariño hacia las inditas de México; me preocupan sus pequeñas grandes tragedias . . . Todo eso he aprendido a apreciar, gracias a los años que estuve ausente'" (Indian problems have always interested me; I feel a great affection for the little Indian women of Mexico; their great little tragedies matter to me . . . I learned to appreciate all of that thanks to the years I was away).[79] As a promotional piece for *María Candelaria*, this article casts del Río's interpretation of the leading role in Fernández's Mexican production as the embodiment of her newfound esteem for Indigenous Mexican women and the inhabiting of her authentic Mexicanness in contrast to her period of alienation in Hollywood.[80] Through this logic, the text elevates the repatriated del Río into "propiamente la intérprete ideal de la india mexicana" (truly the ideal interpreter of the Indigenous Mexican woman). In other words, the article focuses on Hollywood as a categorically un-Mexican environment to collapse the chasmic differences among Mexican women and praise del Río as the quintessential embodiment of Mexican female Indigeneity.

---

76. Martha Elba, "De *Ramona* a *María Candelaria*. Lolita ama a las indias mexicanas. Lolita ya es nuestra," *Cinema Reporter*, February 5, 1944, 8.

77. *Cinema Reporter*, February 5, 1944, 8.

78. *Cinema Reporter*, February 5, 1944, 8.

79. *Cinema Reporter*, February 5, 1944, 8.

80. A similar logic appears to be at work in French critic George Sadoul's assessment of del Río's performance. See López, "From Hollywood and Back," 21.

Maclovia (1948)

Emilio Fernández's 1948 film, *Maclovia*, has received relatively little attention within Mexican film scholarship because it is considered to be repetitive of both his earlier film, *María Candelaria*, and of Carlos Navarro's 1935 film, *Janitzio*.[81] Even a cursory review of *Maclovia*'s plot reveals some redundancies. The film takes place on the island of Janitzio, where the title character (played by María Félix) is the most beautiful Tarascan[82] woman who lives there. Because she is so beautiful, Maclovia's father refuses to allow her to marry her beloved José María (played by Pedro Armendáriz) because of his humble status and even forbids them from seeing one another. In light of this rejection, José María resolves to better himself by attending school. Sara (played by Columba Domínguez) is another Indigenous woman who is in love with José María. She takes advantage of the imposed separation to declare her love to him, but José María rejects her. Dissatisfied with this outcome, Sara tries to use to her advantage the arrival of a sergeant (played by Carlos López Moctezuma) who desires Maclovia. When the sergeant unfairly imprisons José María to try to bed Maclovia, Sara offers to have sex with the officer to negotiate José María's release, but the sergeant also rejects her. Finally, the doubly rebuffed Sara spreads the false rumor that Maclovia has slept with the officer in order to incite the community to put her to death, as is their custom when Tarascan women have sex with outsiders. Instead, military officers intervene to prevent the unjust punishment, and Maclovia and José María escape the island safely.

While *Maclovia* clearly shares many elements with Navarro and Fernandez's earlier films, it also diverges in significant ways.[83] Among these differences is that the film comments on political injustice in more explicitly racial terms[84] and is more heavily invested in the politics of the Revolution that exhorts Indigenous and mestizo men to become participa-

---

81. Emilio García Riera, *Historia documental del cine mexicano*, vol. 4, *1946–1948* (Guadalajara: Universidad de Guadalajara, 1994), 202–4.

82. Though the Purepecha people are the predominant Indigenous group in the region where the film takes place, *Maclovia* does not specify to which linguistic group the community belongs, and instead uses the broader term, Tarascan, that comprises multiple local ethnolinguistic groups.

83. Tierney, *Emilio Fernández*, 96.

84. Tierney, *Emilio Fernández*, 96–97.

tory national subjects. At the same time, the film more intensely defines a moral and aesthetic dichotomy in its representation of diegetic Indigenous womanhood. The key to understanding how the film bolsters the revolutionary message that it applies to men and reinforces the racialized hierarchy rooted in coloniality for the valuing of women lies in the way it uses three categories of characters according to the local racial formation: the white-as-white (the sergeant and the schoolteacher), the white-as-indigenous (Maclovia and José María), and the indigenous-as-indigenous (the other members of the native community who are portrayed as morally and/or ethically deficient).

In *Maclovia*, the ideological condemnation of the prerevolutionary racialized political hierarchy occurs through the presentation of the film's villain, Sargento Genovevo de la Garza, through whiteness-as-whiteness in the Mexican context.[85] Within the plot, de la Garza is the instigator of injustices toward Indigenous peoples. When he first sees the beautiful Maclovia in a local bar, his zeal results in a physical confrontation with her father. As a result, they end up before a local commissioner of Páztcuaro along with most of the Indigenous community. During the hearing, the sergeant claims that the civil authority should side with him because of his rank. Crucially, he also cites his Whiteness (*blancura*) as a factor that should bolster his credibility: "¿Vale más la palabra de una punta de indios muertos de hambre que la mía que soy hombre decente? Soy sargento, mire, y de ojos claros, ¿qué no ve?" (Is the word of a bunch of starving Indians worth more than mine, that of a decent person? I'm a sergeant, look, and with light-colored eyes. Can't you see?). This scene is significant because in it, the contrast between the coloniality of power and the Mexican postrevolutionary national ideology is made clear. In referring to his "light-colored eyes" (the ultimate proof of European heritage within the Mexican racial formation), the sergeant invokes the authority of coloniality according to which his proximity to Europeanness should entitle him to the favor of the law, a position that the film clearly rejects. When the sergeant offers to pay a fine instead of making peace with Maclovia's father and the community, the commissioner gives

---

85. In his comments on the film, García Riera points to the "maldad criolla expresada y representada por los por los ojos claros y piel blanca de López Moctezuma" (criollo wickedness expressed and represented through López Moctezuma's light eyes and white skin). In *Historia documental del cine*, vol. 4: 204.

voice to the postrevolutionary national ideology that the film upholds:[86] "No Señor Sargento, no se trata de dinero. Se trata del respeto que nos merecemos todos los mexicanos" (No Sargeant, this isn't about money. This is about the respect that we Mexicans all deserve). The message of the scene is clear: in the ideal modern Mexican nation under construction (the film's plot takes place in 1914, during the Revolution),[87] no longer will certain Mexicans be privileged for their racial identity, but all will be respected equally as co-citizens. The scene transmits this message on a discursive level through dialogue, and does so visually by presenting male whiteness-as-whiteness that has not been transformed through cultural mestizaje (as, for example, the White male schoolteacher has) as the locus of abuses of power rooted in coloniality in Mexico.

The film further bolsters revolutionary politics in the male sphere through its celebratory representation of José María's entrance into national subjectivity via exposure to Mexican history. In a crucial scene, the schoolteacher delivers a history lecture about José María Morelos,[88] emphasizing both his Indigenous identity and the services he rendered to the nation in hyperbolic fashion, prompting José María to understand his commonality with the hero of Mexican independence:

> Ese indio . . . no fue solamente glorioso por las batallas que peleó, sino porque dio a México su primer congreso y su primera constitución. Fue el primer indígena que se atrevió a desafiar a Europa, y el primero también que sintió el dolor de México . . . Ese indio, ese arriero surgido de una recua de mulas, y que con el andar del tiempo habría de dar su nombre a la ciudad donde nació, y que constituye uno de los más puros arquetipos de México y de América, se llamó José María, como tú, José María Morelos y Pavón.
>
> (That Indian . . . was not only glorious because of the battles

---

86. Tierney, *Emilio Fernández*, 98.

87. Tierney, *Emilio Fernández*, 96, 98.

88. Julia Tuñón contextualizes this moment in the film as evidence of the director's "obsesión por la educación" (obsession with education), which surfaces repeatedly throughout his oeuvre. See "Una escuela en celuloide. El cine de Emilio 'Indio' Fernández o la obsesión por la educación," *Historia Mexicana* 48, no. 2, special issue "Las imágenes en la historia del México porfiriano y posrevolucionario" (October–December 1998): 463–65. See also Báscones Antón, Marta, "La negación de lo indígena en el cine de Emilio Fernándes," *Archivos de la Filmoteca* 40 (2002): 98–100.

he fought, but because he gave Mexico its first congress and its first constitution. He was the first Indian who dared to challenged Europe, and also the first who felt the pain of Mexico . . . That Indian, that mule driver who emerged from the herd, and who with the passing of time would give his name to the city where he was born, and who constitutes one of the purest archetypes of Mexico and of America, was named José María, like you, José María Morelos y Pavón.)

The schoolteacher's praise for Morelos is consistent with the postrevolutionary political and cultural discourse, which sought to afford greater prominence to Indigenous and mestizo peoples within the Mexican republic. The speech demonstrates this affinity by suggesting that if an Indigenous person of the past was capable of participating in the national project, so are the Indigenous people of the present. The clearest way in which the film promotes this idea is through the name of its male protagonist and the technical devices used during the scene, which dramatize José María's coming into national consciousness as a glorious transition. During the schoolteacher's speech, he is presented from a low angle, amplifying his representation as a legitimate source of authority, and his increased use of emphatic gestures bestows greater gravitas to his message. Furthermore, as his gestures and tone grow more animated, triumphant nondiegetic music builds up slowly, culminating at the end. At this precise moment, the teacher interpellates José María by pointing directly at him and indicating that his name is the same as that of Morelos. An eyeline match occurs after he points to José María, emphasizing the exchange between the two and José María's reception of the interpellation in a state of quasi-disbelief. The implication of the scene is clear: Morelos and José María share an Indigenous origin, a name, and also can come to share a love for the Mexican nation. In this way, the film promotes the idea that Indigenous men have important political potential as citizens of the Mexican nation, a position that echoes postrevolutionary cultural discourses and imagery.

In line with the films discussed above, *Maclovia* marks the Indigenous characters who are poised to assume Mexican subjectivity by presenting them visually through whiteness-as-indigeneity. In this case, the white-as-indigenous José María and Maclovia escape from the island, which the film represents in a celebratory tone, signaling their future assimilation.[89]

---

89. Tierney, *Emilio Fernández*, 96.

However, in contrast with the scenario analyzed in *María Candelaria*, in *Maclovia* there *is* a functional modern Mexican state that can step in and rescue these Mexican citizens in the making from both savage Indians and deleterious criollos. The film represents this functional state through the magistrate, the schoolteacher, and the military that shields the couple from lapidation. In this sense, *Maclovia* is fundamentally optimistic with regard to the viability of a mestizo nation-state in that its effective representatives reflect a range of biological and cultural mestizaje.

Beyond signaling the ideal candidacy of Indigenous characters for full citizenship within the Mexican nation, with respect to female characters specifically, *Maclovia* mobilizes whiteness-as-indigeneity to represent various positive characteristics in the protagonist. On-screen, Maclovia's whiteness-as-indigeneity is transmitted through her large, round, light-brown eyes; light skin complexion; and fine facial features, while Sara's indigeneity-as-indigeneity is suggested through her comparatively darker skin color, eye shape and dark brown eye color, dark black hair, thick hair texture, and broader facial features.[90] As we will see, these embodied markers of Whiteness and Indigeneity function according to a racially determined visual logic to create a sharp contrast between the protagonist and Sara, the woman who schemes to separate her from her beloved.

Maclovia clearly establishes a difference in the desirability and physical appeal of Maclovia and Sara. In the film, various characters repeatedly describe Maclovia as being very beautiful. Sara, on the other hand, is marked as being thoroughly undesirable within the diegesis as both José María and the sergeant decline her propositions. When she confesses her love to José María, she explicitly acknowledges the limits of her physical appeal: "Yo no soy bonita José María, pero te quiero como eres" (I am not pretty, José María, but I love you as you are). Later, when she offers herself sexually to de la Garza in exchange for the release of José María, the sergeant's response shows a level of admiration for her commitment to the prisoner but makes it clear that she does not compare physically to the woman he truly desires: "Yo respeto el sentimiento pero no, a mí la que me gusta es la otra, Maclovia . . . ya ve lo que dice el dicho, que a cada quien su gusto lo engorde . . ." (I respect your feelings, but no, the one I like is the other one, Maclovia. Like the saying says: to each his own . . .). Through these rebuffs, the film establishes that Sara is not an equally desirable counterpart to Maclovia, as she experiences rejection from Mexican men across racial and socioeconomic lines. Here the film

---

90. Nutini, *Mexican Aristocracy*.

Revolutionary Politics, Colonized Aesthetics   159

instantiates the dynamics of the coloniality of desire to cement Sara as the diegetically undesirable by presenting her as a Mexican female body that bears the marks of Indigeneity in the local racial formation.

Furthermore, the film's editing reinforces this racialized aesthetic hierarchy by indicating on a visual level which of the two women is the recipient of the desirous male gaze. When the Sergeant first sees Maclovia in a tavern, he devours her with his gaze before attempting to approach her. Two eyeline matches occur, indicating the direction of the Sergeant's insistent gaze toward Maclovia and the pleasure it produces for him as his scowl turns slowly into a grin and his eyes move up and down slowly to admire her (figures 3.12 and 3.13). The film's presentation of Maclovia as the pleasure-producing object of the male gaze firmly establishes her as the desirable woman within the diegesis on a technical level. In contrast, Sara is never visualized through this editing device, which reinforces that the film does not portray her as equally alluring. In this way, the film's technical devices operate to uphold the White Mexican woman as the most desirable female and to locate the spectator within this optical relationship with both women.

In addition to casting the women as aesthetic counterpoints, the film also establishes Sara and Maclovia as *moral* opposites. Maclovia is the

Figure 3.12. De la Garza's gaze toward Maclovia produces pleasure. Screen capture from film.

Figure 3.13. Maclovia is gazed upon by de la Garza and the spectator. Screen capture from film.

innocent victim of Sergeant de la Garza and Sara's malicious intentions through no fault of her own. In addition, she has an intense commitment to chastity by shielding herself continuously from the Sergeant and by refusing to have sexual relations with him to liberate José María from jail. By contrast, Sara uses her sexuality for negotiation and spreads a false rumor in the hope that the Tarascan community will put Maclovia to death. While Sara's is a morally debased character, Maclovia is (in the words of José María) "la más buena y la más pura de todas las mujeres" (the best and purest of all women). This melodrama uses racialized codes put in place through the colonization of subjectivity in that it promotes identification with the benevolent female protagonist and enforces a disassociation with the antagonist by employing whiteness-as-indigeneity to represent the former and indigeneity-as-indigeneity to represent the latter.

Beyond each character's physicality, the film emphasizes the contrast between the two women through mise-en-scène, which places the women on opposing sides of the frame along the vertical or horizontal axis.[91]

---

91. I thank Samuel Cruz for calling my attention to this aspect of the film.

This visual juxtaposition is used precisely in the moments when Sara confronts Maclovia aggressively regarding their shared affection for José María and when Maclovia is in a dejected state, therefore emphasizing Sara's cruelty and Maclovia's victimhood. In the first example, Sara warns Maclovia to stay away from José María. Their visual juxtaposition on opposite sides of the frame visually translates the way in which the film's plot locates them as aesthetic and moral opposites. Later on, after having been propositioned by de la Garza, Maclovia runs to a nearby chapel to pray and weep, where Sara confronts her again. In this scene, the positioning of Sara in the upper right-hand corner highlights the way in which she preys on Maclovia's suffering as she ridicules her prayers and sobs, affirming that she is, in fact, the one who truly loves José María. Conversely, the positioning of Maclovia in the bottom left corner emphasizes her suffering, amplified by Sara's callousness. Through the asymmetrical arrangement of the women's bodies at this moment, the film visibly presents them as occupying antithetical positions aesthetically and morally.

Figure 3.14. Maclovia (María Félix) and Sara (Columba Domínguez) occupying opposite sides of the frame in *Maclovia* (1948). Screen capture from film.

Figure 3.15. Maclovia (María Félix) and Sara (Columba Domínguez) in asymmetrical positions of the frame in *Maclovia* (1948). Screen capture from film.

As in the case of Dolores del Río's interpretation of María Candelaria, María Félix's star text is a significant extradiegetic factor that contributes to the desirability of the female protagonist because Félix's star text presented her as the embodiment of Mexican beauty standards of her day.[92] There is, therefore, a conflation of María Félix's association with feminine Mexican beauty in, for example, the advertisements for the beauty products she endorsed[93] and the way in which the film casts her as a woman of great beauty. Both María Félix and Dolores del Río had star texts that firmly established their star personas as far removed from the humble *inditas* they portray in Fernández's films.[94]

By contrast, Columba Domínguez never garnered comparable accolades with those of María Félix in relation to her physical appearance,

---

92. Julia Tuñón, *Los rostros de un mito. Personajes femeninos en las películas de Emilio Indio Fernández* (Mexico City: CONACULTA, 2003), 132; Dever, *Celluloid Nationalism*, 52–58.

93. Dever, *Celluloid Nationalism*, 52–58.

94. Elba "De *Ramona*," 8–10; Hershfield, *The Invention of Dolores del Río*, 1–16; Dever, *Celluloid Nationalism*, 52–58; Tierney, *Emilio Fernández*, 87.

Figure 3.16. Columba Domínguez as the scorned Indigenous antagonist, Sara, in *Maclovia* (1948). Photo courtesy of Mil Nubes-Foto (Roberto Fiesco). All rights reserved.

nor was she featured as an aspirational model of Mexican beauty or consumption in advertisements. While press coverage of María Félix and Dolores del Río depicted them as categorically beautiful women, mentions of Columba Domínguez's appearance frequently contained qualifiers to her physical appeal that functioned as veiled racial references (to signal her lack of *blancura*). In film magazines of the Golden Age, Domínguez's appearance was described as "mexicanísima"[95] (very Mexican), as having "rasgos autóctonos" (Indigenous features),[96] and as possessing a "belleza netamente mexicana" (distinctly Mexican beauty).[97] In these ways, the print culture of the period signaled the status of Columba Domínguez's body as one that was not-quite-White according to local standards.

Furthermore, even though Domínguez won the Ariel for her role in *Maclovia*, beating out María Félix, who was nominated for the same film, this one award did not remotely position the two actresses on equal

---

95. *Cinema Reporter*, March 9, 1955, 17; *Cinema Reporter*, August 12, 1959, 32.
96. *Cinema Reporter*, August 1, 1956, 18–19.
97. *Cinema Reporter*, October 15, 1958, 12.

footing, as Félix went on to become "la estrella más importante surgida en América Latina y el principal mito creado por el cine mexicano" (the most important star to emerge from Latin America and the primary myth created by Mexican cinema).[98] Félix's loss was most likely related to the fact that in *Maclovia* she was cast against type as a humble and submissive woman while her star text was that of a strong-willed woman who dominates men.[99] In total, Félix won five Arieles during the Golden Age—a testament to her dominant status within the Mexican industry and star power, rivaled only by Dolores del Río (who also won five Arieles in the period). Furthermore, I suspect that Domínguez's one win was granted to her for *Maclovia* because in playing the indigenous-as-indigenous villain and scorned woman, Domínguez's performance—while skillful—also supported race- and gender-based biases.[100]

It is also worth noting that even in the melodramatic films directed by Emilio Fernández in which Columba Domínguez (to whom he was married from 1947 to 1952) did star, she did not function as the universal object of desire as Dolores del Río did in *María Candelaria* or María Félix did in *Maclovia*. For example, in *Pueblerina* (1949),[101] the male protagonist, Aurelio, returns to his hometown after having served a prison sentence for shooting a man, Rómulo, in retribution for kidnapping and raping his girlfriend, Paloma (played by Domínguez). However, rather than placing Paloma at the center of the men's rivalry and dramatizing it (as occurs in *María Candelaria* and *Maclovia*), the point of contention between the two men is not Paloma, but rather Aurelio's right to be in his native town (a point that is made evident through the personification of the hometown through a maternal voice-over that calls out to Aurelio tenderly throughout the film). When the spectator encounters Paloma, far from being presented

---

98. Paulo Antonio Paranaguá, "Mito," in *Tradición y modernidad en el cine de América Latina* (Madrid: Fondo de Cultura Económica de España, 2003), 107; Dever, *Celluloid Nationalism*, 60.

99. Paranaguá, "Mito."

100. In this sense, the institutional recognition of Domínguez's performance in *Maclovia* might be read alongside those of other women of color in the Americas, such as Hattie McDaniel and Rita Moreno, who won Oscars for excellent performances in roles that, nonetheless, reinscribed the racialized and gendered stereotypes of the "mammy" and fiery Latina, respectively.

101. I thank Ernesto Acevedo-Muñoz for bringing Columba Domínguez's leading roles to my attention.

as an imposing beauty and a valuable conquest for multiple men, she is a dejected recluse. Whereas in *Maclovia* the title character is repeatedly referred to as a great beauty, in *Pueblerina*, Paloma is compared to a "cabra bizca" (cross-eyed goat), and Rómulo and his brother conclude that she is worth less than a mare. Furthermore, although the raping of Paloma in the past does suggest that Rómulo may have desired her, the film does not focus on the men's desire for her as a function of her beauty, nor do the film's technical devices fetishize her as the object of the male gaze. Instead, Paloma is presented as a valuable woman for Aurelio to marry because of the suffering she has undergone and her enduring goodness despite her tribulations.

In another Fernández film in which Columba Domínguez starred, *La malquerida* (1949), she plays Acacia, the daughter of Raimunda (played by Dolores del Río) and stepdaughter to Esteban (played by Pedro Armendáriz). In this film, she *is* the object of desire for Esteban; however, she becomes her mother's rival for the love of her stepfather and is portrayed as the film's wicked antagonist in the melodramatic plot. Unlike in *María Candelaria* and *Maclovia*, in which the narrative and stylistic devices of the film encourage the alignment of the spectator with the admiration for the female characters presented as beautiful and good through Whiteness, in *La malquerida* the opposite occurs because the attraction between stepfather and stepdaughter is conveyed as immoral and as the source of torture for the melodramatic film's victim, Raimunda. In this way, *La malquerida* presents Acacia as desirable but discourages the spectator from aligning with the desire for the character. Finally, in Fernández's *Un día de vida*, the male characters do repeat that Domínguez's character, Belén Martí, is "muy guapa" (very beautiful) throughout the film. However, in this film, Domínguez is not playing a Mexican woman, but a Cuban one, a narrative caveat that provides an exoticizing justification for her body's distance from Mexican Whiteness (*blancura*). Therefore, although Columba Domínguez was occasionally a leading lady in Fernández's melodramas, her not-quite-White body within the Mexican racial formation was not used to interpret Mexican characters who were upheld as universally desirable, beautiful, and good and with whom spectators were encouraged to identify, as did occur with her Whiter and more successful counterparts, del Río and Félix.

The inability (or refusal) to represent indigeneity-as-indigeneity as beautiful or desirable in *María Candelaria* and *Maclovia*, as well as in earlier Indigenous-themed films analyzed here such as *El indio* and *La india bonita*, betrays this corpus' investment in coloniality by measuring female beauty in terms of its approximation to Whiteness. In light of Carlos Monsiváis and Jesús Martín-Barbero's observations about the role of Mexican Golden Age cinema in educating Mexicans on how to be Mexican,[102] these narrative films about Indigeneity instructed the public to assess the female Mexican body through a colonial lens, even when these same films articulated a break with the multifaceted injustices of internal colonialism by bolstering revolutionary discourses. In this way, filmic *indigenista* melodramas from the postrevolutionary twentieth century carried with them clearly gendered vestiges of coloniality.

Looking Beyond Industrial Representation: *Janitzio* (1935) and "La potranca" (*Raíces*, 1955) as Counterexamples

In contrast with the industrial Mexican films discussed above in which whiteness-as-indigeneity idealizes the Indigenous Mexican characters whose lives justify the need for a revolutionary check on criollo power, two important indigenista films from the period made outside Mexican cinema's industrial structure take an alternative approach to treating similar themes: Carlos Navarro's *Janitzio* (1935) and the segment titled "La potranca" in Benito Alazraki's 1955 film, *Raíces*. Even though twenty years separate the two films, their avoidance of studio-era conventions results in parallel approaches to representing White male abuse of power among Indigenous Mexicans. I illustrate how specific aspects of these films, including their lack of adherence to the same melodramatic norms, help explain why they use a different strategy for representing diegetically Indigenous women who elicit male desire.

---

102. Jesús Martín-Barbero, *Communication, Culture and Hegemony: From the Media to Mediations*, trans. Elizabeth Fox and Robert A. White (London: Sage Publications, 1993), 165–68; and Carlos Monsiváis, "Se sufre pero se aprende," in *A través del espejo: el cine mexicano y su público*, ed. Carlos Monsiváis and Carlos Bonfil (Mexico City: Instituto Mexicano de Cinematografía, 1994), 99–224. See also Silvia Oroz, *Melodrama: O cinema de lágrimas da América Latina* (Rio de Janeiro: FUNARTE, 1999), 28; Noble, *Mexican National Cinema*, 70–79; and Elena Lahr-Vivaz, *Mexican Melodrama: Film and Nation from the Golden Age to the New Wave* (Tucson: University of Arizona Press, 2016), 16–17.

Janitzio is widely recognized as one of the most significant indigenista films for two reasons.[103] First, it is among the first Mexican films to articulate the injustices faced by the Indigenous communities—a stance universally attributed to *cardenismo*. Second, *Janitzio* constitutes an important link in the often-cited visual genealogy between the influence of Sergei Eisenstein in Mexico and the Indigenous-themed Fernández-Figueroa films. *Janitzio* takes place among the Tarascan people on the island of Janitzio, where the film's protagonist, Sirahuén[104] (played by Emilio Fernández), enjoys a budding romance with his beloved, Eréndira (María Teresa Orozco). Their union provokes the jealousy of another woman who is in love with Sirahuén, Tacha. When a new representative of the company that buys fish from the local fishermen, Manuel Moreno, arrives on the island from Mexico City, he oppresses the fishermen by arbitrarily reducing the price of their fish, eventually causing a violent confrontation between himself and Sirahuén, which lands the latter in jail. To liberate Sirahuén from prison, Eréndira agrees to have sexual relations with Manuel, knowing that the perceived transgression is punishable by death in her community. Although Sirahuén attempts to shield Eréndira from the enforcement of their people's law, Tacha alerts the community to Eréndira's transgression, prompting them to stone her to death. Upon Eréndira's death, Sirahuén drowns himself in Lake Pátzcuaro with her lifeless body.

The film's approach to conveying the oppression of the Indigenous community, like other indigenista films that foreground social, economic, and/or political injustice, is to present the white-as-white male as a predatory person who is removed from Indigeneity. As in *La india bonita*, *Janitzio* emphasizes the white-as-white male antagonist's ties to the city

---

103. See de la Vega Alfaro, "Origins, Development and Crisis"; Podalsky, "Patterns of the Primitive: Sergei Eisenstein's ¡Qué Viva México!," in *Mediating Two Worlds: Cinematic Encounters in the Americas*, ed. John King, Ana M. López, and Manuel Alvarado (London: British Film Institute, 1993), 25–39; Tierney, *Emilio Fernández*, 77–80; Joanne Hershfield, "Race and Ethnicity in the Classical Cinema," in *Mexico's Cinema: A Century of Film and Filmmakers*, ed. Joanne Hershfield and David Maciel (Wilmington, DE: Scholarly Resources, 1999), 81–100; Carl J. Mora, *Mexican Cinema: Reflections of a Society* (Berkeley: University of California Press, 1989), 40–42; 58–69; Aurelio de los Reyes, *El Nacimiento De Que Viva México!* (Mexico City: Universidad Nacional Autónoma de México, Instituto de Investigaciones Estéticas, 2006).

104. Though in several scholarly sources that discuss this film the character's name appears written as "Zirahuén," in the film's credits the name appears as "Sirahuén."

and disdain for rural areas. Manuel's foreignness to the Mexican camposcape surfaces when he first approaches the island and meets with Don Pablo, a local authority. In this exchange, Manuel explicitly regrets that his company has assigned him to the location in the following negative terms: "ha sido mi mala suerte que me hayan aventado hasta por acá" (it's bad luck for me that they flung me all the way out here). Beyond suggesting his lack of familiarity, Manuel's association with the city, as in *La india bonita*, carries with it a clear association with immorality. The connection between the city and wantonness occurs when Manuel suggests that he will immediately find an Indigenous woman to alleviate his loneliness. His choice of words here, "una prietita" (a little darkie), confirms his White self-image. To this, Don Pablo responds by conveying the behavior that is expected of Manuel during his stay, citing the visitor's urban provenance as a factor that may impede his proper conduct: "Hay una palabra que muy pocos hombres de la ciudad recuerdan. Se llama moralidad" (There is a word that very few men from the city remember. It is called morality). By presenting Manuel as being hostile to the Indigenous environment, morally suspect from the outset, as well as ignorant and dismissive of local customs, *Janitzio* establishes the white-as-white male as the violator of Indigenous Mexico.[105]

The most poignant way in which *Janitzio* participates in revolutionary politics is by illustrating the white-as-white male's abuse of power and the damage it causes to the Indigenous community. Once Manuel assumes his duties, he drops the price of fish arbitrarily, putting the fishermen's livelihoods at stake. When one of them complains, Manuel uses excessive force (like Gonzalo in *El indio*) by whipping him vigorously and later does the same to Sirahuén when he steps in to defend his fellow fisherman. Furthermore, Manuel uses his status to have Sirahuén incarcerated despite the fact that he was not the instigator of the confrontation. Finally, Manuel manipulates Eréndira into having sexual relations with him, which eventually causes her death. By highlighting the unchecked power of the white-as-white male as the cause of misery and death among the Indigenous community, the film constitutes a denunciation of social and political injustice in racially inflected terms.

While *Janitzio* was clearly the inspiration for both *María Candelaria* and *Maclovia*, as all three films follow similar stories, *Janitzio* employs

---

105. See also the analyses of *La noche de los mayas* and *Deseada* in chapter 4.

melodramatic conventions differently, and visually favors a kind of aestheticized social realism that also characterizes Emilio Gómez Muriel and Fred Zinnemann's 1936 film, *Redes*. Unlike in the later Fernández-Figueroa films, *Janitzio* does not employ whiteness-as-indigeneity to aesthetically or narratively privilege the leading Indigenous female character in the diegesis over the others. This is the case for several reasons. First, unlike the other films, Eréndira is not the film's true protagonist. Rather than focusing on the dilemma of whether or not to acquiesce to Manuel's sexual demands, in narrative terms, the film privileges Sirahuén's decision of what to do with Eréndira once the transgression has taken place, making *him* the film's emotional center and primary point of identification.[106]

Additionally, the film does not comment in any explicit way on Eréndira's appearance as being exceptional or particularly beautiful (as occurs in *María Candelaria* and *Maclovia*). While she is desired by Manuel and Sirahuén, Manuel is not particularly out to conquer *her* (in the way that Sergeant de la Garza is fixated on Maclovia or that the artist is taken with María Candelaria). Manuel simply seeks sexual gratification from any Indigenous woman he can manage to get it from, a point that is made clear when he gazes desirously at another woman in their community in Don Pablo's office and when he expresses indifference toward Eréndira. This disregard is evident, for example, when, prior to running off with Sirahuén's girlfriend for a week, he tells his assistant that he will return to Mexico City as soon as he is done with her.[107] Later, after Manuel has exploited Eréndira sexually, he conveys his indifference to Sirahuén, saying flatly, "para mí no significa nada" (for me, she means nothing). Therefore, while the film demonstrates that Eréndira receives attention from both men, she is not upheld as an object of wonder, nor is she singled out as particularly beautiful or appealing among other women as occurs with the title characters in *María Candelaria* and *Maclovia*.

Furthermore, *Janitzio* does not create moral distinctions among women, as occurs in the Fernández-Figueroa films. While María Candelaria and Maclovia are always virginal and good, and this difference is portrayed through their somatic Whiteness in comparison with other

---

106. In locating the film's melodramatic center in the male mestizo body of Emilio "El Indio" Fernández, Janitzio does constitute a modest attempt to counter the colonization of subjectivity.

107. "Tan pronto como acabe con ella, renuncio y me voy a México" (As soon as I am done with her, I will quit and go to Mexico City).

scheming, diegetically Indigenous women, *Janitzio* does not idealize Eréndira on moral grounds because she uses her sexuality to negotiate Sirahuén's release (which is ethically problematic within the diegesis). Tacha, Eréndira's rival for Sirahuén's love, is responsible for spreading the news of Eréndira's transgression; therefore, both are presented as being morally imperfect. This moral equivalency corresponds to the fact that neither is privileged over the other aesthetically through a Whiter on-screen presence, costume, or makeup or through filmic devices (such as lighting, editing, or mise-en-scène). Unlike the industrial films from the 1930s discussed in this chapter, *El indio* and *La india bonita*, Eréndira's appearance in *Janitzio* is not curated as a glamorous "deco body" or as white-as-indigenous for the screen, meaning that the studio conventions for displaying female attractiveness, such as manicured eyebrows, full lashes, and glamorous makeup, are absent; nor is she presented through sustained and frequent close-ups that showcase her anguish and display her face, as occurs in those melodramas. Furthermore, *Janitzio* does not use stardom as a tool for conveying Indigenous womanhood. The woman who plays the leading female role, María Teresa Orozco, has no substantial star text and was not distinguished from the rest of the film's actors in the opening or closing credits (as occurred with leading ladies in the Fernández-Figueroa films). Therefore, no efforts were made to present her on- or off-screen as a White Mexican woman, and instead she is simply presented in a matter-of-fact fashion, neither fetishizing her appearance as admirable or commenting negatively on it. In this way, *Janitzio* presents Eréndira and Tacha as moral and aesthetic equivalents without appealing to Whiteness to convey superiority in terms of character or appearance.

Benito Alazraki's directorial debut, *Raíces*, can also be understood as a cultural artifact that is entirely ensconced within the cultural politics of the postrevolutionary period. The film's introductory sequence establishes this fact through voice-over that articulates the narrative of mestizaje as the essence of Mexico, and highlights that Indigenous people are "verdaderamente las raíces del México que germina" (truly the roots of the Mexico that grows). More specifically, the film's four segments focus on the marginality, suffering, and injustice endured by Indigenous populations in Mexico. In this way, *Raíces* is part of the genealogy of politically oriented indigenista films.

In the film's final segment, "La potranca," a European archaeologist, Eric, becomes obsessed with Xanath, a local Indigenous girl whose family is assisting him and his wife during their stay in southern Mexico. Eric chases Xanath desperately day after day hoping to rape her but does not succeed. In a last attempt to sexually impose himself on Xanath, Eric offers to buy her from her father, Teódalo, but is intimidated by his response, which prompts Eric and his wife's departure from the area.

"La potranca" explicitly engages with and criticizes the dynamics of the coloniality of power according to which Whiter social actors are inherently more powerful and more valuable. This occurs when Eric attempts to entice Teódalo to sell Xanath using a racist logic according to which her father would only stand to gain from Whitening his family, "En la costa algunos indios regalan a sus hijas a los hombres blancos como yo para mejorar su raza . . . ganarás un nieto mestizo que valdrá mucho más que este dinero; nieto, hijo de blanco, que será mucho más inteligente que tú" (Along the coast some Indians give their daughters away to White men like me in order to improve their race . . . you will gain a mestizo grandchild who will be worth much more than this money; a grandchild, the child of a White man, who will be much smarter than you). Eric's proposal is in line with the logic of the coloniality of power because it equates Whitening with improvement and superior intelligence. The very notion of purchasing Xanath is predicated on the idea that Indigenous people are inferior to White people and can be bought and sold like cattle. The film makes this point explicit when Eric refers to Xanath as an "animalito" (little animal) that he wants to buy. Furthermore, Eric's attempt to "catch" Xanath throughout the segment, which receives a significant amount of screen time, also supports the fact that he relates to her as if she were an animal and not human.

The film challenges Eric's appeal to the coloniality of power through Teódalo's response, which initially appears to coincide with the idea that Whiteness is superior, but ultimately subverts the notion of Indigenous inferiority: "Tienes razón. Las cruzas son buenas y me conviene mejorar mi raza . . . ¡Te doy el doble por tu mujer!" (You are right. Cross-breeds are good and it's in my interest to improve my race . . . I'll give you double for your wife!). The film's rejection of the coloniality of power is poignant because initially Teódalo repeats and appears to have internalized the widely circulated notion that mestizaje was an improvement of Indigeneity. He then directly contradicts this ideological position by offering to purchase the archeologist's wife. This reversal of the archaeologist's initial offer establishes parallels between Xanath and Eric's wife as purchasable commodities and between Teódalo and Eric as both consumers and sexual agents, suggesting that neither group is superior or inferior to the other.

Figure 3.17. In *Raíces* (1955), Teodalo stands by his daughter, Xanath. Photo courtesy of Mil Nubes-Foto (Roberto Fiesco). All rights reserved.

By juxtaposing an apparent acceptance of racist logic with its outright rejection, Teódalo's response constitutes both an awareness of the way in which Whiteness offers social and economic advantages and an assertion of equality and personal dignity that rejects the dominant racist ideology.

While "La potranca" uses whiteness-as-whiteness to denounce the behavior of White men toward Indigenous people, it does not use whiteness-as-indigeneity to represent virtuous and attractive Indigenous femininity. This is the case for two central reasons. The first is that *Raíces* explicitly aims to distinguish itself from other cinematic renderings of Indigeneity. In its introductory sequence, prior to any of the film's four segments, an expository text asserts the various measures that have been taken to offer a faithful portrayal of Indigenous Mexico: "Los interiores y exteriores de esta película son auténticos. Ninguna escena ha sido filmada en estudios cinematográficos. Los actores no son profesionales, son parte del pueblo mexicano" (The interiors and exteriors of this film are authentic. No scene has been filmed in film studios. The actors are not professionals, they are part of the Mexican people). I believe that these disclaimers constitute an attempt to differentiate *Raíces* from the well-known, Indigenous-themed

Figure 3.18. Close-up of Alicia del Lagos as Xanath in "La potranca" (*Raíces*, 1954). Photo courtesy of Mil Nubes-Foto (Roberto Fiesco). All rights reserved.

Fernández-Figueroa melodramas, among others. Because *Raíces*'s strategy for conveying authenticity depended on rejecting the use of stars, Alicia del Lago, who did not have a robust star text that established her as a glamorous White Mexican actress, was cast in the role of Xanath.

Regarding the segment's textual aspects, Xanath's on-screen presence is not crafted as whiteness-as-indigeneity because the film's aesthetic language is that of social realism and because the film is not a melodrama. Xanath's on-screen presence is conveyed as an instance of indigeneity-as-indigeneity in the context of the local racial formation through the rich tone of her complexion, simple hairstyles, and almost complete lack of verbal articulation in any language. While her dilemma is the central concern of the segment's narrative, it is not presented through the externalization of extreme emotional states visualized in close-ups, as occurs in the Fernández-Figueroa melodramas.[108] Instead of privileging the protagonist visually and verbally to incite the spectator's identification with her in this

---

108. Tierney, *Emilio Fernández*, 91–93.

way, the film relies on the spectator's condemnation of the archaeologist's unsolicited and obsessive behavior to suggest Xanath's vulnerability.

The second reason why "La potranca" does not use Whiteness for the representation of female Indigeneity is that, although it clearly illustrates that the White archaeologist desires Xanath, the film casts the archaeologist's desire as categorically morbid and works to disassociate the spectator from his perspective. Throughout the segment, the film clearly portrays Xanath as being closer to childhood than to womanhood: the archaeologist's wife brushes her hair as if she were a surrogate daughter; Xanath jumps and climbs up trees nimbly; quick-paced nondiegetic music plays as she repeatedly outpaces the archaeologist; and, finally, the very name of the segment, "La potranca," clearly associates her with a filly, or mare, under the age of four (see figure 3.19). Additionally, the fact that the archaeologist is nearing old age and that Xanath has an adolescent Indigenous male suitor points to the inappropriateness of Eric's repeated and even violent advances. Furthermore, the scenes in which he chases after Xanath portray the pursuit in a negative light. As Eric

Figure 3.19. "La potranca" associates the young Xanath with a filly, or mare, under the age of four. Photo courtesy of Mil Nubes-Foto (Roberto Fiesco). All rights reserved.

chases Xanath up ancient monuments, potentially putting both of them in danger, intense nondiegetic music presents the event as suspenseful and fear inducing, while the frenetic movement of Xanath and Eric in and out of the frame conveys Eric's desire as a threatening force. While Fernández's films seek to make the spectator complicit in desiring the diegetically Indigenous woman as beautiful (through the gazes of both villains and heroes), *Raíces* highlights the pure beauty of the Indigenous girl (through close-ups featuring her face), but at the same time the film denounces the archaeologist's inappropriate sexualization of the Indigenous girl as a degenerate tendency. Because of *Raíces*'s claims to authenticity, its social realist aesthetic, and its denunciation of the eroticization of Indigenous girlhood, whiteness-as-indigeneity is not a device used to represent Xanath.

Conclusion

This chapter has focused on films that qualify as indigenista in the sense that they denounce social, political, and/or economic abuses endured by the Indigenous people of Mexico on some level. These films coincide with a general postrevolutionary political and cultural discourse that articulated a need to alter the preexisting social and political racialized hierarchy and its vestiges. While the Indigenous-themed films of the early and high Golden Age (*La india bonita, El indio, María Candelaria,* and *Maclovia*) denounce racialized power structures, their approach to visualizing race does not align with their discursive celebration of Indigeneity. In all of these films, whiteness-as-indigeneity is the visual device used to distinguish the primary Indigenous couple that represents national authenticity and/or ideal Mexican proto-citizenship. Furthermore, there is a significant gendered dimension in how these films deploy Whiteness. On the one hand, these melodramas use whiteness-as-whiteness to denounce White males who (wittingly or unwittingly) exercise the coloniality of power. On the other hand, these films appeal to the colonization of subjectivity and desire, employing whiteness-as-indigeneity to solicit compassion for virtuous, diegetically Indigenous women and corroborate their diegetic attractiveness according to a Eurocentric standard. In sum, these films, whose discourses bolster Indigenous rights and whose visual strategies marginalize Indigenous bodies, are the limit-case of an industry in which the nexus of melodramatic centrality and diegetic desirability has required Whiteness.[109]

This analysis has also taken into consideration as counterexamples significant indigenista films that do not feature whiteness-as-indigeneity because they are not squarely located within this nexus or the industrial filmmaking system. In *Janitzio* and *Raíces*, White males who carry out abuses of power are also conveyed through whiteness-as-whiteness; however, whiteness-as-indigeneity is not used to represent the films' primary Indigenous female characters. In *Janitzio*, the main Indigenous woman is not the central point of identification and is not differentiated aesthetically or morally from other Indigenous women in the film, while in "La potranca," the film works to dissociate the spectator from desire toward the young Indigenous female, which it frames as highly inappropriate and threatening. As indigenista artifacts, these two films are inevitably marked by limitations because by definition, indigenista works are not made by Indigenous people themselves. However, the value of *Janitzio* and "La potranca," within the context of this analysis and within the larger view of indigenista films in Mexico, is that they constitute rare attempts to visualize Indigenous womanhood on-screen that are not rooted in the supposed superiority of the White Mexican female body.

---

109. For historian Natasha Varner, what she calls "cine folkórico" is fundamentally a project of erasing Indigenous bodies. In *La Raza Cosmética*, 13, 97.

4

Reframing *Mestizaje*

White Mayans, Indigenous Spirituality, and Cenote Suicides

As the introduction to this book outlines, the national narrative of *mestizaje* became the privileged construct of Mexican identity in the twentieth century and the basis of the country's "fictive ethnicity."[1] José Vasconcelos's *La raza cósmica* (1925) is representative of a celebratory postrevolutionary understanding of racial mixture in the country. Animated by an antiimperialist perspective of the United States, the text portrays mestizaje during and after Spanish colonialism in a positive light in contrast with English colonists' rejection of intermarriage with Native Americans and Blacks. For Vasconcelos, the Iberian project's superiority lay in ". . . esa abundancia de amor que permitió a los españoles crear una raza nueva con el indio y con el negro; prodigando la estirpe blanca a través del soldado . . ." (that abundance of love that allowed the Spaniard to create a new race with the Indian and the Black, profusely spreading white ancestry

---

1. Etienne Balibar, "The Nation Form: History and Ideology," in *Race Critical Theories: Text and Context*, ed. Philomena Essed Goldberg and David Theo (Malden, MA: Blackwell Publishers, 2002), 223–24; and Joshua Lund, *The Mestizo State: Reading Race in Modern Mexico* (Minneapolis: University of Minnesota Press, 2012).

through the soldier).² Vasconcelos's tendency to euphemistically elide the violence that accompanied miscegenation in the context of conquest and colonialism did not endure in Mexican thought and representation; however, the aura of mestizaje that he helped to create has, both within the national territory and in Greater Mexico.³

Another central contributor to the mestizaje narrative, Octavio Paz's *Labyrinth of Solitude*, does discuss the Mexican origin story of Cortés and La Malinche as having negative implications for the Indigenous woman and the world she represents; however, the author nonetheless recognizes the temporary union as the generative source of the Mexican people.⁴ Similarly to Paz's now canonical writing on *mexicanidad*, other cultural artifacts of the Mexican mid-twentieth century manifest a degree of ambivalence regarding the conquest-era conditions in which mestizaje unfolded while also commemorating that episode as the nation's fateful point of origin. Such artifacts include José Clemente Orozco's 1926 fresco, *Hernán Cortés and "La Malinche"* and Rufino Tamayo's 1952 oil painting, *Nacimiento de nuestra nacionalidad*.⁵ In short, whether overtly or ambivalently celebratory, defining cultural figures of the Mexican twentieth century located the heterosexual union of the Indigenous woman and the Iberian conquistador as the momentous and generative beginning of the Mexican nation.

The films I address in this chapter, *La noche de los mayas* (dir. Chano Urueta, 1939) and *Deseada* (dir. Roberto Gavaldón, 1951), reproduce the premises of the national origin story of mestizaje through their focus on the encounter between a foreign man and an Indigenous woman who experience mutual attraction.⁶ However, in these films, the intrusion of the

---

2. José Vasconcelos, *The Cosmic Race/La raza cósmica: A Bilingual Edition*, trans. Didier T. Jaén (Baltimore: Johns Hopkins University Press, 1979), 17, 57.

3. Federico Navarrete Linares, *México racista: Una denuncia* (Mexico City: Grijalbo, 2016); Gloria Anzaldúa, *Borderlands/La Frontera: The New Mestiza* (San Francisco: aunt lute books, 1987).

4. Octavio Paz, *El laberinto de la soledad* (Madrid: Ediciones Cátedra, 2016), 210–35.

5. Mary K. Coffey, *How a Revolutionary Art Became Official Culture: Murals, Museums, and the Mexican State* (Durham, NC: Duke University Press, 2012), 7–8, 210–35.

6. Though, as Lienhard and Tierney observe, *La noche de los mayas* does have parallels with earlier indigenista films, including *María Candelaria*, I propose that a comparison with *Deseada* is especially apt because both films explore the Indigenous woman's romantic and sexual desire for the Hispanic man, as opposed to a scenario in which the man unilaterally imposes himself on the Indigenous woman through force or

man into Indigenous space and the heterosexual, interracial unions that result are unproductive sources of disruption, suffering, and even death. Furthermore, the use of the melodramatic mode to represent the unhappy outcomes of cross-racial romantic unions in these films underscores that these relationships constitute a tragic circumstance. In this way, *La noche de los mayas* and *Deseada* offer a counterpoint to the commemorative aura that surrounded mestizaje as a productive development in the nation's cultural discourse—as represented, for example, in films such as *Chilam Balam* (discussed in chapter 1). Instead, these two films take up the scenario of cross-racial heterosexual desire as a melodramatic framework in which resolution does not lie in a synthesis with Hispanicity, but instead in consigning oneself entirely to Indigenous values and beliefs.

Although the films distance spectators from an idealized narrative of Mexican mestizaje, they are still very much engaged in *indigenismo-mestizaje* as a cultural project through the explicit and exalting display of a re-created Indigeneity. More unique to *La noche de los mayas* and *Deseada* is the fact that Indigenous beliefs are the principles that explain how and why events unfold without which the spectator cannot follow the melodramatic narratives. In discussing how the films represent Indigenous spiritual beliefs, I am not suggesting that these representations are in any way based on the actual beliefs and practices of Indigenous peoples. Rather, as *indigenista* cultural artifacts, these films transmit non-native constructs of Indigenous religiosity and spiritual beliefs. Still, these films' foregrounding of fictionalized native spirituality as a part of their veneration of Indigeneity is noteworthy given the historical ambivalence regarding Indigenous religious beliefs in Mexico, which persisted into the twentieth century.

While the censuring of native spiritual traditions originates in the religious pretext for the Spanish conquest as a project of evangelization, over time the objections to native beliefs shifted along with subsequent prevailing projects of modernity. In the postrevolutionary context, Indigenous religions presented complications for prominent *indigenistas* who negotiated the celebration of native cultures for nationalist purposes with their modernizing objectives. On the one hand, pre-Columbian religious

---

coercion (as occurs in all of the films discussed in chapter 3). See Martin Lienhard, "La noche de los mayas," *Journal of Latin American Cultural Studies* 13, no. 1 (2004): 35–96; Dolores Tierney, *Emilio Fernández: Pictures in the Margins* (Manchester: Manchester University Press, 2012), 80.

beliefs, practices, and deities were the subject of celebratory pictorial representation, as in Diego Rivera's murals *La leyenda de Quetzalcoatl* (1929), *La civilización Zapoteca* (1942), *La gran Tenochtitlán* (1945), *La civilización Tarasca* (1950), *La civilización Totonaca* (1950), and *La civilización Huasteca y el cultivo del maíz* (1950), all of which are located in the Palacio Nacional. On the other hand, José Vasconcelos, who commissioned the murals, thought some native beliefs were unfortunate superstitions both in the pre-Columbian context and in their twentieth-century syncretized manifestation.[7] True to his Hispanist inclinations, Vasconcelos demonstrated a clear preference for the Catholic tradition.[8]

Echoing some of his reservations, Manuel Gamio also demonstrated a critical view of Indigenous spiritual beliefs. For him, colonization had deprived the Indians of their originally rich mythology, faith, and gods, and the botched attempt at Christian conversion left them with a series of ridiculous superstitions.[9] In particular, native beliefs in the twentieth century were problematic for Gamio when they conflicted with the aims of progress in the areas of science and technology.[10] As Paloma Martínez-Cruz has noted, by the middle of the century, indigenistas perceived traditional medicine rooted in Indigenous spiritual beliefs as a symptom of the nation's backwardness, and extending health services to rural areas became a major focus of the Instituto Nacional Indigenista in the mid-1940s.[11] In short, while indigenistas could largely agree that native religions in the distant past were indicative of the greatness of Mexico's Indigenous civilizations, therefore bolstering the value of the modern mestizo nation, contemporary native beliefs were problematic for the nation's aspirations of modernity and homogeneity.

In light of the ambivalence surrounding Indigenous spiritual beliefs in the twentieth century, as indigenista cultural artifacts, *La noche de los mayas* and *Deseada* put forth an unusual proposal to the Mexican viewer. Because in the films native beliefs structure the melodramatic narratives,

---

7. José Vasconcelos, *Indología: una interpretación de la cultura ibero-americana* (Barcelona: Agencia mundial de librería, 1920), 119.

8. Vasconcelos, *Indología*, 119.

9. Manuel Gamio, *Forjando patria* (Mexico City: Editorial Porrúa, S.A., 1960), 90.

10. Luis Villoro, *Los grandes momentos del indigenismo en México* (Mexico City: El Colegio de México, 1996), 239.

11. Paloma Martínez-Cruz, *Women and Knowledge in Mesoamerica: From East L.A. to Anahuac* (Tucson: University of Arizona Press, 2011), 77–94.

both films assign to the viewer a spectatorial positionality that is located within a (supposedly) Indigenous cosmovision. In this sense, *La noche de los mayas* and *Deseada* recall and appear to take up the charge that Gamio aimed at non-Indigenous Mexicans in his 1916 treatise, *Forjando patria*. Exploring the problems preventing the emergence of a cohesive national culture in Mexico, including a lack of common appreciation for art, Gamio exhorted mestizos and criollos to immerse themselves in Indigenous perspectives: "Hay que forjarse—ya sea temporalmente—un alma indígena" (One must forge—even if temporarily—an Indigenous soul).[12] *La noche de los mayas* and *Deseada* embody the spirit of Gamio's argument in that they are art forms that aspire, with all of the limitations inherent to indigenista cultural production, to draw the spectator into the Other's perspective via spirituality, if only for the duration of the films.

These two industrial films from the early and late Golden Age largely work toward creating spectatorial positioning by mobilizing their white-as-indigenous female protagonists as the conduits for the indigenous worldview that they present as legitimate. The role of the white-as-indigenous protagonists in promoting the spectator's connection to Indigenous beliefs rests on two aspects of the films. First, native beliefs are directly connected to the protagonists' irrepressible desires and suffering, which constitute the basis of the films' melodramatic narratives. Second, in these films the women's sacrificial adherence to their native faith (of their own volition) functions as the ultimate proof of their Indigenous authenticity and leads to the restoration of an order that the White man's intrusion disturbed. In this way, the Indigenous worldviews as constructed in the films operate as a crucial framework through which *La noche de los mayas* and *Deseada* present their protagonists as legitimately Indigenous and resolute characters who reestablish order, and not merely as self-effacing suicides, madwomen, or sinners. Within the broader corpus of Indigenous-themed Mexican films, *La noche de los mayas* and *Deseada* stand out both for their emphasis on mestizaje as a deeply fraught and tragic process and for the credence they lend to their versions of native cosmovisions.[13]

---

12. Gamio, *Forjando patria*, 25.

13. It is possible that the similarities I identify in the films can be linked to the fact that the Mayanist Antonio Mediz Bolio collaborated the on screenplay for *La noche de los mayas* and was also one of three writers who created the screenplay for *Deseada*, which was an adaptation of the play *La Ermita, la fuente y el río*, written by the

La noche de los mayas (1939)

As an Indigenous-themed film of the early Golden Age, *La noche de los mayas* is distinctive both for its departure from a cheerful approach to representing Indigeneity as folklore and for its marked lyrical style. Within the oeuvre of its director, Chano Urueta, one of the most prolific Mexican filmmakers of the twentieth century, the film constitutes a rare reach for artistic value. Multiple factors point to the film's status as an aspirational prestige film, including author Antonio Médiz Bolio's literary source material for the screenplay, the collaboration of authors Alfredo B. Crevenna and Archibaldo Burns on the screenplay, the aesthetic nature of photographer Gabriel Figueroa's compositions, and of course Silvestre Revueltas's musical score for the film, which has endured as a celebrated example of musical nationalism in Mexico, largely overshadowing the film itself in the national cultural memory.[14]

La noche de los mayas takes place during the nineteenth century in a Mayan community that has fled to a remote forest to avoid living under the rule of non-Mayas. Given these parameters, the film appears to represent the period of Maya rebellion that began with the Caste War of Yucatan in 1847 and ended in the early twentieth century during which the Mayas of eastern and southern Yucatan exercised self-governance and renamed themselves Cruzob.[15] A central feature of Cruzob society was its own syncretic religion, which operated independently from the Catholic church and drew heavily from pre-Columbian beliefs and folkways.[16] *La noche de los mayas* represents the idea that this spiritual base provided separatist Mayas with a strong internal cohesion and emphasizes the group's rejection of outsiders and their influences.

In the film, Lol (played by Estela Inda) and Uz (played by Arturo de Córdova) are betrothed from birth according to their community's ancestral custom. However, when a White Mexican man, Miguel, establishes contact with their community to extract gum from nearby trees,

---

Spanish author Eduardo Marquina in 1927.

14. Emilio García Riera, *Historia documental del cine mexicano*, vol. 2, *1938–1942* (Guadalajara: Universidad de Guadalajara, 1993), 103–5.

15. E. Bradford Burns, *The Poverty of Progress: Latin America in the Nineteenth Century* (Berkeley: University of California Press, 1980), 112.

16. Burns, *Poverty of Progress*, 113.

Lol falls deeply in love with him. Because of her feelings for Miguel, Lol rejects Uz's declarations of love, provoking his despair. The witch in the community, Zeb (played by Isabela Corona), who is in love with Uz, takes advantage of the situation by facilitating an encounter between Miguel and Lol in the hope of keeping Uz for herself. After Miguel has sex with Lol, the rain gods punish the entire community for the couple's transgression with a severe drought. When Lol's public thrashing does not return the rains, she and Yum Balam (her father and leader of the community) travel to Chichén Itzá and later to the holy cenote[17] to plead with the gods. In their absence, the townspeople burn Zeb and her mother, whom they blame for their misfortunes. Uz follows Lol and her father to the holy cenote, and upon encountering Miguel near the site, Uz kills the White man. When Lol realizes that Miguel is dead, she ends her life by jumping into the cenote, after which the rains return.

In *La noche de los mayas* a fundamental aspect of how the film reframes mestizaje as a process fraught with tension and tragedy is the dichotomic portrayal of Indigenous and White people, which from the outset stresses the power differential between the two groups. The film's initial expository text establishes the dominant position of Whites in contrast with the political and territorial marginality of the Indigenous population.[18] Furthermore, through the central metaphor of the night, the film transmits a binary view of the interaction between the groups that casts the Whites as menacing and destructive intruders. In the opening expository text, a quote from the *Book of Chilam Balam de Chumayel*, a pre-Hispanic prophetic text fully translated into Spanish in 1930 by Antonio Mediz Bolio, a collaborator on the film,[19] foretells that Maya decline will be an inevitable consequence of White control, "¡Ay! Será el anochecer para nosotros cuando vengan . . . los blancos![20]" (Oh! It will be nightfall for us when White people arrive!). The expository text then suggests that that this prophecy has indeed come to pass when it

---

17. Cenote is the term for deep natural wells found in Mexico and Central America that result when the collapse of surface limestone exposes underlying ground water.

18. "En el siglo XIX huyendo del dominio de los blancos muchos grupos de ellos [los mayas] fueron a refugiarse en los bosques" (In the nineteenth century, fleeing the control of white people, many groups [of Mayans] took refuge in the forests).

19. Lienhard, "*La noche de los mayas*," 46.

20. The quote from the *Book of Chilam Balam de Chumayel* appears here, with ellipses, exactly as it does in the film's expository text.

indicates to the spectator that the Maya in the film are living through "el tiempo de su noche" (their night). The recurring metaphor of the night, whose centrality is apparent in that it constitutes the film's very title, *La noche de los mayas* (*Dark night of the Mayas*), sets the tragic tone and establishes the dramatic framework for the film's representation of Indigeneity and mestizaje. By presenting the two groups as existing in opposition to each other and presenting Whites as a force of destruction for the Mayan world, the film begins by emphasizing tension and separateness as opposed to the idea of generative synthesis that pervades the national narrative of mestizaje.

At the heart of how the film reworks the foundational coupling of the Mexican nation is the depiction of interracial contact (and specifically interracial heterosexual desire and union) as a transgression that leads to destruction. There are numerous ways in which the film conveys Miguel's presence as an intrusion and source of devastation. First, there is a stark contrast between the circumstances of the Mayan community prior to and after Miguel and Lol's affair. When spectators first encounter the settlement of Yuyumil, the town is a joyful and orderly place. Bright daytime lighting and upbeat nondiegetic music set a positive tone. On-screen, each member of the Mayan village seems to be busy carrying out his or her tasks. However, Lol and Miguel's affair causes a drought, which then provokes a scarcity of food and water. These circumstances transform Yuyumil from a place of peace and order into a chaotic environment. The scene in which Yum Balam and Lol set off on their pilgrimage and the townspeople decide to take justice into their own hands by burning the witches is the exact opposite of the cheerful introduction to the town described above. The assembly of angry people in the night, when the town is usually quiet, conveys their state of agitation, which erupts into violence. The film is not subtle in identifying Miguel as the source of the Mayans' misery. For instance, at one point during the drought, Lol's friend declares definitively, "Todas las desgracias vinieron del hombre blanco" (All of the misfortunes have come from the White man). Through the contrast between the town's initial harmony and subsequent agitation, *La noche de los mayas* points to White intrusion as an agent of destabilization.

The film further suggests that Miguel's presence is a source of disruption through his role in obstructing tradition and the generational renewal of Mayan society. Early in the film, Yum Balam (Lol's father and chief of the community) and the Indigenous priest discuss the order according to which future events should unfold: young people should eventually relieve them of their tasks in the community and Lol and Uz are to be married because they have been betrothed since Lol's birth. Miguel's presence interferes with the order that the two Mayan men describe because his arrival provokes Lol's intense desire toward him, which causes her to violate tradition by rejecting Uz as her spouse. It is important to point out that the white-as-white Miguel is not exactly an equivalent suitor to Uz (the way the outsider, Juancho, is presented as a worthy rival for the love of Lupe in *La Zandunga*, discussed in chapter 2). Miguel only displays lust toward Lol and has no intention of marrying her, as Uz does; just as he extracts gum from the trees and quickly leaves, so he uses Lol for sexual pleasure and then abandons her. Furthermore, Miguel's foray among the Maya leads to Lol's death, which also violates the societal order according to which the young are supposed to replace their elders. By characterizing Miguel as an intruder whose physical liaison with Lol only causes suffering, destruction, and the violation of tradition within the Indigenous community, *La noche de los mayas* reframes mestizaje as a tragic scenario in which the White man intrudes upon, deceives, and irreparably damages Indigenous people.

In concert with how Miguel's role in the narrative disturbs the union of the would-be Indigenous couple and disrupts the functioning of the Mayan community, the film employs overt visual symbolism to highlight the character's function as a force of turmoil. For instance, prior to Miguel's arrival, Uz leaves a clay jug containing honey and two flowers before the sacred rock, which for them has an oracular function. According to the community's beliefs, if the flowers remain together, so will the two lovers, but if they are dispersed, the man and woman will be separated. As Miguel approaches the Mayan town, he picks up and accidentally breaks the clay jug, and the close-up of the broken container (which occurs at two different moments in the film) visually symbolizes his role in destroying Lol and Uz's union. Similarly, after Miguel has sex with Lol's unconscious body,[21] the shot of his boot stepping on and crushing a white flower visually symbolizes that Lol is no longer a virgin and the

---

21. According to the contemporary definition, this scene constitutes a rape. However, the film does not portray this sexual act as a violation of Lol's will because it suggests that she wanted to have a sexual encounter with Miguel—the reason she allowed him into her dwelling. Later, Lol seeks out Miguel to have sex. Furthermore, the film does not present Lol as the victim of an unwanted sexual act, but rather as the victim of a tragic fate: loving the White man.

harm that Miguel's actions will bring to her. Perhaps the most explicit symbolism that transmits the destructive implications of the interracial affair is when loud thunder sounds and lightning illuminates the night sky on the evening Miguel visits Lol. In case the spectator happens to miss the overt omen, upon seeing the unusual sight, the community's priest declares with certainty, "Tronó el cielo en seco. Desgracia grande va a venir" (The rainless sky has thundered. Great misfortune will come). Through these various visual and aural cues, *La noche de los mayas* links the White man with destruction, problematizing the notion that mestizaje is a positive and generative beginning.

While the film casts literal mestizaje through sexual interracial union as a circumstance fraught with pain and devastation, *La noche de los mayas* is clearly invested in the project of indigenismo-mestizaje in the sense that it upholds Indigeneity as a locus of cultural value that is worthy of artistic representation and dissemination to a broad Mexican public. Despite the fact that the film explicitly eschews the status of a "documento científico" (scientific document) in its opening expository text, an indigenista sentiment pervades *La noche de los mayas* because of its reverence for Indigenous authenticity, which it strives to reproduce through specific aural and visual strategies.

The film attempts to use language as a means to construct Mayan specificity as alterity. The expository text notes that the author of the screenplay, Mediz Bolio, originally wrote the dialogue in a Mayan language[22] and that in the film, his words have been translated "de modo literal y estricto, con lo que ha conservado integralmente la mentalidad y estilo de expresión del idioma maya auténtico" (in a strictly literal manner, conserving entirely the mentality and style of expression of the authentic Mayan language). Because of this literal translation into Spanish, the utterances of Mayan characters in the film are characterized by an unusual syntax in Spanish and frequent metaphors using nature. Representative examples include Uz's rebuke of Zeb's romantic and sexual advances: "Quítate Zeb . . . mi palabra te dice que los murciélagos no pueden acercarse al sol" (Stand back Zeb . . . my word tells you that bats cannot come close to the sun) and his declaration of love for Lol: "Tengo muchacha que quiero yo" (I have a woman who love I do). In addition to attempting to assert a proximity to Mayan expression, the Mayan

---

22. The film refers to Mayan language in general terms ("lengua maya") without identifying a specific one.

characters' speech has the effect of attributing a stoicism and lyricism to them in contrast to the comparatively prosaic Spanish spoken by Miguel and his men. In this sense, Urueta's film represents a unique solution for rendering Indigenous language within the wide range of approaches that Mexican films have taken.

La noche de los mayas also aims to transmit Mayan authenticity through mise-en-scène. The opening expository text emphasizes that the film was not shot in studios but "totalmente en Yucatán . . . en los lugares y en el ambiente en que se desarrolla la acción" (entirely . . . in Yucatán in the places and environment in which the action takes place). By highlighting that the environments presented on-screen are places in which Mayan people have dwelled, the film mobilizes the indexicality of space as a strategy for crafting itself as an authoritative cultural artifact about Indigeneity. The portion of the film in which Lol and her father travel to Chichén Itzá most explicitly draws on the "aura of ruins" to lend legitimacy to the fictional rendering of Mayan people.[23] The predominant use of the long shot and extreme long shot during this sequence as well as the placing of Mayan sculptures (such as the base of the Pyramid of Kukulcán and the Chac Mool statue) in the foreground visually privilege the archeological setting. Beyond merely including these objects in the frame, *La noche de los mayas* stages fictional religious practices at the site of the ruins, therefore also attempting to re-create the site's spiritual function as a strategy for projecting Indigenous authenticity.

The aestheticized display of dance and ritual is a key aspect of how the film constructs Indigenous essentialism while upholding its cultural value. The Mayan community's feast to celebrate the holy ceiba tree is the pretext for showcasing dance. The length of the dance sequence is disproportionate to its narrative function of establishing the context of the feast and therefore draws attention to the dance as a parenthetical spectacle in and of itself. The dance sequence uses the visual language of the ethnographic mode[24] to create truth effects with repetitive shots of long duration from multiple angles that visualize the dance from various perspectives, tending to emphasize the group. Similarly, the ritual sequence

---

23. Quetzil E. Castañeda, "The Aura of Ruins," in *Fragments of a Golden Age: The Politics of Culture in Mexico Since 1940*, ed. Gilbert M. Joseph, Anne Rubenstein, and Eric Zolov (Durham, NC: Duke University Press, 2001), 452–70.

24. Bill Nichols, *Representing Reality: Issues and Concepts in Documentary* (Bloomington: Indiana University Press, 1991), 205–20.

in which the Mayan community first pleads with the gods for the return of rain uses many of the same shot types and editing techniques to highlight the Mayan ritual as a communal practice. Sharing a shift in their mode of address with respect to the other scenes in the film,[25] the dance and ritual interludes function in a parallel manner, encapsulating how the film constructs Mayanness as an alterity with cultural complexity and worth.

While the presentation of Indigenous dance and ritual is so common in Indigenous-themed Mexican films so as to be a cliché of the genre, the *indigenismo* of *La noche de los mayas* stands out in its portrayal of the religious, spiritual, and magical beliefs that it attributes to Indigenous people. As opposed to discounting such beliefs as elements characteristic of Indigenous backwardness or wayward paganism—a perspective present in several Mexican films as early as *Tepeyac* (1917) and as well-known as Emilio Fernández's *María Candelaria* and Ismael Rodríguez's *Tizoc*—in *La noche de los mayas* Indigenous beliefs explain how the narrative unfolds and turn out to be true within the diegesis.[26] Beyond suggesting that the Mayan beliefs are legitimate, the film's version of the Mayan worldview presented in *La noche de los mayas* is integral to the structure of the film. Because the (supposedly) Indigenous cosmovision is the position from which the progression of the narrative can be explained, the film requires the temporal positioning of the spectator within the film's constructed Indigenous belief system to make sense of the relationship among the events in the story.

One instance that exemplifies how the film suggests that the Mayans' beliefs are credible is when it presents the custom of placing a clay jug with honey and two flowers before the holy rock to find out the fate of a romantic couple. In the film, the holy rock functions as a kind of oracle, and before it, Miguel unintentionally breaks the clay container, causing

---

25. The fact that these two scenes contain a shift in the audiovisual presentation of Indigeneity within the film can be appreciated in film reviews that complained of the length and monotony of these scenes. See García Riera, *Historia documental del cine*, vol. 2: 103.

26. Emilio García Riera signals that the film's take on Indigenous beliefs is unusual when he comments, "Resulta curioso que fuera vista como obra renovadora y aun de vanguardia una película capaz de postular, en definitiva, que los dioses mayas eran tan poderosos como los mayas decían" (It is curious that a film capable of proposing, definitively, that Mayan gods were as powerful as the Maya believed, could be considered innovative and even avant-garde). *Historia documental del cine*, vol. 2: 103.

the separation of the flowers. The rift between the flowers representing Uz and Lol functions as foreshadowing, conveying that Lol and Uz's union will not come to fruition. In displaying how the Mayans' ritual yields a response that corresponds to the development of the central love story, the film lends legitimacy to the Indigenous ritual as a practice that reveals truth.

The film's white-as-indigenous female protagonist, Lol, is central to the many other ways in which the film suggests the veracity of the Mayans' diegetic beliefs. For instance, when a month passes after her first sexual encounter with Miguel, Lol participates in a ritual that Zeb officiates to make him return. The ritual that the film presents as being a part of the Mayan belief system actually works. Soon after, Miguel and his men return to the area near Yuyumil, which makes possible another encounter between the White man and Lol. By showing that Lol's participation in Zeb's incantation yields its intended results (Miguel's return), the film demonstrates the legitimacy of the Indigenous worldview that it constructs via the white-as-indigenous woman.

The most impactful way in which the film ties the veracity of Mayan beliefs to Lol is through the sacrifice of her life to restore rain and sustenance to her community. From the moment her transgression comes to light, the community and its authorities suggest that there must be some atonement for Lol's affair with Miguel to restore the favor of the rain gods. The authorities in the community appeal to the gods' justice through a public thrashing meant to cleanse Lol and by pleading with the gods for clemency at Chichén Itzá, neither of which restores the rain. Finally, when Lol realizes that Uz has shot Miguel, she jumps into the holy cenote, which immediately prompts a rainstorm. Because Lol's sacrifice of her own life causes the rain to return, the film lends credence to what the community had been saying all along: her sexual union with a White man is a disturbance of order with cosmic repercussions.

The film highlights the connection between Lol's immolation and the restoration of the rain on a visual level as well. A shot showing the splash caused by Lol's submergence into the water is followed by a shot of large storm clouds, suggesting a causal connection between Lol's self-sacrifice and the abrupt weather change. Subsequent shots of the cenote's water also suggest a connection between the two when the ripples visible on the water's surface caused by Lol's drowning blend into the smaller ripples caused by the droplets of rain hitting the water. In sum, by making the Mayan beliefs within the film the principles that order how the narrative unfolds, *La noche de los mayas* positions the spectator within that worldview and affords the white-as-indigenous Lol the central role in demonstrating the legitimacy of those beliefs.

Part of what makes *La noche de los mayas* a noteworthy film within the Indigenous-themed corpus of Mexican film production is that although the film ends with Lol's death, the way in which Mayan beliefs are presented does not suggest that Lol is a victim of her people. On the contrary, the men in her community attempt at every turn to spare her from punishment to the point of prolonging their community's distress. For instance, when Lol is to be flogged so that she can be purified, Uz cites a law that allows him to take her place. Similarly, Yum Balam takes Lol on a pilgrimage to Chichén Itzá in the hope that the pilgrimage and the sacrifice of a deer will be enough to appease the gods. Last, it is Lol herself who ultimately follows through with the sacrifice by jumping into a cenote without any prompting from her father or Uz. By showing that the sacrifice is the result of Lol's own will and that her father and lover attempt to spare her from the punishment that their laws and beliefs dictate, *La noche de los mayas* avoids a representation in which Lol suffers as a result of her own people's savagery (the dynamic that prevails in films such as *Chilam Balam*, discussed in chapter 1). Instead, *La noche de los mayas* presents the White man, if anyone, as the cause of Lol's demise, because his oblivious behavior disrupts order and tradition in the Indigenous community (not unlike the painter in *María Candelaria* discussed in chapter 3). Furthermore, Miguel does not represent an alternative order or sense of justice to that professed by the Mayans (as is the case with the conquistadors in *Chilam Balam*, who save Naya by appealing to Christian values, and the Mexican military in *Maclovia*, who save Maclovia and José María by appealing to the secular rights of citizens). Therefore, instead of presenting Indigenous people as practicing barbaric beliefs through the victimization of the Indigenous female[27] (as in *Janitzio*, *María Candelaria*, *Maclovia*, and *Chilam Balam*), in *La noche de los mayas* Lol willingly inflicts punishment on herself to restore order, much to the displeasure of the Mayan men closest to her.

Like the vast majority of industrial Indigenous-themed films made in Mexico, *La noche de los mayas* features whiteness-as-indigeneity through the film's female protagonist. However, not embodying the virtuous virgin

---

27. Ella Shohat and Robert Stam, *Unthinking Eurocentrism: Multiculturalism and the Media* (New York: Routledge, 1994), 156.

to the same extent as her counterparts in other films, Lol's Whiteness carries out another function in the film distinct from the underscoring of infallible morality. While the film follows the colonially inflected aesthetic standard to signal Lol's desirability, her Whiteness, via the colonization of subjectivity, also supports her role as the conduit for the Indigenous worldview that the film legitimizes for a Mexican audience.

To explore how Lol's Whiteness allows her to serve as a vehicle through which Indigenous beliefs are presented as credible in the film, it is necessary to first address in what way Lol constitutes an instance of whiteness-as-indigeneity. On the one hand, her bodily characteristics do not align perfectly with those that anthropologist Hugo Nutini associates with White women in the Mexican context.[28] Emilio García Riera corroborates this fact when he reads Estela Inda's body as mestizo, referring to her "interesantes facciones, más o menos indígenas" (interesting, more or less Indigenous features).[29] The not-quite-White status of Inda's body in the Mexican racial formation and national film industry is also borne out in that, like Columba Domínguez, she receives the veiled racialized qualifiers "mexicanísima" (very Mexican) and "exótica" (exotic) when discussed in film magazines of the Golden Age.[30] Bearing in mind the racialized nature of casting in the Mexican film industry (discussed in the introduction), it comes as no surprise that Inda was not given acting opportunities in proportion to her talent.[31] Relegated largely to unglamorized roles within the rural and urban underclasses, she nonetheless managed to distinguish herself in *Los olvidados* (dir. Luis Buñuel, 1950) and *El rebozo de Soledad* (dir. Roberto Gavaldón, 1952), for which she won silver Ariel awards.

Despite Estela Inda's not-quite-White status, *La noche de los mayas* still endeavors to craft Lol as an instance of whiteness-as-indigeneity in

---

28. "For females these standards include white, alabaster skin; medium blonde or auburn hair, straight or slightly curled; light eyes, preferably blue or greenish blue; medium height and thin body conformation; large, expressive eyes, with long lashes; fine, well-proportioned features; a small mouth and nose; and above all elegance and gracefulness in every movement, from walking and sitting to gesticulating and resting." Hugo Nutini, *The Mexican Aristocracy: An Expressive Ethnography* (Austin: University of Texas Press, 2008), 62.

29. García Riera, *Historia documental del cine*, vol. 2: 102.

30. *Cine mundial*, May 22, 1953; *Cinema Reporter*, December 21, 1946, 21.

31. *Cinema Reporter*, December 21, 1946, 21 and 31.

several ways.[32] First, the opening credits differentiate between the various bodies that appear on-screen. On the one hand, the credits identify the film's characters and the actors who interpret those roles, and, on the other hand, it identifies the "conjuntos de indios mayas auténticos" (groups of authentic Indigenous Mayans) who also appear on-screen. The role that the opening credits play in creating this distinction is a subtle but significant one. Much like the opening credits in *Zítari* (discussed in chapter 1), the reference to the "groups of authentic Indigenous Mayans" suggests that *those* filmed bodies represent Indigeneity through indexicality, while the actors who interpret the main roles do so through dramatization. By naming Estela Inda as the actress who interprets the film's leading role in a manner entirely separate to the mentioning of the "authentic Indigenous Mayans," the film puts her in a category apart from those Indigenous participants.

Furthermore, *La noche de los mayas* crafts Lol as an instance of whiteness-as-indigeneity in visual terms. Physical aspects of her on-screen presence follow studio-era conventions, including highly visible makeup on her eyelids and lips; manicured, pencil-thin eyebrows; full and artificially long eyelashes; a slender body and limbs; and a light complexion—all characteristics that Ageeth Sluis has used to define the "deco body" as a cosmopolitan ideal for the female physique in the first three decades of the twentieth century, which "helped to visualize an urban 'mestizo modernity.'"[33] In the Mexican context, this female physical form can be understood as a manifestation of Whitening to the extent that it exalts aesthetic ideals received from European and North American urban centers and deemphasizes physical characteristics attributed to Indigeneity in the local context, such as brownness and roundness. The film's presentation of the diegetically Indigenous Lol via the "deco body" Whitens the Mayan character according to the dominant visual codes that signified physical feminine appeal at that time.

Beyond Lol's physical characteristics and makeup, the film literally whitens her by using bright lighting throughout.[34] The scene in which Lol participates in the ritual officiated by Zeb to summon the white-as-white

---

32. Lienhard reads Estela Inda as a white actress, "*La noche de los mayas*," 41.

33. Ageeth Sluis, *Deco Body, Deco City: Female Spectacle and Modernity in Mexico City, 1900–1939* (Lincoln: University of Nebraska Press, 2016), 3.

34. While this visual technique is similar to that analyzed by Dolores Tierney in *María Candelaria* (in *Emilio Fernández*, 88–95), here the connotations of purity are not present.

man back to Yuyumil clearly illustrates the whitening of Lol's face through illumination, which the use of the close-up shot on her face throughout the scene emphasizes. Moreover, the white flowers in her hair also reflect the light, further brightening her appearance by creating a brilliant aura around her head. Finally, the water that is poured over her hair and face during the ceremony catches the light, making Lol appear to glisten as it washes over her. The overall visual effect that the lighting, mise-en-scène, and cinematography create is that of Lol's luminosity—a long-established convention in cinema for conveying female beauty and desirability.[35]

The construction of Lol's whiteness-as-indigeneity through her corporeal Whiteness and cinematographic whiteness described above serves to transmit her diegetic function as the film's object of desire for both the Mayan Uz and the White Miguel into visual terms in the cinematic medium and according to the raced hierarchy of female attractiveness. The various shots in which the two central male characters gaze at her longingly and/or lustily further cement the film's representation of Lol as an attractive woman. The moment in the film that most draws attention to Lol's body, inviting its sexualization, is the scene in which she is supposed to be flogged in front of her community. Here Lol appears topless with her bare back facing the spectator as both of her arms are tied around the wide tree. The silhouette of her breast is visible as it is pressed up against the dark tree trunk. Furthermore, the composition of the shots in this scene places Lol's body directly in the center, and the spectatorial presence of the rest of the Mayan community produces the display of her body as a spectacle within a spectacle.[36] *La noche de los mayas* therefore codes Lol's desirability through its Whiteness and showcases her body.

Following the implications of the colonization of desire and subjectivity, Lol's Whiteness functions as the means through which the film conveys her desirability and protagonism and bears important implications for the film's portrayal of Indigenous beliefs. Because, as mentioned above, the credibility of Mayan beliefs in the film rests heavily on Lol's function

---

35. Dyer, "The Light of the World," in *White* (London; New York: Routledge, 1997), 122–44.

36. García Riera corroborates the scene's voyeuristic parameters, suggesting that it promotes ". . . el placer de contemplar la bella espalda de Estela Inda e imaginarla, con regusto sádico, marcada por sabrosos y sensuales latigazos" (the pleasure of contemplating Estela Inda's beautiful back and to imagine her, with a sadistic aftertaste, marked by delicious and sensual lashing.) In *Historia documental del cine*, vol. 2: 103.

in the narrative—with her actions both incurring the gods' wrath and quelling it—the visual devices used to Whiten and privilege Lol *also* serve as a way in which the films presents Indigenous beliefs as legitimate. In other words, *La noche de los mayas* uses the raced semiotic privilege of the White Mexican woman's body to align the Mexican spectator with the cosmovision that it presents as Indigenous,[37] strategically tying the cosmovision of the Other (precisely) to a body that is not too Other to make the Indigenous worldview more palatable in a postcolonial context of reception. In this way, Lol's whiteness-as-indigeneity makes her a colonially inflected conduit for an Indigenous cosmovision. It is in this sense that both films discussed in this chapter are unique with respect to the way in which whiteness-as-indigeneity has functioned in many Indigenous-themed films to signal the good Indigenous woman's alignment with Catholicism (as occurs, for instance, in *María Candelaria*,[38] *Maclovia*, *Chilam Balam*, and *María Isabel*). Thus, *La noche de los mayas* distinguishes itself as a film that confers value on an aspect of Indigenous culture (religious and spiritual beliefs) that was treated ambivalently in many other Indigenous-themed productions, but the film also uses the familiar racialized hierarchy that privileges White bodies to do so.

La noche de los mayas offers a reframing of the circumstances surrounding sexual mestizaje. Far from introducing civilization or a preferable religious order, the intrusion of the White man into the Mayan community brings with it the violation of native tradition, which in turn unleashes suffering and destruction. Only the Mayan woman's willing adherence to Indigenous religious custom in the form of self-sacrifice mitigates the damage caused by White male incursion into the Indigenous space. On the one hand, *La noche de los mayas* clearly problematizes mestizaje's foundational narrative by presenting the cross-racial heterosexual encounter as one that is both tragic and unfruitful. On the other hand, Urueta's film constitutes a noteworthy mediation of cultural mestizaje because it suggests the validity of a native cosmovision and positions the spectator within that worldview, even though it resorts to the semiotic power of

---

37. An equivalent example featuring a male Indigenous character would be Roberto Gavaldón's well-known film *Macario* (1960).

38. Tierney, *Emilio Fernández*, 88–95; Claudia Arroyo Quiroz, "Fantasías sobre la identidad indígena en el cine mexicano del periodo post-revolucionario," in *Identidades. Explorando la diversidad*, ed. Laura Carballido (Mexico City: Universidad Autónoma Metropolitana-Anthropos, 2011), 154.

whiteness-as-indigeneity to do so. The second film addressed in this chapter, Roberto Gavaldón's *Deseada*, engages indigenismo-mestizaje in a manner that similarly presents Indigeneity as a valuable cultural reality that is threatened by contact with westerners. Here, too, the key to understanding how unfortunate events unfold lies in the beliefs presented as part of an Indigenous cosmovision. Markedly different, however, is *Deseada*'s use of a surrealist visual language, which underscores the film's overall portrayal of Indigenous Mexico as a bewitching world apart.

Deseada (1951)

An equally prolific Mexican filmmaker, Roberto Gavaldón enjoyed more critical success than his colleague Chano Urueta, earning multiple Ariel awards as well as nominations at the Cannes and Berlin film festivals and at the Academy Awards in the United States. Despite the extension of his oeuvre and the recognition Gavaldón received in his day, his films have not received robust scholarly attention, perhaps because of their thematic repetition and/or because his reputation at home declined after his controversial 1961 film, *Rosa Blanca*, was banned by the Mexican government—only the second national film to be entirely censored in this way.[39] For the purposes of this study, Gavaldón is of interest because although Golden Age filmmaking largely abandoned Indigenous themes after the mid-1940s, shifting instead to urban topics featuring the moral dilemmas that modern life in the city presented, Gavaldón also took up and elaborated on the proposal of cinematic mexicanidad as crafted in the Fernández-Figueroa unit's indigenista films. In *Deseada* (1951) and *Macario* (1960), Gavaldón evolved the subgenre in a direction that some associate with magical realism.[40]

Like *La noche de los mayas*, *Deseada* is set in the Yucatan peninsula and plays on the tensions among duty, tradition, and desire. The title character (played by Dolores del Río) is a mature Mayan woman who, because of her parents' deaths, is the guardian of her younger sister,

---

39. The first was Julio Bracho's *La sombra del caudillo* (1960), which criticized postrevolutionary political intrigue. See Ariel Zúñiga, "Roberto Gavaldón," in *Mexican Cinema*, ed. Paulo Antonio Paranaguá, trans. Ana M. López (London: British Film Institute, 1995), 195–97.

40. Zúñiga "Roberto Gavaldón," 200.

Nicté. Deseada has postponed her own plans to marry the middle-aged Spaniard Don Lorenzo until she ensures her younger sister's marriage to his nephew, Manuel, who arrives to the Yucatan from Spain for the young couple's wedding. In a kind of Mexican national allegory gone horribly wrong, Nicté's betrothal to Manuel is hampered when a mutual attraction develops between Manuel and her older sister, Deseada. Deseada tries her best to deny that she is attracted to Manuel, but when she realizes that Manuel will no longer marry Nicté and that he has shot his uncle because of their rivalry over her, Deseada ends her life by jumping into a cenote.

Like *La noche de los mayas*, *Deseada* is aware of its indigenista positionality as a cultural artifact that mediates Indigeneity to the nation. The film implies that the Mayan cultural reality is relevant to Mexico as a whole through a message that appears in the opening credits indicating that the film is "dedicada entrañablemente a México" (dedicated fondly to Mexico). Furthermore, the film attempts to present itself as an authentic representation of Indigeneity through the use of on-site filming, which the opening credits also highlight by announcing that it is "Totalmente filmada en los escenarios naturales de la milenaria ciudad maya Chichén-Itzá" (Entirely filmed in the natural setting of the millenary city, Chichén Itzá). Here the words "entirely" and "natural" constitute a claim to authenticity, while the word "millenary" seeks to underscores the importance of the Mayan culture due to its antiquity. *Deseada* further demonstrates a self-consciousness regarding its own mediating function presenting itself as a "poema dramático" (dramatic poem). Like the peculiar syntax and ubiquitous metaphors from nature in the speech of Mayan characters in *La noche de los mayas*, here *Deseada* appeals to lyricism as a means of re-presenting Indigeneity as alterity. Through these explicit mentions in the opening credits, *Deseada* conveys itself as a mediation of Mayans within a national framework, makes claims to authenticity, and seeks to aestheticize alterity through the poetic.

Deseada is a film that clearly echoes the official cultural thrust of indigenismo-mestizaje in that, however problematically, it upholds Indigenous culture as valuable and relevant to the Mexican nation. The film's opening sequence, consisting of numerous shots of Mayan ruins through slow pans, tilts, and pedestals, evokes the "aura of ruins,"[41] exalting the structures as wondrous achievements, a position that Deseada verbally

---

41. Castañeda, "The Aura of Ruins," 452–70.

corroborates when, in her first utterance in the film, she refers to the Mayan "grandeza pasada" (past greatness). Furthermore, although *Deseada* points to Mayan culture as highly valuable, it laughably essentializes Mayan individuals as walking reservoirs of their civilization's cultural knowledge, which flows from them consciously and/or unconsciously. In a conversation that Deseada has with a painter as he completes an image resembling ancient Mayan images of the goddess Ixchel, which he has never seen (see figure 4.1), Deseada explains that such knowledge is innate to the painter: ". . . esas cosas no se aprenden en los libros. Se llevan por dentro, en la sangre, de manera natural, sin que nadie nos las explique. Por eso tú hiciste este dibujo . . . Es como si lo hubieras aprendido antes de nacer" (those things aren't learned in books. They are within you, in the blood, naturally, without anyone explaining them to us. That is why you made that drawing. It is as if you had learned it

Figure 4.1. Deseada (Dolores del Río) explains to a Mayan painter (Wilbert Puerto) that he learned the contents of his artwork "antes de nacer" (before birth) in *Deseada* (1951). Photo courtesy of Mil Nubes-Foto (Roberto Fiesco). All rights reserved.

before birth). Furthermore, Deseada herself functions as a custodian of Mayan knowledge, which the film showcases through her role as teacher to Mayan female youth. At every opportunity Deseada spouts off Mayan prophesies and legends, particularly that of Ixchel, the goddess of the moon, and the sun god Itzamná. She vigilantly ensures that the betrothal of her younger sister follows Mayan custom and is even knowledgeable about her people's weaving techniques, which she displays by teaching them to the young women and weaving her sister's wedding hammock. By exhibiting all of this cultural information about the Mayans, the film explicitly participates in indigenista display.

While *Deseada* certainly portrays Mayan culture as constituting a rich tradition, the film also emphasizes Mayan alterity by associating it with exoticism as well as with magic and occult forces. The film introduces the very space where Mayans live as otherworldly through the experience of Manuel and Don Lorenzo as they arrive. As Manuel gazes from the train, looking out onto the Yucatan for the first time, he compares the land to a "mujer que seduce, que fascina, y que lo arrastra a uno sin que haya fuerza que ponerle . . . Aquí hasta los mismos nombres y palabras parecen tener un embrujo" (woman that seduces, that holds you spellbound, and that pulls you with a force beyond any other . . . Here even names and words seem to bewitch). Through lines of dialogue such as these, which the Spanish characters repeat throughout the film, *Deseada* casts both the Mayan people and their surroundings as mysterious and nonrational.

Beyond the perceptions of the European men, the most important way in which *Deseada* presents the Yucatan and its native inhabitants as otherworldly is by depicting the region as a place where occult forces are at play. These forces are associated specifically with native beliefs and with the woman who personifies Indigenous spiritual knowledge in the film, Quiteria. Far from being presented as an ignorant witch doctor, as is the case with her counterpart in *María Candelaria* (see chapter 3), Quiteria is closer to a sage or guardian of knowledge and is the only person who can explain how the web of unrequited and forbidden love among the primary characters came about. Many years earlier, Don Lorenzo had impregnated an Indigenous woman, and she was brought to Quiteria to give birth; however, when a Western doctor intervened to deliver the baby by cutting open the mother's belly, the mother died. Quiteria preserved the mother's blood, which beckoned her son, Manuel, back to the place of his birth, eventually causing him to rival his father (Don Lorenzo) over a woman (Deseada). Furthermore, the film makes clear that this mysterious force, which is only explicable through the fictionalized Mayan cosmovision, produces the attraction between Deseada and Manuel despite their best efforts to resist each other and fulfill family obligations. After Deseada and Manuel engage in a taboo kiss, Deseada explains that the event must have been rooted in witchcraft: "No fui yo la que te dio ese beso. Fueron nuestras sombras las que se besaron. Una cosa como de brujería" (It was not I who gave you that kiss. It was our shadows that kissed. It was something like witchcraft). By presenting Mayan beliefs as powerful forces that unleash intense desire and displaying their power to move otherwise dutiful characters to act immorally, *Deseada* clearly casts Indigeneity as radical alterity by associating it with occult and magical power.

In concert with the significance of Mayan spiritual beliefs for structuring the film's plot, *Deseada* also clearly suggests their power and strangeness in formal terms, using distinct visual devices to create a surreal effect when Deseda and Manuel partake in an evening encounter and kiss for the first time. When Manuel sees Deseada at a site of Mayan ruins, both characters move and communicate as if in a trance. They have a telepathic conversation. Their dialogue is heard through voice-over while their mouths remain closed during close-up shots.[42] Dramatic and eerie nondiegetic music plays in the background. In addition to the abandonment of the conventions of realism that are used in the rest of the film, the fact that the scene takes place in the evening, and therefore occurs in darkness, also contributes to the dreamlike effect it produces. Furthermore, the Mayan ruins where the scene takes place function as an obvious icon of Indigenous culture. The fact that the covert and surreal encounter occurs here suggests that the event is impelled by occult forces related to Indigeneity, a point that is visually rendered through the shot of Manuel and Deseada's shadows approaching each other and kissing on an ancient Mayan ruin. The connection between the Indigenous spiritual forces at work and the forbidden romance is underscored in Deseada's even more surrealist dream that prefigures the encounter. In it, she stands on a Mayan pyramid as Manuel's large head floats above her in the sky, a literal visualization of the parallel between Manuel and the Mayan sun god, Itzamná, repeated throughout the film. This bizarre mise-en-scène

---

42. These devices also characterize well-known scenes from other Mexican films that scholars have consistently identified as surrealist, such as the scene representing Pedro's dream in Luis Buñuel's *Los olvidados* (1950).

presents Deseada's desire for Manuel as one rooted to an Indigenous worldview that the film associates with the fantastic.

While *Deseada* attributes great power to Mayan beliefs, as in *La noche de los mayas*, these beliefs are not themselves the sources of destruction; rather, it is the intrusion of Hispanic men into the Indigenous space that unleashes chaos. The film introduces this idea early on when Deseada refers to the conquest and postconquest period as "el tiempo malo que todo lo destruyó" (the bad time that destroyed everything)—a statement that foreshadows the continued unhappiness and destruction that foreign male characters cause throughout the film. First is the arrival of Don Lorenzo, who impregnates an Indigenous woman out of wedlock, which eventually costs him the chance of a happy life with his true love, Deseada. Second is the intrusion of the non-Indigenous doctor, who violates Indigenous birthing tradition through his medical practice. The doctor's interference causes the death of the woman and the estrangement between Don Lorenzo and his child, Manuel. Third is the arrival of Manuel to the Yucatán. Manuel disrupts Deseada and Don Lorenzo's nuptial plans as well as Deseada's relationship with her sister, Nicté. Even though *Deseada* does imply that Manuel and Nicté's union will go forward, it is clear that any future Manuel has without Deseada will be marred by unhappiness, as he will spend the rest of his life atoning for the attack on his uncle/father "con el sufrimiento" (with suffering). In this way, while *Deseada* points to the possibility of a mestizo union, the film does not celebrate it as a positive outcome, but rather frames the marriage as a burdensome penance. In short, through the negative impact of non-Indigenous men's presence in the Yucatan and the unhappy outcomes of all of the unions between Mayan women and European men (Don Lorenzo and the nameless Indigenous woman he impregnates, Don Lorenzo and Deseada, Manuel and Deseada, and Manuel and Nicté), *Deseada* too reframes the script of Mexican mestizaje as a problematic, tragic, and damaging affair.

Furthermore, as a bona fide Mexican melodrama—complete with a surprise revelation regarding a central character's birth—a significant amount of screen time is spent on scenes in which the teary characters profess the intensity of their love and suffering. Deseada pines after Manuel and suffers from guilt because he is her younger sister's fiancé. Nicté is distraught because she senses that Manuel does not care for her. Manuel is distressed because he cannot have Deseada and because he becomes the rival of his own uncle/father. The scene in which Manuel sings about his misery in the form of a serenade to Deseada is one of

Figure 4.2. Impossible love between Deseada (Dolores del Río) and Manuel (Jorge Mistral) causes much suffering in *Deseada* (1951). Photo courtesy of Mil Nubes-Foto (Roberto Fiesco). All rights reserved.

the film's most melodramatic moments, compounded by Nicté's mistaking of the serenade as a declaration of love for her. This is the case not only because Manuel expresses his anguish in song form, but also because of the numerous tight close-ups of the three characters that magnify their tears and forlorn expressions, conveying their profound yearning and heartache. The film's foregrounding of the characters' suffering through dialogue and screen time serves as further proof of the devastation that results from the intermixing of Indians and Europeans, which in turn problematizes mestizaje as an ideal.

Although *Deseada* does not take place during the period of conquest, various details in the film echo a first contact scenario, which invites a parallelism between the original pairing of conquistadors and native women and the would-be couples whom the film depicts. For instance, as Don Lorenzo and Manuel ride the train toward the town of Loljá, Don

Lorenzo's comments on the land associate the Spanish men with the project of conquest: "El poder de esta tierra es avasalladora. Pretendes conquistarla y resultas tú el conquistado" (The power of this land is overwhelming. You expect to conquer it, and it ends up conquering you). Also, prior to Manuel's arrival, the Mayan women of Loljá speak about him as if he were a wholly foreign creature and as if they had never encountered Whiteness. Nicté, for example, wonders aloud if her betrothed will be "rubio como el sol" (blond like the sun), expressing amazement that such an appearance is even possible. Furthermore, the film exacerbates Manuel's arrival as a meeting between greatly dissimilar people when Nicté refers to him as "hombre extranjero" (foreign man) and when Deseada explains that his arrival takes time because Manuel is traveling "desde muy lejos, de su tierra de España" (from very far, from his land, Spain), as if Nicté had never heard of the country and as if the trip were some kind of epic voyage. Because *Deseada* presents Manuel's presence in the Yucatan in a manner that recalls the original encounter between Spanish men and Indigenous women in Mexico and then proceeds to cast the meeting as a destructive scenario, *Deseada* can be read as a reframing of Mexican mestizaje's origin story as a detrimental ordeal.

Even though *Deseada* does not reproduce a positive narrative of mestizaje (understood as the romantic and sexual union of the Indigenous woman and Spanish man), the film is in tune with the ideological project of indigenismo-mestizaje in the sense that it not only displays Indigenous culture as valuable, but, like *La noche de los mayas*, it also presents native beliefs as the principles that explain how events unfold and places the spectator within a (supposedly) Indigenous worldview. Part of what makes this portrayal of Indigenous beliefs in *Deseada* significant is that the Catholic tradition is also visible throughout the film (for example, through Deseada's interactions with the local priest and the fact that she wears a cross and goes to the chapel to pray for Manuel and Don Lorenzo). However, the visibility of Christianity in the film does not serve to undermine native beliefs in any way. For instance, when the priest accuses Quiteria of being nothing more than a silly, superstitious woman, Deseada defends her without antagonizing the priest: "Quiteria siempre dice cosas sabias, y escuchar su consejo es buena costumbre" (Quiteria always says wise things, and listening to her advice is a good custom). The film itself takes this position, as Quiteria is the only character who understands and can make sense of the chaos that has erupted, while the local priest remains entirely oblivious to its root causes.

Whereas the film presents Deseada as spiritually mestiza, her character ultimately gives greater weight to the Indigenous spiritual tradition. The film supports this interpretation not only because Deseada seeks out Quiteria for counsel (and not the priest), but most importantly because she opts to solve her dilemma by sacrificing herself. Through her choosing to drown in a cenote (instead of pursuing redemption through her Catholicism), Deseada accepts the curse that Quiteria has explained to her, which is rooted in the non-Indigenous doctor's violation of Manuel's mother during his birth. By acting according to Quiteria's counsel, Deseada conveys her investment in the native tradition as the source of truth that explains her reality, in this way quelling the chaos induced by the presence of foreign men among Indigenous people.

In addition to Quiteria's function in the film as the bearer and revealer of truth, there are other ways in which *Deseada* portrays Indigenous beliefs as legitimate. For instance, the film visualizes proof of the cursed nature of Manuel and Deseada's attraction through strong gusts of wind and birds, which, according to Quiteria, are bad omens—natural signs comparable to the drought in *La noche de los mayas*. Moreover, the most explicit way in which *Deseada* lends credence to Indigenous beliefs is through the repeated allusions to the myth of Ixchel (the moon goddess and creator of weaving) and Itzamná (the sun god). According to the film, Ixchel and Itzamná were in love with each other, but because one belonged to the night and the other to the day, they could not be together. Ixchel would purposely spend her nights weaving her wedding hammock to meet Itzamná at dawn, but she would never finish it to continue seeing her beloved. This myth functions as a central metaphor for Deseada and Manuel's love story, which, like that of Ixchel and Itzamná, is impossible. The film clearly associates Deseada with Ixchel through the act of weaving, which she teaches and carries out during the film. Similarly, through the repeated references to Manuel as being "rubio como el sol" (blonde like the sun), the film creates the association between Manuel and Itzamná. *Deseada* further suggests the correspondence between the two stories when the title character accepts that she and Manuel cannot be together by referencing the myth of Ixchel and Itzamná: "Yo nunca terminé de tejer la hamaca de mi destino. No se llegan a juntar jamás el sol y la luna, aunque vivan en el mismo cielo" (I never finished weaving the hammock of my destiny. The sun and the moon never manage to meet even though they live in the same sky). Through both the visualization of bad omens that prove the cursed nature of the film's primary romance and the centrality of Mayan myth that prefigures the destinies of its protagonists, *Deseada* presents Indigenous beliefs as legitimate sources of understanding.

In concert with how the narrative privileges the diegetic Indigenous spiritual tradition, the film further suggests on a visual level that Deseada's resolution to sacrifice herself is rooted in her Indigenous beliefs. Although Deseada's last encounter with Manuel takes place in a chapel and ends with her making the sign of the cross, the film subordinates this Catholic religious expression through the subsequent visualization of symbols conveying Deseada's Indigeneity just prior to her death. She leaves the chapel and walks through the ruins at Chichén Itzá, pausing to imagine her and Manuel's shadow embracing and kissing on a Mayan pyramid, proof of the occult forces that brought them together. The use of the long shot at this point showcases the Mayan pyramids, icons of Indigeneity in the film, and highlights Deseada's fundamental investment in that identity as she walks among the structures. Furthermore, the shot-reverse-shot of Deseada looking up at the sun longingly just before she jumps to her death functions as a visual reference to her love for Manuel, whom the film is associates with the Mayan sun god, Itzamná. The film's final shots prior to Deseada's death, which emphasize her cultural Indigeneity and belief in Mayan mythology, serve to privilege the Indigenous cosmovision as the belief system within which Deseada's self-sacrificial resolution is rooted and bears meaning.

Although in the film Quiteria is the guardian and revealer of Indigenous beliefs, ultimately it is Deseada who plays the central role in the film's representation of Mayan beliefs as constituting a legitimate perspective that explains truth. This is the case because as a melodrama, the film privileges the display of extreme emotions, particularly those of the protagonist, Deseada. The intense emotions the protagonist endures and which the film showcases are directly dependent on the veracity of native beliefs. Therefore, by dramatizing the protagonist's plight and magnifying its affective implications through melodrama, the film also underscores the legitimacy of the native beliefs that explain the causes of her prolonged suffering. In this way, Deseada's pathos serves a means of conveying the credibility of the fictionalized Indigenous cosmovision.

Deseada's narrative and emotional centrality is coded visually through her whiteness-as-indigeneity, with Dolores del Río playing the role of the distraught Mayan woman. As discussed in chapter 3, Dolores del Río possessed both a White star text (due to her aristocratic pedigree) and socioeconomic position, as well as a phenotype that was read as White within the Mexican racial formation. Following the implications of the colonization of subjectivity in Mexican melodrama, *Deseada* mobilizes Whiteness through a raced visual logic for the purposes of eliciting the commiseration of Mexican audiences with a diegetically Mayan character.

Deseada's whiteness-as-indigeneity is, of course, also the visual strategy through which the film presents her as a desirable Indigenous woman—a key point in the film with both Don Lorenzo and Manuel pining after her vehemently. In addition to the ardor of these two suitors, Don Lorenzo reveals that many others had also courted her throughout her youth but had been unsuccessful in their efforts because of Deseada's determination to ensure her younger sister's marriage prior to her own. In this way, the film establishes Deseada as extremely alluring and elusive: "la mujer que se desea y que no se alcanza nunca" (the woman who is desired and who can never be reached), as Don Lorenzo explains. Because of the enduring implications of the colonization of desire in Mexico and its specific repercussions for the representation of female attractiveness as White in Mexican cinema, the beautiful Mayan Deseada is visualized through whiteness-as-indigeneity to convey her desirability in the context of the Mexican racial formation.

In addition to deploying the visual semiotic privilege of the White Mexican woman to convey the pathos and attractiveness of the Indigenous character, I suggest that in the raced Mexican context, Deseada's whiteness-as-indigeneity (like Lol's in *La noche de los mayas*) also functions to support the credibility of the Indigenous cosmovision. This is the case because (as mentioned above) the extreme emotions Deseada experiences are a direct result of the truths that only the fictionalized Indigenous worldview can explain. In other words, Deseada's extreme emotive intensity is the key proof the film offers to demonstrate the veracity and implications of Mayan beliefs. Deseada's whiteness-as-indigeneity allows the character to function as a conduit through which the film presents Indigenous spiritual beliefs as legitimate. By contrast, while Quiteria reveals these beliefs, she is less significant in demonstrating their credibility because she is not directly influenced by the truths she reveals. For this reason, her presence in the film is limited to a handful of scenes, and more significantly within the context of melodrama, her stoic demeanor and lack of emotional display indicate her marginality in the film. Her lack of narrative and affective significance means that the film does not construct Quiteria as a character with whom the spectator is meant to identify or through whom the implications of native beliefs are emphasized. The film further confirms Quiteria's marginality in all of these respects through the character's physical appearance, which, in contradistinction to Deseada's, coincides with the phenotypical expectations of Indigeneity within the Mexican racial formation.

Deseada is compatible with the cultural project of indigenismo-mestizaje in the sense that it lauds Mayan civilization as a robust source of culture and beauty, insinuates the importance of Indigenous culture for the nation at large, and conveys a self-consciousness about the authenticity of its representation of Indigeneity, which tends toward idealization and essentialization. *Deseada* re-creates a first contact scenario between Indigenous women and Spanish men; however, it reframes the foundational narrative of Mexican mestizaje as a troublesome affair in which the multiple intrusions of foreign men unleash chaos, which can only be explained and quelled through Indigenous spiritual beliefs. Despite the film's reconsideration of literal mestizaje as a destructive scenario, through its privileging of Indigenous spiritual beliefs as the key premises for meaning in the film, *Deseada* promotes the value of cultural mestizaje. The film conveys the legitimacy of the Mayan cosmovision through the language of melodrama, highlighting the validity of the beliefs through the affective implications they have for the white-as-indigenous protagonist, whose Whiteness makes her the privileged site of desire, affect, and also the ideal semiotic device through which to convey Indigenous spiritual beliefs as truth.

Conclusion

As mid-twentieth century Mexican artifacts, both *La noche de los mayas* and *Deseada* transmit a congruence with the official cultural stance of indigenismo-mestizaje, which promoted Indigenous cultures as a fundamental aspect of Mexican national identity. Both films convey their alignment with this position through their depiction of Mayan people as possessing an ancient, elaborate, and rich culture worthy of careful and accurate representation, to which the films self-consciously aspire. The essentialization of Indigeneity (intended to convey its separateness vis-à-vis the foreign male interlopers) takes the form of heightened aestheticization, either through enhanced lyricism (*La noche de los mayas*) or surrealist tendencies (*Deseada*).

While the two Mayan-themed films venerate Indigeneity, their treatment of mestizaje through romantic and sexual couplings is notably ambivalent. Instead of treating the unions of White men and Indigenous women as generative romances—as occurs in *Chilam Balam* (discussed in chapter 1)—in these films the interracial heterosexual desires that follow the incursions of foreign men into Indigenous space wreak havoc on Mayan traditions, relationships, and social and cosmic order, destroying instead of generating.

Despite both films' problematizing of romantic and sexual mestizaje, they do support cultural mestizaje by privileging their versions of Indigenous spiritual beliefs as legitimate sources of truth to which the female protagonists willingly adhere—an unusual perspective for Indigenous-themed Golden Age films. Furthermore, by centering a romanticized Indigenous worldview, the films present the Mayan maidens' cenote suicides as dignified acts that rectify damage unleashed by foreign men's meddling. While the films' presentation of the suicides cast them as meaningful acts of self-sacrifice, the deaths forcefully reframe mestizaje as a tragic scenario in which Indigenous people endure great pain and misfortune.

Less surprising than the pessimistic rewriting of the mestizaje narrative and the legitimization of (supposedly) Indigenous beliefs is the use of whiteness-as-indigeneity in Urueta and Gavaldón's films. Both *La noche de los mayas* and *Deseada* instrumentalize racial masquerade, producing (through Whiteness) visually normative female protagonists who serve as conduits between the fictionalized Indigenous cosmovisions that structure the melodramas and the Mexican spectator.

5

María Isabel

A White *Indita* for Modern Mexico

The majority of this book addresses Mexican Golden Age films because of the ideological and social significance that scholars have attributed to production of that period. However, extending our inquiry beyond this period is productive for achieving a fuller understanding of how the country's cinema continued to mediate race in ways that both drew from and evolved beyond the tropes of the 1930s, 1940s, and 1950s. While scholars largely agree that national production declined in quality beginning in the late 1950s,[1] it did continue to attract audiences after its heyday. In the 1960s, "Mexico had the joint highest per-capita rate of film attendance in the world,"[2] meaning that its contents still enjoyed a considerable degree of dissemination. Second, the visual logic that generated racial

---

[1]. Eduardo de la Vega Alfaro, "The Decline of the Golden Age and the Making of the Crisis," in *Mexico's Cinema: A Century of Film and Filmmakers*, ed. Joanne Hershfield and David Maciel (Wilmington, DE: Scholarly Resources, 1999), 165–91; Carl J. Mora, *Mexican Cinema: Reflections of a Society* (Berkeley: University of California Press, 1989); Jorge Ayala Blanco, *La aventura del cine mexicano en la época de oro y después* (Miguel Hidalgo: Grijalbo, 1993); Andrew Paxman, "Cooling to Cinema and Warming to Television: State Mass Media Policy, 1940–1964," in *Dictablanda: Politics, Work, and Culture in Mexico, 1938–1968*, ed. Paul Gillingham and Benjamin T. Smith (Durham, NC: Duke University Press, 2014), 308–15.

[2]. Paxman, "Cooling to Cinema," 315.

masquerade peristed past the Golden Age. Identifying and examining the continuity of whiteness-as-indigeneity point to its entrenchment as a convention for visually codifying desirability in Mexican cinema as a pervasive phenomenon in the local context. With this objective, chapter 5 explores how in the 1960s, whiteness-as-indigeneity adapts to suit an evolving proposal regarding *indigenismo-mestizaje* in cinema while at the same time maintaining the core functions of visually projecting desirable diegetic Indigeneity in a still racist, postcolonial Mexican context.

The very late cinematic iterations of the suffering, white-as-indigenous *indita*, *María Isabel* (dir. Federico Curiel, 1968) and its sequel, *El amor de María Isabel* (dir. Federico Curiel, 1970),[3] are both based on the *María Isabel* graphic novels by Yolanda Vargas Dulché. Produced during what scholars have termed the Mexican film industry's period of crisis,[4] the *María Isabel* duology lifts many of the clichés from Golden Age films that feature a victimized Indigenous female character and transplants them into the context of the late 1960s, with notable additions. The first film proposes María Isabel as a new, yet very familiar *indita* who embodies what the film suggests are the best aspects of both modernity and tradition. While on the one hand María Isabel opposes aspects of long-standing attitudes—overt racism and antiquated, hacienda-style patriarchy—on the other hand she embodies the traditional values of honesty, sexual modesty, sincerity, abnegation, and Catholic piety. Through these virtues, the film portrays María Isabel as the ideal Mexican woman who can ground the modern and affluent Mexican man amid the disorienting experience of local modernity, which the film represents through a stream of deceptive and self-interested characters. As in previous examples discussed in this book, María Isabel's whiteness-as-indigeneity is the visual device that functions to present her as the physically attractive, primary sufferer in the melodrama with whom the audience is meant to commiserate, and as the female model of good character in the film.

If the first film establishes the white-as-indigenous María Isabel as a paragon of Mexican female virtue, its sequel pits her *indita* goodness against a modern career woman who personifies White Mexican physical and cultural capital (*blancura* and *blanquitud*), Mireya. Even though the

---

3. I thank Enrique García for first bringing these films to my attention.
4. Mora, *Mexican Cinema*, 101–6.

actresses who interpret the roles of the two female adversaries, Silvia Pinal and Lucy Gallardo, both physically conform to the standards of Mexican female Whiteness (with Silvia Pinal's character displaying its darkest variant and a platinum blonde Lucy Gallardo exhibiting Mexican hyper-whiteness), diegetically, the women represent racial "opposites" in the context of the Mexican racial formation.[5] Furthermore, the two women also personify contrasting positions with respect to patriarchal norms, with María Isabel embodying tradition (because her greatest aspiration is to be wife and mother) and Mireya representing the modernity of the 1960s (because of her prolonged avoidance of marriage, indifference to motherhood, affair with a married man, and high-profile career). In setting the two women up as rivals for the love of the modern Mexican man, the film compares the merits of two models of Mexican womanhood in diegetically raced terms, coding liberated modernity as White and Marian traditionalism as Indigenous. The film's resolution upholds the latter as the correct moral and affective choice for the modern Mexican male, prioritizing patriarchy and conservative norms above diegetic Whiteness.

However, the visual plane of *El amor de María Isabel* undercuts the discursive preference that the film affords the Indigenous woman vis-à-vis White Mexican womanhood because it presents the protagonist through whiteness-as-indigeneity in the star body of Silvia Pinal. This instrumentalization of whiteness-as-indigeneity means that while the film's diegesis presents the perseverance of an interracial romantic union, visually it avoids the projection of a coupling that can visually be understood as interracial in the context of the local racial formation. In the end, the *María Isabel* films' farcical representation of Indigenous womanhood and of a mestizo happily-ever-after merely transmit the hegemonic norm of White Mexican endogamy on the visual level, thus nullifying any progressive gesture regarding Mexican race relations that the interracial love plot could have contained. In this way, the *Maria Isabel* duology is a perfect example of the persistence of whiteness-as-indigeneity as a raced mechanism through which Mexican cinema has for decades manifested a discursive idealization of Indigeneity while simultaneously denying its visualization as desirable or love-worthy.

---

5. Claudio Lomnitz-Adler, *Exits from the Labyrinth* (Berkeley: University of California Press, 1992), 263–80.

Figure 5.1. Silvia Pinal playing an Indigenous maid in *María Isabel* (1968). Photo courtesy of Mil Nubes-Foto (Roberto Fiesco). All rights reserved.

María Isabel (1967)

The first *María Isabel* film is a kind of racialized Cinderella narrative whose various (and at times only tenuously related) episodes evidence the film's origin in a serial narrative format. An overview of the film's long and convoluted plot is necessary to be able to follow the in-depth analysis that follows.

María Isabel begins when the title character is a child living as a peasant on the hacienda of Don Félix Pereira, along with her father and unkind stepmother. María Isabel and Don Felix's daughter, Graciela, are close friends despite Don Félix's strict rule that Graciela should not socialize with Indians. Graciela is sent away for school and returns when the two girls have grown. Don Félix attempts to force his daughter to marry the son of a wealthy man with whom he has business dealings, but Graciela falls in love with an engineer, Leobardo, who is working on a highway near the hacienda. After the two have sex, Leobardo dies in an explosion related to the highway project. María Isabel and Graciela run away to Mexico City, where Graciela gives birth to a baby girl, Rosa Isela. As Graciela is dying after having given birth, she gives María Isabel a valuable medallion for the baby, and María Isabel promises to raise Rosa Isela. María Isabel first takes refuge in a church where a priest gives her a letter of recommendation to seek employment. Her first employers are comfortable (but very stingy) spinsters who exploit María Isabel and accuse her of theft upon finding the medallion among her things. Maria Isabel leaves and ends up in the house of another wealthy family, where the son (a young medical student) attempts to rape her. After the student helps María Isabel cure an illness that Rosa Isela contracted, he helps her find other employment.

At this point, María Isabel lands at the house of the well-to-do widower Ricardo Robles, who lives with his young daughter, Gloria. Gloria resents the presence of the Indigenous maid and her daughter. María Isabel uncovers the dishonesty of another maid and the butler and becomes the only employee in the house. After attending the private school where Gloria studies, Rosa Isela becomes embarrassed because María Isabel is an Indigenous maid. Gloria turns into an unruly adolescent. Ricardo makes plans to marry the opportunistic Lucrecia, who is in fact, involved with another man and intends to finance an escape with her secret lover using the valuable gifts Ricardo has given her. María Isabel uncovers the couple's scheme. Gloria elopes with her boyfriend, causing Ricardo great distress. By chance, Rosa Isela meets her grandfather, Don Félix, who identifies the girl as his granddaughter upon recognizing the medallion that Graciela had left her daughter on her deathbed. Don Félix demands that María Isabel give him Rosa Isela, which she does only because Rosa Isela does not want to be the daughter of a poor, Indigenous maid. Grief-stricken by the absence of their daughters, María Isabel and Ricardo recognize their mutual love and marry.

Part of the way in which the first *María Isabel* film constructs its protagonist as the ideal *indita* for modern Mexico is by highlighting that she is averse to two aspects of traditional Mexican society that the film presents as problematic: racism and hacienda-style patriarchy. The film first problematizes Mexican racism when Don Félix sternly forbids the girls from continuing their friendship because María Isabel is Indigenous. The film clearly presents Don Félix's racist position in a negative light when he violently interrupts the two girls as they are playing happily together, yelling with disapproval, "¿Se puede saber qué hace esta india aquí en mi casa?" (What is this Indian doing here in my house?). The hacendado proceeds to rip Graciela's doll from María Isabel's hands and make a gesture suggesting he is ready to strike her as loud nondiegetic music sounds, echoing his violence. By conveying his racist and forceful reaction as entirely disproportionate to the girl's activities, the film criticizes Don Félix's bigotry and establishes him as an antagonist who jeopardizes the cross-racial friendship that both girls hold dear—foreshadowing how he will later obstruct the filial bond between Rosa Isela and María Isabel. However, instead of accepting the racist directives, María Isabel challenges those who seek to enforce segregation. As she grows into adulthood, she preserves her fondness and loyalty to Graciela, despite the fact that Don Félix has sent her away, and opts to resume the friendship when Graciela returns.

Furthermore, María Isabel also defends her friendship with Graciela in the context of her own family, which is not portrayed as bigoted toward the White hacendados, but as having internalized the racist norms of social interaction set by the Whites. The young María Isabel opposes her stepmother, who, not thinking the two girls could actually be friends, accuses María Isabel of stealing Graciela's doll and beats her for it. María Isabel also challenges her father's ideas, which reflect an internalization of Mexican apartheid, when he states firmly, "La hija de un peón, y la hija de un amo, pues, no se llevan" (The daughter of a peasant, and the daughter of the master, well, they don't go together). In forging and maintaining a friendship into adulthood, the girls defy raced-based opposition from both Don Félix and María Isabel's family. In this way, the film presents María Isabel as a character who does not conform to the racist social norms that the film problematizes as impediments to authentic affective bonds.

In addition to the protagonist's defense of her cross-racial affective bonds, *María Isabel* clearly associates its title character with resistance to racist behavior and assumptions through her repeated energetic reactions to the bigotry she encounters as an adult. For instance, when the head maid at Don Félix's house slaps and insults her, saying, "Aprende a respetar, india estúpida" (Learn some respect, you stupid Indian), María Isabel rejects the idea that her race makes her deserving of such disparaging behavior. The protagonist shouts back, "Por muy india y muy burra que sea, ¡a mí no me pega naiden!" (Though I may be a dumb Indian, no one hits me!) and physically assaults the woman. This pattern is repeated in the house of Ricardo Robles, where the other maid in the house refers to María Isabel disrespectfully as "esa india ladina" (that wily Indian), "india patarrajada" (barefoot Indian), and "india salvaje" (savage Indian), which the protagonist ignores. However, when the maid in question hits Rosa Isela because María Isabel is Indigenous, María Isabel again rejects the idea that her Indigeneity justifies such physical abuse. The protagonist instead restates her Indigenous identity as a source of pride and strength before attacking the woman: "Ahora sí se te aparece el nahual, condenada. ¡Vas a probar las manos de las indias!" (You're about to encounter the nahual,[6] you wretch. You will have a taste of Indian hands!). By exhibiting María Isabel's direct verbal and physical confrontation of race-based bigotry and violence, the film celebrates her as a figure who vehemently rejects this long-standing aspect of tradition and upholds the tenets of discursive postrevolutionary *mestizaje* according to which Indigenous people should be recognized and respected as co-citizens.[7]

The other aspect of traditional social attitudes that *María Isabel* problematizes is the hacienda-style patriarchy that Don Félix personifies. The film presents Don Félix's approach to asserting control over Graciela's life as negative and outdated when he begins to carry out his plan for marrying off his daughter. For instance, Don Félix merely informs Graciela whom she is supposed to marry and ignores her reservations because, unbeknownst to her, he had arranged the betrothal when she was a child. *María Isabel* suggests that this arranged marriage is out of step with the comparatively modern concept of the love marriage, represented in the film through Graciela and Leobardo's romantic relationship. The suitor Graciela prefers is, in fact, Don Félix's generational, professional, and ideological male opposite, whose youth and engineering work on a new highway near the

---

6. "Dating back to pre-Columbian times, nahualism asserts that each human is born linked to an animal alter ego, her coessence or nahual (alternatively, *nagual* or *nawal*). The nahual accompanies that human over the course of her entire life. The human and animal pair shares a soul or consciousness; they have the same breath but adopt different bodily forms," in Carolyn Fornoff, "Nahual," in *An Ecotopian Lexicon*, ed. Matthew Schneider-Mayerson and Brent Ryan Bellamy (Minneapolis: University of Minnesota Press, 2019), 164.

7. That the film discursively positions itself as being antiracist and adjacent to María Isabel's race-based plight can be appreciated through a subscript that appears on the film's DVD cover, which explains that the film is "una historia que hace reflexionar sobre la discriminación y los abusos de los cuales son víctimas los indígenas" (a story that makes one reflect on the discrimination and abuses of which Indigenous people are victims).

hacienda cast him as a symbol of the arrival of Mexican modernity.[8] Don Félix's virulent responses to the modern courtship further suggest that his clinging to outmoded values is misguided. The film points in this direction when the hacendado beats Graciela forcefully with a whip for staying out all night with Leobardo, and later when Don Félix reacts to learning that Graciela is no longer a virgin by intending to shoot her lover. The practice of betrothal in infancy, the beating of an adult child, and the use of lethal force in retribution for a daughter's premarital sexual activity all hark back to the social customs of a preindustrial era. In this way, *María Isabel* establishes Don Félix's patriarchal authority as anachronistic and problematic (if not altogether barbaric) in the context of 1960s Mexico.

The film positions María Isabel on the side of modernity vis-à-vis the patriarchal expectations both she and Graciela face. María Isabel mitigates Don Félix's oppressive traditionalism to the extent that she works together with Graciela to defy his patriarchal authority—a move the film portrays as resistance to injustice. When Graciela decides to defy her father's plans for her arranged wedding, María Isabel runs away to the city with her, where, unbeknownst to Don Félix, she raises the child herself in accordance with Graciela's dying wishes. Furthermore, María Isabel's actions also cause her to confront patriarchal norms in her own family. When she stays out all night waiting for Graciela to return from Leobardo's camp, María Isabel's family and fiancé interpret her unexplained nocturnal absence as an indication of her sexual activity, which they regard as unacceptable. However, instead of revealing the truth to preserve her status as a dutiful daughter and faithful fiancée within the patriarchal family arrangement, María Isabel instead takes on the condition of the "fallen woman" to protect Graciela. Because both women's decisions pit them against their families' expectations of sexual and marital propriety, María Isabel and Graciela temporarily function as a cross-racial female alliance that opposes some traditional patriarchal norms. Ironically, María Isabel's defense of the modern value of female agency lands her in the traditional position of abnegated Marian figure.

While *María Isabel* illustrates how its Indigenous female protagonist rejects racist expressions of violence and hacienda-style patriarchy, the

---

8. The conflict between Leobardo and Don Félix is but one cinematic iteration of clashes between Mexican men who represent prerevolutionary and contemporary values in national cinema. See Ernesto R. Acevedo Muñoz's analysis of the male characters in Luis Buñuel's *Él*, in *Buñuel and Mexico: The Crisis of National Cinema* (Berkeley: University of California Press, 2003), 124–42.

film also idealizes her as the embodiment of traditional characteristics that it presents as positive—many of which are recognizable as Golden Age tropes of the virtuous *indita*. Paramount among these is, of course, María Isabel's central position in the melodrama as its primary sufferer. The instances in which María Isabel experiences suffering are numerous and are linked to self-sacrifice. First, she endures the rejection of her father and fiancé because she protects Graciela. Then, after she assumes responsibility for Rosa Isela, María Isabel endures poverty, hardship, and humiliation as she tries to find a stable situation as a single mother. In trying to provide for Rosa Isela, she is exploited by the two spinsters and sexually attacked by the medical student. However, María Isabel's greatest source of suffering occurs when the film takes a turn that is reminiscent of *Imitation of Life* (dir. John Stahl, 1934; dir. Douglas Sirk, 1959). Rosa Isela begins rejecting her adopted mother when she realizes that at school, her White phenotype causes people to assume she is a member of the upper class until her classmates realize that her mother is an Indigenous maid. This racialized and classist rejection of all of María Isabel's maternal sacrifices culminates when Rosa Isela insists on going to live with her grandfather, unleashing María Isabel's deepest expression of distress in the film. In sum, following melodramatic conventions, the film elevates María Isabel as a woman of good character because of her continuous self-sacrifice and suffering for the sake of others.

Another central way in which the film idealizes María Isabel along traditional lines is by constructing her as an embodiment of *marianismo*. In taking on maternal responsibility for Rosa Isela, María Isabel literally becomes a virgin mother—an obvious parallel to the biblical account of the circumstances surrounding Mary's motherhood, which María Isabel's very name reinforces. Furthermore, María Isabel remains celibate until her marriage with Ricardo, exhibiting the traditional Catholic ideal of sexual modesty in women, which she defends by going so far as to forcefully fight off the medical student's sexual advances to protect her virginity.

Moreover, despite being in love with Ricardo, María Isabel does not use sexuality to attract him, in contradistinction to other females who are coded as modern (and White) in the film and who do use their bodies and sexuality to attract men. The duology clearly puts forward this comparison at the beginning of the sequel when María Isabel responds to an indignant secretary at Ricardo's office who cannot believe that an Indigenous maid has managed to marry a wealthy professional man. In María Isabel's response, she contrasts city women who use their bodies for material gain with a virtuous representation of herself as "una pobre india . . . con sus pies descalzos, pero con el corazón más limpio que muchas taquígrafas que se arreglan las medias delante de su jefe, se pintarrajean como payasos y usan unas faldas que parecen taparrabos, y ni así logran nada" (a poor Indian . . . barefoot, but with a heart cleaner than that of many secretaries who fix their pantyhose in front of their boss, make themselves up like clowns and wear skirts that look like loincloths, and even then don't get anywhere). *María Isabel* further underscores the title character's sexual modesty by contrasting her with Lucrecia, Ricardo's scheming fiancée, who first appears on-screen in a pink feathered negligée, signaling her sexual involvement with him. Finally, though not explicitly presented as sexually active, Ricardo's adolescent daughter, Gloria, also serves as an immodest counterpoint to María Isabel's propriety when she appears dancing wildly in a skimpy bathing suit during a party she throws in her father's absence. In short, through her motherhood, abstinence from sexual relations, and modesty, the film constructs María Isabel as the embodiment of traditional feminine virtues vis-à-vis women whose behaviors it presents as more modern and misguided.

Beyond exemplifying the Marian ideal through her actions and attitudes, the film also presents María Isabel as a positive representative of Mexican traditional values by constructing her as a faithful Catholic in her modern context. For one, she is the only character who is ever shown in the act of prayer. Predictably, the primary way in which the film showcases María Isabel's Catholicism is through her devotion to the Virgin of Guadalupe. This long-standing characteristic of good *inditas* (and women in general)[9] in Mexican cinema first surfaces when she takes refuge in a church with Rosa Isela just after Graciela's death. As she sits in the pew of an empty church, María Isabel prays out loud for the Virgin of Guadalupe's intersession: "Tú sí me haces caso, virgencita de Guadalupe. Eres india como yo. No dejes que naiden me la quite . . . Echanos tu bendición, virgencita" (You do listen to me, dear Virgin of Guadalupe. You are an Indian like me. Don't let anyone take her from me . . . Give us your blessing, dear Virgin). As well as showcasing María Isabel's piety, the scene ties her feminine virtue to a specific traditional Mexican role model. The film further underscores this association on a visual level later when María Isabel prays to the Virgin to thank her for curing Rosa Isela. As María Isabel thanks the saint, a tightly framed, out-of-focus image of the Virgin of Guadalupe is shown on-screen, and in its center appears

---

9. Laura Isabel Serna, *Making Cinelandia: American Films and Mexican Film Culture Before the Golden Age* (Durham, NC: Duke University Press, 2014), 140–43.

a sharply focused reflection of María Isabel's face onto the glass that protects the image, blending the two into one visual. By combining the recognizable image of the Virgin of Guadalupe with María Isabel's face, this shot suggests that the character is an extension of the saint because of her Mexican Indigeneity and virtue (see figure 5.2).

Furthermore, *María Isabel* bolsters its idealization of the title character via Marian devotion by implying that the Virgin of Guadalupe is indeed a powerful intercessor and that María Isabel does well to place faith in her. This first occurs when, just after María Isabel utters her prayer to the Virgin in the church, a priest immediately appears, offering María Isabel housing for a month and later providing her with a good recommendation so that she can find work. The film also suggests that the Virgin of Guadalupe's protection explains the happy dénouement of María Isabel's romantic aspirations with Ricardo. This occurs during the final scene when, after a shot of the couple during their wedding ceremony at the altar in the same church where María Isabel had sought refuge earlier, the camera tilts upward to reveal a large image of the Virgin of Guadalupe—the film's final image—as resounding celebratory music plays. By showcasing the image of the Virgin in the context of María Isabel's wedding, the film suggests that the Mexican saint has indeed protected María Isabel and has eventually rewarded her with a rich White Mexican man. In presenting

Figure 5.2. María Isabel is literally reflected in the image of the Virgin of Guadalupe. Screen capture from film.

Ricardo as the *indita*'s compensation for virtue via the Virgin of Guadalupe's intercession, the film instrumentalizes this religious symbol to reinforce wealth and Whiteness as the ideal characteristics in the men whom good Mexican *cenicientas* (Cinderellas) should aspire to marry.

In addition to resorting to familiar gendered and religious tropes to highlight the *indita*'s goodness, María Isabel also idealizes the title character by contrasting her with persons who engage in dishonest behavior in the city. For instance, when María Isabel first arrives at Ricardo's house, the maid and butler who are working there steal part of the money intended for the weekly groceries. Also, Ricardo's fiancée, Lucrecia, deceives him by feigning that she is in love with him when she is in fact romantically involved with another man and is only trying to acquire valuables through her relationship with Ricardo. In both cases, it is María Isabel who uncovers the true actions and motivations of these dishonest characters, which aligns her with truth and sincerity in contradistinction to their duplicitousness. Furthermore, the ways in which these characters attempt to acquire money (involving theft, sexuality, and deceit) cast María Isabel as woman who adheres to the traditional Mexican maxim according to which an underprivileged person can pride themselves in being "pobre, pero honrado" (poor, but honest).

Beyond the other characters' dishonesty, the film also uses characterizations that emphasize affective scarcity to idealize María Isabel for her ability to display love. For instance, Lucrecia's calculated sham relationship with Ricardo most obviously highlights the authenticity of María Isabel's true feelings toward him, but Lucrecia is not alone in her inability to express what the film suggests are appropriate expressions of love. For example, Ricardo's daughter, Gloria, is emotionally indifferent toward her father. Though he repeatedly asks for signs of affection, such as responses to his letters or her company on a trip to Europe, Gloria responds coldly while continuing to use his resources, leading her father to conclude that she only sees him as "una fábrica de dinero" (a money factory). Similarly, in the urban upper-class milieu, Rosa Isela fails to develop an affective bond with her parent, María Isabel. When Rosa Isela realizes her mother's socioeconomic disadvantage, she rejects María Isabel forcefully,[10] instead opting to live with her grandfather because of his wealth and status. The film most clearly articulates María Isabel's distinction as the character who is guided by deep affective

---

10. When María Isabel picks her daughter up during a school celebration of Mother's Day, the teacher realizes that María Isabel is not Rosa Isela's maid, but her mother. The girl reacts by shouting, "¡Me da vergüenza que seas mi madre y no quiero te vean conmigo!" (I am ashamed that you are my mother and I don't want to be seen with you!).

investment as opposed to money and self-interest when she responds to Don Félix's offer to pay her any amount of money she desires in exchange for Rosa Isela: "¡Dinero! Para usted no hay más que su cochino dinero . . . Todo el dinero del mundo no sirve para comprar una hija, ¡y la mía no se vende!" (Money! For you there is only your dirty money . . . All the money in the world can't buy a daughter, and mine is not for sale.) Despite her poverty, María Isabel rejects the offer, insisting that an authentic maternal bond cannot be monetized because it consists of profound love.[11]

Of course, in the context of Mexican melodrama, the ultimate proof of María Isabel's authentic maternal love is her willingness to suffer, which the film suggests supersedes a blood relation that has little affective substance to it. María Isabel asserts the legitimacy of her claim to Rosa Isela in terms of her suffering when she states to Don Félix, "No le di mi sangre, pero le di algo que vale más que eso: harto cariño, sacrificios, cuidados, hasta pedí limosna pa' darle de comer. Ahora trabajo de criada para cuidarla y educarla!" (I didn't give her my blood, but I gave her something that is worth much more: a lot of love, sacrifice, care; I even begged to be able to feed her. Now I work as a maid to take care of her and educate her). Through this display of María Isabel's love and suffering, the film marks her as Rosa Isela's rightful parent vis-à-vis Don Félix, whose wealth did not compensate for his poor parenting of Graciela[12] and who continues to foreground his wealth (instead of his love) to support his claim to his granddaughter.[13] In short, the film presents María Isabel as the most emotionally genuine character in the film amid several affectively stunted individuals who primarily relate to others in financial and material terms. The film's melodramatic mode privileges María Isabel's feelings of love and suffering as noble, positioning her as a traditional female model because of her sincerity in a world where most operate through a logic of monetized, self-centered convenience.

---

11. In this sense, *María Isabel* reproduces a pattern famously disseminated in Ismael Rodríguez's films *Nosotros los pobres* (1948) and *Ustedes los ricos* (1949) in which the nobility of the poor is rooted in their sincere affective bonds, while the rich are largely incapable of creating them.

12. María Isabel points out that Don Félix's wealth did not improve the quality of his daughter's life when she says to him, "Y pá qué le sirvió toda esa fortuna a su hija, no más para hacerla desgraciada" (What good was your fortune to your daughter if it made her miserable?).

13. "Si tanto la quieres, piensa en su felicidad y en su porvenir porque todo mi dinero pasará a sus manos" (If you love her that much, think of her happiness and her future because all of my money will pass to her).

While *María Isabel* updates the Golden Age *indita* as an ideal combination of modernity and tradition for 1960s Mexico, at the same time, the film perpetuates some long-standing essentialisms and racist clichés to mark María Isabel's Indigeneity. These include the idea that Indigenous people, as members of the lower class, lack restraint in their emotional and physical reactions (which the film suggests when María Isabel lashes out physically at overtly bigoted characters).[14] The racist stereotype that *María Isabel* presents most pervasively throughout the film is the notion that Indigenous Mexicans are ignorant people. *María Isabel* engages this stereotype through the title character's *indito* Spanish—a holdover from the Golden Age—whose anachronisms ("naiden," "su merced," "casorio," etc.), limited vocabulary, and simple syntax suggest her lack of fluency in dominant Spanish.[15] This artificial *indito* speech attributes to María Isabel an air of simplicity and affected comicality, especially when compared with the film's overall soundtrack in which standard Mexican Spanish is more pervasive, thus marking her status as Other.[16] The film further underscores María Isabel's alienation from formal uses of language in that she is initially illiterate and later learns to read and write from her adopted daughter when Rosa Isela begins school—a reversal of the typical parent/child dynamic, which infantilizes the Indigenous female character. The film reinforces the idea of María Isabel's ignorance when she is employed at the medical student's family home and believes that the skeleton model he is using to prepare for his medical exams is the skeleton of an actual dead person. The externalization of her fear in an exaggerated, childlike manner,[17] which even her employer's explanation does not quell, suggests

---

14. As Pierre Bourdieu has noted, "the highly censored language of the bourgeoisie" contructs itself in opposition to "popular outspokenness," which in its body language is characterized by "agitation and haste, grimaces and gesticulation . . ." as "opposed to slowness . . .—to the restraint and impassivity which signify elevation." *Distinction: A Social Critique of the Judgement of Taste*, trans. Richard Nice (New York: Routledge, 2010), 172.

15. Dolores Tierney, *Emilio Fernández: Pictures in the Margins* (Manchester: Manchester University Press, 2012), 73–102; Yásnaya Aguilar, "El efecto Tizoc," July 4, 2012, https://web.archive.org/web/20190510094735/http://archivo.estepais.com/site/2012/el-efecto-tizoc/.

16. Ella Shohat and Robert Stam, *Unthinking Eurocentrism: Multiculturalism and the Media* (New York: Routledge, 1994), 192.

17. For the trope of infantilizing nonWhite characters in cinema see Shohat and Stam, *Unthinking Eurocentrism*, 139–140.

that María Isabel's alienation from formal education makes her incapable of discerning between a model that serves an academic purpose and human remains (see figure 5.3). Last, the film conflates María Isabel's general lack of formal education with the idea that she is intellectually deficient when she repeatedly refers to herself as "burra" (dumb) throughout the film. In these ways, *María Isabel* reinforces the racist assumption that Indigenous people are not as knowledgeable or intellectually developed as mestizo and criollo Mexicans.

And yet *María Isabel*'s use of the racist trope that attributes ignorance to Indigenous people is more complex than the above analysis would suggest on its own. While the film points to the fact that María Isabel does not know proper Spanish, arithmetic, or science, the film does not suggest that

Figure 5.3. María Isabel overreacts to a model skeleton. Screen capture from film.

she is a stupid person. On the contrary, María Isabel's awareness of her surroundings allows her to uncover covert machinations such as the maid and butler's theft, Lucrecia's scheme, and Gloria's secret departure from her father's home, of which others are entirely unaware. Counterintuitively, the film's insistence on María Isabel's deficiency in general knowledge is part of the way it attempts to elevate the Indigenous heroine in comparison with other characters because that formal knowledge is unnecessary for María Isabel's accurate perceptions and good actions. Furthermore, the film relativizes the value of formal education because the majority of the characters who do possess it are either morally inferior to the uneducated Indigenous woman, or they are unable to perceive what María Isabel is able to understand *despite* her educational disadvantages.

In this sense, *María Isabel* anticipates the character who would become the most important cinematic *indita* of the following decade, La India María.[18] *María Isabel* and the first *India María* film, *Tonta, tonta, pero no tanto* (dir. Fernando Cortés, 1972), have similar storylines in which humble Indigenous women from rural areas migrate to Mexico City and reveal the dishonest actions of city people. Like María Isabel, La India María lacks formal education, which the film emphasizes for comedic purposes through her *indita* Spanish, illiteracy, and other displays of ignorance (such as assuming that her cousin is physically inside a television camera). Like María Isabel, María's ignorance does not impede her from uncovering various crimes. For instance, when María ends up in the house of a wealthy and eccentric widow who believes that her dead husband is still living and communicating with her, María uncovers the niece's plot to steal from the widow by catering to the old woman's belief that her husband talks to the living. In this way, *Tonta, tonta, pero no tanto*, like *María Isabel*, uses the racist cliché of Indigenous ignorance to celebrate María's ability to reveal truth as a meritorious achievement.

Furthermore, the first India María film also goes a step further than *María Isabel* in that it instrumentalizes the racist cliché of Indigenous ignorance for the purposes of social critique. *Tonta, tonta, pero no tanto* ultimately attributes María's ignorance to the lack of schools in rural areas, which María herself remedies by using the reward money she earns for solving a murder to open a school in her town, San José de los Burros (the name of which is an indirect reference to the supposed mental simplicity

---

18. Seraina Rohrer, *La India María: Mexploitation and the Films of María Elena Velasco* (Austin: University of Texas Press, 2017).

of rural Mexicans). Though the film does present María as an ignorant Indigenous woman, it also suggests that this culturally unsophisticated *indita* manages to step in to provide the basic right and service of education where the state has failed to do so. *María Isabel* stops short of such broader social commentary, but both *María Isabel* and *Tonta, tonta pero no tanto* coincide in that they both reproduce the racist trope of Indigenous female ignorance to celebrate how their protagonists are able to circumvent the channels of cultural and social capital to effectively reveal truth.

I suggest, therefore, that *María Isabel* is partly a precursor to María Elena Velasco's comedic persona, La India María, but that it is still deeply influenced by the conventions of the Golden Age Indigenous woman discussed in previous chapters. The elements that *María Isabel* inherits from the Golden Age are, on the one hand, the fundamentally melodramatic nature of the story that privileges the Indigenous female as the primary sufferer, and, on the other, the fact that María Isabel is physically attractive and desired in the diegesis. I contend that these two elements, which distinguish María Isabel from La India María, are also the ones that explain why *María Isabel* still resorts to the use of whiteness-as-indigeneity to visualize the diegetically Indigenous woman, while La India María does not.

María Isabel attempts to induce the spectator's compassion for its Indigenous female protagonist by presenting her as the virtuous victim of others' misdeeds or selfishness. To align the spectator with the pathos that foregrounds a diegetically Indigenous character, the film appeals to the colonization of subjectivity—the process through which narratives in colonial and postcolonial contexts privilege Whiteness as the locus of protagonism and heroism. The film does this by using the star body of the Silvia Pinal to manifest Indigenous womanhood on-screen.[19] María Isabel is therefore an instance of whiteness-as-indigeneity in that her *indita* Spanish, ignorance, dark braids, and occasional disregard of bourgeois bodily restraint are meant to mark her as Indigenous, while other aspects of her body conform to the expectations of physical female Whiteness

---

19. As Paxman notes, Pinal, like Ignacio López Tarso and Mauricio Garcés, was a star during the twilight of the Golden Age and after, during which there were "few creative and commited directors to coax them beyond the banal." Paxman, "Cooling to Cinema," 314. Without a doubt, the *María Isabel* films belong to this category in contradistinction to the more prestigious roles Pinal had previously landed, most notably in two of Luis Buñuel's films, *Viridiana* (1961) and *El angel exterminador* (1962).

in the Mexican racial formation.[20] Concretely, Silvia Pinal's tall, slender body, fine facial features, large eyes, and light skin tone lend María Isabel an on-screen presence that is aligned with the physical criteria for female Whiteness in Mexico. The only modification that the actress made to her body for it to signify Indigeneity for her performance of María Isabel was to don black tresses (either by dying her hair or wearing a wig) in contrast to the blond to light auburn hair color that she usually wore.

The fact that in the local context Silvia Pinal's physical features align with the Mexican construct of Whiteness is evidenced through her participation in different advertising campaigns in which her Whiteness and bourgeois social status were leveraged to sell everything from toiletries to coffee. In a 1960 television advertisement for Colgate soap, for example, Silvia Pinal appears selling a bar of the soap and smiling with the following text superimposed onto her image: "Blancura, Perfume y Suavidad con un solo Jabón Colagate dice Silvia Pinal" (Whiteness, Perfume, and Softness only with Colgate Soap says Silvia Pinal). Here the advertisement uses the word "Blancura" (Whiteness) in complicated ways. While the latter two characteristics of the soap "Perfume y Suavidad" (Perfume and Softness) clearly refer to qualities that the soap provides for skin when the product is used to wash it, the same cannot be said straightforwardly for "Blancura" (whiteness) because no soap has the ability to make skin whiter in the literal sense. What the advertisement does by using the word is conflate the notion of cleaning the skin with that of lightening its chromatic shade,[21] which, as the introduction to this book indicates, can be a desirable physical shift in the context of the Mexican racial formation. The use of Silvia Pinal's star persona to endorse the soap suggests that her skin possess the qualities that the soap claims to provide in veiled racial terms, among them "Blancura" (see figure 5.4). This advertisement

---

20. Although skirting the issue of race, Emilio García Riera suggests the lack of verisimilitude in the visual presentation of the Indigenous servant, María Isabel, through the body of Silvia Pinal. See *El cine de Silvia Pinal* (Guadalajara: Universidad de Guadalajara, 1996), 121. The María Isabel films function analogously to the telenovelas analyzed by Sofía Rios, which "do not convey a believably indigenous or rural background," in "Representation and Disjunction: Made-up Maids in Mexican Telenovelas," *Journal of Iberian and Latin American Research* 21, no. 2 (2015): 223.

21. As Dyer explains, this conflation has been a commercial strategy used to sell cleansing products aimed at women since the nineteenth century. See Richard Dyer, "Coloured White, Not Coloured," in *White* (London and New York: Routledge, 1997), 76–79.

Figure 5.4. Silvia Pinal in an advertisement for Colgate soap that aligns her with Mexican Whiteness. Screen capture from commercial.

points to the fact that, in the context of the Mexican racial formation, Silvia Pinal's physical appearance was treated as exemplary in part because it was consistent with a local physical White ideal.

Furthermore, by the time Silvia Pinal acted in the *María Isabel* duology, she was arguably the last diva of the Golden Age.[22] Her career included numerous roles that exalted the desirability of her body in addition to gaining critical success in Luis Buñuel's *Viridiana* (1961) and *El angel exterminador* (1962).[23] As in the case of Dolores del Río and María Félix's interpretation of Indigenous women in their respective films, Silvia Pinal's star power, which hinged in part on her image as an attractive Mexican actress who inhabited normative beauty standards, is a factor that imbues the Indigenous character in the *María Isabel* duology with the qualities of desirability that were inseparable from Pinal's star text.[24]

---

22. Paxman, "Cooling to Cinema," 314.

23. García Riera, *El cine de Silvia Pinal*.

24. For instance, the promotional material for *Desnúdate, Lucrecia* (dir. Tulio Demicheli, 1958), in which Silvia Pinal starred, featured the actress's shapely and scantily clad body, building expectations around its exposure in the film.

The same physical characteristics associated with Whiteness in the local context that make Silvia Pinal an example of beauty in Mexican advertisements are used to constitute María Isabel's beauty in the film in which Pinal plays an Indigenous woman. The film repeatedly identifies María Isabel as a physically attractive woman through the comments of several characters, including Graciela, the medical student, Ricardo's friend, and Ricardo. Like the Golden Age films discussed in the previous chapters of this book, *María Isabel* opts to present the diegetically beautiful Indigenous woman using the visual physical signifiers that connote Whiteness in the Mexican racial formation. In this way, the *María Isabel* duology continues to operate according to the pattern of the colonization of beauty and desire. The films manifest the concept of Indigenous beauty through the visual language of Whiteness because coloniality itself determines that Whiteness is the standard by which value is measured (here in the form of beauty), making Indigenous beauty visually unrepresentable within this racist logic.

Raising again a comparison between María Isabel and La India María helps to illustrate more clearly the above explanation of María Isabel's whiteness-as-indigeneity. La India María presents its protagonist in a body that conforms to some of the expectations of physical Indigeneity in the context of the Mexican racial formation (such as short stature, a stout build, and medium skin tone).[25] This occurs, as Charles Ramírez Berg has suggested, because she is a comedic character,[26] which means that, unlike Indigenous-themed melodramas, the *India María* films prod the spectator to laugh at and along with María,[27] but not weep for her. Instead, the act of commiseration that Indigenous-themed melodramas encourage requires a degree of identification with the primary sufferer in the narrative, but because Indigenous people constitute a stigmatized social identity in Mexico, the matter of promoting audience identification with a member of this group is a "problem" in the context of Mexican representation. For this reason, María Isabel and other melodramatic *inditas* appear in a physical form that is consistent with the local construct of Whiteness because the physical Whiteness of the diegetically Indigenous character functions as a semiotic trick to promote identification between the spectator and the character in the still colonially inflected Mexican social reality. The comedic

---

25. Rohrer, *La India María*, 24.

26. Charles Ramírez Berg, *Cinema of Solitude* (Austin: University of Texas Press, 2010), 57.

27. Rohrer, *La India María*, 27, 117–120.

films of La India María, by contrast, are predicated on maintaining the *distance* between the spectator and the comparatively naive María. Because the entire comedic premise of these films is that María is a Mexican who is not entirely assimilated into criollo/mestizo Mexican culture, her supposed physical Indigeneity functions to corroborate her status as an Other who knows less than the culturally assimilated spectator.

Furthermore, the India María films do not attempt to present her as sexually or romantically desirable for other characters or for the spectator, which means that the films can avoid the semiotic "dilemma" of how to visually manifest an Indigenous semblance (according to the parameters of the local racial formation) that can also be understood as beautiful by a Mexican audience. Because the spectator is not meant to identify with La India María, but to understand her as Other (to laugh at her), and because she is not upheld as an object of beauty or desire, La India María is one of the few female protagonists who is not subject to the White imperative of narrative Mexican cinema.

In sum, the first *María Isabel* film constructs its Indigenous female protagonist as an ideal combination of modernity and tradition because she rejects overt racism and antiquated hacienda-style patriarchy while still retaining the values of sexual modesty, honesty, and Guadalupan-centered piety. Through the contrast between María Isabel and the better-educated but self-interested and materialistic characters, María Isabel emerges as morally and affectively superior despite the disadvantages that the film attributes to her race. Visually, the film's strategy for reinforcing María Isabel's compassion-worthy suffering, moral admirability, and beauty through whiteness-as-indigeneity provides continuity with Golden Age precursors. At the same time, María Isabel's triumph through morality despite her racially stereotyped ignorance presented in a comedic vein links the film to an important subsequent *indita*, La India María. Comparing the demands that both Indigenous-themed film franchises make of their audience underscores the conventions of whiteness-as-indigeneity as a strategy that Mexican cinema mobilizes in the context of the melodramatic mode when there is the requirement of desirability.

El amor de María Isabel (1970)

While the first María Isabel film suggests that the protagonist's lack of White cultural capital (*blanquitud*) is ultimately unimportant because of her moral excellence and affective genuineness vis-à-vis Whiter characters, the sequel, *El amor de María Isabel*, takes up cultural competence as a primary component of conflict. The sequel introduces a new character who embodies high culture and becomes María Isabel's rival for Ricardo's love, Mireya. The film therefore pits two models of Mexican womanhood against each other in racialized terms, with Mireya personifying Eurocentric Mexican culture and cosmopolitan modernity and María Isabel representing an Indigeneity that is becoming selectively modernized through mestizaje but retains traditional values. In doing so, the film constructs its entire conflict around the following question: will María Isabel's ignorance in the context of White Mexican society—her comparative lack of *blanquitud*—be the undoing of her marriage with Ricardo?

El amor de María Isabel establishes the protagonist as culturally unequal to her husband and his social sector in various and explicit ways. First, when Ricardo takes her to see the opera *Carmen*, María Isabel ends up falling asleep because she is confused by the conventions of opera and does not understand French. Also, she is initially incapable of valuing classical piano, demonstrating her obliviousness to the object's artistic function when she says, "Entre el piano este y el metate no noto ninguna diferencia" (I don't notice any difference between piano and the metate), equating the musical instrument with the rectangular Mesoamerican tool for processing grain. Furthermore, when María Isabel, Ricardo, Mireya, and Mireya's brother go to a nightclub after the opera, María Isabel is equally alienated from contemporary music. Against a panorama of White Mexicans enjoying the music, which the film attempts to portray as youthful and modern through the band's name, "Los estudiantes," María Isabel stands out, making it clear that she does not like the sound when she covers her ears and refers to it unappreciatively as "el ruidajo ese" (that ruckus).

Beyond the question of aesthetic taste and appreciation, the film marks María Isabel as distinct from bourgeois White Mexicans because she does not engage in two ubiquitous features of the group's recreational *habitus* as presented in the film—smoking and drinking alcohol.[28] The film suggests that María Isabel is a misfit in Ricardo's social scene when each character is smoking and/or drinking during the post-opera outing, but María Isabel does not do either because, as she explains, "El alcohol me marea y el humo me hace toser" (Alcohol makes me dizzy and smoke makes me cough). This point emerges repeatedly throughout the film to

---

28. Bourdieu, *Distinction*, 165–70.

mark María Isabel as comparatively unsophisticated and as an outsider in the White bourgeois milieu. In sum, *El amor de María Isabel* foregrounds the protagonist's cultural incompatibility with Ricardo and his acquaintances by highlighting her divergence from their tastes and mores.

The new character that the sequel introduces, Mireya, is María Isabel's opposite in that she embodies the world of White Mexican culture. While María Isabel is completely lost at the opera or piano performances, Mireya is herself a professional world-famous concert pianist—"la mejor intérprete de Chopin" (the best interpreter of Chopin), no less. Furthermore, even though Mireya is not as young as those dancing energetically to the modern band, her cultural competence allows her to appreciate their music aesthetically as "la expresión de la juventud moderna" (the expression of modern youth). Last, while María Isabel's aversion to alcohol and smoking reveal that she has not been socialized in the White bourgeois Mexican world, Mireya is, on the other extreme, dependent on these substances. As she explains, ". . . Para mí las dos cosas son indispensables. El alcohol me ayuda a olvidar, y el humo me calma los nervios" (For me both things are indispensable. Alcohol helps me forget and smoke calms my nerves). Through her knowledge of Eurocentric and contemporary culture and participation in bourgeois consumption habits, the film presents Mireya as a more worldly and refined counterpoint to María Isabel.

The cultural differences between the two women are not merely ornamental distinctions; rather, they function as components that structure the emergence of a love triangle among María Isabel, Mireya, and Ricardo. For one, Ricardo and Mireya are old friends from university, an educational experience that María Isabel has never come close to experiencing. Furthermore, it is precisely María Isabel's taste in music and social customs that excludes her and enables intimacy and attraction to develop between her husband and Mireya. The film conveys this point when Ricardo and Mireya's first outing alone together to a classical piano concert serves as the context for Mireya's first romantic intimations toward Ricardo. Later, high culture again functions as the pretense for Mireya and Ricardo's intimacy when they go together to visit an obscure but brilliant blind piano composer in a rural area. While on this day trip, they are delayed in returning to the city because of a strong storm, and they embrace and kiss passionately as they wait for the storm to pass. Visually, the moment that most clearly transmits the central role of culture and art in Ricardo and Mireya's attraction occurs when Mireya visits their home and tries out the new piano Ricardo has bought specifically for her to play on. As she plays the instrument with gradually increasing intensity, the numerous cuts between close-ups of Mireya's face, her playing hands, and Ricardo establish her musical display and Ricardo's reception of it as an intense, sensual (if not erotic) experience between the two characters. This scene is a precursor to that of the classical piano concert that Mireya gives in public, in which the impressive theater, Mireya's elegant dress, the duration of her playing, and the alternation of high-angle long shots with close-ups of her hands glorify her as a musical wonder with whom Ricardo is thoroughly infatuated. Finally, Ricardo actually verbalizes the cultural and artistic root of his attraction to Mireya when, as he is weighing his relationships with both women, he explains to her, ". . . me fascinas, me envuelves con tu presencia, con tu música, ¡me vuelves loco!" (You fascinate me, you envelop me with your presence, with your music, you drive me crazy!). In short, the film repeatedly emphasizes that Eurocentric White bourgeois cultural capital, which María Isabel lacks, is precisely the central point of Ricardo's attraction to Mireya.

As in the first film, here María Isabel may be portrayed as ignorant of certain norms, but she quickly becomes aware that discrepancies between her and her husband's customs are a threat to her marriage. While María Isabel waits for Ricardo to return from his outing with Mireya, she decides to teach herself precisely the aspects of cultural behavior that Mireya and Ricardo share: drinking, smoking, and piano playing. In the middle of this attempt, which results in a drunken production of cacophony, María Isabel articulates how her lack of White bourgeois cultural capital, and Mireya's possession of it, separates her from her husband: "La guereja bebe. La guereja fuma, y a ti te gusta, ¿no? Es una mujer de mucho mundo. Está 'in' y estoy 'out' . . . Ella está a tu nivel. Yo no soy más que una india estúpida que una vez creyó alcanzar las estrellas del cielo con las manos" (The blondie drinks. The blondie smokes, and you like her, don't you? She is a very worldly woman. She is in and I am out . . . She is at your level. I am just a stupid Indian who once believed she could reach the stars in the sky with her hands). Both by presenting the women as cultural opposites and linking taste to romantic attraction, *El amor de María Isabel* introduces White Mexican cultural competence as a set of criteria according to which the merit of Mexican women can be measured vis-à-vis the White bourgeois Mexican man.

However, the failed performance of bourgeois cultural norms is not the only standard of comparison that the film puts forth to weigh the viability of the love triangle's two possible outcomes. *El amor the María*

Isabel also establishes the women as opposites regarding their adherence to traditional gender norms. The film creates a contrast between Mireya's ultramodern womanhood and María Isabel's traditional values. First, Mireya has postponed marriage to pursue her career, while María Isabel has no aspirations beyond being a wife and mother. The way in which Mireya responds regarding her marital status conveys her tendency toward independence, reservations with respect to the institution of marriage, and desires that are at odds with its monogamous constraints. When Ricardo asks if Mireya has ever married she replies, "No, todavía no he encontrado al hombre que pueda escalvizarme . . . Me he dedicado por completo a la música . . . Tal parece que todos los hombres que llenan por completo mis aspiraciones están casados" (No, I haven't yet found the man who can enslave me . . . I have devoted myself entirely to music . . . It seems that all of the men who fulfill my aspirations are married). María Isabel's comment during the exchange, on the other hand, aligns her with the traditional idea that marriage is a woman's greatest source of fulfillment: "A mí eso de estar toque y toque no se me hace tan divertido como estar casada" (Trifling with the piano doesn't seem as interesting to me as being married).

Furthermore, while María Isabel remains faithful to Ricardo despite the interest of younger men at the conservatory that she is attending, Mireya deviates from the traditional notion of female modesty and sexual virtue by carrying on an affair with a married man. The film further aligns María Isabel with traditional gender norms by suggesting her talent as an excellent cook when she prepares a meal for Mireya and her brother, and later when she makes a cake for her wedding anniversary, while Mireya is never shown performing domestic tasks of any kind. Finally, the film presents María Isabel as consistent with traditional gender norms by continuing to emphasize her maternal quality. This occurs when she expresses distress on Mother's Day because, despite Rosa Isela's abandonment, María Isabel continues loving her as a daughter,[29] and when María Isabel travels to Monterrey to reunite with Rosa Isela after receiving a letter from her. Mireya, on the other hand, never expresses maternal feeling of any kind. In all these ways, the sequel to *María Isabel* continues to underscore the protagonist's embodiment of traditional gender norms for women

---

29. When explaining her story to her friend and fellow student, María Isabel says that Rosa Isela "me abandonó y aún así la sigo queriendo" (abandoned me, but even so I still love her).

through her roles as wife and mother and her domestic skill, but this time in contradistinction to a woman who incarnates the modern values of professional fulfillment and independence.

If the film sets up María Isabel and Mireya as diametrically opposed figures in terms of their level of cultural capital and adherence to traditional values, this contradistinction becomes more complex throughout the course of the film as María Isabel increases her exposure to criollo/mestizo cultural knowledge and gradually assimilates to Mexican modernity. *El amor de María Isabel* signals this evolution in numerous ways. María Isabel's short 1960s bob and her contemporary clothing in the sequel suggests her adjustment on a visual level. She also loses her *indita* Spanish, which is evident when she visits her father and no longer uses the same verbal anachronisms that he does. Furthermore, her mastering of specific technologies also marks her entrance into the mestizo milieu.[30] María Isabel learns how to drive, demonstrating her acclimation to the modern city. Also, she enters the space of formal education at the conservatory, where she learns to play the piano. Furthermore, the sequel suggests that María Isabel evolves with respect to when she first arrived in the city because by the end of the film, she no longer engages in physical attacks in the context of confrontation.[31] The film highlights this change during the climax when María Isabel finally confronts Mireya about her affair with Ricardo in an exchange that is purely verbal. During the encounter, María Isabel explains that if Ricardo's happiness were not on the line, she would allow "que la india brava que hay en mí saliera para arrancarle con las uñas lo que más quiero" (for the wild Indian in me to come out to tear away from you with my nails what I most love). Through the contrast between María Isabel's verbalized desire to lash out physically and her restraint on this occasion, the film suggests that her time in the city has had a "civilizing" effect on her.

The idea that María Isabel undergoes a transformation while in Ricardo's house is not merely left to the spectator's imagination, but is also made explicit through Mireya's direct comparison of the relationship between Ricardo and María Isabel with that of Pygmalion and his statue when she says to him, "Tienes una esposa a la que quieres mucho. La

---

30. David S. Dalton, *Mestizo Modernity: Race, Technology, and the Body in Postrevolutionary Mexico* (Gainesville: University of Florida Press, 2018), 1–30.

31. In other words, María Isabel has internalized the laws of bourgeois restraint as Bourdieu describes them in *Distinction*, 172.

has sacado de la nada para formarla. La has labrado en mármol para convertirla en una estatua maravillosa" (You have a wife whom you love very much. You have plucked her out of nowhere to form her. You have cut her from marble to make her into a marvelous statue). Furthermore, the film does not present María Isabel's changes in a value-neutral fashion, but instead suggests that these steps toward bourgeois criollo/mestizo culture are improvements on her previous condition. Mireya's equating of María Isabel's rural Indigenous life before living with Ricardo with "la nada" (nowhere)—as if bourgeois Mexican social reality constitutes the only sphere of existence—clearly suggests that the acculturated María Isabel is superior to her comparatively more Indigenous previous self. In sum, although María Isabel is initially presented as Mireya's cultural inferior, the sequel also displays María Isabel's ability to "remedy" some of the aspects of her persona that mark her as Other in Ricardo's social context.

Importantly, at the same time that the film evidences María Isabel's process of acculturation, it also explicitly continues to essentialize her Indigenous identity. However, precisely because the film displays how María Isabel disposes of the hallmarks of her Indigeneity from the previous film (ignorance, *indito* speech, braids, and physical agitation) and because it uses whiteness-as-indigeneity to present María Isabel as a compassion-worthy sufferer and desirable woman, her Indigeneity in the sequel consists purely of verbalized sentimentality. This occurs on more than one occasion, including María Isabel's "india brava" (wild Indian) comment discussed above. For instance, on the evening that María Isabel tries to teach herself to drink alcohol, smoke, and play the piano while Ricardo is out with Mireya, the protagonist voices her despair in self-racializing terms: "¡Yo nunca debí haber dejado a mis indios ni a mi raza!" (I never should have left my Indians and my race!). Another sentimental iteration of her Indigeneity occurs when María Isabel expresses that the mere thought of Ricardo's infidelity makes her want to ". . . correr al monte y ponerme a llorar como lloramos los indios, tristemente y en silencio" (. . . run off to the hills to weep like we Indians weep, sadly and silently). Through these lines of dialogue, the film attempts to reassert María Isabel's Indigeneity, which is no longer culturally perceptible and was never visually tenable to begin with. In this way, *El amor de María Isabel* is an extreme example of farcical ethnic masquerade in Mexican cinema, functioning as a limit case for what whiteness-as-indigeneity asks its audience to accept as representative of Indigenous Mexicans.

While María Isabel evolves throughout the course of the film to approximate criollo/mestizo cultural norms, Mireya undergoes no parallel transformation, remaining stagnant as the representative of Eurocentric Mexican culture and nontraditional attitudes toward marriage and motherhood. Furthermore, the film casts her as the vehicle that leads to Ricardo's moral descent and his distancing from traditional values. When María Isabel has left for Monterrey to reunite with Rosa Isela and Ricardo's daughter, Ricardo and Mireya are finally alone. However, instead of bringing about the beginning of Ricardo and Mireya's happy life together, María Isabel's absence results in a scene of bourgeois excess, instability, and moral decay, which the film indicates in multiple ways. At Mireya's home, Ricardo no longer appears as the composed and elegant man he has been throughout the *María Isabel* duology. He is completely inebriated, which is apparent through his markedly slurred speech, stumbling, disheveled hair, and aggressive tone. His demeanor helps to mark the contrast between the couple's desired outcome and the tense unhappiness in which they find themselves, when he states drunkenly, "Brindemos por nuestro triunfo. ¿No es eso lo que queríamos? . . . Vamos a principiar nuestra felicidad." (Let us toast to our triumph. Isn't that what we wanted? . . . Let us begin our happiness). The scene's cinematography also suggests that something is amiss in the couple's new life together. The use of the tracking shot, in contrast with the immobile shots used to film Ricardo's home environment with María Isabel, suggests the instability of Ricardo and Mireya's relationship and establishes a general sense of unease. Furthermore, the use of the oblique angle as Mireya sits with Ricardo eerily hovering over her visually manifests that something in the relationship between the characters is amiss. Finally, Ricardo's aggressive requests that Mireya play the piano liken her display of high culture to alcohol when he says, "Tu música me embriaga, me hechiza" (Your music intoxicates me, bewitches me). This display of excessive alcohol consumption and its parallel with piano music—both of which are symbols of bourgeois behavior in the film—suggest that, if left unchecked, White Mexican bourgeois modernity spirals into decadence, which is precisely the path that Ricardo's affair with Mireya has taken.

The scene that dramatizes the end of Ricardo and Mireya's affair concludes by displaying the fate of the childless and unmarried career woman as a pitiful end as she is left to weep alone with her musical instrument. Against this backdrop, the white-as-indigenous María Isabel functions as the paragon of traditional values who anchors the modern

Mexican man to family and marital fidelity. The cut from the lone, weeping Mireya to the subsequent scene of María Isabel and Rosa Isela's reunion highlights the contrast between the modern mistress and María Isabel's personification of the maternal mestiza ideal. María Isabel takes up her motherly role by embracing Rosa Isela and later reuniting with Gloria (Ricardo's daughter) and her baby. Furthermore, the film suggests that María Isabel leads Ricardo to reassume his position as family patriarch when (now sober) he too appears at Gloria's house, and all are reunited as a big, happy mixed-race family. The melodramatic nondiegetic music that plays throughout these reunions celebrates them as the best possible outcome, particularly in contradistinction to Ricardo's previous scene of drunken isolation from his family at Mireya's side. Because Ricardo's recovery of María Isabel is inseparable from his full return to family life, *El amor de María Isabel* presents the diegetically Indigenous protagonist as the factor that is capable of grounding the White bourgeois Mexican man in traditional values, which the film presents as morally and affectively superior to more modern alternatives.

Through Ricardo's choice of María Isabel over Mireya, the film appears to uphold the Indigenous woman as preferable to the White Mexican woman by subordinating the importance of elite White cultural capital to that of traditional values. In other words, María Isabel's partial acculturation is "good enough" for Ricardo because she is unsurpassed in her display of wifely and motherly excellence. However, while, according to the narrative, the Indigenous woman's virtue allows her to triumph over the White Mexican woman, producing a coupling that is consistent with the Mexican twentieth-century celebration of mestizaje, the film's *visual* plane tells a different story. Although in the narrative Mireya and María Isabel are racial "opposites," the on-screen presences of both characters conform to the bodily standards of Whiteness (*blancura*) for Mexican women in the context of the Mexican racial formation. Mireya displays blond hyperwhiteness, and María Isabel personifies the limit of physical Whiteness with her dark hair and eyes and light skin (which is, in fact, chromatically lighter than Ricardo's). Although *El amor de María Isabel* upholds the notion of interracial romance, through its use of whiteness-as-indigeneity the film in fact *visually* reinforces the hegemonic norm of White endogamy. In this way, the film's visual plane, which persists in its celebration of the unity between White Mexican heterosexual bodies, undercuts the narrative's progressive aspirations to exalt cross-class, interracial love.

Conclusion

The *María Isabel* duology is a noteworthy cinematic artifact because of how it engages the theme of Indigeneity in the context of 1960s Mexican modernity. The first film draws on Golden Age *indita* conventions with some notable updates, resulting in an Indigenous female protagonist who opposes racism and hacienda-style patriarchy but preserves sexual modesty, honesty, and religiosity. Furthermore, María Isabel's capacity for exhibiting love and revealing truth distinguishes her from the self-interested, deceptive, and materialistic individuals around her, suggesting that her cultural deficits are of minor importance. Like its Golden Age predecessors, visually, *María Isabel* employs whiteness-as-indigeneity to transmit the title character's heroism, nobility, beauty, and melodramatic centrality to a Mexican audience.

The sequel delves more deeply into María Isabel's cultural insufficiency in Ricardo's White bourgeois Mexican world by generating an antagonist who incarnates its values and performs them perfectly. Even though initially María Isabel and Mireya personify extremes—Indigenous traditionalism on the one hand, and White cosmopolitan modernity on the other—throughout the course of the film María Isabel undergoes a process of acculturation. This transformation allows her to approximate mainstream criollo/mestizo social and cultural expectations while retaining her traditional values tied to marriage and motherhood, as Mireya remains alienated from such values. In the end, traditional gendered values outweigh sophisticated cultural capital when the film casts Mireya as the choice that leads the Mexican man down a path of moral decadence and María Isabel as the catalyst for the recovery of his patriarchal position.

The discrepancy between the film's narrative plane, in which the women are racial "opposites," and its visual dimension, in which both women project versions of Mexican Whiteness, undermines the diegetic triumph of the Indigenous woman. By promoting acculturation through María Isabel's evolution and Whiteness through her on-screen presence in the star body of Silvia Pinal, the *María Isabel* duology ultimately celebrates Indigenous womanhood as an abstract essence that is not culturally or visually perceptible and is only verbalized sentimentally from time to time.

6

Indios, Desire, and the White Mexican Woman

As has been widely noted, in the foundational allegory of the Mexican nation, Indigenous Mexico is feminine and unites with masculine Hispanicity to generate the Mexican mestizo nation. The twentieth-century exaltation of Indigenous culture exhibited the premises of this narrative by largely showcasing Mexican Indigeneity in the form of Indigenous women. While the majority of this book has been dedicated to discussing how Mexican film promoted Indigeneity as relevant for national identity by representing it through White Mexican womanhood, here I address how the colonized dynamics of desire and subjectivity also affect the representation of the Indigenous man in Mexican cinema.

Whereas the centrality and desirability of the white-as-indigenous female is so common in Indigenous-themed Mexican films as to be a cliché of the genre, the protagonism and appeal of the Indigenous man in Mexican cinema is much rarer. This comparative dearth is rooted in the racial and gendered structure of the nation's foundational narrative in which the Indigenous woman is sexualized as the Spanish male's partner[1] and the Indigenous man has no discernable function other than that of an ancient and deceased heroic figure. The centrality of the figure of Cuauhtémoc (the last Aztec ruler who endured torture at the hands of

---

1. Analisa Taylor, *Indigeneity in the Mexican Cultural Imagination* (Tucson: Arizona University Press, 2009), 100.

the Spanish and refused to divulge the location of large quantities of treasure) in artistic production during the nineteenth and twentieth centuries throughout ideologically diverse currents of Mexican nationalism indicates the extent to which the Indigenous male primarily occupies the function of the glorious, defunct hero in the national imaginary.[2] Such recurring instances of Cuauhtémoc's veneration include the 1869 bust of Cuauhtémoc,[3] Leandro Izaguirre's 1892 painting *The Torture of Cuauhtémoc*,[4] the 1887 Porfirian-era Monument to Cuauhtémoc,[5] David Alfaro Siqueiros's 1951 mural *Torment and Apotheosis of Cuauhtémoc*;[6] and extend to *el México de afuera* (Greater Mexico) in the form of Chicano nationalist works such as Guillermo Aranda's mural *La Dualidad*.[7]

Furthermore, the notion of the Indigenous male's marginality in the project of *mestizaje* can be identified in the conventions of casta painting from the colonial period in New Spain. These visual representations of interracial heterosexual pairings usually began with the depiction of the Spanish man and Indigenous woman[8] (while the opposite racial and gender configuration was rarer and not as prominently featured). This convention points to how elite colonial culture—of which casta painting was an emanation[9]—promoted the coupling of the Spanish man and Indigenous woman while deemphasizing the inverted arrangement. In this sense, the pictorial genre reflected the colonial social landscape in which White men maintained "privileged access to non-white women's sexuality" while at the same time obstructing non-Whites' access to White women's sexuality.[10]

---

2. Ana María Alonso, "Conforming Disconformity: 'Mestizaje,' Hybridity, and the Aesthetics of Mexican Nationalism," *Cultural Anthropology* 19, no. 4 (November 2004): 464.

3. Stacie G. Widdifield, *The Embodiment of the National in Late Nineteenth-Century Mexican Painting* (Tucson: University of Arizona Press, 1996), 90–91.

4. Widdifield, *Embodiment*, 117–19.

5. Rebecca Earle, *The Return of the Native: Indians and Myth-Making in Spanish America 1810–1930* (Durham, NC: Duke University Press, 2007), 75.

6. Mary K. Coffey, *How Revolutionary Art Became Official Culture: Murals, Museums and the Mexican State* (Durham, NC: Duke University Press, 2012), 53–56.

7. Guisela Latorre, *Walls of Empowerment: Chicana/o Indigenist Murals of California* (Austin: University of Texas Press, 2008), 77–81.

8. Widdifield, *Embodiment*, 125.

9. Ilona Katzew, *Casta Painting: Images of Race in Eighteenth-Century Mexico* (New Haven: Yale University Press, 2004).

10. Peter Wade, *Race and Sex in Latin America* (New York: Pluto Press, 2009), 83.

The establishment of the Spanish man and Indigenous woman as the normative interracial arrangement in Mexico and the endurance of this pattern in the local imaginary can also be observed in public reaction to a highly visible couple that consisted of an Indigenous man and White Mexican woman after independence—that of Benito Juárez (president of Mexico from 1861 to 1872) and Margarita Maza, who were married in 1843. Public opinion that cast Juárez as inferior to his wife[11] smacked of a colonially inflected indignation. In short, the notion of mestizaje coalesced in the Mexican cultural imagination in specifically gendered and racialized terms that privileged the pairing of the Spanish man and the Indigenous woman. Indigenous-themed Mexican films evidence the influence of this convention in that Indigenous male characters tend not to be protagonists, nor are they frequently presented as desirable men—a trend that contrasts sharply with Mexican cinema's representation of Indigenous women as desirable, albeit through colonized standards of beauty.

This chapter focuses on a group of films across the long Golden Age that depart from the general trend of avoiding central Indigenous male characters: the colonial-age drama *Tribu* (dir. Miguel Contreras Torres, 1935), the nineteenth-century foundational romance *Lola Casanova* (dir. Matilde Landeta, 1949), the interracial drama starring María Félix and Pedro Infante, *Tizoc* (dir. Ismael Rodriguez, 1957), and the parodical film *El violetero* (dir. Gilberto Martínez Solares, 1960) starring the comedic personality Tin Tan (Germán Valdés). In these films, Indigenous men are central to the narratives, and in the majority of them, whiteness-as-indigeneity functions to mark the Indigenous male protagonists as noble savages. Furthermore, in these films, Indigenous men are involved in romantic relationships with White Mexican women, which end in one of two ways: the death of the Indigenous male or his transformation into a criollo/mestizo figure. The rareness of this cross-racial heterosexual coupling in Mexican cinema[12] and the endings of the films in which it

---

11. Widdifield, *Embodiment*, 124.

12. In contrast to the United States where the Motion Picture Production Code (the Hays Code) prohibited the production of films showing miscegenation, in Mexico no such official proscription existed, however, I propose here that there was cultural pressure against filmic representations of couples made up of Indigenous men and White Mexican women. See Roby Wiegman, "Race, ethnicity, and film," in *The Oxford Guide to Film Studies*, eds John Hill and Pamela Church Gibson, (New York: Oxford University Press, 1998), p. 163.

does occur point to a cultural anxiety (if not a taboo) with regard to this particular racial and gender composition of the romantic couple because these films preclude the possibility of the couple's continuity as racial and cultural "opposites."[13] In other words, twentieth-century Mexican cinema tends to reaffirm the dynamics of the nation's foundational narrative—a dynamic that the White Mexican woman's desire for the Indigenous man directly contradicts. As a result, when this desire does appear on film, it is extinguished through tragedy or allayed through acculturation. Golden Age Mexican cinema therefore does not imagine a possible future for the Indigenous man and White Mexican woman as a romantic couple, a pattern that, when read allegorically, contributes to a rigid and colonially inflected narrative of Mexican national identity.[14]

Tribu (1935)

Miguel Contreras Torres's 1935 conquest-era melodrama, *Tribu*, takes place in a fictitious settlement in Spanish America, Santa Fe de Otul. When the film begins, Spanish troops have been unable to subdue a rebellious Indigenous tribe that lives nearby, and a captain convinces the governor, Duke Alfónso del Moral, to attack them. As a result of the skirmish, the governor's wife, his daughter (Leonor, played by Medea de Novara), and the priest (Fray Juan de Oviedo) are all taken as prisoners of war. Even though a prominent warrior in the Indigenous community, Zotil, suggests that they be sacrificed to the gods, the leader of the tribe, Tumitl (played by the director, Miguel Contreras Torres), protects the Spanish prisoners and sees that they return safely to their settlement, after which he and Duke Alfonso del Moral sign a peace agreement between the Spanish and the tribe. During Tumitl's stay as the Duke's guest, a faction of the Indigenous tribe led by Zotil attacks a group of Spanish soldiers and later kidnaps Leonor. To demonstrate his personal honor and loyalty to the treaty he signed with the Spanish, Tumitl pledges to return Leonor to her

---

13. Lomnitz-Adler, *Exits*, 263–80.

14. My reading of the romantic outcomes in the films discussed in this chapter is indebted to Doris Sommer's analysis of love plots in nineteenth-century Latin American fiction involving characters from disparate social sectors as allegories for the foundation of nations in the region. *Foundational Fictions: The National Romances of Latin America* (Berkeley: University of California Press, 1991).

family safely. However, upon delivering the unharmed Leonor, Tumitl is attacked by Zotil's faction and dies in Leonor's arms.

In a similar manner to Contreras Torres's 1931 short film *Zítari* (discussed in chapter 1), *Tribu* distances the story's content from the rigors of history and romanticizes its characters and plot, which has specific implications for its presentation of Indigeneity. Nowhere is this clearer than in the film's opening expository text, which both indicates the absence of a fixed geographical and historical referent and aggrandizes its characters: "*Tribu* ocurre en cualquier parte de América, sin apego a los cánones históricos. Es un romance de amor en la virgen tierra americana cuando el indio aún era amo y señor de la selva; y el español, legendario caballero de la aventura temeraria" (*Tribu* takes place in any part of America, without adherence to historical canons. It is a romance of love in the virgin American land when the Indian was still lord and master of the jungle; and the Spaniard was the legendary knight-errant of temerarious adventure). The combination of eschewing history and referencing the literary genre of the romance, a piece of writing telling of heroic or marvelous deeds usually in a historical or imaginary setting, frames the film's content as the stuff of legend. The language used also presents colonial-era figures as idealized and larger than life. Through these gestures, the film puts forth the Indian of the colonial period as a feature of local lore in romanticized terms. Like *Zítari*, *Tribu* elevates the tragedies of temporally removed Indigenous protagonists to the level of legendary dramas, ennobling colonial-era natives and, by extension, positioning the twentieth-century Mexican nation as the inheritor of fabled, Indigenous-themed lore.

The film's idealization of colonial-era Indigeneity occurs largely through its crafting of Tumitl as a quintessential noble savage. *Tribu* positions him as an inherently good native on several occasions. When the tribe takes four prisoners from the Spanish settlement (Leonor, Elvira, her mother, and the Friar), Tumitl discards the possibility that they be sacrificed to the gods, which a prominent warrior, Zotil, raises. The film underscores Tumitl's benevolence toward the Europeans when he proudly reassures the Spaniards: "Jefe Tumitl defiende blancos" (Chief Tumitl defends Whites). Later, Tumitl patiently and respectfully negotiates a peace agreement with the Spanish, suggesting that he is reasonable and amicable, unlike the belligerent natives led by Zotil, who attack the Spanish by surprise and kidnap the Duke's daughter. Furthermore, Tumitl keeps his word to the Duke and Duchess by bringing Leonor back to safety when she is captured by Zotil. After completing this honorable task, the friar,

Figure 6.1. While held as prisoners by the Indigenous tribe, Leonor (Medea de Novara, center left) and her circle are treated well by Tumitl (Miguel Contreras Torres, center right). Playing the translator, Itzul, Emilio Fernández stands just behind the film's main couple. Photo courtesy of Mil Nubes-Foto (Roberto Fiesco). All rights reserved.

who is also the voice of Christian religious authority in the film, declares his definitive and positive judgment of Tumitl: "Yo leo en el fondo de los corazones. Ese indio es bueno" (I read in the depths of men's hearts. That Indian is good). In short, *Tribu* idealizes Tumitl by producing him as a noble leader who acts honorably in all of his dealings with the Spanish, particularly in contrast to the figure of the bad savage that Zotil embodies.

The film conveys the difference between the morally polarized Indians on visual and aural levels by presenting Tumitl through whiteness-as-indigeneity and his antagonist through characteristics that do not embody Whiteness in the Mexican context. Of the physical characteristics that anthropologist Hugo Nutini identifies as being desirable for males to possess in order to be perceived as belonging to the aristocracy, a class identity that is inseparable from the Mexican construct of Whiteness,

Tumitl possesses a light complexion, large eyes, elegance of movement, and a grave demeanor.[15] He maintains stoic bodily and facial comportment throughout the dramatic events that occur throughout the film. By contrast, Zotil possesses a darker complexion and broader facial features and is shown scowling and shouting angrily in the film's fictitious Indigenous language. Tumitl is further associated with Whiteness because he learns to speak some Spanish, which underscores his alignment with the Iberian characters, especially the Duke and Leonor, whose pacifist values are consistent with his. In sum, Tumitl's whiteness-as-indigeneity, which consists of visual and aural markers, works alongside his inherent benevolence in the plot to establish him as the good savage

Furthermore, like the valiant warrior and virtuous princess in *Zítari*, Tumitl's honorable character and whiteness-as-indigeneity also identify him as a noble native of legendary status who is fit for appropriation into national lore. *Tribu* ascribes a monumentality to Tumitl through his centrality to the melodramatic aspect of the film, which reaches its height in the moment that Tumitl's selfless restitution of Leonor to her parents ends in his death. The film elevates Tumitl as a heroic figure by dramatizing how he is punished for a well-intentioned act: the rescuing of the Spanish aristocrat in the service of preserving peaceful relations between the European and Indigenous groups. As a "good" Indigenous leader whose life ends because of the greed and ambition of other men in the early stages of the colonial project, the film locates Tumitl as a glorious and tragic Indigenous symbol whose virtues resonate in the present, not unlike the much-venerated figure of Cuauhtémoc.

Tribu's blatant contrast between the "good' and "bad" Indians, Tumitl and Zotil, is a well-worn cliché in the representation of Indigeneity from its earliest rendering by non-Indigenous people; however, this is not the only comparison that the film establishes to highlight Tumitl's inherent goodness. The film also establishes parallels and contrasts with Spanish characters in a manner that presents nobility and honor as characteristics that are not inherent to one specific group but instead are a question of personal character.

Concretely, the film aligns Tumitl with the Duke, who both embody honor and virtue, and contrasts the two righteous figures with the Spanish

---

15. Hugo Nutini, *The Mexican Aristocracy: An Expressive Ethnography* (Austin: University of Texas Press, 2008), 62.

captain Bazán, whom the film associates with greed, violence, and dishonor. First, *Tribu* suggests that Captain Bazán is motivated by a greed that alienates him from his own group's moral code. Upon arriving at the seemingly abandoned Indigenous settlement, Orimbo, he proposes that the Spanish appropriate all of their belongings as booty, to which the Duke responds with a corrective: "Los soldados de España sólo han disfrutado de un botín después de una batalla ganada en buena ley" (Spanish soldiers have only taken booty after a fairly fought battle). Furthermore, when the Spanish first planned to attack the tribe but discovered that they were in mourning because their chief had died unexpectedly, the Duke decides not to attack in order to respect their grief, which frustrates the captain, who is eager to annihilate the natives: "La guerra es la guerra" (War is war). Here again, the Duke indicates the path of honor, signaling the captain's debased instincts when he responds, "La gloria sin honor no es gloria" (Glory without honor is not glory). The Duke's pursuit of peace and insistence on honorable behavior mirrors Tumitl's actions and values discussed above, while Captain Bazán's tendency toward violence, ambition, and greed align him with the "bad savage," Zotil. In this way, the film eschews a representation in which the Spanish are the unconditional exemplars of virtue, and instead crafts a depiction of idealized Indigeneity, not only in contradistinction to the "bad' savage but also vis-à-vis morally polarized Europeans.

Building on parallels and contrasts between Tumitl and other characters, the central way in which the film points to Tumitl's value is by emphasizing his suitability as a love match for the film's female protagonist, the white-as-white Leonor. *Tribu* points to the affinity between the two characters in multiple ways. First, both characters favor peace between the Spanish and the Indigenous people amid the climate of conflict stirred up by the antagonizing forces that Captain Bazán and Zotil personify. Second, the film suggests their affinity in various instances in which Tumitl and Leonor have excursions in natural settings. The same nondiegetic romantic score featuring string instruments plays when they are alone together, conveying the fondness they feel for one another. These nature scenes constitute the only in-between space in which they can exist together in harmony, beyond Spanish or Indigenous objectors in Santa Fe de Otúl or Orimbo. Furthermore, their conversations in rudimentary Spanish suggest their willingness and ability to bridge the differences between them. The intimacy between the two characters reaches its peak on the evening after Tumitl has rescued Leonor, and they stop to sleep for the night in a cave. They hold each other closely as a storm rages outside (the externalization of the troubled climate in which they love each other), physically conveying their mutual desire and affection. Last, the intensity of Leonor's love and desire for Tumitl is evident in her deep distress when he is shot and she holds his agonizing body in her arms. Here, Tumtil's compatibility with the White female aristocrat serves to underscore his exceptionality with respect to the other Indigenous people of his tribe, and the desire of the White proto-Mexican woman for the Indigenous male functions as the ultimate indicator of his value.

Even though the religious difference between the characters surfaces as a potential obstacle to their union,[16] the film downplays this discrepancy as one that is circumstantial to the characters' locations and cultures of origin and ultimately points to their overwhelming compatibility. In fact, Leonor demonstrates flexibility even when it comes to religious matters, which serves to indicate her exceptionality among the more orthodox Spaniards. After she and her mother return to the Spanish settlement following their brief imprisonment by the Indigenous tribe, Leonor suggests an equivalency between the Spanish project of conquest and the Indigenous people's defense of "su patria y su religión" (their homeland and their religion). Leonor even goes a step further, alarming her mother when she states that worshiping the sun and moon is "más romántico" (more romantic) than Christianity, which points to her affinity with Tumitl. Moreover, the film formalized their mutual understanding through an ephemeral quasi-marriage when, precisely as Leonor is holding Tumitl's agonizing body, the friar blesses the couple from afar, declaring, "Ante Dios están unidos. Sólo el amor podrá lograr la paz del mundo" (They are united before God. Only love will achieve peace in the world). Through this validation of their mutual affection by the Christian priest, the film suggests that the religious differences between the characters are secondary to their love.

For all of their compatibility and shared tenderness, Leonor and Tumitl's relationship—a reversal of the foundational Mexican coupling of the Indigenous woman and the Spanish conquistador—does not materialize into a universally recognized union, nor does it have a projected future. Therefore, though in *Tribu* the desire of the White woman for the Indigenous male functions to underscore his worth, the film ultimately respects the normative gender and race pattern of heterosexual unions

---

16. *Tribu* suggests that religion may be an impediment to Tumitl and Leonor's union when she offers him a bejeweled cross and he rejects it.

Figure 6.2. Though Leonor and Tumitl do not share the same religion, *Tribu* suggests that "ante Dios están unidos" (they are united before God). Photo courtesy of Mil Nubes-Foto (Roberto Fiesco). All rights reserved.

that was established in the colonial period and became embedded in the dominant Mexican narrative of mestizaje. By conveniently and melodramatically killing off Tumitl, *Tribu* cements the Indigenous male's status as the quintessential noble savage through martyrdom, therefore promoting his mythological, but not biological, contribution to Mexican mestizaje.

Lola Casanova (1949)

In Matilde Landeta's 1949 film, *Lola Casanova*,[17] the context for the antagonism between Indigenous and White people is not the sixteenth-century period of colonial settlement, but the nineteenth-century conflict between

---

17. For a discussion of the evolution of the legend of Lola Casanova from local oral accounts to cinematic renditions, see Robert McKee Irwin, "Lola Casanova: La Malinche invertida en la cultura nacional mexicana," *Literatura Mexicana* 18, no. 1 (2007): 59–87 and Anne Doremus, "Indigenism, Mestizaje, and National Identity in Mexico during the 1940s and the 1950s," *Mexican Studies/Estudios Mexicanos* 17, no. 2 (2001): 375–402.

the Seri people and the Spanish and criollo settlers near the city of Guaymas in the northeastern state of Sonora. Despite the three centuries that separate the periods in which the films are set, *Lola Casanova* echoes many of the strategies through which *Tribu* produces the Indigenous male as noble savage and transmits his compatibility with the White Mexican woman, while still ultimately thwarting the possibility of the interracial couple's future together. Regionally focused, *Lola Casanova* explicitly frames the central love story as the point of departure for mestizaje in the local context around Guaymas.[18] However, while in this film the white-as-indigenous male serves as the worthy Seri contributor to the beginning of mestizaje in the area, he must die as a martyr for this future to fully come to fruition.

The narrative in *Lola Casanova* progresses from the themes of separation and antagonism to those of synthesis and peace. Framed as a flashback, the film's story begins with the burning of a Seri village and the subsequent migration of the Seris toward the Pacific Ocean. The Spanish man responsible for the attack, Don Nestor, returns to Guaymas and gifts Lola Casanova (Meche Barba) a young Seri boy, Indalecio. The Seris regroup after the tragedy they have endured, and, through feats of strength, several warriors vie for the position of chief, among them Lobo Zaíno. Coyote Iguana (Armando Silvestre) prevails in these contests and becomes the new Seri leader. Don Diego Casanova, Lola's father, experiences financial ruin and later loses his house to Don Nestor in a game of cards. Although interested in a suitor, Juan, Lola decides to marry Don Nestor to save the family's finances. En route to Hermosillo for the wedding, the Seris attack the wedding party's carriages, killing most of the *yoris*—the Seri term for Whites—and abducting Lola. Coyote Iguana wishes to marry Lola. Although his tribe's council, led by Tórtola Parda (Isabela Corona), objects to the union, the council is forced to accept the marriage when Coyote Iguana brings back Don Nestor's severed head, avenging the burning of their town. Even though Lola has the opportunity to flee when Juan finds her, she chooses to stay with the Seris and marry Coyote Iguana. Lola introduces *yori* clothing and healing practices. She also establishes trade with non-Seris, all of which lead to the formation of a rival faction within the Seri community led by Tórtola Parda and

---

18. As Robert McKee Irwin has noted, *Lola Casanova* operates as an inverted account of the genesis of the Mexican people found in the Malinche/Cortés narrative. See "Lola Casanova."

Lobo Zaíno. Lola and Coyote Iguana have a son. They travel to Guaymas to sign a peace agreement in the town, and upon returning to the Seri village, they find that their rivals have burned their homes. In the ensuing skirmish, Coyote Iguana dies. The film ends with a flash forward showing Lola and the new chief, Aguila Blanca, in the mestizo town of Pozo-Coyote. By establishing peaceful mestizaje as the end result, the film presents the earlier phase of interracial violence as a step in the process of forging national and ethnic cohesion in Mexico.

In *Lola Casanova*, the centrality of mestizaje is not merely suggested by the events of the plot or left to be inferred by the spectator, but explicitly stated in the form of voice-over commentary. As the film opens, an authoritative masculine voice describes the process of blending that is taking place in Pozo-Coyote, which the spectator later learns is the result of Coyote Iguana and Lola's efforts: "Así se prepara el advenimiento del mestizo, preciada floración humana del continente. Los viejos mueren sin dejar de ser Seris. Los adultos envejecen sin dejar de ser yoris. Los niños maduran con atributos de ambos. Se habla en español y se piensa en indio."[19] (This is how the coming of the mestizo, the continent's precious human flowering, is prepared. The elderly die while still Seris. The adults age while still *yoris*. Children mature with the attributes of both. One speaks in Spanish and thinks in Indian). Through this initial narration, the film clearly frames the narrative as the story of how mestizaje came to be in the area around Guaymas. Furthermore, *Lola Casanova* links the process of ethnic and racial synthesis to nation-building in a manner that suggests that the dilution of Indigeneity is necessary for progress when Lola concludes the film by pronouncing, "Terminó el brioso señorío de los Seris. En cambio, ahora todos somos México, y México entero es nuestro. La patria de los hijos se hizo inmensa, rica y apacible" (The vigorous dominance of the Seri ended. Now we are all Mexico and all of Mexico is ours. The homeland of our children became immense, rich and placid). In this way, the film both insinuates Indigeneity's contribution to

---

19. The use of the word "indio" as it appears in the quotations and film titles discussed in this chapter, as well as in the chapter's title, reflects the fact that in the mid-twentieth century the term was not necessarily deployed as a racial slur in Mexico. See Antonio Zirión Pérez, "Hacia una descolonización de la mirada: la representación del indígena en la historia del cine etnográfico en México (1896–2016)," in *Repensar la antropología mexicana del siglo XXI*, ed. Maria Ana Portal Ariosa (Mexico City: Universidad Autónoma Metropolitana, 2019), 366.

mestizaje while also suggesting that, in its purest form, it is incompatible with the modern nation. This tension, conveyed in the initial and final commentaries on mestizaje, points to the process of selection and differentiation of Indigeneity that the film itself dramatizes.

As in *Tribu*, *Lola Casanova* puts forth an idealized representation of the good savage through the overt contrast with "bad" Indians; however, in Landeta's film, the nobility and savagery of the Indigenous people is conveyed in part through their degree of compatibility with the mestizo nation that Lola describes at the end of the film. In short, "good" Indians defend a social order in which mestizaje is possible, while the "bad" Indians do not. The idealized noble savage who personifies the first group in the film is Coyote Iguana. *Lola Casanova* first suggests Coyote Iguana's nobility when he achieves the position of chief through competition and points to his code of honor when he takes Lola prisoner during the Seri ambush, declaring that he does not kill women. This act turns into one linked both to peace and to mestizaje when Coyote Iguana explains to

Figure 6.3. Coyote Iguana (Armando Silvestre) takes Lola Casanova (Meche Barba) prisoner with the intention of marrying her. Photo courtesy of Mil Nubes-Foto (Roberto Fiesco). All rights reserved.

Lola that he wishes to become "cuñado de tus hermanos" (brother-in-law to your brothers), demonstrating that although he is a capable warrior, his ultimate goal is peace. The length to which Coyote Iguana goes to silence the tribal council's opposition to the marriage underscores his commitment to achieving peace through mestizaje. This conviction materializes most clearly when, as the leader of the Seris, he establishes a peace agreement in Guaymas, for which he later pays the ultimate price. Coyote Iguana's death while defending his decision to make peace with the *yoris* positions him as an Indigenous martyr of mestizaje. By presenting Coyote Iguana as a legitimate leader who follows a code of honor, desires peace, and pursues mestizaje, the film crafts him as a noble savage whose heroism makes Mexican mestizaje possible. In this way, Coyote Iguana, like Tumitl, fulfills the symbolic function of the glorious but defunct Indigenous male hero in the Mexican cultural imagination, of which Cuauhtémoc is the quintessential example.

In contrast, the "bad" natives, Lobo Zaíno and Tórtola Parda, are antagonistic forces in the sense that they oppose Lola's presence among the Seri, any peaceful interaction with the *yoris*, and sow disunity among the Seri themselves—actions that are all linked to their opposition to mestizaje. For instance, in her role as the head of the council, Tórtola Parda tries to obstruct the interracial marriage in every way and gives voice to her prejudice against Lola with unfounded statements such as "las mujeres blancas traen desgracia" (White women bring misfortune). Furthermore, she and Lobo Zaíno organize the unprovoked attack against the peace-supporting Seris precisely because they had mended the tribe's relationship with the *yoris*. Furthermore, Tórtola Parda shoots the lethal arrow that kills Coyote Iguana, suggesting that she and Lobo Zaíno's desire for control and power in the tribe is greater than their sense of internal solidarity, which contrasts with Coyote Iguana's code of honor. In this way, the film's portrayal of "good" and "bad" Indians is shaped by the characters' attitudes toward mestizaje.

Visually, the film produces Coyote Iguana's on-screen presence through whiteness-as-indigeneity, which serves to transmit both his position as the noble savage who defends mestizaje and his desirability in the eyes of the White Mexican female, Lola Casanova. The male protagonist is played by the Mexican-American actor Armando Silvestre, whose film career consisted of many low-budget Mexploitation films featuring his toned, masculine physique. In the context of *Lola Casanova*, which was his first film, the display of Silvestre's body throughout the majority of the film functions as part of the character's aesthetic embodiment of Whiteness. Coyote Iguana's body reflects the White ideal for Mexican males described by Nutini, which details that, according to local raced and classed bodily ideals, males should be "broad shouldered, well-muscled, but lean and well proportioned" as well as "elegant and graceful in every aspect of physical behavior."[20] Furthermore, the display of Coyote Iguana's body can be understood as an instance of what Richard Dyer has called "the white man's muscles," which draws on the "white representational traditions" of "[c]lassicism, Californianism, barbarianism and crucifixionism," and because it is an "achieved" body, signals wealth and leisure.[21] Coyote Iguana's physique incarnates these ideals, and its ubiquitous display throughout the film through his near-nakedness calls attention to his body.

The film also underscores Coyote Iguana's desirability by showing that the White woman choses him, forgoing the possibility of escaping from captivity and returning to her white-as-white suitor and their criollo world. The language Lola uses to describe her choosing Coyote Iguana suggests that her decision is the result of intense desire as opposed to logic or esteem: "Me entregué al instinto. El y solo él condujo mis pasos definitivos" (I surrendered to instinct. He and only he drove my definitive steps). While the second sentence of this confession may appear to suggest that Coyote Iguana forces her hand, what occurs in film on the visual plane suggests otherwise. As Lola's words sound through voice-over narration, she walks toward Coyote as if in a trance, conveying how he "drives" her steps through attraction and not by force. By visually presenting Coyote Iguana through whiteness-as-indigeneity, the film marks him as the good Indian who is most compatible with the ideals of the future mestizo nation. At the same time, Coyote Iguana's white-as-indigenous on-screen presence reinscribes colonially inflected standards for male desirability because the film transmits Indigenous masculine appeal through embodied Whiteness in the Mexican context.

Although Coyote Iguana's male Seri rival, Lobo Zaíno, has a similar build to Coyote Iguana's, Lobo Zaíno's body is not exhibited on-screen with either the same frequency or through the same variety of shot types. Furthermore, Lobo Zaíno (whose name means "dark wolf") is made up

---

20. Nutini, *Mexican Aristocracy*.

21. Richard Dyer, "The White Man's Muscles," in *White* (London and New York: Routledge, 1997), 145–55.

in a manner that gives him the appearance of having notably darker skin, and his facial expressions and language are more aggressive. By attributing physical darkness and inelegance to Lobo Zaíno, his on-screen presence is more removed from the embodiment of male Whiteness in the Mexican context compared with Coyote Iguana. In ascribing to the antagonist visual and aural markers associated with Indigeneity in the local context, *Lola Casanova* marks the Indian who overtly opposes the project of Mexican mestizaje in embodied, raced terms that tie him to stereotypes regarding Indigeneity.

"Bad" Indians are not the only means through which the film underscores Coyote Iguana's virtues and portrays him as the desirable Indigenous candidate for mestizaje. In a manner similar to *Tribu*'s condemnation of Captain Bazán, *Lola Casanova* presents Don Nestor Ariza as equally dishonorable and incompatible with mestizaje as Lobo Zaíno and Tórtola Parda. This White man, whose accent indicates that he is from Spain, is responsible for the initial attack against the Seris, which is motivated by his endless greed.[22] The film adds to this negative characterization by demonstrating how Don Nestor tries to take advantage of Don Diego Casanova's financial ruin in order to marry his daughter. Beyond his avarice and dishonesty, Don Nestor opposes the ideal of mestizo synthesis that the film's opening commentary glorifies when, upon returning to Guaymas from his attack on the Seri, he gifts Lola an Indigenous boy, whom he regards as an animal and suggests should be kept in a cage. In this way, the film crafts Don Nestor as the personification of a retrograde, Eurocentric worldview that must be left behind for the future mestizo nation to emerge. Through his character flaws, the film presents him as an unsuitable match for the criolla Lola, whose choice for a mate is allegorically representative of the nation's destiny.[23]

Furthermore, *Lola Casanova* conveys Don Nestor's unsuitability for the protagonist by visualizing the irredeemably flawed character in an undesirable White male body that is old, rotund, and unattractive compared with Coyote Iguana's white-as-indigenous embodiment, which is toned

---

22. Upon Don Nestor's return from the attack, Lola attributes his violent act to the fact that Don Nestor is "insaciable de riquezas" (insatiable in his thirst for riches).

23. As Patricia Torres de San Martín observes, in Matilde Landeta's Golden Age films, the director "employs allegory to construct her symbolic discourses." See "Adela Sequeyro and Matilde Landeta: Two Pioneer Women Directors," in *Mexico's Cinema: A Century of Film and Filmmakers*, ed. Joanne Hershfield and David Maciel (Wilmington, DE: Scholarly Resources, 1999), 44.

and almost always exposed. The film reveals how Don Nestor functions to highlight Coyote Iguana's compatibility with Lola when she explicitly compares the two as she considers what a future with Coyote might be like: "Coyote es joven, brutal, pero ingenuo. Ariza era viejo, demoníaco, lleno de pasiones deformes. Los vicios son repugnantes, en cambio, la rusticidad no es asquerosa" (Coyote is young, savage, but naive. Ariza was old, demoniacal, full of deformed passions. Vices are repugnant whereas rusticity is not revolting). By presenting Don Nestor as the dishonorable and physically unappealing Spanish oppressor of the Seri, the film avoids a blanket idealization of diegetic Whiteness and condemnation of Indigeneity. Instead, Don Nestor and Lobo Zaíno both constitute extremes through which the film portrays the Indigenous Coyote Iguana and the criolla Lola as the compatible forgers of a Mexican mestizaje in contradistinction to the instigators of violence in their groups of origin.

To underscore the allegorical weight of Lola and Coyote's union as a representation of the future Mexican nation, the film aggrandizes their coupling by presenting it through the melodramatic mode, which lends to it a heightened momentousness.[24] While the film does not begin in the "space of innocence"[25] that frequently characterizes melodrama, it certainly casts Lola and Coyote's mutual love as this kind of space, which serves as a refuge from the ongoing tensions within and between their respective groups of origin. The film conveys the depth of their affection for each other both verbally (through declarations of love and esteem)[26] and visually (when the characters hold each other affectionately or gaze lovingly into each other's eyes[27]). A nondiegetic, string-based romantic score sounds during such loving instances, indicating that these scenes are moments of affectively charged tenderness. Beyond the film's idealization of the characters' emotional bond, the melodramatic representation of the love story is also evident in that the characters' union is threatened by hostile forces from both the White and Seri groups, which culminate in Coyote Iguana's death at the hands of the opposing faction in his own tribe. This

---

24. Peter Brooks, *The Melodramatic Imagination: Balzac, Henry James, Melodrama, and the Mode of Excess* (New Haven: Yale University Press, 1995), 13.

25. Brooks, *The Melodramatic Imagination*, 29.

26. The film's hyperbolic declarations of love include Coyote Iguana's verbalized delight when the council approves his marriage to Lola: "Eres el mejor premio que haya ganado guerrero alguno" (You are the best prize ever attained by any warrior).

27. This occurs, for example, in the marriage scene.

tragic ending to the central love story imbues it with pathos, heightening its emotive magnitude. In sum, through affective displays, idealization, and tragedy, *Lola Casanova* crafts the central interracial relationship as a love story of epic proportions to evoke the allegorical birth of the Mexican nation as a grandiose development.

For all of its glorification of mestizaje, *Lola Casanova* plainly suggests that its contributors are not on unequal footing by casting Lola as the criolla savior who is the only one capable of leading the Seris into Mexicanness. The film explicitly articulates the subordinate position that Coyote Iguana occupies in this project during the peacemaking trip that the couple and those loyal to Coyote Iguana make to Guaymas. As Lola walks through the streets of her former city, she strengthens her resolve to Mexicanize the Seri, explaining, ". . . yo era para él [Coyote Iguana] la ilusión, y para su pueblo la esperanza . . . Seguiría con los Seris llevando el afán de incorporarlos con mi amor y mi paciencia a México, a la patria grande" (For him [Coyote Iguana] I was joy, and for his people, hope. I would continue with the mission of incorporating them into Mexico, the homeland, with my love and patience). Thus, while Coyote Iguana's actions demonstrate that he is compatible with the mestizaje project, the film suggests that only Lola is capable of leading it—a protagonism underscored by the title of the film. Even though Coyote is instrumental in generating mestizaje by choosing a White wife and making peace with the *yoris*, through his death he is cut off from existing within the consolidated mestizo milieu that appears in the opening and closing scenes. The alternative that *Lola Casanova* puts forth, that Coyote Iguana lives on through his mestizo child, is consistent with the fundamentally Whitening intention of both nineteenth- and twentieth-century Mexican mestizaje, which (as discussed in the introduction) ultimately sought to mitigate Indigeneity through dilution.

Coyote's death is consistent with the Hispanicizing impulse of liberal and postrevolutionary Mexican mestizaje (indicating that pure Indigeneity must end or be transformed so that Mexican modernity can emerge). At the same time, his death (like that of Tumitl's in *Tribu*) conforms to the taboo regarding the coupling of the White woman and Indigenous male in the Mexican context by thwarting the mestizo marriage's projection into the future.[28] Therefore, although the film employs whiteness-as-indigeneity and the desire of the White Mexican woman to signal the ideal

---

28. This outcome for the romantic interracial couple contrasts sharply with that of Naya and Francisco de Montejo in *Chilam Balam*, whose normative union does endure into the future (see chapter 1).

Indian who plays a role in the creation of mestizaje, ultimately, even this Whitened Indian dies because, as the Indigenous male partner in a heterosexual mestizo marriage, he violates the gendered and raced norms of the traditional mestizo arrangement.

Tizoc (Amor indio) (1957)

Also taking place in the nineteenth century, Ismael Rodríguez's *Tizoc* similarly focuses on interracial love that ends in tragedy; however, instead of celebrating an emergence of mestizaje, *Tizoc*'s drama points to the impossibility of such a project at that time in southern Mexico. In the film, Tizoc (played by Pedro Infante) is the "último descendiente de príncipes tacuates" (last descendent of Tacuate princes). He lives in relative isolation and has limited contact with Mixtec natives who bear a long-standing hatred toward his people. Tizoc and Machinza (a Mixtec woman played by Alicia del Lago) like each other, but her brother and father are virulently opposed to their courtship. The criollos, María (played by María Félix) and her father, Don Enrique, arrive in Oaxaca after María has refused to go through with her wedding because of her fiancé's indiscretion. María and Tizoc begin to interact as they encounter each other in the town and after Tizoc saves her father's life. These interactions lead to Tizoc falling in love with María. In one of their meetings, María gives Tizoc her handkerchief, which, unbeknown to her, represents betrothal according to an Indigenous custom. Realizing that Tizoc believes himself to be engaged to María, Don Enrique tricks Tizoc into postponing the wedding for a month, during which he arranges María's marriage to her previous fiancé, Arturo. When María finally does forgive Arturo and he arrives in Oaxaca for their wedding, Machinza sees the couple kissing and then mistakenly informs Tizoc that María has deceived him. During this meeting with Tizoc, Machinza's father and brother surprise them and shoot Machinza for her interest in Tizoc. Believing that María has lied to him, Tizoc kidnaps her and is eventually followed by Don Enrique, Arturo, and an Indigenous man who is helping them. When Tizoc learns that María did not intentionally deceive him, he lets her go, but Arturo shoots at Tizoc anyway. Disgusted with her own people, María asks Tizoc to take her away with him. As they flee, Don Enrique's Indigenous assistant shoots an arrow at them and hits María, wounding her lethally. Tizoc then stabs himself with same arrow and dies.

If Tizoc and María's participation in mestizaje is limited because death precludes them from sharing a future and producing mestizo offspring (as occurs in *Lola Casanova*), the film points to the possibility of cultural mestizaje by highlighting the characters' affinity in a manner that parallels the compatibility of Leonor and Tumitl in *Tribu*. *Tizoc* constructs this rapport in part by crafting Tizoc as a clear exception to all the other Indigenous characters in the film. First, Tizoc is of noble descent and a non-Mixtec. He has exceptional knowledge of nature and skill in hunting, which allows him to sell animal furs that aren't adulterated with bullet wounds like those of the Mixtec hunters. Despite this opportunity to gain wealth, Tizoc refuses to exploit nature for his personal gain beyond his most basic needs and also shuns material compensation for favors,[29] whereas the Mixtec hunt to accumulate wealth.

Perhaps the most prominent way in which the film suggests Tizoc's difference with respect to the other Indigenous characters is through his devout Catholicism.[30] Whereas Tizoc appears in the chapel at the feet of the statue of Mary (in this sense he is María Candelaria's male equivalent with regard to Marian devotion), the Mixtec Indians, motivated by their jealousy and desire to disrupt a union between Tizoc and Machinza, are superstitious and seek out a shaman to help them kill Tizoc. The film presents the two scenes with the shaman as spaces of wickedness because of the Mixtec groups' intention to cause harm through those gatherings. Furthermore, *Tizoc* associates the shamanistic practices with maleficence through the scene's low-key lighting, the very dark (and clearly artificial) pigment worn by the shaman, his dramatic gestures, shouting, the growth of the fire as the shaman engages in "witchcraft" (he himself uses the term "brujería"), and the sounding of loud and dramatic nondiegetic music as he calls for evil to befall Tizoc. This scene could not be more different from the brightly lit chapel scene in which Tizoc sings sweetly to the Virgin while placing flowers at the statue's feet. In sum, while other Indians in the film are common, self-interested, vengeful, and pagan, Tizoc is of noble birth, generous, peaceful, and Catholic. It is only this exceptional Indigenous male who can elicit the admiration of the White Mexican woman.

---

29. When Arturo offers to pay Tizoc for a favor, the Indigenous man suggests that accepting montary compensation in exchange for his help goes against his personal code of honor: "Tizoc no cobra por favores que hace" (Tizoc doesn't charge for the favors he does).

30. Associating "good" natives with devout Catholicism is a trope of Golden Age cinema commonly associated with Indigenous female characters. See Dolores Tierney, *Emilio Fernández: Pictures in the Margins* (Manchester: Manchester University Press, 2012), 91–94.

Indios, Desire, and the White Mexican Woman   259

Figure 6.4. Pedro Infante as the title character in *Tizoc* (1957). Photo courtesy of Mil Nubes-Foto (Roberto Fiesco). All rights reserved.

For her part, María distinguishes herself from the rest of the criollos in various ways. First, she is clearly a misfit within her patriarchal and sexist society, chafing against the sexual license afforded to Arturo and her father's attempts to impose his will on her by, for example, pressuring her to go through with the marriage. Second, María does not display the bigoted attitudes toward Indigenous people that her father exhibits by referring to the Indigenous people disparagingly. Furthermore, *Tizoc* suggests María's comparative proximity to Indigeneity through her sartorial transformation upon arriving in Oaxaca. María promptly abandons her restrictive corset, high-collared shirt, and skirt in exchange for a variety of Indigenous huipiles—a first step in her evolution toward "going native,"[31] which culminates

---

31. This analysis is indebted to Patricia Arroyo Calderón's conference paper presented at The Society of Cinema and Media Studies' annual conference in 2016 titled "Screening Indigeneity: Tourism, Anthropology, and the Ethnographic Gaze during the Lost Decade of Mexican Cinema (1955–1965)."

at the end of the film when she attempts to flee with Tizoc and abandon her criollo world entirely. The final and perhaps most significant way in which María stands out from other criollos is her astonishment and admiration for the local flora and fauna. During her arrival trip to Oaxaca, María insists on stopping her father's carriage numerous times to contemplate the scenery. The film transmits her strong affinity with nature through her compulsion to paint landscapes and Indians during her stay. Furthermore, *Tizoc* clearly transmits the idea that María has been transformed through her contact with nature in Oaxaca—in large part through her interactions with Tizoc—while other criollos remain indifferent to its beauty and power. For instance, upon hearing the Mexican mockingbird's singing, María interrupts a kiss with Arturo and asks him, "¿No crees que los pájaros, las flores, del agua que corre por el río y toda la naturaleza nos dice algo que no podemos comprender?" (Don't you think that the birds, flowers, the water that flows through the river and all of nature tells us something that we cannot understand?). The fact that Arturo dismisses this idea as fanciful nonsense foregrounds María as a White woman with unusual sensibilities. Therefore, like Tizoc, María stands out for exhibiting attitudes and beliefs that distinguish her from the rest of her ethnoracial group.

It is precisely by emphasizing Tizoc and María's exceptionalism that the film suggests their affinity and promotes mestizaje as an aspiration. Their compatibility is rooted in their shared valuing of Catholicism and nature. The film indicates that both Tizoc and María take their religious life seriously, as they both have multiple individual conversations with the priest. Furthermore, while María is fascinated by nature, Tizoc is represented as being one with nature: he lives far from the town near a mountain and is presented as having an extraordinary knowledge of the land and the ability to communicate with wildlife because "los animales del monte le cantan y le lloran al indio" (the mountain animals sing and weep to the Indian). Similar to *Tribu*, *Tizoc* emphasizes on a visual level that María and Tizoc's appreciation of nature is central to their bond by displaying them in natural settings when they have personal conversations alone (see figure 6.5). As they discuss intimate thoughts and feelings, foliage, a lake, and mountains surround them, suggesting that only here, far away from the "bad" Indians and criollos, can they express their mutual fondness. The film conveys how both nature and religious beliefs function as the basis for a cultural mestizaje that allows the characters to bond when it combines the religious discourse and the characters' admiration for local nature in one of Tizoc's lines to María during a picturesque encounter:

Figure 6.5. The criolla María (María Félix) dressed as a Tehuana and Tizoc (Pedro Infante) find common ground in nature. Photo courtesy of Mil Nubes-Foto (Roberto Fiesco). All rights reserved.

". . . buena es la tierra, el sol, el aire, el agua del río, mesmamente como tata Dios" (. . . good is the earth, the sun, the air, the water in the river just like God the father). María's response, "Me encanta oírte hablar, Tizoc" (I love hearing you speak, Tizoc), cements that the characters' veneration of nature and their religious beliefs—precisely the points that distinguish María and Tizoc from their groups of origin—function as the shared values that make their mutual appreciation possible. In this way, *Tizoc* points to the possibility of mestizaje not only through the characters' affection for each other, but also through their respective degrees of acculturation.

For all the fondness that Tizoc and María share, there is a central consideration that sets *Tizoc* apart from the two interracial love stories discussed in this chapter thus far, which is meaningful for discussing the representation of Indigenous male desirability in Mexican cinema. Tizoc's romantic love and desire for María is unidirectional—a fact that is apparent in the film's full title, *Tizoc (Amor indio)* (Tizoc [Indian love]). Furthermore, while Tizoc makes explicit declarations of romantic love to

María, perhaps most clearly when after kidnapping her, he releases her, saying, "... pa' siempre te quedarás como lumbre prendida en el corazón del indio Tizoc" (you will forever remain like a burning fire in the Indian Tizoc's heart), María only ever conveys fondness for Tizoc, but not romantic desire. Though she says that she feels affection for him using the verb "querer" in Spanish, whose meaning can encompass liking, loving, or generally feeling affection for someone, María makes it clear that her feelings are not romantic in nature when she explains to the priest why she used this word: "Lo quiero como una criatura o como un ser desdichado" (I love him like a child or like a wretched person). In other words, "querer" for María in the context of her relationship with Tizoc denotes a kind of paternalistic sympathy.

There are other moments in which María displays affective intensity toward Tizoc, but these displays consist of either admiration or worry, not romantic desire.[32] Even the film's climax, the moment in which María decides to flee with Tizoc, lacks a romantic confession. Instead, María exhibits a different form of emotional intensity: disdain for her father and fiancé when she declares with indignation, "¡Vengativos, traicioneros! Nunca te perdonarán, pero jamás volveré con ellos. Tizoc, ¡llévame contigo!" (Vengeful, treacherous men! They will never forgive you, but I will never go back with them. Tizoc, take me with you!). In sum, though the film suggests the possibility of mestizaje through Tizoc and María's affinity and cultural common ground, diegetically (and in contradistinction to *Tribu* and *Lola Casanova*), *Tizoc* presents the Indigenous male as undesirable for the White Mexican woman, thus precluding a representation of the two characters as a viable romantic mestizo couple. In this way, the unilateral nature of Tizoc's attraction sets up a scenario that conforms to the Mexican taboo surrounding interracial relationships between White women and Indigenous men.[33]

---

32. María exhibits her strong esteem for Tizoc when calls him "un hombre bueno" (a good man) and an "espíritu poético" (a poetic spirit). She demonstrates anxiety and guilt regarding his well-being when she fears that her father and fiancé will kill him even after Tizoc returns her to them. Even if these affective displays convey a degree of emotional investment in Tizoc, they do not mirror the romantic love and desire that Tizoc expresses toward María.

33. *Tizoc* also conveys the Indigenous male's irrelevance within the traditional racial and gendered configuration of *mestizaje* when María's criollo father, Don Enrique (who expresses bigoted opinions about Indigenous people and is one of Tizoc's antag-

While the film's narrative firmly suggests Tizoc's undesirability, what occurs on the visual plane is much more complex. On the one hand, the film's plot underscores the desirability of the White Mexican male vis-à-vis the Indigenous Mexican male through María's acquiescence to marry her white-as-white former fiancé, whom she kisses on-screen (the only man with whom this occurs in the film). *Tizoc* later reinforces the implications of race for male desirability in the Mexican context in a much more obvious way when, during a sequence that showcases a local Indigenous festivity, a white-as-white man asks María to dance. At this point, Tizoc has already fallen in love with María, and, as he watches them dance, he imagines himself in the place of the man and María reciprocating his desire. When he imagines this, he appears not as Pedro Infante in brownface (the way in which the film visualizes Tizoc), but instead in the form of Pedro Infante, the White Mexican star, dressed in a smart mid-twentieth-century suit and tie and showing off his masculine signing voice—a hallmark of performing Mexican masculinity (see figures 6.6 and 6.7).

This is the only moment in the entire film that expresses and indulges in mutual desire between the two characters. María and White Tizoc dance closely, their faces touch, and their hands are clasped intimately. María fixes her desirous gaze on him and manifests her excitement with the subtle raising of her left eyebrow. In all the other scenes, María's character shows restraint in her treatment of Tizoc, maintaining a physical distance compared with the intimacy she displays in this scene. Furthermore, the cinematography presents White Tizoc in the person of Pedro Infante as desirable, privileging his figure in the frame and using the close-up throughout the scene to display his dapper appearance and musical talent. Also, it is only in this daydream that Tizoc appears as the dominant

---

onists in the film), conveys his sexual interest toward Indigenous women. At a festive celebration where many Indigenous women are present, Don Enrique's friend, Don Pancho, explains that the local Indigenous women become betrothed when they gift a handkerchief to a man. Don Enrique conveys sexual interest in the women when he responds, "Oye, pues con gusto lo recibiría de aquella chaparrita que hay allí, o de cualquiera de esas tres" (Listen, I would gladly receive one from that little woman over there, or from any of those three). When Don Pancho responds with confusion because he is familiar with Don Enrique's disdain for Indigenous people, Don Enrique's response perfectly captures the sexual criollo male entitlement that is a feature of the specifically gendered and racial dimensions of coloniality in Mexico: "Un momento, yo aborrezco a los indios, ¡pero no a las indias!" (Wait a minute, I abhor Indigenous men, but not Indigenous women!).

Figure 6.6. Tizoc (played by Pedro Infante in brownface) daydreams that María is dancing with a Whitened version of himself in *Tizoc* (1957). Screen capture from film.

Figure 6.7. In Tizoc's daydream, María gazes desirously at a Whitened version of himself. Screen capture from film.

figure in the couple, physically leading María's body firmly and elegantly, whereas in their interactions throughout the film, Tizoc is submissive and deferential. The fact that the film conveys Tizoc's reciprocated desire for the White Mexican woman *only* when he imagines himself as a White Mexican man indicates how the film reproduces the hierarchization of male appeal in Mexico based on the coloniality of desire.

Whereas Maria's nonreciprocation of Tizoc's desire, except when he is Whitened, underscores the racialized hierarchy of male attractiveness, the casting of Pedro Infante in the role of Tizoc requires a more nuanced analysis of the character's desirability in the film. Pedro Infante was a major figure of the Mexican star system, and, as Sergio de la Mora has observed, Infante personified some of the ideals of mid-twentieth-century Mexican masculinity such as emotional intensity, virility, and strength.[34] He was able to personify these ideals in part because he was a White Mexican man whose star text foregrounded his working-class relatability, combining the aesthetic privilege of the former with the appeal to authenticity from the latter.[35] Infante cultivated his image through multiple melodramatic roles and his self-fashioning as an athletic person, making him an iconic Mexican version of "the white man's muscles."[36] Infante's interpretation of Tizoc is an instance of brownface featuring the Golden Age's *indito* pidgin Spanish,[37] infantile emotional reactions, unbecoming hairstyle, and unintentionally comical, hop-like gait. Infante's brownface performance (for which he won an award for best actor at the Berlin International Film Festival in 1957) is different from what this book calls whiteness-as-indigeneity. While brownface and whiteness-as-indigeneity are both forms of racial impersonation, whiteness-as-indigeneity seeks to retain the markers of Whiteness that are advantageous in the context of the local racial formation for the sake of featuring a character as both romantically and sexually desirable. Brownface relinquishes some or all of these markers for the sake of a verisimilitude that it pursues disingenuously.

---

34. de la Mora, *Cinemachismo: Masculinities and Sexuality in Mexican Film* (Austin: University of Texas Press, 2006).

35. de la Mora, *Cinemachismo*, 70. In this sense, Pedro Infante's star text parallels that of Elvis Presley in the United States.

36. Dyer, "The White Man's Muscles," in *White*, 145–83.

37. Tierney, *Emilio Fernández*, 84–85; Yásnaya Aguilar, "El efecto Tizoc," July 4, 2012, https://web.archive.org/web/20190510094735/http://archivo.estepais.com/site/2012/el-efecto-tizoc/.

Thus, while Tumitl and Coyote Iguana are examples of whiteness-as-indigeneity because their respective films present them as desirable for the White woman, the presentation of Tizoc through Infante's brownface performance underscores his undesirability in María's eyes.

Now, Infante's interpretation of Tizoc contains a fundamental tension. On the one hand, we have the emasculating trappings of his brownface performance, and on the other, we have the film's attempts to feature elements of Infante's attractive star persona (concretely, his muscled torso and famous virile singing voice). This tension is most obvious at specific points when the film endeavors to capitalize on these two aspects of Infante's star text but within the constraints of a brownface performance: the scenes in which a shirtless Tizoc energetically builds a house by hand for himself and María, and the scene in which he sings to María as his Indigenous self (and not as the imagined White version of himself). Even though María does not express desire for his body, the film's lengthy exhibition of the shirtless Tizoc at work clearly aims to display Infante's body as appealing—a recurring aspect of his numerous cinematic performances. At the same time, Tizoc maintains the high-pitch *indito* speech and racially caricatured bodily movements that are the exact opposite of the deeper voice, curt verbal style, and confident movements that defined most of Infante's on-screen performances. Furthermore, in *Tizoc* there are no women swooning over his appearance, which is part of the way in which Infante's films produced his "to-be-looked-at-ness."[38] The point is that the film's exhibition of Infante's virile torso clashes with the *indito* affectations.

A similar conflict occurs aurally when the film features Infante's singing ability, which is also a regular occurrence in his film performances. When Tizoc sings "Te quiero más que a mis ojos" to María, the spectator/listener simultaneously hears the actor's trademark virile voice *and* Tizoc's *indito* Spanish. This blending of Infante's masculine tone with the laughable imitation of Indigenous people's Spanish, which connotes childishness and ignorance in the film, inhibits the projection of Infante's usual brand of masculinity and appeal. *Tizoc*'s failed mobilization of the main points of Infante's star appeal (his body and voice) in this brownface performance highlights both the absurdity and racist nature of Golden Age brownface conventions but also the extent to which the desirability of Golden Age

---

38. Laura Mulvey, "Visual Pleasure and Narrative Cinema," in *Literary Theory. An Anthology*, ed. Julie Rivkin and Michael Ryan (New York: Blackwell, 1998), 585–96.

stars in their performances was predicated on their embodiment of Mexican standards of Whiteness (*blancura* and *blanquitud*).

Like *Tribu* and *Lola Casanova*, *Tizoc* uses the affective bonds between the White Mexican woman and Indigenous man to promote the possibility of mestizaje. However, the film stops short of conveying the characters' mutual romantic love and ends with their deaths, thus suggesting that a reversal of the gender and racial configuration of the Mexican origin story is not a viable model for Mexican mestizaje. Despite their respective portrayals of Tumitl, Coyote Iguana, and Tizoc as exceptional Indigenous men who embody honor and virtue, in one way or another, the three films uphold Whiteness as the standard of Mexican male attractiveness. While *Tribu* and *Lola Casanova* do this by distinguishing the white-as-indigenous male as the only desirable native, *Tizoc* reinscribes White male desirability because in the film the White Mexican woman can only desire the Indigenous male if he *becomes* a White Mexican man.

El violetero (1960)

Gilberto Martín Solares's comical film starring Tin Tan, *El violetero*, diverges in that, unlike the three films discussed thus far, it does not end in the death of the Indigenous male who is in love with the White Mexican woman. However, its romantic happy ending does require the extinguishing of the Indigenous male in a different sense that also underscores Whiteness (in this case, *blanquitud*) as a necessity for Mexican male attractiveness and appeal.

The film is a parody of both *María Candelaria* (dir. Emilio Fernández, 1944) and *La violetera* (dir. Luis César Amadori, 1958), borrowing the backdrop of Xochimilco from the former and the storyline of class transformation from the latter—while also taking a few jabs at *Tizoc*. In the film, Germán Valdés (known professionally as Tin Tan) plays an *indito* from Xochimilco, Lorenzo Miguel, who sells flowers with his friend María Candela. While doing some gardening for a wealthy local White family, the younger daughter, Teresa, insults Lorenzo, making disparaging comments about Indigenous people. Her older sister, Lucía, decides to take Lorenzo on as a project while Teresa is away in the United States, converting him into a respectable gentleman to teach Teresa a lesson. This transformation involves teaching him to read and write, pronounce Spanish according to dominant standards, speak English, change his eating habits, dance, as well as set him up in a respectable flower shop. When Teresa returns, she is smitten with the new Lorenzo, whom she does not recognize. Through Teresa's attraction to the former *indito*, Lucía reveals to her sister the ignorance of her bigoted opinions. Lorenzo also surprises the family's administrator by revealing to all his fraudulent management of the family's wealth. During the process of teaching Lorenzo how to behave according to bourgeois Mexican standards, Lucía and Lorenzo fall in love and by the end of the film become a couple.

Through parody, *El violetero* takes aim at Mexican Golden Age cinema's representation of Indigeneity. First, it ridicules the trope of presenting the Amerindian protagonist as a representative of Indigenous nobility. The observation that Lorenzo "desciende de Apochquiyauhtzin, el ultimo rey de Xochimilco" (descends from Apochquiyauhtzin, the last king of Xochimilco) recalls both the comparison of María Candelaria with "las antiguas princesas que vinieron a sojuzgar los conquistadores" (the ancient princesses that the conquistadores came to conquer) and the affirmation that Tizoc is the "último descendiente de príncipes tacuates" (the last descendant of Tacuate princes). In this way, *El violetero* pokes fun at these films' attempts to elevate their protagonists by connecting them to aristocracy while visualizing them as tattered Indians.

El violetero also mocks the Golden Age convention of idealizing Indigenous characters as exemplary Christians. In the film's opening scene, María Candela and Lorenzo Miguel's morning greeting to each other includes excessive religious references, which presents them as exaggeratedly devout:

María Candela: Buenos días le dé Dios, Lorenzo Miguel. ¿Cómo amaneció su merced?

Lorenzo Miguel: Bien en lo que cabe, gracias a Dios. ¿Y asté cómo amaneció, María Candela?

María Candela: Bien, con el favor de Dios.

Lorenzo Miguel: Bendito sea su santo nombre

María Candela: Amén.

(María Candela: Good morning and God bless you, Lorenzo Miguel. How are you today?

Lorenzo Miguel: As well as I can be, thank God. And how are you today, María Candela?

María Candela: Good, thank God.

Lorenzo Miguel: Blessed be his holy name.

María Candela: Amen.)

The redundant religious language in this exchange references the staging of María Candelaria and Tizoc's piety during their respective prayer scenes and multiple encounters with local priests.[39] Now placed outside melodramatic conventions and in the banal context of a routine morning greeting, the pious gestures of Indigenous characters are entirely recast in a comedic light.

Furthermore, in *El violetero*, María Candelaria's beautiful "pregón (street cry) in a high soprano register, more reminiscent of a singer trained in the art-music tradition than in a folkloric singing style,"[40] becomes a shrill musical duet by Lorenzo Miguel and María Candela that is hilarious by comparison. Moreover, *El violetero* also reproduces the conventions of *indito* performances, including a submissive demeanor, hop-like gait, higher-pitched voice, and anachronistic Spanish words and pronunciation. In the absence of the narrative and nondiegetic conventions of filmic melodrama (such as the victimization of the protagonists and the musical accentuation of pathos), *El violetero*'s reproduction of these racial Golden Age tropes functions as pure comedy.

Even though the film ridicules the way in which Golden Age Mexican cinema represents Indigenous people, it reiterates the racist core of twentieth-century Mexican *mestizaje*: the idea that all Mexicans are mestizos and equals, but that the *habitus* of White bourgeois Mexicans is the standard to which all should aspire.[41] The film's alignment with this position can be appreciated by juxtaposing what Lucía says about Indigeneity and how she approaches the diegetically Indigenous Lorenzo. In

---

39. Tierney, *Emilio Fernández*, 91–94.

40. Jacqueline Avila, *Cinesonidos: Film Music and National Identity During Mexico's Epoca de Oro* (Oxford: Oxford University Press, 2019), 143.

41. Pierre Bourdieu, *Distinction: A Social Critique of the Judgement of Taste*, trans. Richard Nice (New York: Routledge, 2010).

Figure 6.8. The parodic film *El violetero* (1960) reproduces the visual motifs of *María Candelaria* for comedic effect. Filmoteca UNAM Collection. All rights reserved.

contrast to her unabashedly racist sister, Lucía gives voice to the official doctrine of mestizaje: "Todos los mexicanos somos iguales. El que más el que menos llevamos sangre india y debemos estar orgullosos de ello" (All we Mexicans are equal. We all have some Indigenous blood and we should be proud of that). However, for all of her espousal of Mexican equality, Lucía's project of transforming Lorenzo is predicated on the idea that Whitening him (through *blanquitud*) is an improvement compared to his Indigenous condition. For instance, when she explains how she wants to change Lorenzo, she explains, "Usted es como tierra virgen. Yo voy a transformarlo en un jardín" (You are like virgin land. I am going to transform you into a garden). Beyond equating Indigeneity with a more primitive condition, which reveals that Mexicans are not precisely equal after all, Lucía also displays the paternalistic positioning of White Mexicans who believe themselves to personify the teleological endpoint of Mexican progress.

Like Lola Casanova, Lucía functions as the leader and authority of Lorenzo's transformation. In a scene in which, midway into his metamorphosis, Lorenzo feels that he will never be able to repay Lucía for everything she is doing for him, Lucía answers him with a perfect articulation of the racist core and asymmetrical positioning of Indigenous and White Mexicans in the twentieth-century project of mestizaje: "La forma de agradecerme es llegar a ser lo que yo quiero que sea" (The best way to thank me is to become what I want you to be). This statement manifests that Lucía's undertaking (and the Whitening ambitions of the broader project of mestizaje that it represents) is the result of her volition and disregards the possibility of Indigenous agency. Therefore, while *El violetero* presents Lucía as the heroine who opposes overt racism, this film also acritically reiterates (and even celebrates) the racist mestizaje discourse because the heroine's method for quelling Teresa's bigotry is predicated on the inferiority of Indigeneity and the subordination of the Indigenous person to White will.

Perhaps *El violetero*'s greatest contribution to revealing the intricacies of Mexican racism is that it demonstrates the extent to which this racism is tied to the question of desirability. The film introduces a tension between Indigenous masculinity and attractiveness in one of Teresa's dismissive remarks about Lorenzo in which she scoffs at the idea that an Indigenous male could ever be an alluring socialite: "Sí, ya me imagino al chichimeca ese convertido en un playboy" (Sure, I can see that Chichimec transformed into a playboy). This sarcastic statement establishes the parameters for Lucía's project in which making the *indito* desirable for the White Mexican woman constitutes victory. In fact, Teresa's desire for Lorenzo at the end of the project (which she demonstrates by kissing him) is the proof that Lucía uses to determine the success of her undertaking. Of course, Lorenzo can only elicit the desire of the White Mexican woman when he himself is able to perform Whiteness (*blanquitud*) successfully and is no longer recognizable as an *indito* to those in White Mexican society. In this way, the desire of the White Mexican woman means that the *indito* has been definitively transformed and functions as the ultimate mark of success.

Although it is outside the realm of melodrama, the parodic film still unfolds according to the colonially inflected logic of whiteness-as-indigeneity. While Germán Valdés's performance contains some characteristics of brownface in Lorenzo Miguel's speech and movements prior to his transformation, the performance lacks the actual *brown face* precisely because the character must eventually elicit the desire of the white-as-white Teresa and Lucía once Lorenzo Miguel leaves his cultural Indigeneity behind. In other words, while *Tizoc*'s full-on brownface approach

Figure 6.9. At the end of *El violetero* (1960), neither Teresa nor the bourgeois party guests suspect that Lorenzo Miguel (Germán Valdés) is an Indigenous man. Filmoteca UNAM Collection. All rights reserved.

underscores the undesirability of the protagonist, *El violetero*'s retention of Germán Valdes's White male Mexican appearance supports Lorenzo Miguel's diegetic appeal at the end of the film. In this way, despite *El violetero*'s ridiculing of the conventions of cinematic Indigeneity, it ultimately reiterates (both on the diegetic and visual planes) the colonially informed hierarchy of Mexican male appeal.

In the end, Lucía herself falls in love with Lorenzo, which leads to the happy romantic ending. Although this cheerful outcome may, on its face, appear more progressive than the panorama that *Tizoc* affords the interracial would-be couple, on close examination the films have more in common than what their opposite endings might suggest. *Tizoc* and *El violetero* put forth the same racialized requirement for male desirability: the Indigenous male must be able to embody Whiteness (*blancura* and *blanquitud*) to be desired by the White Mexican woman.

Beyond the Golden Age

While this book focuses on Indigenous-themed films leading up to and during the Golden Age because of the ideological weight that scholars have attributed to cinema during this period, I wish to address how the cultural anxiety surrounding the desire of the White Mexican woman for the Mexican man of color—no longer presented as Indigenous, but as a lower-class brown mestizo man—has continued to surface in Mexican cinema and continues to speak to a colonial wound that is bound up with the question of desire. Films throughout the second half of the twentieth century and the beginning of the twenty-first have pointed to the Mexican man of color's yearning for the White Mexican woman in ways that echo the dynamic present in *Tizoc* and *El violetero*.

In *El juicio de Martín Cortés* (dir. Alejandro Galindo, 1974), a detective investigates a theater group that is performing a play about Hernán Cortés's mestizo son with doña Marina, Martín Cortés. The detective is carrying out the investigation because during one performance, the actor who plays Martín kills the actor who plays his fully European half-brother, don Martín. The theater group puts on the play for the detective, and one of its subplots is a love triangle among Martín, don Martín, and a Spanish noblewoman, Lucía María. Don Martín is in love with Lucía María, but she is in love with the mestizo Martín. In what the actors refer to as the "bodega scene," Lucía María declares her love for Martín, but he rejects her because he wants to return to New Spain and establish himself as a ruler there. Prior to presenting the scene to the detective, the stage workers (characterized as mestizo working-class men of color through their appearance and speech patterns) approach the director to say that they refuse to set up the "bodega scene" and that they plan to complain to the union about it. When the director and author of the play ask them to explain their grievance, they say that they consider it "denigrante para México" (denigrating for Mexico) and cite the mestizo character's missed opportunity to have intercourse with a White woman as the reason why the scene is insulting to Mexicans:

STAGE WORKER 1: . . . ¡Pues ya parece que el mexicano iba a dejar que se le fuera viva la güerita! Pues si están solos allí . . .

STAGE WORKER 2: Seguro. Ella está muy bien y se ve muy dispuesta, Además, ¡es gachupina! ¡Ya parece que el mexicano iba a dejar pasar la oportunidad!

STAGE WORKER 1: . . . As if the Mexican was going to let the blondie get away! They are all alone there . . .

STAGE WORKER 2: For sure. She is very attractive and seems quite willing. And besides, she is Spanish! As if the Mexican was going to miss that chance!

The stage workers' objections foreground the coloniality of desire from the male perspective because they cast intercourse with the White woman as a rare achievement that is linked to self-respect and personal dignity. Their attitude speaks to the endurance of the coloniality of desire because it demonstrates the workers' subscription to a normative discourse generated by the colonial and postcolonial reality. This normative discourse hierarchizes bodies, constructing White ones as ideal and casting romantic and sexual connections with White bodies as accomplishments, particularly for the Mexican man of color because he has been written out of the national foundational couple.

While in *El juicio de Martín Cortés* the effects of coloniality erupt in the murder of the figure that personifies White male power (the fully Spanish don Martín), in Carlos Reygadas's 2005 film *Batalla en el cielo*, the mestizo Mexican man purges his pent-up frustration by violently murdering the White Mexican woman. In the film, Marcos is an overweight, mestizo, working-class man of color in Mexico City who is a chauffeur for Ana, a well-to-do young White woman who works as a prostitute just for the thrill of it. Marcos is attracted to Ana and is servile and deferent, scarcely daring to speak to her, while she is dismissive and apathetic toward him. At one point in the film, Ana decides to have sex with Marcos, not because she is interested in him, but as a part of her pursuit of new experiences. During sexual intercourse, Ana maintains her indifference toward Marcos and her dominance in their dynamic, insisting that he "calm down" when he attempts to show physical initiative and that he be entirely still throughout intercourse.[42] This emasculating experience contrasts sharply with Marcos's fantasy about Ana, which opens and closes the film. In these two scenes, Ana performs oral sex on Marcos. The slow movement of the camera, the whitish-gray background, and the instrumental score

---

42. As Mariano Paz has observed, the film constructs Marcos and Ana as aesthetic opposites. "Las leyes del deseo: sexualidad, anomia y nación en el cine de Carlos Reygadas," *Bulletin of Spanish Studies* 92, no. 7 (2015): 1071.

featuring a violin during these scenes establish Marcos's experience of this fantasy as a sublime dream.[43]

Marcos's fantasy parallels Tizoc's daydream of dancing with María because both represent the Mexican man of color's yearning to engage in mutual desire with the White Mexican woman, and both films suggest the impossibility of that desire. In the closing version of this hallucination, Ana looks up at Marcos and says, "Marcos, te quiero" (Marcos, I love you), and he responds, "Yo también te quiero" (I love you too). This scene reveals that Marcos's deepest desire is to be reified as a man, and how because of the mechanisms of the coloniality of desire, only the desire of the White Mexican woman can be the antidote to his social and economic marginality and lack of agency. By murdering Ana, Marcos unleashes centuries of raced, classed emasculation and rejection, which Ana has perpetuated through her utter indifference toward him.

The racial and gender dynamics of *Batalla en el cielo*, as well as those in *Tizoc*, *El violetero*, and *El juicio de Martín Cortés* illustrate Fanon's observation about how, for the man of color, being desired by the White woman is connected to the attainment of a legitimate position in postcolonial societies. "When my restless hands caress those white breasts they grasp white civilization and dignity and make them mine."[44] Evidencing the vestiges of the coloniality of desire, these films convey a dynamic in which the consolidation of masculine dignity and self-respect for the Mexican man of color is linked to the White woman's reciprocation of his desire for her.

Perhaps Alonso Ruizpalacios's 2014 film, *Güeros*, begins to heal this colonially determined wound. The film follows two disenchanted student protesters, Santos and Sombra, who are "en huelga de la huelga" (on strike from the strike) that has stretched on for many months at the Universidad Autonóma de México, where they both study. The two friends are jolted out of their paralysis when Sombra's brother, Tomás, is sent to stay with them, and they embark on a search to find a would-be Mexican rock legend, Epigmenio Cruz. Along their journey through Mexico City, they pick up a friend and fellow student who is also Sombra's crush, the light-skinned, blue-eyed, and upper-middle-class Ana.

---

43. As Ignacio Sánchez Prado notes, the graphic rendering of sexual acts involving Ana and Marcos "directly confronts the notions of male and female beauty and desireability in Mexican media." *Screening Neoliberalism: Transforming Mexican Cinema, 1988–2012* (Nashville: Vanderbilt University Press, 2014), 204.
44. Frantz Fanon, *Black Skin, White Masks* (New York: Grove Press, 2008), 63.

While the film does not present Sombra as an Indigenous man, *Güeros* does explicitly mark him as a dark-skinned Mexican mestizo who is low on the socioeconomic ladder. The film repeatedly calls attention to Sombra's rich skin color in comparison to his much lighter brother. For instance, when both Santos and Ana first meet Tomás, they ask him, "Por qué no eres prieto como el Sombra?" (Why don't you have dark skin like Sombra?). Furthermore, *Güeros* marks Sombra as lower class in contradistinction to Ana, who is marked as upper-middle-class. The film draws this distinction in various ways. When the two characters are moving through the student protestors' headquarters in the university, Ana identifies herself as belonging to the "Lomas pinche" (dodgy Lomas) group, which points to her proximity to privilege. Also, Sombra mentions that while his mother only completed middle school, Ana's parents had access to a university education and that Ana would be able to afford tuition if the public university began charging, while he would not be able to.[45] *Güeros* also points to how the disparity in Ana and Sombra's socioeconomic realities in the twenty-first century is linked to the legacy of coloniality. While mocking the stylistic conventions of Golden Age Mexican cinema, the two ridicule how *Tizoc* represents the speech of Indigenous Mexicans. When Ana says that Sombra can represent that accent quite well, Sombra's response creates an analogy that positions himself as the poor Indigenous man and Ana as the privileged criolla: "Como el indio Tizoc, y tú eres la niña María" (Me as indio Tizoc, and you as Miss María).[46] Because *Güeros* sets up the romantic relationship between Sombra and Ana as one characterized by a socioeconomic distance that is rooted in coloniality, it is possible to read *Güeros* within a genealogy of films that address interracial relationships between the Indigenous man and the White woman in Mexican cinema.

Like *Tizoc*, *El juicio de Martín Cortés*, and *Batalla en el cielo*, *Güeros* highlights the desirability of the White Mexican woman for the Mexican man of color. Sombra's infatuation with Ana is perhaps clearest when, along with Santos and Tomás, he enters a student assembly in which Ana is urging the student protestors to come to a consensus regarding their

---

45. As Jacobo Asse Dayán observes, *Güeros* both reflects on the impact that neoliberal tendencies have on the young characters and is itself a self-aware product of neoliberal policies that have stymied Mexican film production and exhibition. "*Güeros*: Social Fragmentation, Political Agency, and the Mexican Film Industry under Neoliberalism," *NORTEAMÉRICA* 12, no. 1 (January–June 2017): 137–68.

46. The source of this translation is the film's English-language subtitles.

own objectives. As Sombra enters the auditorium, the film presents Ana from his perspective. The camera zooms slowly toward her, concluding with a close-up of Ana's face and then cuts to a reverse shot that zooms back toward Sombra slowly and ends with a close-up capturing his infatuated gaze as he watches her. For the duration of both of these shots, romantic, nondiegetic music plays over Ana's impassioned speech, which transmits Sombra's enamored subjective state. Similarly, when Ana puts on makeup in the car prior to going to her posh friends' gathering, the use of the extreme close-up on her mouth and eye, as well as the tight close-up on the profile of her face, present her from the perspective of Sombra's admiring gaze, which the film then makes explicit when Ana asks, "¿Qué me ves Sombrilla?" (What are you looking at, Sombrilla?). In short, *Güeros*'s presentation of Ana from Sombra's adoring perspective is not new in its veneration of the White Mexican woman as desirable.

As in *Tribu*, *Lola Casanova*, and *Tizoc*, the film points to the affinity and romantic potential that exists between the White woman and the Mexican man of color. Sombra and Ana's playful energy, evident both in how they interact physically (pushing each other into a fountain near the posh gathering, for example) and verbally (through continuous jokes, banter, and laughter) indicates their mutual attraction. However, Ana and Sombra are not a couple because Sombra did not ask Ana out during their first semester at university, allowing Furia (her current boyfriend) the opportunity to do so. The tension between Sombra and Ana increases when she presses him for an explanation of why he failed to ask her out. Near the end of the film, Sombra finally responds by mouthing voiceless words, so that the spectator cannot access a direct answer to the question. However, Sombra's comments at the gathering held by Ana's friends reveal a likely explanation. His suggestion that Ana probably avoids introducing Furia to her bourgeois acquaintances because he would reflect negatively on her in that environment[47] indicate Sombra's own feelings of marginality in that space. *Güeros* transmits this point visually when Ana sits and socializes with her bourgeois, light-skinned friends, and Sombra stands

---

47. When Ana asks Santos, Tomás, and Sombra if they are ready to leave the posh gathering, Sombra responds, "Estás muy a gusto ¿no? Aquí no necesitas al Furia para encajar. No creo que a ese güey te lo traigas acá ¿no? No te vaya a quemar con tus amigos" (How about you? You seem right at home. You don't need Furia to fit in here. I mean, I don't think you'd bring him here. He might ruin your reputation with your friends). The source of this translation is the film's English-language subtitles.

outside the circle of seated people and then steps out of the lounge. The spectator can surmise that Sombra's hesitance to ask Ana out is linked to their difference in socioeconomic class. *Güeros* chooses to present this socioeconomic discrepancy visually through the difference in the tones of Ana and Sombra's bodies, which in fact does mirror the raced nature of socioeconomic inequality in the country. In this way, *Güeros* reproduces the scenario of cross-racial heterosexual attraction that this chapter has traced; however, it offers a novel resolution.

Sombra's mouthed but mute response to Ana's question is the beginning of a playful, voiceless conversation between the two in which they gradually bring their faces closer together and kiss each other's mouths. When they begin to kiss, the film cuts to an extreme close-up of Sombra and Ana's lips and tongues as they engage, entirely filling the left half of the screen with Sombra's rich skin color and the right half of the screen with Ana's lighter skin, magnifying their enmeshment as they repeatedly place their lips and tongues over and inside of the other's mouth. The extreme close-up, slow motion, and the absence of diegetic sound, except for the amplified noise of the lovers' breathing, presents Sombra and Ana's kiss as a moment of sublime and intimate connection. This moment of mutual love and desire between the White Mexican woman and the Mexican man of color is not merely imagined (like in *Tizoc* and *Batalla en el cielo*), nor does it end in his death (like in *Tribu* and *Lola Casanova*), nor does it require that he be transformed into a Whitened bourgeois success (like in *El violetero*). The presentation of Sombra's desirability and lovability in *Güeros* constitutes a decolonial gesture because it rejects two key aspects of the dynamics of the coloniality of desire in Mexican film: the favoring of the White male/Indigenous female coupling and the extinguishing of White female desire for the Mexican man of color through his death or transformation. Ana and Sombra's intense kiss (see figure 6.10) conveys the mutual desire and love of the White Mexican woman and the Mexican man of color *as he is*. In doing so, *Güeros* begins to heal an aspect of colonial violence in cultural representation that has marked the Mexican man of color as undesirable—and therefore as lacking equal value compared with the White Mexican man.

Conclusion

This chapter's point of departure has been that the racial and gender configuration of the Mexican foundational narrative—the coupling of the Spanish man and Indigenous woman—constitutes an entrenched script

Indios, Desire, and the White Mexican Woman   279

Figure 6.10. Sombra and Ana kiss in *Güeros* (2014). Screen capture from film.

in the Mexican cultural imagination in which the Indigenous Mexican male has no discernable procreative function. This tendency toward the simultaneous feminization of and sexualization of Indigeneity is apparent in the predominance of women who are presented as desirable in Indigenous-themed Mexican films and in the comparative dearth of films that feature Indigenous men and/or suggest their desirability, especially in relation to the White (proto-) Mexican woman.

Though a handful of films from the long Golden Age contemplated the scenario of attraction between the Indigenous man and the White Mexican woman (*Tribu, Lola Casanova, Tizoc, El violetero*), these films exhibit an investment in coloniality both because they do not envision a future for the mestizo couple and because they suggest that the Indigenous male's desirability requires Whiteness—either in the form of whiteness-as-indigeneity (*Tribu* and *Lola Casanova*) or through the character's transformation into a White Mexican male (*Tizoc* and *El violetero*).

Films after the Golden Age have continued to evidence the colonial wound that casts the Mexican man of color as undesirable. Both *El juicio de Martín Cortés* and *Batalla en el cielo* display the mestizo man's yearning for the White Mexican woman's desire to reify his manhood and value. In showing the Mexican man of color's desirability and lovability in reciprocal terms vis-à-vis the White Mexican woman, *Güeros* subtly but powerfully rejects this colonial legacy.

Conclusion

This book's proposal for thinking about the representation of Indigeneity in Mexican film rests on the idea that cinematic Indigeneity in narrative film itself has constituted a kind of cultural "problem" in twentieth-century Mexico. This "problem" arises from the overlapping of two distinct race-based discourses during the postrevolutionary era. On the one hand, postrevolutionary cultural nationalism championed the project of *indigenismo-mestizaje*, which both foregrounded Indigeneity and *mestizaje* as being symbolically representative of the country and sought to acculturate Indigenous people into an essentially capitalist and Hispano-centric national order. On the other hand, through the ever-evolving discourses of modernity/coloniality, White Mexican privilege continued to exist despite the dissemination of official *indigenisimo* and *mestizaje* rhetoric. The coloniality of power remained particularly entrenched in attitudes surrounding long-term, socially visible coupling and aesthetic standards, especially for women (a fact that this book refers to as the colonization of desire). Furthermore, as a consequence of its postcolonial condition, Mexico's historical narratives tended to center the non-native as protagonist and victor, therefore promoting the Mexican subject's adoption of a Western subject position (a process this book refers to as the colonization of subjectivity).

Situated in this ideologically layered milieu in which Indigenous people were still socially stigmatized, Indigenous-themed twentieth-century Mexican film required a semiotic "solution" to represent virtuous and desirable diegetically Indigenous protagonists to a Mexican audience. Specifically, this "solution" needed to be a visual one, both because of the importance of the optical in the medium of cinema and because of the role that phenotype plays in assigning racial categorization. In other words, because the physical schemata associated with Indigenous people in the local context were an immediate visual marker of still-stigmatized Indigeneity, filmmakers largely implemented a nonindexical visual option to manifest Indigeneity on-screen when films aspired to engage their audiences through melodramatic identification and desire.

The semiotic "solution" for which Mexican filmmakers opted before, during, and after the Golden Age is what this book has termed whiteness-as-indigeneity. Whiteness-as-indigeneity is a colonially inflected semiotic trick that depends on the splitting of the diegetic and visual planes of cinema; on a disavowal of indexicality. It uses the physical markers of Whiteness in the local racial formation to incite identification and desire in spectators through colonized social and visual habits while retaining the diegetic Indigeneity of the narrative context. Though it is also a form of racial impersonation, whiteness-as-indigeneity is distinct from brownface, which disingenuously pursues indexicality, resulting in a different kind of racial farce that is almost always infused either with comicality or villainy. Instead, whiteness-as-indigeneity retains key signs that mark Whiteness in the local racial formation for the purposes of directing commiseration, as well as romantic and sexual desire, toward diegetically Indigenous protagonists whom spectators consume in a postcolonial Mexican context.

In exploring the longevity and the varied applications of whiteness-as-indigeneity in Mexican cinema, this study has also reconsidered the perimeters of *indigenista* cinema as a concept by taking on as objects of study films that are unrelated to social realism, overt political messaging, or artistic prestige. Whatever their limitations, such films are loci that reveal how Mexican cinema has functioned as a space for the negotiation of local assumptions about race in ways that bear some consistency through time. The examination of these films as cultural artifacts exposes both the durability and ubiquity of whiteness-as-indigeneity as a tool for screening race in Mexico. It also proposes the flexibility of whiteness-as-indigeneity as a device that facilitates the emitting of a range of messages and positions regarding Indigeneity, diverse among themselves but all operating within the broader framework of the indigenismo-mestizaje cultural climate, which promoted the relevance of Indigeneity for the nation.

The discursive specificity of the films, on the one hand, and their thematic and aesthetic overlap, on the other, has determined the interrelatedness of the analyses put forth throughout this study. In this way, for instance, the first two chapters have highlighted how the Whitening of

Indigenous female characters functioned as a device to integrate chronologically remote and geographically dispersed types into a broader *indigenista* national discourse. On the one hand, chapter 1 considered how *Zítari* (dir. Miguel Contreras Torres, 1931) and *Chilam Balam* (dir. Iñigo de Martino, 1955) Whiten precolonial and conquest-era Indigenous women in their fabrication of glorified, prenational, Indigenous-themed lore. On the other hand, chapter 2 examined the Whitening of the Tehuana in *La Zandunga* (dir. Fernando de Fuentes, 1938) and *Tierra de pasiones* (dir. José Benavides Jr., 1943) as a central component of how the films perform an overall revision of the regional type's mythic reputation, generating a nonthreatening cinematic regional type for broad consumption.

Delving more deeply into how different Indigenous-themed films have engaged the discourse of indigenismo-mestizaje itself, chapters 3 and 4 argue that the use of whiteness-as-indigeneity as an aesthetic strategy has crucial implications for cinema's ideological positioning within that race-based project. Along this line, chapter 3 discussed how the films *La india bonita* (dir. Antonio Helú 1938), *El indio* (dir. Armando Vargas de la Maza, 1938), *María Candelaria* (dir. Emilio Fernández 1944), and *Maclovia* (dir. Emilio Fernández 1948) are consistent with the awareness of racialized political inequality that animated much indigenismo-mestizaje rhetoric. In such narrative studio films, however, whiteness-as-indigeneity constitutes a point of continuity with coloniality that contradicts the films' decolonial messages with alternative approaches surfacing outside the industrial matrix in films such as *Janitzio* (dir. Carlos Navarro, 1935) and *Raíces* (dir. Benito Alazraki, 1955). While these films adhere to the political core of the indigenismo-mestizaje discourse, those discussed in chapter 4 (*La noche de los mayas* [dir. Chano Urueta, 1939] and *Deseada* [dir. Roberto Gavaldón, 1951]) contest two of its Hispano-centric underpinnings: the notion that the conquest was generative despite its destruction and the marginalization of native religious and spiritual beliefs. While both films position Indigenous beliefs as legitimate sources of truth-knowing that explain events in the narrative, they too capitulate to coloniality by relying on whiteness-as-indigeneity as the vehicle for the spectator's suspension of disbelief.

Subsequently, the final two chapters expanded, in chronological and gendered terms, the study's analysis of whiteness-as-indigeneity as a racist crutch for cinematizing values and beliefs tied to indigenismo-mestizaje. In exploring post–Golden-Age iterations of the suffering *indita* in *María Isabel* (dir. Federico Curiel, 1968) and *El amor de María Isabel* (dir. Federico Curiel, 1970), chapter 5 points to the endurance of whiteness-as-indigeneity as a feature of Mexican racial masquerade even as these films modernize the archetype's attitudes toward some aspects of local society. Shifting the focus to desirable and virtuous representations of Indigenous men during the long Golden Age (which, because of the gendered configuration of the Mexican origin story, are rare), chapter 6 demonstrates how whiteness-as-indigeneity has also surfaced as a means of projecting Indigenous male virtue and appeal. Furthermore, the endings to love stories involving these Indigenous male characters—which consist either in tragedy or transformation—reinscribe the Indigenous male's marginality in the national narrative of *mestizaje*.

While it would be comforting to think that whiteness-as-indigeneity is a bizarre racist relic of the early to mid-twentieth century, its continued emergence in Mexican audiovisual production suggests otherwise. In 1997, the media conglomerate Televisa aired a telenovela adaptation of *María Isabel* starring Adela Noriega, and in 2012, the network also aired the telenovela *Un refugio para el amor*, which employed the same racist visual logic to idealize the protagonist, Luciana, as a desirable, virtuous rural woman with Indigenous ancestry.

The racial masquerades that these chapters have explored are the direct result of twentieth-century Mexican cinema's overarching, raced norm of cinematic signification by which it generated a celluloid illusion of White Mexican near-universality. The circumstances of racial representation in Mexican cinema today can be understood in connection with the transformation of Mexican film production as a result of neoliberal policies.[1] As Ignacio Sánchez Prado has argued, these policies have resulted in a tendency for local productions with commercial ambitions to center the middle and upper-middle urban class through genres and modes of address that these sectors prefer because of their consumption of media from abroad, namely from the United States.[2] Mexican films that align with this contemporary tendency, such as the entire Manolo Caro dramedy

---

1. Misha MacLaird, *Aesthetics and Politics in the Mexican Film Industry* (New York: Palgrave Macmillan, 2013); Ignacio Sánchez Prado, *Screening Neoliberalism: Transforming Mexican Cinema, 1988–2012* (Nashville: Vanderbilt University Press, 2014).
2. Sánchez Prado, *Screening Neoliberalism*, 62–104.

universe,[3] are currently promoting the myth of White Mexican universality and enacting its idealization.

Despite the many productions that continue to perpetuate the farce of White Mexican preponderance, several films since the 2000s (often, but not always, independent and auteur films) have resisted this norm, instead problematizing Mexican Whiteness as a locus of privilege, willful obliviousness, and tyranny both for those who are outside its limits as well as for those within them. These films include *Y tu mama también* (dir. Alfonso Cuarón, 2001), *Batalla en el cielo* (dir. Carlos Reygadas, 2005), *Güeros* (dir. Alonso Ruizpalacios, 2014), *¿Qué le dijiste a Dios?* (dir. Teresa Suárez, 2014), *Hilda* (dir. Andrés Clariond, 2014), *Roma* (dir. Alfonso Cuarón, 2018), *Las niñas bien* (dir. Alejandra Márquez Abella, 2018), just to name a few. By beginning to visually corroborate the raced nature of class difference in Mexico, such films constitute an important step in that they, at the very least, refuse to perpetuate the negation of Mexicans of color in the realm of audiovisual representation. In the best cases, these films deliver poignant critiques of raced classism as a social phenomenon in Mexico and, in so doing, address the root cause of White hypervisualization in the Mexican mediascape.[4]

The contrast between these critical contemporary films and those discussed in the book's chapters evidences a degree of evolution in Mexican cinema's representation of race and race relations. While much of twentieth-century Mexican cinema reinscribed the colonially derived value of White Mexican physical capital—generating, for example, the visual, raced logic of whiteness-as-indigeneity—contemporary productions like those mentioned above are challenging White predominance in representation and denouncing the underlying racism in Mexico that has made such representations normative for so long. Sadly, as the racist reactions to Yalitza Aparicio's performance in *Roma* have made apparent, in Mexico,

---

3. Illustrative examples from his filmography include *No sé si cortarme las venas o dejármelas largas* (2013), *Amor de mis amores* (2014), and *La vida inmoral de la pareja ideal* (2016).

4. Mónica García Blizzard, "Whiteness Wars in *Las niñas bien*," *Latin American and Caribbean Ethnic Studies* (June 2021): 1–14, https://www.tandfonline.com/doi/full/10.1080/17442222.2021.1944483; García Blizzard, "Marking Race and Class Privilege in Contemporary Mexican Cinema," in *Poetics of Race in Latin America*, ed. Mabel Moraña (London: Anthem Press, forthcoming).

there remains a widespread expectation of Whiteness (*blancura*) in local audiovisual productions (particularly as it applies to women). The deeply entrenched nature of this expectation is apparent in the passionate reactions that surface when the White norm is not adhered to. The intensity and ubiquity of such reactions indicates the degree of effort and intention required to create a visual landscape in which bodies are not placed on a hierarchy based on racialized understandings of aesthetics. Hopefully, the continued interrogation of artificial White ubiquity and racial masquerade in Mexican visual mediums (as well as those in other parts of the world) can contribute to dismantling such forms of disingenuous representation, which although comical in their absurdity, corrosively reinforce inequality.

Bibliography

Acevedo Muñoz, Ernesto R. *Buñuel and Mexico: The Crisis of National Cinema*. Berkeley: University of California Press, 2003.

Aguilar, Yásnaya. "El efecto Tizoc." *Este país*. July 4, 2012. https://web.archive.org/web/20190510094735/http://archivo.estepais.com/site/2012/el-efecto-tizoc/.

Aguilera Skvirsky, Salomé, and Carl Good. "Las cargas de la representación." *Hispanófila* 177 (June 2016): 137-54.

Aleiss, Angela. *Making the White Man's Indian: Native Americans and the Hollywood Movies*. Westport: Praeger Publishers, 2005.

Alonso, Ana María. "Conforming Disconformity: 'Mestizaje,' Hybridity, and the Aesthetics of Mexican Nationalism." *Cultural Anthropology* 19, no. 4 (November 2004): 459-90.

Alonso, Ana María. "Territorializing the Nation and 'Integrating the Indian': 'Mestizaje' in Mexican Official Discourses and Public Culture." In *Sovereign Bodies: Citizens, Migrants, and States in the Postcolonial World*, edited by Thomas Blom Hansen and Finn Stepputat, 39-60. Princeton: Princeton University Press, 2005.

Altamirano, Ignacio M. *El Zarco*. Mexico City: Editorial Porrúa, 2010.

Amador, María Luisa, and Jorge Ayala Blanco. *Cartelera cinematográfica 1950-1959*. Mexico City: CUEC, 1985.

Anderson, Benedict. *Imagined Communities: Reflections on the Origins and Spread of Nationalism*. London: Verso, 2006.

Anzaldúa, Gloria. *Borderlands/La Frontera: The New Mestiza*. San Francisco: aunt lute books, 1987.

Arroyo Quiroz, Claudia. "Fantasías sobre le identidad indígena en el cine mexicano del periodo post-revolucionario." In *Identidades. Explorando la diversidad*, edited by Laura Carballido, 149-70. Mexico City: Universidad Autónoma Metropolitana-Anthropos, 2011.

Asse Dayán, Jacobo. "*Güeros*: Social Fragmentation, Political Agency, and the Mexican Film Industry under Neoliberalism." *NORTEAMÉRICA* 12, no. 1 (January-June 2017): 137-68.

Avila, Jacqueline. *Cinesonidos: Film Music and National Identity During Mexico's Epoca de Oro*. New York: Oxford University Press, 2019.

Ayala Blanco, Jorge. *La aventura del cine mexicano en la época de oro y después*. Miguel Hidalgo: Grijalbo, 1993.

Balibar, Etienne. "Is There a "Neo-Racism?" In *Race, Nation, Class: Ambiguous Identities*, by Etienne Balibar and Immanuel Wallerstein, 17–28. New York: Verso, 1991.

Balibar, Etienne. "The Nation Form: History and Ideology." In *Race Critical Theories: Text and Context*, edited by Philomena Essed Goldberg and David Theo, 220–31. Malden, MA: Blackwell Publishers, 2002.

Bartra, Roger. *The Cage of Melancholy: Identity and Metamorphosis in the Mexican Character*. Translated by Christopher J. Hall. New Brunswick: Rutgers University Press, 1992.

Báscones Antón, Marta. "La negación de lo indígena en el cine de Emilio Fernándes." *Archivos de la Filmoteca* 40 (2002): 91–106.

Benjamin, Walter. "The Work of Art in the Age of Mechanical Reproduction." In *Illuminations*, edited by Hannah Arendt, translated by Harry Zohn, 217–52. New York: Schocken Books, 1969.

Bhabha, Homi K. "Dissemination: Time, Narrative, and the Margins of the Modern Nation." In *Nation and Narration*, edited by Homi K. Bhabha, 291–322. London and New York: Routledge, 1990.

Bhabha, Homi K. "The Other Question: Stereotype, Discrimination and the Discourse of Colonialism." In *The Location of Culture*, 94–120. New York: Routledge, 1994.

Bonfil Batalla, Guillermo. "Andrés Molina Enriquez y la Sociedad Indianista Mexicana: El indigenismo en vísperas de la Revolución." *Anales del Instituto Nacional de Antropología e Historia* 47, tome XVIII (1965): 217–32.

Bonfil Batalla, Guillermo. "El concepto del indio en América: Categoría de situación colonial." *Anales de Antropología* 9 (1972): 105–25.

Bonfil Batalla, Guillermo. *México profundo: Una civilización negada*. Mexico City: Secretaría de Educación Pública, 1987.

Bourdieu, Pierre. *Distinction: A Social Critique of the Judgement of Taste*. Translated by Richard Nice. New York: Routledge, 2010.

Brooks, Peter. *The Melodramatic Imagination: Balzac, Henry James, Melodrama, and the Mode of Excess*. New Haven: Yale University Press, 1995.

Bukholder de la Rosa, Arno. "El periódico que llegó a la vida nacional. Los primeros años del diario *Excelsior* (1916–1932)." *Historia Mexicana* 58, no. 4 (April–June 2009): 1369–1418.

Burns, E. Bradford. *The Poverty of Progress: Latin America in the Nineteenth Century*. Berkeley: University of California Press, 1980.

Burton-Carvajal, Julianne. "Mexican Melodramas of Patriarchy: Specificity of a Transcultural Form." In *Framing Latin American Cinema: Contemporary*

Critical Perspectives, edited by Ann Marie Stock, 186–234. Minneapolis: University of Minnesota Press, 1997.
Butler, Judith. "Precarious Life, Grievable Life." In *Frames of War: When Is Life Grievable?* New York: Verso, 2016.
Camhaji, E., S. Corona, and G. Serrano. "El racismo que México no quiere ver." *El País*. November 27, 2019. https://elpais.com/sociedad/2019/11/27/actualidad/1574891024_828971.html.
Castañeda, Quetzil E. "The Aura of Ruins." In *Fragments of a Golden Age: The Politics of Culture in Mexico since 1940*, edited by Gilbert Joseph, Anne Rubenstein, and Eric Zolov, 452–70. Durham, NC: Duke University Press, 2001.
Castellanos Guerrero, Alicia. "Para hacer nación: discursos racistas en el México decimonónico." In *Los caminos del racismo en México*, edited by José Jorge Gómez Izquierdo, 89–115. Mexico City: Plaza y Valdés, S.A., 2005.
Castellanos Guerrero, Alicia, Jorge Gómez Izquierdo, and Francisco Pineda. "Racist Discourse in Mexico." In *Racism and Discourse in Latin America*, edited by Teun A. Van Dijk, 217–58. New York: Rowman & Littlefield, 2009.
Cerón-Anaya, Hugo. *Privilege at Play: Class, Race, Gender, and Golf in Mexico*. New York: Oxford University Press, 2019.
Chavez, Daniel. "The Eagle and the Serpent on the Screen: The State as Spectacle in Mexican Cinema." *Latin American Research Review* 45, no. 3 (2010): 115–41.
Coffey, Mary K. *How a Revolutionary Art Became Official Culture: Murals, Museums, and the Mexican State*. Durham, NC: Duke University Press, 2012.
Cope, R. Douglas. *The Limits of Racial Domination*. Madison: University of Wisconsin Press, 1994.
Couret, Nilo. *Mock Classicism: Latin American Film Comedy 1930–1960*. Oakland: University of California Press, 2018.
Cuellar, Manuel. *Choreographing Mexico: Festive Performances and Dancing Histories of a Nation*. Austin: University of Texas Press, 2022.
D'Lugo, Marvin. "Aural Identity, Genealogies of Sound Technologies, and Hispanic Transnationality on Screen." In *World Cinemas, Transnational Perspectives*, edited by Nataša Durovicová and Kathleen E. Newman, 160–85. New York: Routledge, 2009.
Dalton, David S. *Mestizo Modernity: Race, Technology, and the Body in Postrevolutionary Mexico*. Gainesville: University of Florida Press, 2018.
Dawson, Alexander S. *Indian and Nation in Revolutionary Mexico*. Tucson: University of Arizona Press, 2004.
Dawson, Alexander S. "'Wild Indians,' 'Mexican Gentlemen,' and the Lessons Learned in the Casa del Estudiante Indígena, 1926–1932." *The Americas* 57, no. 3 (January 2001): 329–61.
de la Mora, Sergio. *Cinemachismo: Masculinities and Sexuality in Mexican Film*. Austin: University of Texas Press, 2006.

de la Mora, Sergio. "Roma: Repatriation Versus Exploitation." *Film Quarterly* 72, no. 4 (summer 2019): 46–53.

de la Peña, Guillermo. "The End of Revolutionary Anthropology?: Notes on Indigenismo." In *Dictablanda: Politics, Work, and Culture in Mexico, 1938–1968*, edited by Paul Gillingham and Benjamin T. Smith, 279–98. Durham, NC: Duke University Press, 2014.

de la Vega Alfaro, Eduardo. "The Decline of the Golden Age and the Making of the Crisis." In *Mexico's Cinema: A Century of Film and Filmmakers*, edited by Joanne Hershfield and David Maciel, 165–91. Wilmington, DE: Scholarly Resources, 1999.

de la Vega Alfaro, Eduardo. "Origins, Development and Crisis of the Sound Cinema (1929–64)." Translated by Ana M. López. In *Mexican Cinema*, edited by Paulo Antonio Paranaguá, 79–93. London: British Film Institute, 1995.

de la Vega Alfaro, Eduardo. "La transición del 'mudo' al 'sonoro' en México y el caso de *Zítari* (Miguel Contreras Torres, 1931)." In *Cine mudo latinoamericano: Inicios, nación, vanguardias y transición*, edited by Aurelio de los Reyes and David M. J. Wood, 235–50. Mexico City: UNAM, 2015.

de los Reyes, Aurelio. *Cine y sociedad en México*. 2 vols. Mexico City: Universidad Nacional Autónoma de México, 1981.

de los Reyes, Aurelio. *El nacimiento de* Que Viva México! Mexico City: Universidad Nacional Autónoma de México, Instituto de Investigaciones Estéticas, 2006.

de los Reyes, Aurelio. *Medio siglo de cine mexicano (1896–1947)*. Mexico City: Editorial Trillas, 1987.

DeGuzmán, María. *Spain's Long Shadow: The Black Legend, Off-Whiteness, and Anglo-American Empire*. Minneapolis: University of Minnesota Press, 2005.

Dever, Susan. *Celluloid Nationalism and Other Melodramas: From Post-Revolutionary Mexico to Fin De Siglo Mexamérica*. Albany: State University of New York Press, 2003.

Domínguez-Ruvalcaba, Héctor. *Modernity and the Nation in Mexican Representations of Masculinity: From Sensuality to Bloodshed*. New York: Palgrave Macmillan, 2007.

Doremus, Anne. "Indigenism, Mestizaje, and National Identity in Mexico during the 1940s and the 1950s." *Mexican Studies/Estudios Mexicanos* 17, no. 2 (2001): 375–402.

Dyer, Richard. *The Matter of Images: Essays on Representation*. New York: Routledge, 1993.

Dyer, Richard. *White*. London; New York: Routledge, 1997.

Dyer, Richard. "Whiteness: The Power of Invisibility." In *White Privilege: Essential Readings on the Other Side of Racism*, edited by Paula Rothenberg, 9–14. New York: Worth Publishers, 2005.

Eakin, Marshall C. *Becoming Brazilians: Race and National Identity in Twentieth-Century Brazil*. Cambridge: Cambridge University Press, 2017.

Earle, Rebecca. *The Return of the Native: Indians and Myth-Making in Spanish America 1810–1930*. Durham, NC: Duke University Press, 2007.
Echeverría, Bolívar. *Modernidad y blanquitud*. Mexico City: Ediciones Era, 2019.
Elba, Martha. "De *Ramona* a *María Candelaria*. Lolita ama a las indias mexicanas. Lolita ya es nuestra." *Cinema Reporter*, February 5, 1944, 8.
Falicov, Tamara. "The Interlocking Dynamics of Domestic and International Film Festivals." In *The Routledge Companion to Latin American Cinema*, edited by Marvin D'Lugo, Ana M. López, and Laura Podalsky, 266–78. New York: Routledge, 2018.
Fanon, Frantz. *Black Skin, White Masks*. Translated by Richard Philcox. New York: Grove Press, 2008.
Félix-Didier, Paula, and Andrés Levinson. "The Building of a Nation: La guerra gaucha as Historical Melodrama." In *Latin American Melodrama. Passion, Pathos, and Entertainment*, edited by Darlene J Sadlier, 50–63. Urbana: University of Illinois Press, 2009.
Flores, René, and Edward Telles. "Social Stratification in Mexico: Disentangling Color, Ethnicity, and Class." *American Sociological Review* 77, no. 3 (2012): 486–94.
Fornoff, Carolyn. "Nahual." In *An Ecotopian Lexicon*, edited by Matthew Schneider-Mayerson and Brent Ryan Bellamy, 163–75. Minneapolis: University of Minnesota Press, 2019.
Fregoso, Rosa Linda. *MeXicana Encounters: The Making of Social Identities on the Borderlands*. Berkeley: University of California Press, 2003.
Gaines, Jane. "'White' Privilege and Looking Relations." In *Feminist Film Theory: A Reader*, edited by Sue Thornham, 293–307. Edinburgh: Edinburgh University Press, 1999.
Galindo, Alejandro. *Una radiografía histórica del cine mexicano*. Mexico City: Fondo de Cultura Popular, 1968.
Gamio, Manuel. *Forjando patria*. Mexico City: Editorial Porrúa, S.A., 1960.
García Blizzard, Mónica. "Whiteness Wars in *Las niñas bien*." *Latin American and Caribbean Ethnic Studies* (June 2021): 1–14. https://www.tandfonline.com/doi/full/10.1080/17442222.2021.1944483.
García Blizzard, Mónica. "Marking Race and Class Privilege in Contemporary Mexican Cinema." In *Poetics of Race in Latin America*, edited by Mabel Moraña. London: Anthem Press, forthcoming.
García Canclini, Néstor. *Hybrid Cultures: Strategies for Entering and Leaving Modernity*. Translated by Christopher L. Chiappari and Silvia L. López. Minneapolis: University of Minnesota Press, 2005.
García Riera, Emilio. *El cine de Silvia Pinal*. Guadalajara: Universidad de Guadalajara, 1996.
García Riera, Emilio. *Historia documental del cine mexicano*. 13 vols. Guadalajara: Universidad de Guadalajara, 1993–1994.

García Riera, Emilio. "The Impact of Rancho Grande." Translated by Ana M. López. In *Mexican Cinema*, edited by Paulo Antonio Paranaguá, 128–32. London: British Film Institute, 1995.

Garrigan, Shelley E. *Collecting Mexico: Museum, Monuments, and the Creation of National Identity*. Minneapolis: University of Minnesota Press, 2012.

Gledhill, Christine. "Signs of Melodrama." In *Stardom: Industry of Desire*, edited by Christine Gledhill, 207–32. New York: Routledge, 1991.

Gómez Izquierdo, José Jorge. "Racismo y nacionalismo en el discurso de las élites mexicanas: Historia patria y antropología indigenista." In *Los caminos del racismo en México*, edited by José Jorge Gómez Izquierdo, 117–81. Mexico City: Plaza y Valdés, S.A., 2005.

González Navarro, Moisés. "El mestizaje mexicano en el período nacional." *Revista Mexicana de Sociología* 30, no. 1 (1968): 35–52.

Greeley, Robin Adèle. "Muralism and the State in Post-Revolution Mexico." In *Mexican Muralism: A Critical History*, edited by Alejandro Anreus, Leonard Folgarait, and Robin Adèle Greeley, 13–36. Berkeley: University of California Press, 2012.

Gunckel, Colin. "*El signo de la muerte* and the Birth of a Genre: Origins and Anatomy of the Aztec Horror Film." In *Sleaze Artists: Cinema at the Margins of Taste, Style and Politics*, edited by Jeffrey Sconce, 121–43. Durham, NC: Duke University Press, 2007.

Gunckel, Colin. *Mexico on Main Street: Transnational Film Culture in Los Angeles before World War II*. New Jersey: Rutgers University Press, 2015.

Hall, Stuart. "Race, Articulation and Societies Structured in Dominance." In *Essential Essays/Stuart Hall Vol. 1*, edited by David Morley, 172–213. Durham, NC: Duke University Press, 2019.

Hall, Stuart. "The Spectacle of the 'Other.'" In *Representation: Cultural Representations and Signifying Practices*, edited by Stuart Hall, 223–90. London: Sage Publications & Open University, 1997.

Hellier-Tinoco, Ruth. *Embodying Mexico: Tourism, Nationalism & Performance*. New York: Oxford University Press, 2011.

Hernández Cuevas, Marco Polo. *African Mexicans and the Discourse of the Modern Nation*. New York: University Press of America, 2004.

Hershfield, Joanne. *Imagining la Chica Moderna: Women, Nation, and Visual Culture in Mexico, 1917–1936*. Durham, NC: Duke University Press, 2008.

Hershfield, Joanne. *The Invention of Dolores Del Río*. Minneapolis: University of Minnesota Press, 2000.

Hershfield, Joanne. *Mexican Cinema/Mexican Woman, 1940–1950*. Tucson: University of Arizona Press, 1996.

Hershfield, Joanne. "Race and Ethnicity in the Classical Cinema." In *Mexico's Cinema: A Century of Film and Filmmakers*, edited by Joanne Hershfield and David Maciel, 81–100. Wilmington, DE: Scholarly Resources, 1999.

Bibliography 293

Hill, Matthew J. K. "The Indigenismo of Emilio 'El Indio' Fernandez: Myth, Mestizaje, and Modern Mexico." MA thesis, Brigham Young University, 2009.

Hoetink, Harry. *Caribbean Race Relations*. Oxford: Oxford University Press, 1967.

hooks, bell. *Ain't I a Woman: Black Women and Feminism*. New York: Routledge, 2015.

hooks, bell. "The Oppositional Gaze: Black Female Spectators." In *Feminist Film Theory: A Reader*, edited by Sue Thornham, 307–20. Edinburgh: Edinburgh University Press, 1999.

Irwin, Robert McKee. "Lola Casanova: La Malinche invertida en la cultura nacional mexicana." *Literatura Mexicana* 18, no. 1 (2007): 59–87.

Irwin, Robert McKee, and Maricruz Castro Ricalde. *Global Mexican Cinema: Its Golden Age*. London: British Film Institute, 2013.

Iturriaga, Eugenia. "La ciudad blanca de noche: Las discotecas como espacios de segregación." *Alteridades* 25, no. 50 (July–December 2015): 105–15.

Iturriaga, Eugenia. *Las élites de la Ciudad Blanca: Discursos racistas sobre la otredad*. Mérida: UNAM, 2016.

Joseph, Gilbert M., Anne Rubenstein, and Eric Zolov. "Assembling the Fragments: Writing a Cultural History of Mexico Since 1940." In *Fragments of a Golden Age: The Politics of Culture in Mexico Since 1940*, edited by Gilbert M. Joseph, Anne Rubenstein, and Eric Zolov, 3–22. Durham, NC: Duke University Press, 2001.

Katzew, Ilona. *Casta Painting: Images of Race in Eighteenth-Century Mexico*. New Haven: Yale University Press, 2004.

King, John, Ana M. López, and Manuel Alvarado, eds. *Mediating Two Worlds: Cinematic Encounters in the Americas*. London: British Film Institute, 1993.

Knight, Alan. "Racism, Revolution, and Indigenismo; Mexico, 1910–1940." *The Idea of Race in Latin America, 1870–1940*, edited by Richard Graham, 71–113. Austin: University of Texas Press, 1990.

Knowlton, Timothy. *Maya Creation Myths: Words and Worlds of the Chilam Balam*. Boulder: University Press of Colorado, 2010.

Lahr-Vivaz, Elena. *Mexican Melodrama: Film and Nation from the Golden Age to the New Wave*. Tucson: University of Arizona Press, 2016.

Latorre, Guisela. *Walls of Empowerment: Chicana/o Indigenist Murals of California*. Austin: University of Texas Press, 2008.

"Ley de la industria cinemátografica." http://dof.gob.mx/nota_to_imagen_fs.php?cod_diario=196431&pagina=3&seccion=2.

Lienhard, Martin. "*La noche de los mayas*." *Journal of Latin American Cultural Studies* 13, no. 1 (2004): 35–96.

Lomnitz-Adler, Claudio. *Exits from the Labyrinth*. Berkeley: University of California Press, 1992.

López, Ana M. "Are All the Latins from Manhattan?: Hollywood, Ethnography and Cultural Colonialism." In King, López, and Alvarado, eds. *Mediating Two Worlds*, 67–80.

López, Ana M. "Early Cinema and Modernity in Latin America." *Cinema Journal* 40, no. 1 (fall 2000): 48–78.

López, Ana M. "From Hollywood and Back: Dolores del Río, A Trans(National) Star." *Studies in Latin American Popular Culture* 17 (1998): 5–28.

López, Ana M. "Tears and Desire: Women and Melodrama in the 'Old' Mexican Cinema." In King, López, Alvarado, eds. *Mediating Two Worlds*, 147–63.

López, Rick A. *Crafting Mexico: Intellectuals, Artisans, and the State after the Revolution*. Durham, NC: Duke University Press, 2010.

López, Rick A. "The India Bonita Contest of 1921 and the Ethnicization of Mexican National Culture." *American Historical Review* 82, no. 2 (2002): 291–328.

López Caballero, Paula. *Indígenas de la nación: Etnografía histórica de la alteridad en México*. Mexico City: Fondo de Cultura Económica, 2017.

López Sánchez, Olivia. "La mirada médica y la mujer indígena en el siglo XIX." *Ciencias* 60 (October–March 2001): 44–49.

Lund, Joshua. *The Mestizo State: Reading Race in Modern Mexico*. Minneapolis: University of Minnesota Press, 2012.

MacLaird, Misha. *Aesthetics and Politics in the Mexican Film Industry*. New York: Palgrave MacMillan, 2013.

Maldonado-Torres, Nelson. "The Decolonial Turn." Translated by Robert Cavooris. In *New Approaches to Latin American Studies: Culture and Power*, edited by Juan Poblete, 111–27. New York: Routledge, 2018.

Martín-Barbero, Jesús. *Communication, Culture and Hegemony: From the Media to Mediations*. Translated by Elizabeth Fox and Robert A. White. London: Sage Publications, 1993.

Martínez, María E. *Genealogical Fictions: Limpieza de Sangre, Religion, and Gender in Colonial Mexico*. Stanford: Stanford University Press, 2008.

Martínez Casas, Regina, Emiko Saldívar, René D. Flores, and Christina A. Sue. "The Different Faces of Mestizaje: Ethnicity and Race in Mexico." In *Pigmentocracies: Ethnicity, Race, and Color in Latin America*, edited by Edward Telles, 36–80. Chapel Hill, NC: University of North Carolina Press, 2014.

Martínez-Cruz, Paloma. *Women and Knowledge in Mesoamerica: From East L.A. to Anahuac*. Tucson: University of Arizona Press, 2011.

Marubbio, M. Elise. *Killing the Indian Maiden: Images of Native American Women in Film*. Lexington: University Press of Kentucky, 2006.

Memmi, Albert. *The Colonizer and the Colonized*. Boston: Beacon Press, 1991.

Méndez, Luis. "México es racista—Poniatowska." *El Norte*, January 28, 2015. https://www.elnorte.com/aplicacioneslibre/articulo/default.aspx?id=450888&md5=a7d9542d2e1168fcf306d6434e7adb2c&ta=0dfdbac11765226904c16cb9ad1b2efe.

Mignolo, Walter. "The Conceptual Triad: Modernity/Coloniality/Decoloniality." In *On Decoloniality: Concepts, Analytics, Praxis*, by Walter D. Mignolo and Catherine E. Walsh, 135–52. Durham, NC: Duke University Press, 2018.

Mohanty, Satya P. "Drawing the Color Line: Kipling and the Culture of Colonial Rule." In *The Bounds of Race: Perspectives on Hegemony and Resistance*, edited by Dominick LaCapra, 311–43. Ithaca: Cornell University Press, 1992.

Monsiváis, Carlos. "Cantinflas: That's the Point!" In *Mexican Postcards*, translated and edited by John Kraniauskas, 88–105. New York: Verso, 2000.

Monsiváis, Carlos. "Ernesto García Cabral y el nuevo darwinismo: 'El hombre desciende de la caricatura.'" In *La vida en un volado: Ernesto el Chango García Cabral*, edited by María José Moyano, 15–30. Mexico City and Barcelona: CONACULTA-INAH/Lunwerg Editores, 2005.

Monsiváis, Carlos. "Mexican Cinema: Of Myths and Demystifications." Translated by Mike González. In King, López, Alvarado, eds. *Mediating Two Worlds*, 139–46.

Monsiváis, Carlos. "Se sufre pero se aprende." In *A través del espejo: el cine mexicano y su público*, edited by Carlos Monsivías and Carlos Bonfil, 99–224. Mexico City: Instituto Mexicano de Cinematografía, 1994.

Mora, Carl J. *Mexican Cinema: Reflections of a Society, 1896–1980*. Berkeley: University of California Press, 1989.

Moraña, Mabel, Enrique D. Dussel, and Carlos A. Jáuregui. *Coloniality at Large: Latin America and the Postcolonial Debate*. Durham, NC: Duke University Press, 2008.

Moreno Figueroa, Mónica. "Displaced Looks: The Lived Experience of Beauty and Racism." *Feminist Theory* 14, no. 2 (2013): 137–51.

Moreno Figueroa, Mónica. "Distributed Intensities: 'Whiteness,' Mestizaje and the Logics of Mexican Racism." *Ethnicities* 10, no. 3 (2010): 387–401.

Mörner, Magnus. *Race Mixture in the History of Latin America*. Boston: Little Brown and Company, 1967.

Mraz, John. *Looking for Mexico: Modern Visual Culture and National Identity*. Durham, NC: Duke University Press, 2009.

Mraz, John. "Today, Tomorrow and Always: The Golden Age of Illustrated Magazines in Mexico, 1937–1960." In *Fragments of a Golden Age: The Politics of Culture in Mexico Since 1940*, edited by Gilbert M. Joseph, Anne Rubenstein, and Eric Zolov, 234–72. Durham, NC: Duke University Press, 2001.

Mulvey, Laura. "Visual Pleasure and Narrative Cinema." In *Literary Theory: An Anthology*, edited by Julie Rivkin and Michael Ryan, 585–96. New York: Blackwell, 1998.

Navarrete Linares, Federico. *México racista: Una denuncia*. Mexico City: Grijalbo, 2016.

Nesvig, Martin Austin, ed. *Religious Culture in Modern Mexico*. Lanham, MD: Rowman & Littlefield, 2007.

Nichols, Bill. *Representing Reality: Issues and Concepts in Documentary*. Bloomington: Indiana University Press, 1991.

Noble, Andrea. "Latin American Visual Cultures." In *The Companion to Latin American Studies*, edited by Philip Swanson, 154–71. London: Arnold, 2003.

Noble, Andrea. *Mexican National Cinema*. London and New York: Routledge, 2006.

Núñez Becerra, Fernanda. "La degeneración de la raza a finales del siglo XIX. Un fantasma 'científico' recorre el mundo." In *Los caminos del racismo en México*, edited by José Jorge Gómez Izquierdo, 67–88. Mexico City: Plaza y Valdés, S.A., 2005.

Nutini, Hugo. *The Mexican Aristocracy: An Expressive Ethnography*. Austin: University of Texas Press, 2008.

O'Gorman, Edmundo. *La invención de América: El universalismo de la cultura de Occidente*. Mexico City: Fondo de Cultura Económica, 1958.

Omi, Michael, and Howard Winant. "Racial Formation." In *Race Critical Theories: Text and Context*, edited by Philomena Essed and David Theo Goldberg, 123–45. Oxford: Blackwell Publishers, 2002.

Omi, Michael, and Howard Winant. *Racial Formation in the United States: From the 1960s to the 1990s*. New York: Routledge, 1994.

Oroz, Silvia. *Melodrama: O cinema de lágrimas da América Latina*. Rio de Janeiro: FUNARTE, 1999.

Pagden, Anthony. *The Fall of Natural Man: The American Indian and the Origins of Comparative Ethnology*. Cambridge: Cambridge University Press, 1982.

Palou, Pedro Ángel. *El fracaso del mestizo*. Mexico City: Ariel, 2014.

Pani, Erika. *Para pertenecer a la gran familia mexicana: Procesos de naturalización en el siglo XIX*. Mexico City: El Colegio de México, 2015.

Paranaguá, Paulo Antonio. *Tradición y modernidad en el cine de América Latina*. Madrid: Fondo de Cultura Económica de España, 2003.

Paxman, Andrew. "Cooling to Cinema and Warming to Television: State Mass Media Policy, 1940-1964." In *Dictablanda: Politics, Work, and Culture in Mexico, 1938-1968*, edited by Paul Gillingham and Benjamin T. Smith, 299–320. Durham, NC: Duke University Press, 2014.

Paz, Mariano. "Las leyes del deseo: Sexualidad, anomia y nación en el cine de Carlos Reygadas." *Bulletin of Spanish Studies* 92, no. 7 (2015): 1063–77.

Paz, Octavio. *El laberinto de la soledad*. Madrid: Ediciones Cátedra, 2016.

Pilcher, Jeffrey M. *Cantinflas and the Chaos of Mexican Modernity*. Wilmington, DE: Scholarly Resources, 2001.

Podalsky, Laura. "Disjointed Frames: Melodrama, Nationalism, and Representation in 1940s Mexico." *Studies in Latin American Popular Culture* 12 (1993): 57–74.

Podalsky, Laura. "Patterns of the Primitive: Sergei Eisenstein's ¡Qué Viva México!" In King, López, Alvarado, eds. *Mediating Two Worlds*, 25–39.

Podalsky, Laura. "Unpacking Periodization." In *The Routledge Companion to Latin American Cinema*, edited by Marvin D'Lugo, Ana M. López and Laura Podalsky, 62–74. New York: Routledge, 2017.

Poole, Deborah. "An Image of 'Our Indian': Type Photographs and Racial Sentiments in Oaxaca, 1920–1940." *Hispanic American Historical Review* 84, no. 1 (2004): 37–82.
Quijano, Aníbal. "Coloniality of Power, Eurocentrism, and Latin America." *Nepantla: Views from the South* 1, no. 3 (2000): 553–80.
Quijano, Aníbal. "Modernity, Identity, and Utopia in Latin America." Translated by John Beverly. *Boundary* 20, no. 3 (1993): 140–55.
Rabasa, José. "Postcolonialism." In *Dictionary of Latin American Cultural Studies*, edited by Robert McKee Irwin and Mónica Szurmuk, 252–57. Gainesville: University Press of Florida, 2012.
Radcliffe, Sarah, and Sallie Westwood. *Remaking the Nation: Place, Identity and Politics in Latin America*. London; New York: Routledge, 1996.
Ramírez, Gabriel. *Miguel Contreras Torres, 1899–1981*. Guadalajara: Centro de Investigación y Enseñanza Cinematográficas, Universidad de Guadalajara, 1994.
Ramírez Berg, Charles. *Cinema of Solitude: A Critical Study of Mexican Film, 1967–1983*. Austin: University of Texas Press, 2010.
Ramírez Berg, Charles. *The Classical Mexican Cinema: The Poetics of the Exceptional Golden Age Films*. Austin: University of Texas Press, 2015.
Ramírez Flores, Roberto. "La Ley federal de cinematografía de 1949: La consolidación de un paradigma censor." *El ojo que piensa. Revista de cine iberoamericano*, no. 13 (2016). http://www.elojoquepiensa.cucsh.udg.mx/index.php/elojoquepiensa/article/view/246.
Ramos, Samuel. *El perfil del hombre y la cultura en México*. Madrid: Espasa Calpe, S.A., 1951.
Rios, Sofia. "Representation and Disjunction: Made-up Maids in Mexican *Telenovelas*." *Journal of Iberian and Latin American Research* 21, no. 2 (2015): 223–33.
Rogin, Michael. "Making America Home: Racial Masquerade and Ethnic Assimilation in the Transition to Talking Pictures." *Journal of American History* 79, no. 3 (December 1992): 1050–77.
Rogin, Michael. *Blackface, White Noise*. Berkeley: University of California Press, 1998.
Rohrer, Seraina. *La India María: Mexploitation and the films of María Elena Velasco*. Austin: University of Texas Press, 2017.
Rollins, Peter C., and John E. O'Connor, eds. *Hollywood's Indian: The Portrayal of the Native American in Film*. Lexington: University Press of Kentucky, 2003.
Rony, Fatimah Tobing. *The Third Eye: Race, Cinema, and Ethnographic Spectacle*. Durham, NC: Duke University Press, 1996.
Ruétalo Victoria. *Violated Frames: Armando Bó and Isabel Sarli's Sexploits*. Berkeley: University of California Press, 2022.
Sánchez-Rivera, Rachell. "What Happened to Mexican Eugenics?: Racism and the Reproduction of the Nation." PhD diss., University of Cambridge, Queens College, 2019.

Schroeder Rodríguez, Paul. *Latin American Cinema: A Comparative History*. Berkeley: University of California Press, 2016.

Serna, Laura I. *Making Cinelandia: American Films and Mexican Film Culture Before the Golden Age*. Durham, NC: Duke University Press, 2014.

Shilling, Chris. *The Body and Social Theory*. London: Sage Publications, 1993.

Shingler, Martin. *Star Studies: A Critical Guide*. London: British Film Institute, 2012.

Shohat, Ella, and Robert Stam. *Unthinking Eurocentrism: Multiculturalism and the Media*. New York: Routledge, 1994.

Sluis, Ageeth. *Deco Body, Deco City: Female Spectacle and Modernity in Mexico City, 1900–1939*. Lincoln: University of Nebraska Press, 2016.

Sommer, Doris. *Foundational Fictions: The National Romances of Latin America*. Berkeley: University of California Press, 1991.

Sontag, Susan. "Notes on Camp." In *Camp: Queer Aesthetics and the Performing Subject—A Reader*, edited by Fabio Cleto, 53–65. Ann Arbor: University of Michigan Press, 1999.

Spivak, Gayatri Chakravorty. "Can the Subaltern Speak?" In *Marxism and the Interpretation of Culture*, edited by Cary Nelson and Lawrence Grossberg, 271–314. Urbana: University of Illinois Press, 1988.

Stam, Robert, and Louise Spence. "Colonialism, Racism and Representation." *Screen* 24, no. 2 (March 1983): 2–20.

Stavenhagen, Rodolfo. "El Indigenismo mexicano: Gestación y ocaso de un proyecto nacional." In *Raza y política en Hispanoamérica*, edited by Tomás Pérez Vejo and Pablo Yankelevich, 219–45. Madrid: Iberoamericana Vervuert, 2018.

Stern, Alexandra. "Mestizofilia, biotipología y eugenesia en el México posrevolucionario: Hacia una historia de la ciencia y el Estado, 1920–1960." *Relaciones* 21, no. 81 (2000): 53–91.

Strecher, Lucía. "Las máscaras del deseo interracial: Fanon y Capécia." In *Frantz Fanon desde América Latina: Lecturas contemporáneas de un pensador del siglo XX*, edited by Elena Oliva, Lucía Strecher, and Claudia Zapata, 225–79. Buenos Aires: Ediciones Corregidor, 2013.

Sue, Christina A. *Land of the Cosmic Race: Race Mixture, Racism, and Blackness in Mexico*. Oxford: Oxford University Press, 2013.

Taylor, Analisa. *Indigeneity in the Mexican Cultural Imagination*. Tucson: University of Arizona Press, 2009.

Taylor, Analisa. "Malinche and Matriarchal Utopia: Gendered Visions of Indigeneity in Mexico." *Signs: Journal of Women in Culture & Society* 31, no. 3 (spring 2006): 815–40.

Tierney, Dolores. *Emilio Fernández: Pictures in the Margins*. Manchester: Manchester University Press, 2012.

Torres de San Martín, Patricia. "Adela Sequeyro and Matilde Landeta: Two Pioneer Women Directors." In *Mexico's Cinema: A Century of Film and Filmmakers*,

edited by Joanne Hershfield and David Maciel, 37-48. Wilmington, DE: Scholarly Resources, 1999.
Tovey, David G. "The Role of the Music Educator in Mexico's Cultural Missions." *Bulletin of the Council for Research in Music Education*, no. 139 (winter 1999): 1-11.
Tuñón, Julia. "Femininity, *Indigenismo*, and Nation: Film Representation by Emilio 'El Indio' Fernández." In *Sex in Revolution: Gender, Politics, and Power in Modern Mexico*, edited by Jocelyn H. Olcott, Mary Kay Vaughan, and Gabriela Cano, 81-98. Durham, NC: Duke University Press, 2006.
Tuñón, Julia. *Los rostros de un mito. Personajes femeninos en las películas de Emilio Indio Fernández*. Mexico City: CONACULTA, 2003.
Tuñón, Julia. "Una escuela en celuloide. El cine de Emilio 'Indio' Fernández o la obsesión por la educación." *Historia Mexicana* 48, no. 2, special issue "Las imágenes en la historia del México porfiriano y posrevolucionario" (October-December 1998): 437-70.
Urías Horcasitas, Beatriz. *Historias secretas del racismo en México (1920-1950)*. Mexico City: Tusquets Editores México, 2007.
Urías Horcasitas, Beatriz. "Medir y civilizar." *Ciencias*, no. 60 (October-March 2001): 28-36.
Varner, Natasha. *La Raza Cosmética: Beauty, Identity, and Settler Colonialism in Postrevolutionary Mexico*. Tucson: University of Arizona Press, 2020.
Vasconcelos, José. *The Cosmic Race/La raza cósmica: A Bilingual Edition*. Translated by Didier T. Jaén. Baltimore: Johns Hopkins University Press, 1979.
Vasconcelos, José. *Indología: Una interpretación de la cultura ibero-americana*. Barcelona: Agencia mundial de librería, 1920.
Vidal Bonifaz, Rosario. *Surgimiento de la industria cinematográfica y el papel del estado en México, 1895-1940*. Mexico City: Miguel Angel Porrúa, 2010.
Villarreal, Andrés. "Stratification by Skin Color in Contemporary Mexico." *American Sociological Review* 75, no. 5 (2010): 652-78.
Villoro, Luis. *Los grandes momentos del indigenismo en México*. Mexico City: El Colegio de México, 1996.
Wade, Peter. *Race and Sex in Latin America*. New York: Pluto Press, 2009.
Widdifield, Stacie G. *The Embodiment of the National in Late Nineteenth-Century Mexican Painting*. Tucson: University of Arizona Press, 1996.
Wiegman, Roby. "Race, Ethnicity, and Film." In *The Oxford Guide to Film Studies*, edited by John Hill and Pamela Church Gibson, 158-68. New York: Oxford University Press, 1998.
Williams, Linda. *Playing the Race Card: Melodramas of Black and White from Uncle Tom to O.J. Simpson*. Princeton: Princeton University Press, 2001.
Williams, Linda. "'Tales of Sound and Fury . . .' or, the Elephant of Melodrama." In *Melodrama Unbound Across History, Media, and National Cultures*, edited

by Christine Gledhill and Linda Williams, 205–18. New York: Columbia University Press, 2018.

Williams, Raymond. *Marxism and Literature*. Oxford: Oxford University Press, 1977.

Woods Peiró, Eva. *White Gypsies: Race and Stardom in Spanish Musicals*. Minneapolis: University of Minnesota Press, 2012.

Zavala, Adriana. *Becoming Modern, Becoming Tradition: Women, Gender, and Representation in Mexican Art*. University Park: Penn State University Press, 2011.

Zirión Pérez, Antonio. "Hacia una descolonización de la mirada: la representación del indígena en la historia del cine etnográfico en México (1896–2016)." In *Repensar la antropología mexicana del siglo XXI. Viejos problemas, nuevos desafíos*, edited by María Ana Portal, 361–407. Mexico City: Universidad Autónoma Metropolitana, 2019.

Zúñiga, Ariel. "Roberto Gavaldón." Translated by Ana M. López. In *Mexican Cinema*, edited by Paulo Antonio Paranaguá, 195–97. London: British Film Institute, 1995.

Index

Note: page numbers followed by *f* indicate figures

acculturation, 16, 18, 46, 235, 237–38, 242, 261
Allá en el Rancho Grande (de Fuentes), 4n16, 98, 126, 127n9, 133
Altamirano, Ignacio, 16, 47
alterity: Indigeneity as, 196, 198–99; Mayan, 186, 188; national regimes of, 6; radical, 1, 199
El amor de María Isabel (Curiel), 59, 210–11, 230–32, 234–35, 237, 284
Aparicio, Yalitza, 2, 285
Armendariz, Pedro: *El indio* and, 134; *Maclovia* and, 154; *La malquerida*, 165; *María Candelaria* and, 39*f*, 138
Arroyo Calderón, Patricia, 2n8, 259n31
Arroyo Quiroz, Claudia, 74n41, 142, 144
assimilationism, 14–16
Avila, Jaqueline, 127n9, 142

Barba, Meche: *Lola Casanova* and, 249, 251*f*
Bartra, Roger, 49, 54
Batalla en el cielo (Reygadas), 60, 274–76, 278, 280, 285

Bhabha, Homi, 3, 7, 8n32, 17n89, 23
beauty, 4, 29, 52; colonized codes of, 40; female, 59, 106, 117, 122, 136, 147, 166, 193, 275n43; feminine, 39, 105, 162; Indian, 27n135, 146n58; Indigenous, 131, 133, 145, 147, 175, 206, 228, 241; *María Isabel* and, 228–29, 238; Mexican, 162–63; Tehuana and, 93; Vélez and, 103; White, 43, 47
blackface, 5nn18–19, 6
Blackness, 1n2, 9, 42n197, 44
blancura, 8, 22–23, 50, 120, 165, 226, 237, 286; *blanquitud* and, 17, 20–21, 30, 46, 51, 75, 103, 210, 272; in *Maclovia*, 155; in *María Candelaria*, 141; Vélez's, 105
blanquitud, 8, 22, 60, 229–30, 267, 270–71; *blancura* and, 17, 20–21, 30, 46, 51, 75, 103, 210, 272
Bonifant, Cube, 95, 110
Bourdieu, Pierre, 21, 222n14
Brooks, Peter, 72n36, 116
Buñuel, Luis, 191, 199n42, 216n9, 225n19, 227

Calles, Plutarco Elías, 19, 81

Index

Campillo, Anita, 131; *La cruz y la espada* and, 131, 132f; *La india bonita* and, 125, 129
camposcape, 28, 93, 96, 99–100, 102, 128–29; Mexican, 168
Cardenas, Lázaro, 35, 81; government of, 33
cardenismo, 35, 167
casta painting, 9, 240
Caste War of Yucatan, 12, 182
Catholicism, 39n185, 194; *Chilam Balam* and, 80–81, 84, 86, 88–90; conversion to, 44; *Deseada* and, 203; *María Isabel* and, 218; Mesoamericans and, 65; *Tizoc* and, 258, 260
Cerón-Anaya, Hugo, 1n2, 23
Chilam Balam (de Martino), 36, 59, 64–68, 71n34, 79–92, 179, 183, 190, 194, 207, 283
cinema, 54n256, 60, 83, 85n71, 281–82; auteur, 2; classical, 42; European, 39; Golden Age, 41, 52–53, 56, 58, 97, 110, 166, 175, 258n30, 269, 273 (*see also* Golden Age of Mexican cinema); Hollywood, 41, 54, 55n264; indigenismo-mestizaje and, 210; indigenista, 40, 64, 282; Latin American, 55, 64n6; narrative, 51, 68; race and, 37, 41–43; racial dynamics of, 41–42; Spanish, 6 (*see also* Roma people); spectatorship, 42, 47; twentieth-century, 6, 30–31; White female beauty and, 106, 193
Clavijero, Francisco Javier, 65, 66n10
colonialism, 5, 44, 178; Iberian, 56, 140; internal, 166; Spanish, 3, 9, 177
coloniality, 3, 6, 29, 56, 124, 155, 276; of desire, 43, 159, 265, 274–75, 278; Indigenous people as objects of, 58; *María Candelaria* and, 145n54; in Mexico, 54, 123, 156, 263n33; modernity/coloniality, 7, 281; Whiteness and, 48, 166, 228, 279, 283
coloniality of power, 3, 5n20, 38, 43, 123, 155, 281; Whiteness and, 48, 144, 146, 171
colonization of desire, 51, 60, 92, 120, 239, 281; *Deseada* and, 205; *La india bonita* and, 131; *La noche de los mayas* and, 193; Whiteness and, 43, 47–48, 68, 123; whiteness-as-indigeneity and, 105
colonization of subjectivity, 38, 60, 68, 97, 239, 281; *Deseada* and, 205; Fanon and, 48; *Janitzio* and, 169n106; *Maclovia* and, 160; *María Candelaria* and, 141, 144; *María Isabel* and, 225; *La noche de los mayas* and, 191, 193; Whiteness and, 43, 50–51, 53, 91, 119, 141, 144; whiteness-as-indigeneity and, 40, 92, 123, 135, 175, 191, 193; *La Zandunga* and, 105, 108
colonized, the, 7–8, 44, 48
colonizer, the, 6–7, 44, 84
comedias rancheras, 98–99, 114, 121, 124, 126
Contreras Torres, Miguel, 69, 75, 242, 244f; *De raza Azteca*, 32, 69. See also *Tribu*; *Zítari*
Corona, Isabela: *Lola Casanova* and, 249; *La noche de los mayas* and, 183
Cortés, Hernán, 44, 63, 65, 178, 249n18, 273
Cortés, Margarita: *Tierra de pasiones* and, 120, 150, 151f
Crevenna, Alfredo B., 134n21, 182
criollos, 10, 22, 45–46, 68, 123, 139–41, 158, 181, 223; in *Tizoc*, 257, 259–60
La cruz y la espada (Strayer), 131, 132f

cultural production, 4, 23–25, 35, 38, 46, 93, 110; Afro-Mexican population's erasure and, 7; indigenista, 25, 181; Whiteness and, 48, 50, 51n239, 146

Dalton, David S., 28, 38
deco bodies, 28, 96, 136, 170, 192
De Córdova, Arturo: *La noche de los mayas* and, 182; *La Zandunga* and, 99
Del Lago, Alicia: *Raíces* and, 173; *Tizoc (Amor indio)* and, 257
Del Río, Dolores, 54, 56, 102–103, 124, 146, 163, 227; *Deseada* and, 195, 197f, 201f, 204; *La malquerida* and, 165; *María Candelaria* and, 39f, 138, 143f, 144, 147–48, 152–53, 162, 164; *Ramona* and, 152–53
De Novara, Medea: *Tribu* and, 77f, 242, 244f; *Zítari* and, 67, 69, 75–76
Deseada (Gavaldón), 59, 168n105, 178–81, 195–207, 283
desire, 4, 44, 46n219, 273, 282; coloniality of, 159, 265, 274–75, 278; *Deseada* and, 195; female, 150n70, 278; male, 166; racial(ized) dynamics of, 30, 43, 179, 184; representation of, 94; stardom and, 53n253. See also colonization of desire
De Zayas Enriquez, Rafael, 11, 13
Díaz, Porfirio, 13, 16
Domínguez, Columba, 191; *Maclovia* and, 154, 161f, 162, 163f, 164; *La malquerida* and, 165; *Pueblerina* and, 164–65
Dyer, Richard, 8n32, 30, 37, 42, 47n226, 56, 75, 106, 226n21, 253

Echeverría, Bolívar, 8, 103. See also *blanquitud*

Eisenstein, Sergei, 95, 146, 167; *¡Qué viva México!*, 32, 96, 97n25, 109n55, 110, 113, 148
epidermal schemas, 1n2, 2, 37; European, 1; racialized, 8, 23; Tehuana, 95, 97n25; White, 30, 96, 120, 141

Fanon, Frantz, 1n2, 43–44, 48–49, 275
Félix, María, 54, 124, 165, 227; *Lola Casanova* and, 241; *Maclovia* and, 154, 161f, 162–64; *Tizoc* and, 257, 261f
femininity: ethnic, 147; Indigenous, 172; Indigenous-looking, 43; Mexican, 126, 133n16; performed Indigenous, 96, 131; White Mexican, 46n219, 75, 133
Fernández, Emilio "El Indio," 74n41, 145, 162, 164, 173, 175; indigenista films of, 31n154, 32, 35–36, 38, 40, 195; *Janitzio* and, 36, 167, 169–70; *La malquerida*, 165; *Río Escondido*, 34; *Tribu* and, 244f. See also *Maclovia*; *María Candelaria*
fictive ethnicity, 17, 177
Frank, Consuelo: *El indio* and, 134, 136, 138f
Fregoso, Rosa Linda, 102, 108n54

Gamio, Miguel, 19, 24, 125, 180–81
García Riera, Emilio, 79, 98, 99n36, 136n22, 147n59, 155n85, 188n26, 191, 193n36, 226n20
Gavaldón, Roberto, 195; *Macario*, 194n37, 195; *El rebozo de Soledad*, 191. See also *Deseada*
gender, 41, 52, 102; bias, 164; heterosexual pairings and, 240, 241, 247, 267, 278–79; identities, 85; norms, 103, 110, 113, 233, 247
Golden Age of Mexican cinema, 4–5, 33–34, 40, 52, 55, 57, 124, 210, 225,

Index

Golden Age of Mexican cinema (*continued*)
241, 268–69, 273, 279, 282, 284; brownface and, 266; decline of, 79; desire and, 60; film magazines of, 163, 191; Tehuana and, 93

Gómez Izquierdo, José Jorge, 17n87, 20, 49

Güeros (Ruizpalacio), 60, 275–80, 285

Gutiérrez, Rodrigo, 67, 74

Hall, Stuart, 3, 17n89, 28n138

Hershfield, Joanne, 4, 28–29, 38, 93n2, 146

hooks, bell, 41–42, 52, 120n76

Inda, Estela: *La noche de los mayas* and, 182, 191–92, 193n36

La india bonita (Helú), 35, 123–33, 141, 145, 167–68, 170, 175, 283

Indigeneity, 1n1, 5–9, 11, 13–14, 16–17, 20, 27, 30, 41, 65–67, 91–93, 124, 166, 175, 210, 279, 281–82; ancient, 66–67, 74; Catholicism and, 39n185; *Chilam Balam* and, 83, 89, 91; cinematic, 141, 272, 281; *Deseada* and, 195–96, 199, 204, 206; female, 147, 153, 174; *La india bonita* and, 129, 131; indigenismo-mestizaje and, 179, 186; indigenista films and, 40; *Janitzio* and, 167; *Lola Casanova* and, 250–51, 254–56; *Maclovia* and, 158–59; *María Candelaria* and, 147, 150–51; *María Isabel* duology and, 211, 215, 219, 222, 228–30, 235, 238; Mexican, 239; Mexican films about, 31–32, 43, 64; *La noche de los mayas* and, 182, 184, 186–87, 188n25, 192; poverty and, 49; *Raíces* and, 171–72, 174; Rivera and, 25; Tehuana and, 96; *Tizoc (Amor indio)* and, 259; *Tribu* and, 243, 245–46; *El violetero* and, 268–72; Whiteness and, 46, 55, 57–59, 158; Whitening and, 38; *La Zandunga* and, 105; *Zítari* and, 69, 71–74, 76–79

indigenismo, 25, 36, 38, 65, 72, 123; cinematic, 40, 78; mestizaje and, 17, 124, 138 (*see also* indigenismo-mestizaje); of *La noche de los mayas*, 188; pictorial, 27, 147

indigenismo-mestizaje, 20, 24–25, 40–41, 65–66, 179, 281–83; *Deseada* and, 195–96, 202, 206; discourse, 59, 66, 78, 283; *La noche de los mayas* and, 186, 206; whiteness-as-indigeneity and, 210

indigenista films, 40, 58, 166–67, 170, 176, 178n6; Fernández's, 31n154, 32, 35–36, 38, 40, 195

Indigenous Mexicans, 31, 66, 140–41; *El amor de María Isabel* and, 222; death and, 49; Del Río and, 152–53; education and, 15; *Tizoc* and, 276; White actors playing, 39f, 105, 136; White male abuse of power and, 166

Indigenous womanhood, 58, 64; *La india bonita* and, 129, 131; *Janitzio* and, 170, 176; *Maclovia* and, 155; *María Isabel* and, 211, 225, 238

Indigenous women, 30, 37, 41, 64, 96, 125–26, 224, 241, 283; diegetically, 123, 175, 177; *La india bonita* and, 128; male desire and, 166, 263n31; Mexican Indigeneity and, 239; Spanish men and, 44–45, 202, 206; White Mexican women presented as, 43, 227

El indio (Vargas de la Maza), 123–24, 133–37, 138f, 141, 145, 165, 168, 170, 175, 283

inditas, 133, 162, 210, 213, 217–18, 220, 222, 224–25, 228–29, 284

indita genre, 59, 238

Infante, Pedro, 4n16, 51; in *Nosotros los pobres*, 54; in *Tizoc*, 241, 257, 259f, 261f, 263–66
interracial marriage, 44–45, 177, 252. See also Whitening

Janitzio (Navarro), 32, 35–36, 123–24, 154, 166–70, 176, 190, 283; *María Candelaria* and, 134n20
Juárez, Benito, 16, 241
El juicio de Martín Cortés (Galindo), 60, 273–76, 280

Kahlo, Frida, 95–96

limpieza de sangre (purity of blood), 9–11
Lola Casanova (Landeta), 60, 71n34, 241, 248–56, 258, 262, 267, 277–79
López, Ana M., 56, 59, 93
López Moctezuma, Carlos, 82, 87f; *La india bonita* and, 125–26, 127f; *Maclovia* and, 154, 155n85

Maclovia (Fernández), 59, 123–24, 154–65, 198–69, 175, 190, 194, 283
Malinche/Malintzin, 63, 89, 178, 249n18
María Candelaria (Fernández), 31n154, 39f, 59, 73n38, 76, 101, 105n48, 120nn75–76, 123–24, 134, 138–54, 158, 164–65, 168–69, 175, 178n6, 188, 190, 192n34, 198; indigenismo-mestizaje and, 283; white-as-indigenous nudity and, 110n61; Whiteness and, 38; whiteness-as-indigeneity and, 194. See also *El violetero*
María Isabel (Curiel), 59, 194, 210–26, 228–29, 284
María Isabel duology, 210–11, 227–28, 236, 238

Martín-Barbero, Jesús, 52–54, 118n74, 166
Martínez Casas, Regina, 17, 22
Martínez Gracida, Manuel, 94–95
masculinity, 115n70; Indigenous, 253, 271; Indigenous-looking, 43; Infante's, 266; Mexican, 129, 263, 265
Mayan belief system: *Chilam Balam* and, 84, 86, 87f, 90; *Deseada* and, 199–200, 204–205; *La noche de los mayas* and, 188–90, 193
Mayan cosmovision, 84, 86, 206; fictionalized, 199
Mediz Bolio, Antonio, 181n13, 182–83, 186
melodrama, 37, 54–55, 68, 72–73, 77–78, 93, 97, 108, 115n69, 116, 124, 206, 221, 269; cinematic conventions of, 136; colonization of subjectivity and, 135, 205; Whiteness and, 53, 118–19, 137. See also *Chilam Balam*; *Deseada*; *Maclovia*; *María Candelaria*; *Tierra de pasiones*; *Tribu*; *El violetero*; *La Zandunga*; *Zítari*
Mesoamerican ruins, 70, 83, 187; in *Deseada*, 196, 199, 204
Mesoamericans, 65–67, 88, 91; ancient, 78–79, 82, 85; pre-Columbian, 74, 92. See also *Chilam Balam*; *Zítari*
mestizaje, 14–15, 17–19, 123–25, 177–79, 181, 240–41, 281, 284; *El amor de María Isabel* and, 230, 237; *Chilam Balam* and, 89; cultural, 59, 156, 158, 194, 206–207, 258, 260; *Deseada* and, 201–202; *Lola Casanova* and, 249–52, 254, 256; *María Candelaria* and, 138; *La noche de los mayas* and, 183–86, 194; postrevolutionary, 215; *Raíces* and, 170–71; sexual, 194, 207; *Tizoc*

mestizaje *(continued)*
  (Amor indio) and, 257–62, 267; *El violetero* and, 270–71. See also indigenismo-mestizaje; Mexican mestizaje
mestizos, 10, 12, 17, 25, 45, 66, 141, 181, 269
Mexican film industry, 98, 108, 191; crisis of, 210; development of, 33, 40; Mexican government and, 33–34; racism in, 2
Mexican film production, 37, 40, 55; Indigenous-themed corpus of, 190; neoliberal policies and, 276n45, 284; state's role in, 34; Whiteness in, 47
Mexican independence, 10–11, 46, 48, 66, 156
Mexican mestizaje, 15, 20, 59, 78–79; *Chilam Balam* and, 80–81, 84, 90–91, 179; *Deseada* and, 200, 202, 206; *Lola Casanova* and, 252, 254–56; *Tizoc* and, 267; *Tribu* and, 248; *El violetero* and, 269. See also whiteness-as-indigeneity: desirability and
Mexican national identity, 40–41, 56, 66, 69, 103, 242; Indigeneity and, 239; Indigenous cultures and, 206; post-revolutionary, 28; racial categories and, 6
Mexicanness/*mexicanidad*, 1, 29, 68, 73, 77, 96, 153, 256; cinematic, 195; Paz on, 178
mexicano, lo, 27n136, 95n12
Mexican racial formation, 23, 108, 155, 165, 191; Indigeneity and, 55, 131, 206, 228; Whiteness and, 30, 135, 144, 204, 211, 225–28, 237; whiteness-as-indigeneity and, 205
Mexican Revolution, 17–18, 25, 57, 81, 96, 113–14, 117, 123; *La india bonita* and, 126; *El indio* and, 134–35, 137; *Maclovia* and, 154, 156; *María Candelaria* and, 139–40; *La rebelión de los colgados* and, 134n21; *Río Escondido* and, 34
Mexicans of color, 2, 29–30, 273–80, 285
Mexican Whiteness, 21n113, 23, 31, 47n224, 53, 60, 165, 238; boundaries of, 2, 22, 51; as indigeneity, 56, 94; Pinal and, 227f; privilege and, 9, 285; Spanish origins and, 103. See also White Mexicans; White Mexican woman, the; White Mexican womanhood; White Mexican women
Mignolo, Walter, 3, 7
miscegenation, 14, 178, 239. See also mestizaje
modernity, 17, 49, 52, 56, 96–97, 179–80; indigenismo and, 25, 38; *María Candelaria* and, 139–41; *María Isabel* duology and, 59, 210–11, 216, 222, 229–30, 234, 236, 238; mestizo, 192; Mexican, 18, 22, 28–31, 216, 234, 238, 256; modernity/coloniality, 7, 281; Roma people and, 57n273; Western, 8, 30, 39, 140; *La Zandunga* and, 102; *Zítari* and, 70
modesty, 135; female, 233; sexual, 210, 217–18, 229, 238
Modotti, Tina, 95–96
Monsiváis, Carlos, 27n134, 52, 166
Mora, Margarita: *Tierra de pasiones* and, 114, 119f
Morelos, José María, 16, 156–57
Moreno Figueroa, Mónica, 20, 47
Mulvey, Laura, 41–42, 149

nationalism, 24, 123, 152, 240; cultural, 36, 281; musical, 182; popular, 66, 125

Navarrete Linares, Federico, 17n87, 30n148, 46, 49–50
Negrete, Jorge: *Tierra de pasiones* and, 114–15
New Spain, 10, 45; casta painting in, 9, 240
Nieves. *See* Orozco, Nieves
Noble, Andrea, 4, 142, 146, 147n61
La noche de los mayas (Urueta), 59, 71n33, 75n41, 168n105, 178–94, 196, 200, 202–203, 205–207, 283
Nosotros los pobres (Rodríguez), 54, 221n11
nudity: *María Candelaria* and, 147–49; *Tierra de pasiones* and, 115–17; *La Zandunga* and, 93, 97, 108, 110, 117
Nutini, Hugo, 60–61, 75, 191, 244, 253

Obregón, José, 67–68, 74
Omi, Michael, 16, 21
Orozco, José Clemente, 25, 178
Orozco, María Teresa: *Janitzio* and, 167, 170
Orozco, Nieves, 146–47nn58–59. *See also* Rivera, Diego

Paxman, Andrew, 34–35, 225n19
Paz, Octavio, 63, 178
piety, 144, 218, 229, 269; Catholic, 210; filial, 106
Pimentel, Francisco, 11, 15
Pinal, Silvia, 59, 226–28, 238; *El amor de María Isabel* and, 210–11; *María Isabel* and, 212f, 225–26
Podalsky, Laura, 38n181, 64n6, 109n55, 147n60
Poniatowska, Elena, 50, 95
Poole, Deborah, 95, 97
Porfiriato, 13, 16

positivism, 11, 13

race, 29, 36, 126, 226n20, 247, 282–83; bias, 164; cinema and, 37, 41–43, 175, 209; class and, 23; essentialist representations of, 16; male desirability and, 263; Mexican Whiteness and, 53; relations in Mexico, 5, 41, 211, 285; Whiteness and, 75
racial formation, 21, 155; indigeneity-as-indigeneity and, 173; Indigenous Mexican womanhood and, 159, 229; US, 55–56; White Mexican womanhood and, 37, 47, 91, 120, 130; whiteness-as-indigeneity and, 211, 265, 282. *See also* Mexican racial formation
racial masquerade, 5, 40, 57, 209–10; in *Deseada*, 207; in *María Candelaria*, 141, 146; Mexican, 38, 284, 286; in *La noche de los Mayas*, 207. *See also* blackface; whiteness-as-indigeneity
racism, 3, 50n237, 210, 229, 238; biological, 16, 19; Mexican, 14, 18, 42n197, 213, 271, 285
Radcliffe, Sarah, 17n89, 23
Raíces (Alazraki), 36, 59, 123–24, 166, 170–76, 283
Ramírez Berg, Charles, 1, 4, 42, 50, 228
Redes (Zinnemann), 32, 35, 124
Rivera, Diego, 25, 27, 95–96, 147n59, 180
Roma people, 6, 57n273

Sánchez Prado, Ignacio, 275n43, 284
Sánchez-Rivera, Rachell, 11, 19
Said, Edward, 17n89, 28n138
Sierra, Justo, 14–15
Silvestre, Armando: *Lola Casanova* and, 249, 251f, 252

Siqueiros, David Alfaro, 25, 240
Sluis, Ageeth, 28, 38, 93, 96–97, 99, 112, 128n11, 192. *See also* camposcape; deco bodies
Soler, Julián: *La india bonita* and, 125–26, 127f
Spanishness, 9, 15, 105
Spence, Louise, 37, 58
Stam, Robert, 37, 58

Tehuana, the, 59, 93–97; *Tierra de pasiones* and, 117–18, 120–21; whiteness-as-indigeneity and, 102, 122; Whitening of, 108, 283; *La Zandunga* and, 105–109, 112–13, 283
Tehuantepec, Isthmus of, 59, 95, 109n55, 113, 114n66, 121; as camposcape, 102; *Tierra de pasiones* and, 115–16. See also *La Zandunga*
telenovelas, 1, 50n235, 52, 226n20, 284
Teresa de Mier, Servando, 65, 66n10
Tierney, Dolores, 1, 4, 38, 41–42, 59, 76, 134n20, 141, 144, 147n59, 178n6, 192n34
Tierra de pasiones (Benávides), 59, 94, 97, 113–22, 133, 150n71, 283
Tin Tan (Germán Valdés), 60, 241, 267, 271–72. See also *El violetero*
Tizoc (Amor indio) (Rodríguez), 60, 71n34, 73n38, 188, 241, 257–67, 272–73, 275–79
Tonta, tonta, pero no tanto (Cortés), 224–25
Tribu (Contreras Torres), 35–36, 60, 75, 77f, 241–49, 254, 256, 258, 260, 262, 267, 277–79

Urueta, Chano, 182, 195. See also *La noche de los mayas*

Valdés, Germán. See Tin Tan

Varner, Natasha, 28, 30, 38, 124, 145n54, 176n109
Vasconcelos, José, 18, 25, 31, 46, 66, 177–78, 180
Vélez, Lupe, 56; *La Zandunga* and, 99, 101f, 102–109, 111f, 121
Villoro, Luis, 40, 65, 72
El violetero (Martínez Solares), 60, 241, 267–73, 275, 278–79
Virgin of Guadalupe, 218–20

Westwood, Sallie, 17n89, 23
White Mexicans, 4, 21n113, 29–30, 48, 230, 270–71
White Mexican womanhood, 75, 91; Indigeneity and, 211, 239; Vélez and, 105
White Mexican woman, the, 277; Indigenous man and, 242, 249, 256, 258, 262, 267, 271–72, 279; in *Maclovia*, 160; Mexican man of color and, 273, 275–76, 278, 280; semiotic privilege of, 205
White Mexican women, 43, 132, 148, 241
whiteness-as-indigeneity, 5–6, 31, 35–36, 40, 55–57, 59, 61, 92, 122–24, 166, 175–76, 207, 210, 241, 266, 279, 282–85; brownface and, 265; *Chilam Balam* and, 91; *Deseada* and, 204–205; desirability and, 91, 106, 122, 145–46, 205, 210, 229, 239, 252–53, 279 (*see also* colonization of desire); *La india bonita* and, 126, 128–31, 133; *El indio* and, 135–37; *Janitzio* and, 169; *Lola Casanova* and, 252–53, 256; *Maclovia* and, 157–58, 161; *María Candelaria* and, 141, 144–47, 152; *María Isabel* duology and, 210–11, 225, 228–29, 235, 237–38; *La noche de los mayas* and, 190–95; *Raíces* and, 172–73, 175; *Tierra de pasiones* and, 118–20;

Tribu and, 244–45; *El violetero* and, 271; *La Zandunga* and, 102, 105, 108; *Zítari* and, 74, 76
whiteness-as-whiteness, 123, 128, 135, 155–56, 172, 175–76
Whitening, 10, 16, 23, 38, 44, 46, 68; in Golden Age cinema, 97; in *La india bonita*, 131; of Indigenous female characters, 282–83; mestizaje and, 256, 271; in Mexican melodrama, 54; in *La noche de los mayas*, 192; in *Raíces*, 171; of Roma people, 6; in *El violetero*, 270–71; in *La Zandunga*, 108, 283

White womanhood, 42, 60–61, 108, 120
Williams, Linda, 83n66, 99n34, 116, 137
Winant, Howard, 16, 21
Woods Peiró, Eva, 6, 57n273

La Zandunga (de Fuentes), 35, 59, 94, 97–102, 105–13, 115–18, 121–22, 185, 283
Zavala, Adriana, 27n135, 133n17, 146n58
Zítari (Contreras Torres), 68–72, 78, 80, 83, 243

www.ingramcontent.com/pod-product-compliance
Lightning Source LLC
Chambersburg PA
CBHW051600230426
43668CB00013B/1920